D1713439

THE
ALL-VOLUNTEER FOR[
THIRTY YEARS OF SER[

THE
ALL-
VOLUNTEER
FORCE
THIRTY YEARS OF SERVICE

EDITED BY

Barbara A. Bicksler
Curtis L. Gilroy
John T. Warner

Foreword by Donald H. Rumsfeld

 BRASSEY'S, INC.
Washington, DC

Hardcover ISBN: 1-57488-919-2
Softcover ISBN: 1-57488-920-6

(alk. paper)

Printed in the United States of America on acid-free paper that meets the American National Standards Institute Z39-48 Standard.

Brassey's, Inc.
22841 Quicksilver Drive
Dulles, Virginia 20166

First Edition

10 9 8 7 6 5 4 3 2 1

CONTENTS

FOREWORD   vii
  Donald H. Rumsfeld

PREFACE   xi

PART I
THE ALL-VOLUNTEER FORCE IN PERSPECTIVE

Introduction 3
        Melvin R. Laird

Chapter 1   Reflections From the Gates Commission 8
             Frederick B. Dent, Milton Friedman, Stephen E. Herbits,
             Theodore M. Hesburgh

Chapter 2   The Making of the All-Volunteer Force 15
             Martin Anderson

Chapter 3   The Gates Commission: Right for the Wrong Reasons 22
             Bernard D. Rostker

Chapter 4   Reflections on Managing the All-Volunteer Force:
             Past and Future 33
             John P. White

Commentary No More Greetings 45
             Walter Y. Oi

PART II
SUSTAINING THE FORCE:
RECRUITING AND RETENTION

Introduction 55
        Christopher Jehn

Chapter 5   Sustaining the Force in an Era of Transformation 57
             Paul F. Hogan, Curtis J. Simon, John T. Warner

Chapter 6   Manpower Quality in the All-Volunteer Force 90
             David J. Armor, Paul R. Sackett

Chapter 7   The Effects of Socioeconomic Change on the
             All-Volunteer Force: Past, Present, and Future 109
             Martha Farnsworth Riche, Aline Quester

Commentary 142
             Dennis D. Cavin, Gerry Hoewing, Garry L. Parks, Kenneth T. Venuto

PART III
RESERVE COMPONENT CONTRIBUTIONS
TO THE ALL-VOLUNTEER FORCE

Introduction 167
William A. Navas Jr.

Chapter 8   The All-Volunteer Force: An Employer's Perspective...................... 169
Robert K. Steel

Chapter 9   From the Home Front to the Front Lines:
U.S. Reserve Forces Answer the Call to Duty 191
Edward L. Schrock

Chapter 10   Manning the Force While at War:
A Critical Challenge 199
James R. Helmly

Chapter 11   The Reserves and Guard: Standing in the Civil-Military Gap
Before and After 9/11 206
Peter D. Feaver, David P. Filer, Paul Gronke

Commentary 237
Reginald J. Brown, Thomas F. Hall

PART IV
TRANSFORMATION IN MILITARY MANPOWER
AND PERSONNEL POLICY

Introduction 255
Ken Krieg

Chapter 12   Looking to the Future: What Does Transformation
Mean for Military Manpower and Personnel Policy? 257
Beth J. Asch, James R. Hosek

Chapter 13   A "Continuum of Service" for the All-Volunteer Force.................. 297
John D. Winkler, R. Wayne Spruell, Thomas L. Bush, Gary L. Crone

Chapter 14   Toward a New Balance in Military Capabilities 308
Arthur K. Cebrowski

Commentary 317
Patricia A. Tracey, Michael L. Dominguez, Heather Wilson

PART V
THE NEXT DECADE

Chapter 15   Observations on a Remarkable Transformation 331
Paul Wolfowitz

Chapter 16   Thirty Years of an All-Volunteer Force:
Personal Observations 335
John W. Vessey Jr.

Chapter 17   A Bigger Force or a Smaller Empire 343
Ed Dorn

Chapter 18   The All-Volunteer Force: Resilient and Perishable 348
Rudy de Leon

Chapter 19   Looking Ahead: The 40th Anniversary 350
David S. C. Chu

Editors and Contributors 353

Glossary 371

Index 375

★ ★ ★ ★ ★ ★ ★ ★ ★ ★ ★

FOREWORD

My interest in the all-volunteer force goes back a long time. In the mid-1960s, I attended a conference at the University of Chicago on the all-volunteer force. My friend Milton Friedman was there. He was such an enthusiast for the all-volunteer force that it was contagious. Everyone there seized the issue, myself included.

I returned to Washington, D.C. and introduced legislation in the Congress on the all-volunteer force. I testified before the House and Senate Armed Services Committees, which was an intimidating thing to do as a junior congressman — to explain to giants like Eddie Hebert and Richard Russell why the current system was not the right system. Despite strong opposition and through the efforts of many dedicated people, the goal of implementing an all-volunteer force was ultimately achieved. President Richard Nixon embraced the concept of the all-volunteer force and, with encouragement from Secretary of Defense Melvin Laird, persuaded Congress to approve it.

The most enjoyable part of my job as secretary of defense is to meet with the U.S. troops stationed around the world — to look them in the eye and thank them for volunteering, for signing up and saying "send me." These men and women chose to serve their country, to put their lives at risk in order to preserve the freedoms in America. Their willingness to serve is a wonderful thing. It is a great strength of the armed services — of the all-volunteer force.

The United States may have the most precise weapons on earth. We may have the most lethal capabilities and vast resources at our disposal. But certainly the greatest resource the nation has is the character, the courage, and the spirit of our men and women in uniform. We, as a nation, are so fortunate that so many young men and women are willing to sign up, with such a remarkable sense of mission.

★

Over the past 30 years, our all-volunteer force has liberated millions of people. It has won the cold war, liberated Grenada, liberated Kuwait, removed the Taliban from power in Afghanistan, and ousted the forces of Saddam Hussein from Iraq. Today it is helping to put terrorists on the run all across the globe. The fight against terrorism is not the same as fighting armies, navies, or air forces. Our armed services are working with law enforcement officers, intelligence specialists, and the Treasury Department in this war against terrorism. It takes time to adjust to new and different responsibilities and to confront a new and different enemy. Yet our men and women in uniform are doing so successfully.

On a recent visit to Mosul, Iraq, I was able to witness about 150 soldiers in the legendary 101st Airborne Division reenlist as a group. This reenlistment ceremony was conducted on the front lines — at one of Saddam Hussein's palaces in the former stronghold of one of the world's most repressive and brutal regimes. Those soldiers chose to reenlist because they know that the mission they are performing is important to our country, to the 23 million people of Iraq, to the entire Middle East region, and to the world. These are the kind of men and women who are in the all-volunteer force today.

The armed forces are currently under a great deal of stress. Nevertheless, the services are successfully meeting their recruiting and retention targets — indicators that are crucial to watch. Without the ability to attract and retain the best men and women, the armed forces will not be able to do their job. Compensation, health care, housing, and other family support services are critically important in the recruiting and retention equation, and must be constantly attended to.

We in the department also need to be mindful of personnel tempo, given the demands that are being placed on the force. Personnel tempo has to be set at a level that is rational, that does not wear people out, and that does not drive people away, because we need to continue to attract the best people available. Our part-time force, in the reserve components, is particularly busy, yet it is doing an amazing job despite the high operational tempo. To ensure a ready, capable, and available reserve component in the future, I believe some degree of rebalancing between the active and reserve components is needed. We must provide our reserve forces with more predictability and take care to use this important component of the force judiciously — in a way that is fair to our reservists, to their families, and to their employers.

While the force is successfully accomplishing all the tasks it is being assigned, it is also transforming into a more agile, lethal force. This transformation is not only about weapon systems and force structure, however. It is also about transforming our policies and practices, to include manpower and personnel policies. Changes to personnel policy cannot be made quickly; they take thought, analysis, and discussion. But it is clear that the world has changed, the force has changed, and some of our policies and practices must change as well.

The all-volunteer force has succeeded at every challenge it has faced. The nation owes a debt of gratitude to these volunteers. Today, 30 years after the inception of the all-volunteer force, we can look back and say that the decision to rely on volunteers was the right one. It was not an easy decision to make and it was a hard-fought battle at the time. Nevertheless, it was the right decision in the end. And those who were involved in making that decision in the early years are to be thanked.

I am often asked about what has changed since I left the Department of Defense after my first tenure as secretary. The answer, of course, is that many things have changed. Within the department, the bureaucracy has grown; many of our processes, such as the acquisition process, have become more complex; the legislative agenda is far more extensive. The world has changed as well. During the cold war we faced a familiar enemy, one that we had studied for many years and that we knew well. Our enemy today is elusive and complex, skilled at denial and deception, and able to draw on modern technology and powerful weapons to advance its cause.

There is one thing, however, that has not changed—and that is the people. The military and civilian staffs in the Department of Defense are still dedicated, talented professionals. The men and women in uniform today are, without question, the finest military in the world—probably the finest military the world has ever seen. This concept of an all-volunteer force has been a booming success. It works and it works well.

DONALD H. RUMSFELD

★ ★ ★ ★ ★ ★ ★ ★ ★ ★ ★

PREFACE

This volume contains papers presented at a conference held on September 16 and 17, 2003, at the National Defense University in Washington, D.C., to commemorate the 30th anniversary of the all-volunteer force. This volume is the third in a series of conference proceedings evaluating the performance of the nation's volunteer military and the challenges that it may face in the future.

The first volume, entitled *The All-Volunteer Force After a Decade: Retrospect and Prospect*, reported on the early success of the volunteer force and the difficulties it faced later in its first decade. Many of the 1983 conference participants were not optimistic about the future of a volunteer military. But 10 years later, the tide had turned. The Department of Defense had learned many lessons from its experiences during the first decade, and the outcome of the 1993 conference — 20 years after the inception of the all-volunteer force — was to declare that force a success. The presentations contained in *Professionals on the Front Line: Two Decades of the All-Volunteer Force* exuded a sense of confidence, yet cautioned against overoptimism.

Rapidly changing world events make the 30th year of the all-volunteer force a particularly important time. As the department's military strategy evolves in the face of complex and uncertain adversaries, it is essential to also assess the implications of these changes for manpower and personnel policies. While the September 2003 conference included reflections on the early years of the all-volunteer force, its focus was primarily forward-looking, covering topics that include sustaining the force in the future, the changing role of the reserve component, and transforming military personnel policy.

With regard to future challenges in sustaining the force, this volume focuses on the importance of understanding the civilian labor market and changes in the demographic composition of the population; of proactively employing the appropriate mix of compensation and personnel policies to address particular problems; and of maintaining high-quality standards for the force. The volume then addresses the changing roles and missions of the reserve component and the need to "rebalance" both the active and reserve components within the total force. The series of papers on policy transformation stress how the department will need to manage personnel differently in the future in order to provide the flexibility necessary for a more agile and lethal force. Finally, the closing chapters highlight key challenges facing the department in the decade ahead.

In bringing the military manpower community together for this conference, we were pleased with the overwhelming interest and level of participation among senior leaders. Secretary of Defense Donald Rumsfeld and Deputy Secretary of Defense Paul Wolfowitz joined former Secretary of Defense Melvin Laird and former Chairman of the Joint Chiefs of Staff General John W. Vessey Jr., U.S. Army (Retired), in reflecting on the history of our volunteer military and in celebrating its success in defending our nation. Also participating were several members of the President's Commission on an All-Volunteer Armed Force (the Gates Commission). Two former deputy secretaries of defense, five former under secretaries, three current assistant secretaries of the military departments, all armed forces personnel chiefs (including the Coast Guard), and two members of Congress spoke about the accomplishments of the all-volunteer force and the challenges that lie ahead. They were joined by distinguished guests from the Defense Department, other government organizations, academia, and the research community.

Many individuals contributed to the success of this project, and we are grateful to them all. David Chu, Under Secretary of Defense for Personnel and Readiness, and Charles Abell, Principal Deputy Under Secretary, provided support and counsel for the conference. William Carr, Acting Deputy Under Secretary of Defense for Military Personnel Policy, also contributed to the conference, along with Major Heidi Schwenn of the Office of Accession Policy, who provided staff work over many months. Special thanks are extended to Lieutenant General Michael M. Dunn, president of the National Defense University, and his staff for providing facilities to host the conference. We are especially grateful to Walter Oi, Bernard Rostker, and Stephen Herbits for their assistance in recommending topics and participants.

Strategic Analysis, Inc. provided outstanding support not only in preparation for the conference itself but also during publication of this volume. Barbara Smith and Jesse Durham served as coordinators for the conference, supported by their staff in the Meeting Services Group. Mary Ann Walsh provided cover and layout design and Amy Cauffman worked tirelessly on the many graphics. Kevin Huff and Lisa Nolan proofread drafts and helped prepare the final manuscript. Thanks go to each member of this team for their important contributions. Special thanks are due to Jocelyn Gibbon, whose advice and critical editing were invaluable.

Publication of this volume would not have been possible without the assistance of Don McKeon of Brassey's, Inc.

★ ★ ★ ★ ★ ★ ★ ★ ★ ★ ★

PART I

The All-Volunteer Force in Perspective

★ ★ ★ ★ ★ ★ ★ ★ ★ ★ ★

INTRODUCTION

MELVIN R. LAIRD

I want to begin by applauding the Department of Defense (DOD) for celebrating the 30th anniversary of the all-volunteer force (AVF) with a conference that brought together both those who were present at the start of the all-volunteer force, such as myself, and those who share responsibility for sustaining this force into its next decade. Hosting such an event is important for the future of the all-volunteer force. It reminds us of where we started, of the success we have achieved over the years, and of what we need to do to ensure continued success in the future.

Looking back to the early years reminds me of the many individuals who supported the concept of a volunteer army some three decades ago: individuals like William Steiger and Donald Rumsfeld who were young members of Congress at that time; David Packard, Roger Kelley, and the many others on my team at the Department of Defense; and of course President Richard Nixon, who had the vision and willingness to carry the volunteer concept forward. I personally have a great deal of gratitude for the energy these people devoted to making this great all-volunteer force come to be. Although I have been called the "father of the all-volunteer force" it was through their dedication and support that our country succeeded in this effort.

In the mid-1960s, some of the earliest supporters of the concept of an all-volunteer force began to emerge. One of them was a young congressman from Wisconsin, William Steiger, who pressed Gerald Ford and me to put the idea in the 1968 Republican platform. At the time, I was the ranking member of the House Appropriations Subcommittee on Defense and chairman of the House Republican Conference. Ford was the House minority leader. Although Steiger was very persistent, Ford and I did not think the upcoming Republican Convention was the proper time to take up the issue. Steiger and a number of other young members of Congress strongly believed that the draft was unfair.

★

They worked hard to circulate the idea of volunteer service and gain support for the concept. In October 1968, after seeking input from a large group of people, Nixon did adopt the all-volunteer force as an element of his personal campaign platform, as we campaigned in Pennsylvania. He gave me support for this effort throughout his presidency.

VIETNAM AND THE AVF

After Nixon was elected to the presidency, I joined him and others who had traveled with him during the campaign in Key Biscayne, Florida, where we discussed a program for the Department of Defense. Of course, ending the conflict in Vietnam on an honorable basis was a prominent issue. More than half a million American ground combat troops were in Vietnam. Another million service personnel in the Navy, the Air Force, the Marines, and support forces were in the region—more troops than make up the whole of the armed forces today. The conflict in Southeast Asia was costing the nation some $20–25 billion per year, an amount that approached 25–30 percent of the defense budget. But Vietnam was not only a dominant issue in terms of the nation's overall national security posture; it was also important because of the questions it raised about how the military manpower burden was being borne—who was serving, who was taking the risks, who was bearing the personal burden for America's security.

So in many respects, the necessity for spending time and effort to develop a "Vietnamization" strategy to resolve the Vietnam conflict played a key role in how the administration addressed the all-volunteer force. The draft supported the Vietnam operation. President Johnson had made a decision not to use the guard and reserve to any significant extent in Vietnam. As a result, the new administration had to develop the "total force concept" along with the idea of the "all-volunteer force." We decided to place more emphasis on the role of the guard and reserve, to give them the kind of equipment they needed so that they could be called upon to serve. Today, this concept of the "total force" has truly come to fruition. Almost 40 percent of the U.S. forces in support of the Iraq war are guard and reserve—a fact many people do not realize.

MANAGING THE ALL-VOLUNTEER FORCE DEBATE

In late 1968 and into 1969, there was a growing consensus within the administration on the importance of an all-volunteer force. At issue, however, was how to lay a proper framework for study, introduction, and congressional consideration of the initiative. It was an emotional subject. Many people had taken hard positions on a variety of draft and volunteer-force issues—people within the Defense Department, the White House, and the Congress. A forum was needed through which many views could be aired and a consensus built. Thus, it was my belief that the administration should take a year to study the many complex issues involved in military personnel procurement, to consider alternatives, and to provide a set of recommended directives. There was no room to mishandle the issue for risk of scuttling the entire idea. So, it was suggested in Key Biscayne, in the third week of December 1968, that a commission be set up to study the idea of an all-volunteer force.

There were several alternatives to creating the commission. One approach was to conduct the study within DOD—an approach that could have been viewed as less than objective. It would also have required a considerable amount of my time as secretary of defense, which was not particularly appropriate. With Vietnam such an important national issue, the need to develop and implement a coherent Vietnam strategy was compelling. The nation was impatient. It was clear that Vietnam had to be my top priority as secretary. In the end, it was probably the issue on which I spent more time than any other, especially during the early months of my tenure.

Another approach would have been to submit the issue to the National Security Council (NSC) process. However, the NSC was itself overloaded with a myriad of issues. The AVF could readily have been suffocated by that crowded environment, if not by the generally strong opposition to the all-volunteer force among the White House staff. At the time, many leaders in the White House were influenced by individuals who did not approve of a volunteer Army. Alexander Haig, a military assistant to the President's National Security Advisor, was one of those opponents. His views, as expressed in a May 2, 1969 memorandum to Henry Kissinger, are an example of the challenges the AVF concept faced. He wrote: "You will note the Army's feelings which I share that an all-volunteer force under certain concepts would be totally incompatible with the tradition of the military and our society, a judgment that I think even Sam Huntington would support. It will be interesting to see what the President's panel comes up with in this area. The only reason I am not more concerned about this campaign promise is the fact that I know a Republican budget could not sustain the simple economics of such a force, even if the Vietnam conflict were settled tomorrow."

A third possible approach was to establish an independent commission. Those present in Key Biscayne decided that this approach was the best, particularly given the considerable opposition to the concept of all-volunteer service in the military, especially from the Joint Chiefs and the service secretaries. The opposition was so intense that at one point I had to direct the Joint Chiefs to stop making speeches on volunteer service. I explained to them that this concept was going to be adopted and that they were going to support it. I am glad we made that decision in Key Biscayne. The creation of a commission, independent of the Department of Defense and the National Security Council, helped to dispel much of the opposition over the all-volunteer force, not only in the military but also among the general public. I believe the commission was a key to building the needed support for the AVF.

On January 30, 1969, President Nixon sent me an order requesting the plan for a special commission, to develop a detailed plan for action on ending the draft. The people who served on the Gates Commission gave their work a tremendous amount of time and effort. I recall that Thomas Gates did not want to chair the commission initially. When I first raised the issue with him, he said he just couldn't do it. I then asked him, "If the President of the United States calls you, will you do it?" Gates said that he had never turned down a president with regard to anything. That was his way of saying yes. And he did a tremendous job.

PROCEEDING CAREFULLY:
GAINING SUPPORT

One had to proceed carefully down the path toward implementing an all-volunteer force, as the draft had many constituents. Early on, I convened three luncheons with groups of college presidents. Why? The draft was a very important recruiting tool for universities, because college deferments were available at the time. During these luncheons, I announced that I was going to go to Congress to get approval for a lottery system, which would significantly curtail college deferments.[1] The lottery system was instituted by Congress, despite its opponents, and was a prelude to the work of the Gates Commission.

Gaining support in Congress for the all-volunteer force was another challenge. I worked very closely with many members of the House Armed Services Committee — Les Arends, Eddie Hebert, and Mendel Rivers, to name a few. The committee was divided over the all-volunteer force, and the initiative had lost momentum. There appeared to be nothing that could restore the dwindling support. I talked privately with Eddie Hebert about an issue that the committee had unsuccessfully raised before Congress and the Office of Management and Budget for six years — that of building an armed forces medical university on the Bethesda campus of the U.S. Naval Hospital. I agreed to testify on behalf of this idea in exchange for the committee's support for the AVF. Although I received a letter authorized by the President directing me not to testify, I was able to explain to him the importance of the legislation to our efforts on the AVF: that such a university would help provide a source for military doctors, who would no longer be supplied through the draft. In the end, the President told me to do what I thought was best, and I testified for the medical university before Congress. The medical university was built in Bethesda, and the all-volunteer force sailed through the House Armed Services Committee — an example of how the consensus-building process sometimes worked.

It was critically important to make sure that the all-volunteer force had sufficient support in the Congress — to make sure it had the votes. I was fortunate to have served as a member of the House Appropriations Subcommittee on Defense for nine terms, so I knew the members well. I was perhaps the only secretary of defense who was routinely invited to sit in on the committee markup of the defense budget — whether it was the defense bill or a supplemental. During my tenure, the department never lost a vote in the Congress. My staff, including Assistant Secretary of Defense for Manpower and Reserve Affairs Roger Kelley, worked hard to track the votes for the all-volunteer force on a regular basis. Every Wednesday, I received a report on the status of members' positions on the issue — each member, by name, by district. I personally phoned each member whose position was borderline. I commend my staff for their efforts. They were the kind of team who made it possible for the department to get the votes it needed.

IN CONCLUSION

From 1939 through October 1972, the Department of Defense regularly used the draft to man its force. It was the easiest way to meet its manpower requirements, but it was not the best way. Back in 1973, the department was successful in implementing the all-volunteer force because we were selective about our objectives and relentless in their pursuit; because I had a strong management team; and because we obtained support from Congress, from the media, and from the American public. These were the key ingredients in our recipe for success.

Part 1 of this volume explores further some of the issues that I have touched on here and others that surrounded the all-volunteer force in its early years. Among the topics addressed in these chapters are how Nixon came to embrace the all-volunteer force concept; rationale for the conclusions reached by the Gates Commission and various perspectives on whether they were right; and implementation challenges, particularly in recruiting and compensation. These papers draw from the personal experiences of the authors, many of whom were participants in the initial years of transition from conscription to an all-volunteer force. As a consequence, they are rich in history and offer valuable insight for the future.

Establishing the all-volunteer force was a great accomplishment. The draft has no place in today's era of warfare, where our troops face a complex and challenging enemy. It does not lead to the kind of high-quality and highly capable force that the nation needs and that the all-volunteer force has produced. The dedicated service of our men and women in uniform is the clearest evidence of the wisdom of our nation's decision, 30 years ago, to return to a volunteer force.

NOTES

1. The first lottery was conducted on December 1, 1969. It included all males born between 1944 and 1950. Individuals were assigned random sequence numbers from 1 to 365 based on a random drawing of birth dates. In 1970, draft calls were issued for individuals holding numbers below 196. The rest were exempted from any future military obligation.

★ ★ ★ ★ ★ ★ ★ ★ ★ ★ ★

CHAPTER 1

REFLECTIONS FROM
THE GATES COMMISSION

FREDERICK B. DENT

Let me say at the outset of my recollections regarding President Nixon's Commission on an All-Volunteer Armed Force that I am very proud of the results of our recommendations to President Nixon as well as his political courage and wisdom in accepting and executing them. His action brought to a halt the unfortunate protests nationwide, which were threatening the very fabric of our society. Additionally, his action resulted in the development of the nation's fine all-volunteer forces on land, at sea, and in the air. The points made below reflect my view of the most important positions taken by the commission that are relevant for the future of the all-volunteer force—the inequity of the draft, low pay for military members, the question of national service, and the significance of a standby draft.

President Nixon's charge to the commission in 1969 was clear: "I have directed the Commission to develop a comprehensive plan for eliminating conscription and moving to an all-volunteer armed force." He also laid out certain criteria for achieving the goal and warned that "the transition to an all-volunteer force must, of course, be handled cautiously and responsibly so that our national security is fully maintained" (Nixon 1970, vii). A remarkable thing to me was that President Nixon undertook this initiative just two months into his first term.

EDITORS' NOTE:

Each of the authors in this chapter was invited to participate in the 30th anniversary conference. Frederick Dent and Stephen Herbits participated in the opening panel and presented their papers. Milton Friedman and Theodore Hesburgh were unable to attend, but forwarded the statements included in this chapter. At the conference, their remarks were read by Secretary Melvin Laird.

★ ─────────────────────────────────────

The makeup of the commission was very sound and diverse. It was headed by a former secretary of defense, Thomas S. Gates, a wonderful, experienced man who previously served as chairman of J. P. Morgan and Company and president of the University of Pennsylvania. The commission also included three other prominent business executives, including Dr. Alan Greenspan, currently chairman of the Federal Reserve Board; two former supreme allied commanders, Europe, Generals Alfred Gruenther and Lauris Norstad; three university presidents; a boarding school headmaster; two university professors, including Nobel Prize winner Dr. Milton Friedman; a former distinguished member of Congress; the executive director of the National Association for the Advancement of Colored People; and a college student, Stephen Herbits, who is one of my fellow commentators in this chapter. The commission had a total of 15 members.

A key to the successful execution of President Nixon's charge was the splendid commission staff operating under the truly remarkable leadership of Dr. William H. Meckling, a dean from the University of Rochester. The large staff, consisting of scholars, military personnel, and consultants, produced important and pertinent studies that became the basis of the commission's report to the President. These studies made up four sizable volumes, which were subsequently made available to the public. Many of these studies were nothing short of brilliant. A great collegial atmosphere prevailed among the commission members and the staff. We were determined to carry out the President's mandate, but also kept open minds, and ultimately reached a truly unanimous recommendation to present to President Nixon.

My most compelling personal recollection of our findings was the maladministration of the draft, which led to social unrest and protests on campuses and in the streets. Because of deferrals granted to certain individuals, the draft encouraged students to stay in college and graduate school, to flee to Canada, or to take other actions to avoid being drafted. It interfered with the operation of the civilian labor market and the choices individuals typically make about careers, marriage, and other life decisions. A draft, whether under selective service or a lottery, was inequitable.

Those who were drafted not only put their lives at risk for the country, but were compensated at a level equal to only 60 percent of the average compensation of their peers in the private sector. How could the nation force some individuals to work at far less than the going wage at something they did not want to do, while others could escape that responsibility? I personally felt that the draft was a national disgrace, a failure of representative government.

The commission recommended that Congress correct the inequity in basic pay for first-term enlisted men and officers at an estimated cost of about $2.7 billion. Additional costs of moving to an all-volunteer force, such as outlays for proficiency pay, reserve forces pay, medical corps pay, and recruiting in general, were estimated to be about $560 million. Because most of this budget increase took the form of personal income, about $540 million of it would be recovered by the U.S. Treasury in the form of income tax collections (Gates 1970, 124).

The commission estimated that the additional annual budget cost required to maintain a 2.5 million-man force would total $2.1 billion, after reflecting personal income tax collections for higher paid military members. But savings would result from going to an all-volunteer force in the form of lower training costs due to increased retention and reduced turnover with the end of the two-year draft, as well as increased productivity through higher individual and unit performance with a more experienced force. On net, the costs of moving to a volunteer military were quite modest and well worth correcting a very inequitable system.

An important problem for the commission was the maintenance of the required number of medical doctors in the services. Fortunately, the number of medical students already committed to military service at that time gave the Department of Defense the leeway to entertain several possible solutions. It was clear that special recruiting and retention incentives, such as stipends for students, as well as a special career progression for physicians, would be needed.

We also gave consideration to mandatory national service—which would require all youth to enter the military or some other form of public service—as an alternative to the draft. We concluded that implementation of such a system would amount to trying to correct an inequitable situation by simply expanding it. Mandatory national service would be coercive and involuntary, much as the draft we recommended abolishing. Such a solution would also be excessively disruptive to young people's lives and contrary to the nation's traditional respect for individual freedom and choice.

I was impressed with the projection for fiscal year 1975 that 6.1 percent of the male population between 18 and 45 years of age would be required to man an all-volunteer force of 2.5 million men, considerably fewer than under a mixed force of conscripts and volunteers. More impressive was the smaller number of projected accessions needed to sustain a volunteer force. If the draft were abolished, we argued that an all-volunteer force with the same effective strength as a 2.5 million-man mixed force would require 25 percent fewer recruits per year (who meet the same mental, physical, and moral standards) than the mixed force (Gates 1970, 42). The percentage of males required for enlistment could be reduced further by population growth, female enlistments, or transfers of some jobs to the civilian sector.

Our final recommendation to the President was that the nation's interests would be best served by an all-volunteer force, yet supported by an effective standby draft that could be activated by the President with congressional approval. We recommended that legislation be enacted to provide a register of all males within a certain age, a system for selection and processing inductees, and an organization to maintain the register and administer procedures.

Commission members were invited to meet in the Cabinet Room with President Nixon when Chairman Tom Gates presented our report to him. The President's courageous decision to move to an all-volunteer force was executed smoothly and effectively by the successful efforts of the Department of Defense under the leadership of Secretary Melvin Laird. The efforts of the Secretary and his staff led to today's superb all-volunteer force.

As we look to the future, we must be alert as a nation to avoid the mistakes of the past, such as pay inequity, and to craft personnel policies that will make volunteer service attractive to both the active and reserve forces. It may also be time to review the status of the standby draft.

While those who reached the age of required draft registration between 1940 and 1973 generally assumed that the draft was a normal component of our nation's fabric, history teaches us to the contrary. Conscription was the primary means of securing personnel during World Wars I and II as well as during the Korean conflict, but throughout most of the United States' history, its military has been composed of volunteers.

This is a national tradition that I hope we can maintain.

REFERENCES

Nixon, Richard M. 1970. Statement by the President announcing the creation of the commission. In *Report of the President's Commission on an All-Volunteer Armed Force*, by Thomas S. Gates. Washington, D.C.: U.S. Government Printing Office.

Gates, Thomas S. 1970. *Report of the President's Commission on an All-Volunteer Armed Force*. Washington, D.C.: U.S. Government Printing Office.

MILTON FRIEDMAN

No public policy debate in which I have engaged has given me as much satisfaction as serving on the all-volunteer commission headed by Thomas Gates. The draft was a major stain on our free society. I had talked and written against it for more than a decade. Membership on the commission enabled me to contribute to ending the draft more directly, and in addition was intellectually stimulating and personally rewarding. To cap it all, it was crowned with success, not only in the sense that legislation was enacted to end the draft but, more important, that by general consent, the all-volunteer military has displayed in practice for three decades the advantages that we claimed for it in our report. Afghanistan and Iraq are the most recent demonstrations that an all-volunteer force can be both highly effective militarily and compatible with a free society.

STEPHEN E. HERBITS

General Jack Keane is known not only as a great leader, but also as a great intellect. In his 37 years in the Army, he has seen the full scope of the all-volunteer force and its implications. He made the following statement before the Senate Foreign Relations Committee while testifying about the Army, particularly its involvement in Iraq: "The Volunteer Force, which I personally believe is the most significant military transformation since World War II, and the enormous success of the United States Military, I think is largely attributable to the fact that the people are in because they want to be, and they come to us smart and confident, with dedication to serve their country, and that has literally changed our Force" (Keane 2003).

There are many people who were involved at the end of the 1960s and early 1970s as the nation considered the idea of a volunteer force, set policy to institute such a force, and then moved toward implementation. The giant among them is Secretary of Defense Melvin Laird. He is to be thanked for his vision, leadership, and guidance. He is a true hero of the all-volunteer force, as it would not have come to fruition without his involvement. I am going to discuss in my comments something that happened just after Secretary Laird left the Department of Defense. It is illustrative of both the importance and the difficulty of the transformation to the volunteer force.

In May 1973, Roger Kelley, the assistant secretary of defense for manpower and reserve affairs—the equivalent of today's under secretary of defense for personnel and readiness—planned to return to the private sector. He asked if I would come spend some time at the Department of Defense. In 1973, there was significant turnover among the civilian leadership in the department, and, in that vacuum, a variety of specific problems developed. The "numbers" were not looking good; there were problems, and it was not clear why. In a period of transition, the leadership was concerned.

The military manpower system can be compared to an oil refinery or petrochemical facility. In the control room of these facilities are many knobs, switches, dials, and mechanisms that control the process of refining raw petroleum. How the knobs and dials are managed determines the kind of product that is produced.

The military manpower system is similar in that there are many "dials" that work the system—perhaps 30 or more that are very important. These dials can be categorized into three groups: leadership, managerial, and technical. Leadership comes in the form of guidance set by the political and military leaders, such as deciding on the size of the active duty force or adding substantial numbers of women to the uniformed services. Managerial decisions are of the second order and are generally responsive to policy guidance, such as deciding on the number of new recruits needed to sustain the force (also called driving turnover) or changing monthly goals for recruiters. Technical decisions involve operational issues handled by the recruiting commands, such as how to achieve that monthly goal or changing testing requirements.

From the later months of 1972, when the last draft call was issued, to the early months of 1974, the Secretary and the Chief of Staff of the Army made a series of decisions affecting most of the dials in the manpower system. While each decision was perhaps justified on its own merits, together they resulted in turning each dial a slight degree in the wrong direction. By the spring of 1974, the cumulative impact of those individual decisions threatened the very viability of the volunteer force.

THE ALL-VOLUNTEER FORCE IN PERSPECTIVE

Further, the public statements made by the Army's leadership in the early months of the all-volunteer force reached a crescendo in June 1973. In that month, the Secretary and the Chief of Staff of the Army made a total of 12 public statements which unambiguously signaled that the voluntary Army would not succeed. Moreover, they left the impression that it would be acceptable to them if that happened. This pattern continued until Deputy Secretary of Defense William Clements addressed their behavior directly.

By 1974, Deputy Secretary Clements had reviewed a comprehensive analysis of the problems of the all-volunteer force and summoned the Secretary and Chief of Staff of the Army to his office. He reminded them that national policy had been set by the Congress of the United States, the President of the United States, and the Secretary of Defense. He instructed them to *turn the dials back* and to do so within 30 days. It was just as easy to turn the dials back as it was to turn them in the wrong direction in the first place. The dials were turned back and the volunteer force survived a serious crisis.

That same spring, Milton Friedman—one of the guiding lights of the all-volunteer force policy—rejoined the public fray. In his 1963 book, *Capitalism and Freedom*, Friedman had outlined the desirability of an all-volunteer armed force. He later served on the Gates Commission from which came the *Report of the President's Commission on an All-Volunteer Armed Force* (1970). In May 1974, Friedman wrote an article for his regular *Newsweek* column describing the Army's questionable managerial decisions, referring to its actions as "sabotage." That indictment piqued interest in Washington. It alienated some people, and caused me to be summoned to the office of Roger Kelley's successor.

I was asked two questions. First, was Milton Friedman's article in the national interest? I responded: "Yes, I do think it is in the national interest that the Army's efforts were put on the record." The second question was whether I had provided the information to Dr. Friedman for his article. My answer was this: "If anyone can be called the father of the volunteer force, it's Milton Friedman." I referred to his book. I referred to the advice he had given to candidate Richard Nixon in 1967 and 1968, to his service on the Gates Commission, and to the fact that he was a Nobel laureate. I asked the Assistant Secretary whether he thought that Milton Friedman would rely on a young staffer at the Pentagon for information that would appear under his name in an international magazine. And I exited. That was the end of that.

I tell this story not to set a negative tone about the volunteer Army, but rather to raise a caution. Much time and care were put into creating the volunteer force—by President Nixon, Secretary Laird, and many others. The concept of a volunteer military was first studied by a presidential commission. It was then studied for a year within the Department of Defense, and that study was followed by a national policy discussion. All of these steps were extremely important because the public, the Congress, and the military opposed the concept of a volunteer force when it was introduced.

Today is a different world. The vast majority of the military supports a volunteer force and, in fact, would vigorously fight a reinstitution of the draft.

The public understands the all-volunteer force and supports it. The number of people even talking about returning to the draft is minimal. However, despite this support, public debate will not decide the future of the volunteer force. Its future will be determined by how we manage the little knobs and dials. It will be determined, for example, by how the department handles the National Guard and reserves over the next few years—by how they are integrated into the total force and by how the total force is adjusted so that members of the guard and reserve are not overused, disrupting their lives and particularly their roles as first responders.

The future of the all-volunteer force will not be determined by the large public policy issues. It will be determined by how the leadership in the Department of Defense manages the specifics. History reminds us of what we need to remember as we go forward.

REFERENCES

Keane, Jack. 2003. General Jack Keane, Acting Chief of Staff of the Army, statement before the Senate Foreign Relations Committee, July 29.

Gates, Thomas S. 1970. *Report of the President's Commission on an All-Volunteer Armed Force.* Washington, D.C.: U.S. Government Printing Office.

THEODORE M. HESBURGH

Shortly after President Nixon's inauguration, I was visiting with him, one-on-one, in the Oval Office. I mentioned several things I thought he could accomplish and that would be good if he did. One of these, of course, was the all-volunteer Army. The other was the vote for 18-year-olds, since they could be drafted at that age and should be able to vote for their commander in chief. Fortunately, the President was able to accomplish the latter with a new amendment to the Constitution, for which I think he did not receive adequate credit.

I have followed with great pride and satisfaction the birth and flowering of the all-volunteer Army. I believe it was an idea whose time had come, and the past years have certainly justified its creation.

★ ★ ★ ★ ★ ★ ★ ★ ★ ★ ★

CHAPTER 2

THE MAKING OF THE ALL-VOLUNTEER FORCE

MARTIN ANDERSON

Ever since the founding of our country in 1776, the military draft has been a controversial issue. The United States drafted men during the Civil War, during World War I, and during World War II. Not too many years ago, during the 1960s, the military draft was one of the issues that dominated political debate, as hundreds of thousands of teenage males were forced to serve in the Vietnam War. And when those young draftees began dying, the rising opposition to the draft divided our country dangerously. It was a nasty time.

Over the past 30 years, the military draft has vanished from American politics. It was a non-issue when Ronald Reagan was elected president in 1980, and it remained a non-issue right up through the election that George W. Bush won in 2000. Except for occasional calls for conscription by politicians such as Fritz Hollings and Charles Rangel, it has been many, many years since most politicians have raised the idea of drafting young men into the armed forces.

The abolition of the military draft in 1973, however, was historic, in that it marked the first time in United States history that the nation officially adopted a national policy of an all-volunteer force. Ending the draft was controversial. When President Nixon proposed the end of the draft, the idea was opposed by most of the military establishment, by many in Congress, by most of Nixon's national security advisers, and by a large segment of the media.

Conscription involves some of the most basic questions of individual rights and the relationship between the state and the individual. The ending of the draft was preceded by years of debate in intellectual circles, in the Congress, in political campaigns, and in the media. The question of the military draft has troubled our society from its very beginning, flaring into controversy during times of war and subsiding during times of peace.

During the 1950s and the early 1960s, a number of articles appeared arguing the case for an all-volunteer force. Senator Adlai Stevenson called for the abolition of the draft in 1956, and Senator Barry Goldwater called for it in 1964—both to no avail. But within the intellectual world, the idea was spreading and gaining converts across the ideological spectrum, from John Kenneth Galbraith to Milton Friedman. The Vietnam War brought the issue to a head.

In December 1966, my wife and I were invited to dinner at the house of a colleague of mine at Columbia University in New York. His other guests included a young lawyer, George Anderegg, who had recently joined Richard Nixon's law firm on Wall Street. As the evening progressed, so did the intensity of the political discussion. Finally, in exasperation, Anderegg looked at me and said, "With views like that you should be working for my boss."

I didn't think any more about it, but he did. A few days later I got a telephone call from Leonard Garment, one of Nixon's law partners. He said he had heard there was some crazy professor at Columbia who thought like Nixon, and he invited me to join him and a few others for dinner later that week. Intrigued, I accepted, took the subway down to Wall Street, and soon became part of a small informal group that had begun plotting Nixon's 1968 presidential campaign. The group included Garment, Pat Buchanan, John Sears, Raymond Price, and Alan Greenspan.

In March 1967, at one of our weekly meetings in a tiny room at the law offices of Nixon, Mudge, Rose, and Guthrie, someone raised the issue of the military draft. For as long as anyone could remember, Nixon had supported the draft, and since 1952, when he became Dwight Eisenhower's running mate, he had loyally supported Eisenhower's idea of universal military training, which would ensure that all young males, not just a select few, would serve in the military.

The question before the group was, what should Nixon's position be in the upcoming presidential campaign? Should he stay with the idea of universal military training? Should he propose changes to the current draft system—a system that was under increasing attack for being unfair? Or should he propose a radical new plan of mandatory universal national service for everyone?

I was familiar with the debate on the military draft, and had just finished reading an article by Milton Friedman that brilliantly summed up the arguments in favor of ending the draft and moving toward an all-volunteer system. As I looked around the table it was clear that no one thought having Nixon call for universal military training was going to be much of a political plus in 1968. But it was also clear that unless he had a new alternative, he would be stuck with the position he had held for 15 years.

"I have an idea," I said, thinking about the powerful arguments in Friedman's article. "What if I could show you how we could end the draft completely—and increase our military power at the same time?" They just looked at me. So I barreled along and said, "Look, let me take a crack at putting together a paper on this that would explain how it would work." They were obviously more than a little skeptical, but probably figured it wouldn't hurt to have the professor write a little paper. So they agreed that I should go ahead.

During the next few days I combed my files for material on the draft, and spent many hours researching the issue in the Columbia University library. The result, finished a few weeks later, was a 17-page policy memorandum for Nixon that spelled out the essential arguments, pro and con, for ending the draft and establishing an all-volunteer force.

Nixon read it, indicated he found it "very interesting," and said he wanted to think more about it. Nothing seemed to happen for the next four months. Few of the campaign staff expressed any interest in the idea, and the ones who did — like Pat Buchanan — thought it was a bad idea.

But later I found out that Nixon was intrigued with the idea. He set up a 30-man task force of his old friends in the military and the political world, and sent them copies of the proposal.

During the next four months the comments rolled in. About half of the commentators liked the idea, and the other half were strongly opposed. Some thought it was dangerous. No one seemed to be neutral. But Nixon never mentioned the issue, and nothing happened until one day in late 1967.

On November 17, 1967, Nixon was returning to New York City from Washington on the Eastern Airlines shuttle. In addition to myself, he was accompanied by a young reporter, Robert Semple, from the *New York Times*. In November 1967, Nixon's chances of winning the Republican nomination, let alone the election, were considered so dim that covering his budding campaign did not seem to warrant the attention of one of the more senior reporters from the *Times*. Semple was new at the paper and had just recently been assigned to cover Nixon.

After the plane took off I switched seats with Semple so he could conduct the interview with Nixon that had been arranged earlier. Semple's interview ranged over a variety of domestic and foreign issues. As the interview was winding down, Semple suddenly changed the subject. "What would you do about the military draft?" he asked, knowing that Nixon had openly and consistently supported both the draft and universal military training when he was vice president.

Nixon smiled and replied evenly, "I think we should eliminate the draft and move to an all-volunteer force."

And then Nixon continued to elaborate on his new idea. Semple, somewhat stunned, hurriedly scribbled notes. For Nixon was calmly reversing his long-standing position on an issue that could be critical in the next year's presidential campaign, and was confidently explaining just why he now favored such a move.

It had taken four months, but Nixon apparently had been persuaded by the arguments to end the draft. And from that day on, his policy was to end the draft. But there was much opposition to that idea even within the campaign; and as the campaign gained momentum, his primary victories piled up, and he won the nomination at the convention, Nixon did not make it one of his major issues. There was no major speech given about an all-volunteer force.

At least not until October. As the campaign swung into its final weeks in 1968, the polls showed a very close race, and Nixon decided on a policy blitzkrieg. One afternoon he called a staff meeting and announced that he intended to make a new major policy speech every day for the next 10 days. He asked for suggestions.

We were all near exhaustion, and after the third or fourth idea was put on the table, there was silence. So I spoke up, saying, "Well, you could always do one on the draft."

Nixon looked around at the others and said, "That's a good idea. Is that okay with everyone?"

There was silence.

Nixon said, "Okay—next?"

I knew that everyone in the room thought it was a lousy idea but, with about three weeks left to go in the campaign, we were acutely short of finding 10 new major issues. And no one said a word.

Ray Price, Nixon's senior speech writer, got the assignment to write the first draft, and he and I worked together on it. Nixon checked and edited the speech, and, on October 17, 1968, he laid out his full policy on military manpower in an address to the nation on the CBS Radio Network.

Early in his speech Nixon said simply, "We have lived with the draft so long . . . that too many of us now accept it as normal and necessary. . . . I say it's time we took a new look at the draft—at the question of permanent conscription in a free society." And he ended that speech with these lines: "So I say, it's time we looked to our consciences. Let's show our commitment to freedom by preparing to assure our young people theirs."

Nineteen days later, on November 5, Richard Nixon defeated Hubert Humphrey—by a whisker—and became the 37th president of the United States. The all-volunteer force was no longer simply an issue for debate among intellectuals. It was now a major commitment of a newly elected president.

But there was a little problem.

Turning that idea, that campaign promise, into the law of the land was going to be extremely difficult. Key members of Congress, many military leaders, and many of Nixon's own appointees, including his secretary of defense and his national security adviser, had long supported the draft. The public's support for an all-volunteer force was growing, but in early 1969 that support was no match for the opposition.

Faced with certain defeat if he submitted legislation to end the draft to the Congress in early 1969, Nixon accepted a suggestion I made to keep the issue alive by studying it for a year or so.

So, on March 27, 1969, Nixon appointed a presidential commission to review the idea and report to him within a year. The members of the commission were carefully chosen. It is relatively easy to select the members of a commission so that the result is predetermined. We deliberately—at some risk—chose not to do that.

Instead, we decided to appoint five people who were for the idea, five who were against it, and five who, while they had no clear position, were men and women of integrity. Two of the members who we knew were in favor of the idea were Alan Greenspan and Milton Friedman. Two of the members who had serious reservations were General Alfred Gruenther and General Lauris Norstad.

Nixon wanted Thomas Gates, the former secretary of defense under President Eisenhower, to head the commission, but he was reluctant. I remember accompanying Gates when he met with Nixon in the Oval Office.

Gates protested that he was not the man for the job, saying, "But Mr. President, I'm opposed to the whole idea of a volunteer force. You don't want me as the chairman."

"Yes I do Tom," the President replied, "that's exactly why I want you as the chairman. You have experience and integrity. If you change your mind and think we should end the draft, then I'll know it's a good idea."

What could Gates do? He accepted the chairmanship.

Over one million dollars was appropriated for the work of the commission, and soon the members and their staff of 44 experts were hard at work. As a special assistant to President Nixon, I got the task of being the White House liaison to the commission. The internal debate was intense and, as they sometimes say in the diplomatic world, "frank." But they drove to meet the deadline.

A little less than a year later, on February 20, 1970, the President's Commission on an All-Volunteer Armed Force submitted its report to President Nixon. Every single member of the commission agreed that the military draft should be abolished. Here is an excerpt from the report: "We unanimously believe that the nation's interests will be better served by an all-volunteer force, supported by an effective standby draft, than by a mixed force of volunteers and conscripts; that steps should be taken promptly to move in this direction . . . We have satisfied ourselves that a volunteer force will not jeopardize national security, and we believe it will have a beneficial effect on the military as well as the rest of our society" (Gates 1970, iii).

That report, unlike many government reports, was distributed widely to the media and key policy makers. The Macmillan Company published a hard-cover edition, which found its way into every major library in the country, and tens of thousands of a small paperback edition went on sale across the country.

The next step was to draft legislation, and I chaired a White House working group that helped craft it. Finally, after a long and difficult struggle in the Congress, the legislation passed. Induction authority officially ended on July 1, 1973.

It was five and one-half years from the time Nixon announced his idea to a young *New York Times* reporter to the death of the draft and the birth of a new defense manpower policy. The policy is one of the most important legacies that Nixon left. It is also an example of the kind of power a determined and skillful president can exercise. It does make a difference who sits in that Oval Office.

What I have just described is but one small slice of all the forces that created the all-volunteer force in this country 30 years ago. The draft was an issue that had bedeviled us since the founding of our country. Thousands of men and women have been involved in the movement that created a truly professional force of warriors: a force of men and women who all freely choose to become part of the military might that protects us and preserves our liberty.

The all-volunteer force is no ordinary force. It is extraordinary and its power is awesome. Let me just conclude by saying a few words about what was created.

Today, in the year 2003, the military might of the United States of America is unchallenged. Yes, the world is a dangerous place, and we are not beloved by many of its inhabitants—not because we are evil, but because we are good. If they could, our adversaries would conquer and enslave us. But they cannot for one simple, clear reason.

No other nation in the world—not Russia, not China, not Iraq or Iran or North Korea—has military power that comes even close to matching that of the U.S. armed forces.

Part of the United States' military strength comes from the equipment that a prosperous economy can buy. But that is only part of what has made the nation invincible. Yes, our tanks and our guns, and our planes and our ships, and our nuclear-tipped intercontinental missiles are unmatched. But this armada does not operate itself.

Our military strength requires extraordinary skill and dedication and passion. Our full military power is much more the men and women in our armed forces than the hardware they employ. What has changed most dramatically in our armed forces over the past 30 years is not the equipment but the skills and judgment of the men and women who use it.

And we know why. It's pretty simple. We should have known it all along. It is because they are volunteers. They freely join. They have the spirit and morale of people who choose their own destiny. And they have the judgment and skill of those who prepare and practice and who take pride in what they do.

The all-volunteer force is no longer an intellectual theory. We now have a history of what it can do. The might of the all-volunteer force was first clearly revealed during the Persian Gulf War in 1991. It was the first serious test of an all-volunteer force that had been building for almost 20 years. The result was stunning. Millions of Americans watched in living color on television as our military force calmly and deliberately crushed the enemy forces and liberated Kuwait. And they did so with astonishing speed and very few American casualties. Every nation in the world took careful note and recalculated its view of U.S. might.

And then again in Afghanistan in 2001, and in Iraq in 2003, the prowess of our forces was demonstrated to be even more powerful than it was in 1991. The all-volunteer force of America is an awesome fighting machine. When it came back from the Persian Gulf War in 1991, President Bush (the first one) called it "the finest fighting force the nation has ever known." He was right. Now his son is the commander in chief of the most powerful fighting force the world has ever known.

The possessors of this military might have never shown the slightest inclination to lust for political power. They are not any threat to our liberty. They are liberty's guardians. The idea of civilian control of all that power is still embedded deep in our culture, in the military and outside the military.

Today our armed forces are quite an extraordinary group of men and women. Not only are they warriors who take on difficult and dangerous tasks, risking their lives. Not only do they have respect and reverence for the free society we have built. They are also wonderful people. They are intelligent, skillful, and compassionate—men and women we are proud of, men and women others want to join.

Let me end with a short story about President Reagan.

Reagan loved to read and write, and when he came across something by a person who deeply impressed him he would carefully copy the statement by hand onto a three-by-five-inch index card. He kept these little white cards in the drawer of his desk.

Recently, I was given access to these cards while writing a book about Reagan's private letters. While we found 6,500 handwritten letters, which he had authored over a period of 70 years, we found only a few index cards on which he had written quotations.

One of the quotations that he had copied and kept in his desk drawer was about the U.S. armed forces. It said: "The vital element in keeping the peace is our military establishment. Our arms must be mighty, ready for instant action, so that no potential aggressor may be tempted to risk its own destruction." The man who said that was General Dwight D. Eisenhower.

Eisenhower was right to write it, and Reagan was right to keep it as a reminder of what our armed forces must be if we want to protect our liberties and this incredible country we have inherited.

The key to doing it is the all-volunteer force.

REFERENCES

Gates, Thomas S. 1970. *Report of the President's Commission on an All-Volunteer Armed Force.* Washington, D.C.: U.S. Government Printing Office.

CHAPTER 3

THE GATES COMMISSION:
RIGHT FOR THE WRONG REASONS

BERNARD D. ROSTKER

INTRODUCTION

It is wonderful that after three decades we can celebrate the continued success of the all-volunteer force (AVF) — that this experiment in social and military manpower policy has been successful. Never before had any country tried to maintain such a large standing military without a draft. Moreover, many can remember the dark days of 1979 when the misnormed Armed Services Vocational Aptitude Battery (ASVAB) resulted in a force that even the most ardent supporters of the AVF concluded was not sustainable. And yet, today, there is no question that the AVF has succeeded in producing a superb military force, tested in two wars and the pride of our nation. It is often said that imitation is the highest form of flattery. In this case the foreign countries, such as France and Spain, that have followed our lead and moved to an all-volunteer force attest to our success.

THE "SOCIAL WELFARE" ARGUMENT
OF THE GATES COMMISSION

As we commemorate the work of the Gates Commission and the wisdom of its unanimous recommendation to end conscription, it is worthwhile to reflect on the reasons that it gave the American people for embarking on this potentially risky path. It invoked a social welfare argument. A whole chapter in the commission's report (chapter 3) was devoted to conscription as a hidden tax (Gates 1970). The conscription tax is the earnings that a draftee forgoes by being drafted into the military. Because under a draft, the military would pay much less than what an individual could earn in the civilian sector, this tax can be considerable. For example, if in a year the military pays $10,000 to a draftee who could earn $15,000 in a civilian job, the draftee must forgo $5,000 of income. This draftee, then, would be paying a hidden tax of $5,000 for each year of service.

★ ⎯⎯⎯⎯⎯⎯⎯⎯⎯⎯⎯⎯⎯⎯⎯⎯⎯⎯⎯⎯⎯⎯⎯⎯⎯⎯⎯⎯⎯⎯⎯⎯⎯⎯⎯⎯⎯⎯⎯

The commission recommendation to move to an AVF echoed the arguments that had been heard at the University of Chicago Conference on the Draft in 1966 (Tax 1967). First, using the paradigm of conscription as a tax, the commission found the tax to be inequitable and regressive. Second, it argued that a full accounting for the true cost of the draft meant that, even given the higher budget costs of an all-volunteer force, a mixed system of volunteers and conscripts was more costly to society than an all-volunteer force would be. Third, because the Department of Defense did not account for the true cost of the military labor it employed, the armed forces were "inefficient" and were wasting society's resources.

The commission invoked Benjamin Franklin's writings on the impressing of American sailors at the time of the Revolution to ask if it was "just . . . that the richer . . . should compel the poorer to fight for them and their properties for such wages as they think fit to allow, and punish them if they refuse" (Gates 1970, 24)? The importance of this argument was highlighted in the report. The commission noted: "This shift in tax burden lies at the heart of resistance on 'cost' grounds to an all-volunteer armed force. Indeed, this shift in tax burden explains how conscription gets enacted in the first place. In a political democracy conscription offers the general public an opportunity to impose a disproportionate share of defense costs on a minority of the population" (Gates 1970, 25).

The commission found morally questionable the discriminatory form that this implicit tax takes and the abridgement of individual freedom that is involved. The commission argued, "The extent of the discrimination resulting from conscription depends on the proportion of the population forced to serve, and on the level of compensation provided to those who serve . . . In addition to being discriminatory, conscription as a tax is also generally regressive, falling on individuals whose income is low" (Gates 1970, 27–28).

Now looking back over these 30 years we might ask if the redress of this discrimination and inefficiency, which proved compelling to the commissioners in their unanimous vote to recommend the end of conscription, was also central to the success we celebrate today. In other words, are we here today because we eliminated this hidden tax of conscription? Are we here today to celebrate the gross product gained by allowing those who would have been drafted to contribute to society via their best free market alternative? Are we even here today because, as Milton Friedman said at the landmark 1966 Chicago conference, "a draft is inconsistent with a free society" (Tax 1967, 200)? With due respect to the commission and Professor Friedman, I think not.

ALTERNATIVE VIEWS OF CONSCRIPTION

It should be noted that even at the time of the Gates Commission's report, there were those, like Senator Sam Nunn, who were certain that it was not the hidden tax argument embraced by the Gates Commission but the public's growing opposition to the war in Vietnam that was responsible for ending the draft. In 1973, Nunn told the Georgia state legislature, "the concept [of the all-volunteer force] is a clear result of the Vietnam war because it caused the President and

Congress to yield to the tremendous pressure to end the draft at almost any price" (Nunn 1973). In 1978, he argued before a Senate subcommittee, "The AVF is to a large extent a political child of the draft card burning, campus riots, and violent protest demonstrations of the late 1960s and early 1970s" (Nunn 1978, 50).

Moreover, the notion that the state had a right to take service involuntarily had a long and honorable history. Conscription is implied in the Bible when specific exemptions from military service—who "may leave and return home"—are listed (Deut. 20:5 The Holy Scriptures). Moreover, the effectiveness of conscripts is questioned, as it is written, "Whoever, is afraid and faint-hearted must leave and return home, so that his fellows may not become faint-hearted like him." In 1783, George Washington wrote Alexander Hamilton that "every Citizen who enjoys the protection of a free Government, owes not only a proportion of his property, but even of his personal services to the defense of it" (O'Sullivan and Meckler 1974, 27). Conscription was accepted throughout most of the world to provide personnel to staff armed forces, and is still used in our country today to select citizens to sit on a jury.

Recent foreign converts to an all-volunteer force, such as France and Spain, do not appear particularly moved by the argument that conscription is "inconsistent with a free society." In fact, many in these countries still believe it is the obligation of every citizen to perform some service at the call of the state. Despite these beliefs, these nations found universal military service both unaffordable and inconsistent with maintaining a competent, modern military. Ultimately, the compelling arguments against conscription for them were the cost of universal service, the poor efficiency and low effectiveness of a military force of conscripts, and the unfairness perceived by the citizenry in a system that selects so few to serve (Jehn and Selden 2002). These same reasons that moved countries such as France and Spain to adopt an all-volunteer force are the reasons that the U.S. AVF has been so successful.

WHY HAS THE AVF BEEN SUCCESSFUL?

The AVF has been successful not because of the rationale the Gates Commission used to justify its arguments to end the draft, but because the product of its recommendation, the all-volunteer force, after many growing pains, became a military force unsurpassed in its efficiency and effectiveness. I know of no military leader in uniform, nor civilian leader charged with the management and maintenance of the national defense, who would choose to return to conscription in any form—universal service, selective service, or random selection—because these leaders perceive that this great experiment has been a success. They support the all-volunteer policy because of the force it has produced.

With the most profound respect for the Gates Commission and all of those who participated in the grueling battles to end conscription, I humbly suggest that they made the right recommendation for a reason that they did not fully understand. In the final analysis, we do not today celebrate the capturing for society of the productivity that would have been lost to the country by those young men who would have been forced to work for the military at less than market wages.

Rather it is the productivity of those young men and women who voluntarily joined the military over the last 30 years that we celebrate today.

In the final analysis, as we look back over these 30 years, the problem with the draft was not what it did to society in the form of lost social welfare, but what it did to the military. By providing an unlimited supply of males for short periods of time, the draft established a military force of limited capability. The first thing the end of conscription did was to force the military to "clean up its act," and not just one act, but many acts. From recruiting to barracks life, the military needed to select policies and programs that were cost effective in terms of recruiting, retaining, and motivating the people who voluntarily joined. Over the last 30 years, the cohorts that joined the military responded by reenlisting in unprecedented numbers to form the most professional and effective force in the history of the world.[1]

Not long ago, the Chief of Naval Operations confided in me that he had a terrible personnel problem. Too many sailors at the end of their first term wanted to stay in the Navy. The very existence of such a problem is remarkable given the 15 percent first-term retention of the pre-AVF years (Lee and Parker 1977, 358). What was he to do? The sailors were all qualified. The Chief had cut accessions as far as he dared without destroying the infrastructure needed to ensure the ability of the Navy to operate in the future. He had cut back on recruiting and training to levels that threatened the viability of those institutions, and still he had more who wanted to stay. Surely the economy has something to do with the state of retention. But, I submit, more importantly, it is the volunteer force and all that has resulted in terms of quality of life for service members and their families that produced today's military.

BOTH EARLY PROPONENTS AND CRITICS GOT IT WRONG

I find it ironic that both the early proponents and critics of the volunteer force failed to foresee the superb force that would develop once the military no longer relied on the draft to fill its ranks. The reasons they both "got it wrong" are instructive as the department continues to manage the all-volunteer force into the future.

THE PROPONENTS OF THE AVF GOT IT WRONG BECAUSE . . .

The Gates Commission based its recommendation on a broad notion of social welfare, employing arguments that themselves were modified over the years as additional scholars built and critiqued argument after argument. The elegant arguments so cogently put forward by those who participated in the original Pentagon study of the draft almost 40 years ago (for example, those articulated by Walter Oi [1967]) today seem somewhat less certain. A consistent theme of both the 1964 Pentagon draft study and the Gates Commission report was that economic, rather than budget, costs should be considered when assessing the cost of the military and that any additional costs were simply an acceptable transfer of the burden of payment for national defense from draftees and reluctant volunteers to the population at large.

More recently, however, Lee and McKenzie (1992), building on the work of Browning (1987), demonstrated that such transfer payments were not neutral, and that a volunteer force, with its greater budgetary cost, could impose higher "deadweight" losses from taxation than a draft force of equal size. Warner and Asch (1996) extended Lee and McKenzie's model to distinguish between first-term and career members of the military. They acknowledged that the social costs of a draft force could actually amount to less than the social costs of a volunteer force. Parenthetically, this point was also acknowledged by Milton Friedman (1967, 203) when he noted, "When a very large fraction of the young men of the relevant age group are required . . . in the military . . . it might turn out that the implicit tax of forced service is less bad than the alternative taxes that would have to be used to finance a voluntary army. Hence for a major war, a strong case can be made for compulsory service."

Warner and Asch showed that, while the issue is ultimately empirical and hinges on questions about the deadweight loss from taxation, the elasticity of supply, and the productivity differences between volunteer and conscripted forces, the case for an AVF was more compelling than suggested by Lee and McKenzie. Their analysis is particularly insightful as to why several European countries with strong historic ties to the draft as a legitimate form of national service decided to abandon conscription. Clearly, the Gates Commission did not fully comprehend the positive impact that the all-volunteer force would have on the military itself. For example, it downplayed the dramatic effect it would have on participation of minorities and women. In fact, at the conference commemorating the 10th anniversary of the AVF held at Annapolis in 1983, Bill Meckling, the staff director of the commission, admitted his shock when Marty Binkin noted that the commission never discussed the role of women in its report (Binkin and Bach 1977). Meckling described in his address at Annapolis how he had gone back to the report to prove Binkin wrong, only to find, to his surprise, that Binkin was right (Meckling 1986, 112). At the same conference, the keynote speaker, Secretary of Defense Caspar Weinberger, pronounced the changed role of women in the armed services to be one of the most profound results of the all-volunteer force (Weinberger 1986, 3).

Finally, the Gates Commission had no way of knowing how well the volunteer force would prove itself in battle. In the words of the Chairman of the Joint Chiefs of Staff at the time of Desert Storm, "The Gulf War also demonstrated the significance of having good people. The main reason we did so well once we got there was the skill of our people. That was the result of many factors, but primarily it is the great benefit of having a volunteer professional force. The men and women who participated in Desert Shield and Desert Storm were members of the oldest, most experienced (in length of service) fighting force the United States has ever fielded" (Crowe 1993, 324).

In terms of the critics of the all-volunteer force one has only to read the article in the 1974 inaugural edition of *Armed Forces and Society* by Morris Janowitz and Charles Moskos, the nation's two leading military sociologists, to see what was missed. This article was written at a time when the issue of race was, in the words of the official Army history of the period, "of deep concern to many of the Army's leaders, [and] this sensitive subject . . . played a part in the Army's approach to the transition" (Griffith 1997) to an all-volunteer force. Moreover, this article was circulated through the White House even before it was published (Rumsfeld 1974).

In 1974, Janowitz and Moskos expressed concern for the large number of blacks who had joined the volunteer Army and questioned the "political legitimacy" of the military under the all-volunteer force. They asked if "a political democracy [can] . . . have a legitimate form of government if its military is not broadly representative of a larger society. [Moreover], can a military force whose combat units are overweighed with a racial minority have credibility in the world arena?" (Janowitz and Moskos 1974, 110). The answer, obvious to them, was no. For Janowitz and Moskos, the culprit here was the Gates Commission, "which programmed the all-volunteer force by emphasizing visible and competitive monetary compensation, rather than a series of steps and strategies dealing with the organizational climate and professional integrity of the military as a social institution" (Janowitz and Moskos 1975, 40).

Moskos carried the arguments further in the form of his institution-occupation (I/O) model. First put forward in October 1976 at the Regional Conference of the Inter-University Seminar on Armed Forces and Society in Alabama, this model drew a sharp distinction between the military as an institution and the military as an occupation. For Moskos, "an *institution* is [reflective of] transcending self-interest in favor of a presumed higher good. Members of an institution are often seen as following a calling. . . . An *occupation* is [reflective] of the marketplace, i.e., prevailing monetary rewards for equivalent competencies" (Moskos 1977, 42–43). Moskos argued that the military was being transformed from an institution to an occupation with "consequences in the structure and perhaps, the function of the armed forces" (Moskos 1977, 45).

While Moskos's formulation of the I/O model attracted nationwide attention, it was based on neither sound logic nor empirical observation. At the time, even Janowitz wrote, "There is no basis—analytic and empirical—to apply such a formulation, for either the short-term or long-term trends in military organizations and military profession in the United States. . . . The formulation of the shift from institution to occupation . . . has overtones of an ideological appeal to return to the 'good old days.' But," he noted, "there is no return" (Janowitz 1977, 54).

Moskos's formulation of the I/O model is a classic "false dichotomy." While Moskos acknowledges that there are elements of both institution and occupation in the all-volunteer force military, he argues, "the social science analyst must always use pure types to advance conceptual understanding" (Moskos

1988, 15). In truth, if Moskos allowed for the coexistence of elements of institution and occupation, it would weaken his claim that there are dire consequences for the military if it incorporates such occupational notions as higher pay, a salary system, or the all-volunteer force. He claims that "members of an institution are often seen as following a *calling*," and then, with a clever play on words, claims that an induction notice is a calling "in the almost literal sense of being summoned by a local draft board" (Moskos 1981, 6). But when is a true calling based on a commitment enforced by the threats that if one does not serve he will be hunted down, put in jail, and fined? Moreover, Moskos's accounts of the draft Army of the 1950s paint a picture far from the reality that others saw. One history of the period noted that between the Korean and Vietnam Wars, which was the time during which Moskos served, the draft Army did not demonstrate the "clubbiness of the old Army. Characteristics of the Army after World War II— . . . composed largely of short service draftees . . . —virtually ensured that its ethos would be centralized, bureaucratic, and impersonal" (Bacevich 1986, 119).

Moskos's criticism of the all-volunteer force, he tells us, is based on his opposition to the "marketplace philosophy" that underpinned the rationale of the 1970 Gates Commission (Moskos 1988, 19). Recently, the sociologist James Burk considered whether "the move to an all-volunteer force . . . reflects a shift in American culture away from an emphasis on the duties of citizenship to an emphasis on the rights of citizenship and the pursuit of individual interests" (Burk 2002, 2). He notes that this is an empirical question, and asks, "Has there been a withering of civic virtues?" (Burk 2002, 3). He found, however, "evidence [that] casts doubt on the proposition that members of the current generation suffer from a deficit of civic virtue . . . Citizen-soldiers in the all-volunteer force possess civic virtues and political beliefs that are largely indistinguishable from those held by their civilian counterparts who failed to volunteer for military service" (Burk 2002, 4).

History has shown that the I/O model may be descriptive of the uniqueness of military service, but it is not predictive of the kind of military personnel we are likely to have or the implied negative "consequences" that Moskos warned against. Looking back over the last 30 years of the all-volunteer force, one can see that none of the direct or implied dire "outcomes"—a lack of motivation, low commitment, a loss of professionalism, or a drop in the overall performance—Moskos anticipated if the military became even more like an occupation (Moskos 1977, 44) has come to pass. Quite the opposite has occurred. Performance, if anything, has improved, a trend that has held true since the advent of the all-volunteer force.

In 1975, an attitudinal study of "junior enlisted personnel who had direct combat responsibilities" conducted by Colonel Charles Brown and Moskos found that "the transition to the volunteer Army has been generally successful. The volunteer combat soldier in today's Army [1975] can be expected to perform as well if not better than his counterpart of the early 1970s" (Brown and Moskos 1997). More recently, in 2003, Moskos told the acting Secretary of the Army, after a visit to the Middle East, that soldiers in Iraq had achieved "exceptional levels of performance under very demanding conditions" (Moskos 2003). In retrospect, either the all-volunteer force did not move the Army towards an occupation, as Moskos feared it would, or his contention that "institutional identification fosters greater organizational commitment and performance than does occupational commitment" (Moskos and Wood 1988, 5) was wrong.

In fact, what has come to pass, as a direct result of the AVF, is the professionalism of the military, demonstrated not only by their sterling performance on battlefields worldwide, but also by the explosion in the size of the career military. Since the beginning of the AVF, more people then ever — officers and enlisted — have decided to make the military their career.

In 1969, when President Nixon established the Gates Commission, only 18 percent of Army personnel had served in the armed forces for more than four years. The corresponding percentages for the Navy, Marine Corps, and Air Force were 31, 16, and 46 percent, respectively (U.S. Department of Defense 1978, 82). In 2002, in the all-volunteer force, the number of members who had served for more than four years equaled 51 percent for the Army, 49 percent for the Navy, 35 percent for the Marine Corps, and 66 percent for the Air Force (U.S. Department of Defense 2001). In the early 1970s, before the all-volunteer force, the services routinely retained about 15 percent of the cohort of true volunteers, draft-motivated volunteers, and draftees who were eligible to reenlist (Lee and Parker 1977, 358). Today, the corresponding number is about 53 percent.

The most disturbing aspect of Moskos's I/O thesis was the implication that a calling should be associated with low wages. According to Moskos, "Extrinsic rewards . . . can weaken intrinsic motivation" (Moskos and Wood 1988, 5), and the people needed in the military — the white middle class — are not motivated by higher pay. The logical conclusion is that soldiers who are paid well cannot be trusted because one can never be sure if they are just serving for the money. If low pay forces dedicated soldiers to leave because they cannot support the quality of life they want for their families, then, Moskos's logic would say that is all right because they really did not have the calling in the first place. Low wages are not an indication of dedicated service. Wages reflect the value that the American people put on military service. Many in the Congress who voted for the large military pay raises in the early 1970s did so not because they favored the all-volunteer force, but because they valued military service and thought that it was unconscionable for military wages to be below comparable civilian wages.

THE AVF IS REPRESENTATIVE OF THE AMERICAN PEOPLE

Aside from the test of military prowess, the one test of the all-volunteer force that seems to have maintained currency with the American people is representativeness. This is a shifting concept. In the 1840s, when Congress debated the fate of the United States Military Academy at West Point, representativeness meant regional representativeness and resulted in the congressional appointment system we have today. In more recent years, representativeness has meant social representativeness. Each year the Office of the Under Secretary of Defense for Personnel and Readiness publishes a report on the representativeness of the force. It consistently shows that today's force is broadly representative of the middle of American society. Those in the upper socioeconomic class are under-represented and those in the lower socioeconomic class are underrepresented. It is the lack of representatives from the upper class that is usually questioned, especially when the country goes to war. Unfortunately, you cannot have it both ways. No one has yet devised a "little draft" to correct one problem of under-representation that might pass the tests of fairness, legality, feasibility, and affordability. Moreover, after two wars, today's force, with whatever degree of under- or overrepresentativeness it possesses, certainly does not lack credibility among the American people.

CONCLUSION: ENDING THE DRAFT WAS IN THE BEST INTEREST OF THE AMERICAN PEOPLE

In closing, let me reiterate: seldom if ever has the recommendation of a presidential commission been so forcefully acted upon or had such a profoundly positive effect on this country. Even if the members of the Gates Commission did not quite understand the eventual outcome of their recommendation, they were confident that ending the draft was in the best interest of the American people. They were right. It is my pleasure to salute their achievement, and that of the men and women of our armed forces — all volunteers — who through their dedicated service prove after 30 years how right the Gates Commission was.

NOTES

1. The Gates Commission did expect to see some reduced turnover because of an all-volunteer force. It thought that this would result in a smaller training base (Gates 1970, 40). What it did not perceive was the increase in productivity that would result from an older and more experienced force. In fact, well into the 1980s, the services still did not understand, or account for in their personnel planning, the impact that the volunteer force would have on the military (Hosek, Fernandez, and Grissmer 1984).

REFERENCES

Bacevich, A. J. 1986. *The pentomic era: The U.S. Army between Korea and Vietnam.* Washington, D.C.: National Defense University Press.

Binkin, Martin, and S. J. Bach. 1977. *Women and the military.* Washington, D.C.: Brookings Institution Press.

Brown, Charles W., and Charles C. Moskos. 1997. The American soldier: Will he fight? *Military Review* 77(1): 1–9.

Browning, Edgar. 1987. On the marginal welfare cost of taxation. *American Economic Review* 77(1): 11–23.

Burk, James. 2002. *The civic virtue, rights and opportunities of citizen-soldiers.* Paper prepared for the Conference on All-Volunteer Armed Forces and Citizenship, June 19–21, held at the American Center, Science PO, Paris.

Crowe, William J. Jr. 1993. *The line of fire: From Washington to the Gulf, the politics and battles of the new military.* New York: Simon & Schuster.

Friedman, Milton. 1967. Why not a volunteer Army? In *The draft: A handbook of facts and alternatives*. Edited by Sol Tax, 200–7. Chicago: University of Chicago Press.

Gates, Thomas S. 1970. *Report of the President's Commission on an All-Volunteer Armed Force*. Washington, D.C.: U.S. Government Printing Office.

Griffith, Robert K. Jr. 1997. *The U.S. Army's transition to the all-volunteer force 1968–1974*. Washington, D.C.: Center of Military History, United States Army.

Hosek, James R., Richard L. Fernandez, and David W. Grissmer. 1984. *Active enlisted supply: Prospects and policy options*. Santa Monica, Calif.: RAND Corporation.

Janowitz, Morris. 1977. From institutional to occupational: The need for conceptual continuity. *Armed Forces and Society* 4(1): 51–54.

Janowitz, Morris, and Charles C. Moskos. 1974. Racial composition in the all-volunteer force. *Armed Forces and Society* 1(1): 109–23.

———. 1975. Racial composition of the volunteer armed forces. *Society* May-June: 37–42.

Jehn, Christopher, and Zachary Selden. 2002. The end of conscription in Europe? *Contemporary Economic Policy* 20(2): 93–100.

Lee, D., and R. McKenzie. 1992. Reexamination of the relative efficiency of the draft and the all-volunteer Army. *Southern Economic Journal* 59: 640–54.

Lee, Gus C., and Geoffrey Y. Parker. 1977. *Ending the draft: The story of the all volunteer force*. Washington, D.C.: Human Resources Research Organization.

Meckling, William H. 1986. Comment on women and minorities in the all-volunteer force. In *The all-volunteer force after a decade: Retrospect and prospect*. Edited by William Bowman, Roger Little, and G. Thomas Sicilia. New York: Pergammon-Brassey's International Defense Publishers.

Moskos, Charles C. 1977. From institution to occupation: Trends in military organization. *Armed Forces and Society* 4(1): 41–50.

———. 1981. *Institution versus occupation: Contrasting models of military organization*. Department of Sociology, Northwestern University, Evanston, Ill.

———. 1988. Institutional and occupational trends in armed forces. In *The military: More than just a job?* Edited by Charles C. Moskos and Frank R. Wood. New York: Pergamon-Brassey's International Defense Publishers.

———. 2003. *Preliminary report on Operation Iraqi Freedom (OIF)*. Presented to the Acting Secretary of the Army, December 14, 2003.

Moskos, Charles C., and Frank R. Wood. 1988. Introduction. In *The military: More than just a job?* Edited by Charles C. Moskos and Frank R. Wood. New York: Pergamon-Brassey's International Defense Publishers.

Nunn, Sam. 1973. *Remarks by U.S. Senator Sam Nunn before the Georgia General Assembly*. March 5 news release. Washington, D.C.: Office of Senator Sam Nunn.

———. 1978. *Costs of the all-volunteer force*. Hearing before the Senate Armed Services Subcommittee on Manpower and Personnel. 95th Congress, Second Session, February 6, 1978.

Oi, Walter Y. 1967. The economic cost of the draft. *American Economic Review* 57(2): 39–62.

O'Sullivan, J., and A. M. Meckler. 1974. *The draft and its enemies: A documentary history*. Chicago: University of Illinois Press. Quoting George Washington, Sentiments on a peace establishment.

Rumsfeld, Donald. 1974. Janowitz study on racial composition. Presented to the Secretary of the Army, November 15, 1974.

Tax, Sol. 1967. *The draft: A handbook of facts and alternatives.* Chicago: University of Chicago Press.

U.S. Department of Defense. 1978. *America's volunteers: A report on the all-volunteer armed forces – summary.* Washington, D.C.: Office of the Assistant Secretary of Defense (Manpower, Reserve Affairs, and Logistics).

———. 2001. *DOD personnel update.* Washington, D.C.: Office of the Under Secretary of Defense (Personnel and Readiness).

Warner, John T., and Beth J. Asch. 1996. The economic theory of a military draft reconsidered. *Defense and Peace Economics* 7: 297–312.

Weinberger, Caspar W. 1986. The all-volunteer force in the 1980s: DoD perspective. In *The all-volunteer force after a decade: Retrospect and prospect.* Edited by William Bowman, Roger Little, and G. Thomas Sicilia. New York: Pergamon-Brassey's International Defense Publishers.

★ ★ ★ ★ ★ ★ ★ ★ ★ ★ ★

CHAPTER 4

REFLECTIONS ON MANAGING THE
ALL-VOLUNTEER FORCE: PAST AND FUTURE

JOHN P. WHITE

The Department of Defense (DOD) conference on September 16–17, 2003, commemorating the first 30 years of the all-volunteer force (AVF), afforded an opportunity to look back at accomplishments and forward to challenges.

The AVF is the very foundation of today's magnificent military. The United States' accomplishments since the initial phases of the Gulf war, in combat and noncombat military missions all around the world, are in large measure attributable to the quality of U.S. soldiers, sailors, airmen, and Marines. It is the quality of these forces that has made the U.S. military so effective. High-technology weapons are important, but they are not the fundamental reason for our success. People are.

Looking back, the AVF is one of the most successful social policies of the last 50 years. The policy decision to staff the military based on fairness and quality was both simple and stunningly powerful. It is difficult to describe all of the enormous benefits of this policy for both the volunteers and the total force.

Looking forward, recent unexpected geopolitical events signal the need to rethink DOD's human resource strategies. Both the civilian world from which the forces are drawn and the role of those forces in defending the United States and its interests are evolving in ways that present new challenges to sustaining a high-quality military force. These challenges are numerous and include the need for more ground combat forces. The force management difficulties that are manifest in Iraq reflect a serious shortage in end strength. The Army and Marine Corps together need between about twenty and forty thousand additional troops. Meeting this need will test the capacity of the department's manpower and personnel systems and demand innovations in recruitment, retention, and overall management of the total force.

★

Secretary Rumsfeld plans to expand combat capability by finding and making improvements in efficiency across the DOD that will free uniformed personnel for combat units. Such a broad assessment is needed. But it will meet with resistance from those comfortable with the status quo, as have such reviews in the past. The more promise offered by innovative changes, the more difficult they are to implement. This is not a reason to avoid thinking broadly – quite the reverse. But it is a reminder that payoffs from such exercises are often fewer than first envisioned and come later than first forecasted.

An effective response to the evident need for more ground forces must include some increase in end strength.

LESSONS FROM THE AVF EXPERIENCE

Consistent with the theme of this volume, I will focus my remarks on lessons from the AVF experience to date that seem relevant to its future. I have drawn upon my personal experience dealing with this issue for over 35 years, first as an economist at RAND beginning in the late 1960s; then as assistant secretary of defense for manpower, reserve affairs, and logistics and deputy director of the Office of Management and Budget in the late 1970s; and then as deputy secretary of defense in the mid-1990s.

Today, much of the discussion about conscription is rather abstract. Most people who deal with AVF issues have no experience with a conscripted force. You do not know what you missed. I was a platoon commander in the U.S. Marine Corps between 1959 and 1961. The young men in my platoon were good Marines, but many of them were in the Marine Corps because a judge back home had given them a choice: either go to jail or join the Marines. Few of them would meet the quality standards required to serve in today's Marine Corps.

Why was the argument for an AVF persuasive in the late 1960s and early 1970s? First, the tragedy of Vietnam had convinced the American people, many in Congress, and, most importantly, President Nixon that conscription was inherently unfair. There were so many horror stories of mistreatment of draftees, so many young men in military jails, and so much inefficiency apparent in the military that people were searching for a change.

Second, and in my view most important, the demographics had changed. The small cohorts of eligible draftees born in the late 1930s and early 1940s had given way to the "baby boomers," who were becoming eligible for service. The military force had many more recruits available than it needed. A volunteer force had become a feasible option.

Finally, the economic arguments that were at the center of the Gates Commission's report were necessary to winning the policy debate (Gates 1970).

But it should be remembered that the arguments we economists cherished – that conscription was a hidden tax on the young that also caused major inefficiencies in the Department of Defense – were not persuasive unto themselves. Many people, including no less an expert than Senator Sam Nunn, saw military service as a citizen's obligation. The uniformed leadership of the services relied on the draft and was opposed to such a radical change. Leaders in the Army feared that they could not attract enough recruits without conscription. Leaders in the other services, particularly the Air Force, were concerned that their practice of "creaming" "draft-induced" volunteers would be thwarted. (That is, attracting to their service young men facing the less desirable option of conscription into the Army.) All were concerned about what would happen in time of war.

The importance of the economic arguments was that, when taken in their entirety, they presented a totally new paradigm for evaluating military organizations. In contrast to the social and psychological models of testing and evaluation that grew out of World War II, this free market model could deal effectively with the macro operational issues of manning the force. It was coherent, integrated, and intellectually sound. It could address all the issues of demand and supply, attrition and retention, the mix of career and noncareer members, and the like in the context of management efficiency and personal equity.

The AVF proponents were able to muster persuasive arguments regarding its efficacy just when the need for change was strongly felt and the demographics made change feasible.

The initial years of the AVF were fraught with difficulty, and returning to conscription was a real possibility. The troubles of the early years even affected President Nixon's view, as he wrote in *The Real War:* "I had considered the end of the draft in 1973 to be one of the major achievements of my administration. Now, seven years later, I have reluctantly concluded that we should reintroduce the draft" (Nixon 1980).

The expected difficulties of implementing such a massive change were aggravated by two events, a technical mistake and a major policy decision made in a broader context. As described by Chu and White (2000, 206), "The technical mistake was mis-norming the shift to a new Armed Services Vocational Aptitude Battery (ASVAB) in fiscal year 1976, with the result that actual quality was substantially below measured quality. (Policy makers ignored, to their regret, the complaints of sergeants that recruit quality was declining: a lesson for present and future decision-makers.)"

The policy error was the result of President Carter's strategy for fighting inflation, which included limiting all federal pay raises, including those for the military. I have a clear recollection of the anti-inflation policy debate, having been an active participant as the deputy director of the Office of Management and Budget. First, the President felt very strongly about his anti-inflation stance and was not open to considering major exceptions. Second, those of us involved in the AVF transition did not appreciate the magnitude and rapidity of the damage that would be done. The force was already in a much more fragile state than we realized because of the general difficulties in making the transition from a draft compounded by the misnorming errors. This, it should be noted, is also a caution to present and future decision makers. The AVF is both robust and fragile. It requires an ongoing institutional commitment to assure its continued success. The current force management difficulties portend much more serious problems in the near future if they are not corrected.

I believe that the country would have returned to conscription if the recruiting difficulties had persisted into the 1980s. Fortunately, the commitment and professionalism of those responsible for managing the AVF saved it. The central issue in military recruiting was always the Army's ability to attract recruits in the numbers and quality required. Success there meant success everywhere. That success was engineered by General Maxwell Thurman at the Army Recruiting Command during the late 1970s and early 1980s. If the AVF has a hero in its past, the hero was Max.

The Congress also played a key role in solving the problem, as it has done so often in support of the AVF. It increased the administration's military pay raise recommendations in 1980 and provided an added raise in 1981. The percentage increases in pay for those years were 11.7 and 14.3 percent, respectively (U.S. Department of Defense 1996, 51).

The early crisis has been followed by over 20 years of success. That success is the product of an array of policies and programs that responded effectively to the changing needs of the force. The success has been apparent, foremost, in military performance. It is also reflected in the racial integration, gender integration, professional competence, and overall structure of the force. All of these accomplishments are remarkable but none are complete, nor will they continue without sustained management attention.

David Chu and I previously presented an assessment of the status of the AVF that stated:

> The successes of military personnel management over the last generation offer four potential explanations for success and lessons to learn from this experience.
>
> First, in each area a clear, measurable set of objectives was set, such as quality standards for enlistees and promotion equity for minorities. Equally important, these objectives were accepted (indeed, sometimes directed) by the political leadership of DOD. The leadership received regular reports on success in meeting these objectives — or the lack thereof — and took action accordingly.
>
> Second, military personnel outcomes were seen to be the product of a system, and attention was focused on management of the system.
>
> Third, quantitative analysis was employed widely and aggressively, to try to understand the relationships between causes and effects. Equally important, policymakers were focused on outcomes, not inputs, and they were willing to use experiments to test, evaluate, and adjust policies.
>
> Fourth, policymakers came to understand early that incentives — bonuses, compensation, promotion opportunity, and the like — rather than "rules and regulations" would be the main instruments

to achieve the outcomes they desired. They also understood that rules and regulations might have to be changed or reshaped to produce the incentives they needed (Chu and White 2000, 212–13).

Imagine what could be done if the civil service were managed using these practices.

It is right to celebrate AVF successes, but it is critical to prepare for the future. Changing force needs and labor market characteristics will require changes in how the force is managed. The effective management practices listed above are useful guidelines, but they carry within them serious biases and weaknesses that need to be corrected. Three such weaknesses are discussed below:

- a strong supply-side, or market-centric, bias in the approach to recruiting and retention issues

- dependence on a traditional compensation structure, particularly with respect to retirement

- insensitivity to personnel costs, including the cost of quality-of-life programs

THE SUPPLY-SIDE BIAS

The success of the volunteer concept depended, first and foremost, on meeting the market test for both recruiting and retention at affordable budget levels. The Gates Commission determined that this standard could be met: "Our studies show that the increments in pay, and therefore the incremental budgetary outlays necessary to provide a voluntary force in the 1970s of about the same size as our pre-Vietnam force are fairly small" (Gates 1970, 50).

Meeting the recruiting goals in both number and quality was the most visible, and difficult, test of the transition period. Both the problems and the solutions associated with this challenge were seen in terms of achieving recruiting goals through increases in compensation. As with other management systems, the DOD personnel system concentrates on what it measures. The emphasis on recruiting and retention metrics carries with it an overemphasis on supply-side changes at the expense of parallel assessments of demand-side program performance, which includes the effectiveness of advertising, the efficiency of the recruiting organization, the value of quality-of-life programs, and the magnitude of first-term attrition rates.

Shortfalls in recruiting and retention are usually first defined in terms of exogenous events. The failure to meet DOD goals is attributed to market forces such as civilian wage increases, expanding civilian employment, and so on. Consequently, the proposed remedies stress compensation adjustments while leaving DOD's human resource management programs largely unexamined.

This problem is exacerbated by two lags in remedial action. First, it takes some time for the system to detect any important shifts in program effectiveness. Monitoring mechanisms are "weak and imperfect, leading to an unfortunate lag between changes in conditions and changes in policy. This can be seen in both the failure during the 1970's ASVAB mis-norming episode to pick up promptly on the sergeants' complaint about enlistee quality" (Chu and White 2000, 213) and the belated response to the persistent decline in recruit quality during the 1990s. Second, once the remedies are fashioned there is a further, inevitable, lag in the time it takes to make either internal, programmatic adjustments or legislative changes such as authorizing pay increases. These lags make program assessment more difficult but do not diminish its importance.

Market supply shifts are also important factors in program productivity changes, but new program management problems are usually the result of a combination of external and internal factors. The labor market may have changed, but there are usually program management deficiencies as well. This was true as recruiting became more difficult in the mid-1990s. The initial reaction was to define the problem in terms of increased civilian competition in the labor market. Higher economic growth meant declining unemployment and rising wages. Consequently, the proposed solutions, principally increases in various forms of compensation, were aimed at readjusting DOD's position in the market.

It was only after further analysis and debate that internal problems were identified and corrections proposed. This was true of the Army's recruiting problem in 1996, for example. The labor market had become tighter, but it was also true that the Army had reduced its recruiting budget to address other priorities. Sharp increases in Air Force pilot attrition in the same period provide another illustration of this phenomenon. It was true that the airlines were increasing the demand for experienced pilots. But it was also true that the Air Force had previously reduced the number of pilots in its training pipeline, thus leaving it vulnerable to external pressures.

Internal review should be the first priority when faced with a drop in program effectiveness. Management must ask whether program practices can be adjusted to address the failure to meet recruiting and retention goals. This is not only good management practice but is necessary given the program implementation lags discussed above. The best immediate option for addressing shortfalls in recruiting and retention is often to make program adjustments in, for example, recruiters, advertising, and/or bonuses being offered. These adjustments do not usually constitute a complete response but will ameliorate the situation, at a minimum, and buy time for making more fundamental corrections.

The supply-side recruiting problems of the 1990s were real, but so was the need to modify service recruiting programs. Over time, an array of responses to the recruiting shortfalls were made, including increases in pay and bonuses, but so were changes in advertising and the services' recruiting programs. Many of the internal reforms were instituted prior to the so-called TRIAD pay increases in 2000 and 2001.[1] It is impossible to isolate the impact of each of the number of changes made. But it is my impression that the institutional changes were very important to the recruiting improvements (in both quality and quantity) achieved. Pay matters, but it is not all that matters. The system responded appropriately to the challenges, but the complete correction took several years.

(For a general discussion of the response to the 1990s recruiting problems, see Asch et al. 2002.)

In some cases, recruiting and retention problems reflect pervasive organizational issues of DOD's own making. For example, according to a recent report of the Defense Science Board (U.S. Department of Defense 2000, 63), an informal survey of junior officers suggests that retention difficulty is directly linked to the following factors:

- a lack of confidence in leadership
- decreased job satisfaction
- confusion about the purpose and importance of missions
- frequent and unpredictable deployments
- apparent low priority given to quality-of-life initiatives and programs by senior leadership

The Defense Science Board report recommended that DOD develop a comprehensive strategic plan that addresses systemic issues such as the ones listed above. Strategic planning of the overall personnel management system will be central to meeting future challenges.

THE TRADITIONAL COMPENSATION STRUCTURE

The problem of responding to market changes has been made more difficult by the traditional structure of the compensation system. The Gates Commission supported a major change in the compensation system. "A Department of Defense study group recommended the introduction of a 'salary' system of pay in which allowances for quarters and subsistence would [be] combined with basic pay to provide a 'salary.' The Commission supports this recommendation" (Gates 1970, 61). Obviously, this recommendation was not accepted, and the traditional system, designed for a different time with different needs, is still in place.

The Report of the Ninth Quadrennial Review of Military Compensation (QRMC) commented on this problem. "About two-thirds of all compensation is generated by a single set of tables of basic pay and allowances for all Services and occupations. Thus, there are limits on how much flexibility the military Services have in differentiating pay among their members. These limits can in turn increase the difficulty of attracting the required numbers and types of personnel — the basic purpose of the compensation system" (U.S. Department of Defense 2002, xxi–xxii).

The QRMC went on to emphasize two fundamental themes: balance and flexibility. It noted the need to have "the appropriate balance between basic pay and special and incentive pays" as well as the critical need to "get basic pay right first" (U.S. Department of Defense 2002, xxii). The DOD's record regarding the latter imperative is uneven at best.[2]

The QRMC also proposed increased flexibility via new tools for shaping the force. "New force-shaping tools such as alternative career lengths, changes in 'up-or-out' policies, or even a more voluntary assignment system would add great flexibility to the military compensation system" (U.S. Department of Defense 2002, xxii). The previously cited Defense Science Board study also recommended an array of force-shaping tools including a strategic human resource plan for the total force, pay for performance, seamless integration of active and reserve components, military retirement reform, and increased emphasis on quality-of-life programs (U.S. Department of Defense 2000).

A review of current and prospective programs reveals a rich array of tools that could assist in force shaping as well as improve the effectiveness and equity of the force. The prospect of retirement reform illustrates both the deficiencies of the compensation system as it now exists and the opportunities for improvement in the future.

RETIREMENT REFORM

Retirement reform has been repeatedly analyzed and recommended beginning with the Gates Commission. The reasons given for suggesting reform are consistent across the various reviews, as are many of the principles specified to guide the reformers. The 1978 President's Commission on Military Compensation (the PCMC or Zwick Commission) made the case succinctly. "While the cost of military retirement represents a substantial proportion of all defense expenditures, cost alone does not provide a case for change. Rather, the Commission concluded that change is needed because of three inherent deficiencies in the existing retirement plan" (Zwick 1978, 26–27). The deficiencies described are as follows:

- The current system is inequitable.
- The current system inhibits effective and flexible force management.
- The current system is inefficient.

The Zwick Commission's retirement reform proposals were rejected by much of the senior uniformed leadership. This leadership supported the existing system because it was familiar, operational, and equitable, i.e., all members were subject to the same rules, from senior career noncommissioned officers to the newest recruits. The institution voted for tradition over innovation.

It is interesting to note that at the time of the Zwick Commission report, the Carter administration adopted the so-called "offset strategy," which emphasized U.S. military force quality to check traditional Soviet force quantity. The fruits of that policy were revealed in the first Gulf War and successively since then in joint military operations. The technological and operational innovations introduced as part of the offset strategy have required changes in personnel skill mix and force mix. The force transformation ongoing in the department today makes such skill and force changes even more important. The skills needed in the future will be different in kind, mix, and longevity from those of the past.

Meanwhile, the continuing mismatch between a force that responds to retirement incentives designed for the pre–World War II era and the preferred force for the transformed military grows worse each year.

The retirement system "is a 'one-size-fits-all' system that permits personnel managers little flexibility to shape different rank-experience structures in different Services and different skills. Jobs such as those in the combat arms require 'youth and vigor.' In contrast, other jobs involve high training costs and are learned over fairly long periods of time. Future automation and substitution of capital for labor will increase the need for skilled labor relative to unskilled labor and will, on balance, reduce the need for 'youth and vigor.' It seems unlikely that 20 years is the optimal career length across the whole spectrum of military occupations" (U.S. Department of Defense 2000, 73; Asch and Warner 1996).

In contrast, a reformed retirement system would allow shaping and managing the force using differentiated incentives to meet changing career profiles and force structure. For example, Rostker (2002, 34) has proposed a new personnel structure for officers with the following salient features:

> The recommended system for the 21st century will be a competitive up-or-out system in junior grades with relatively high selection rates, and then stringent selection into a career force, e.g., a 30 percent selection rate. Once in the career force the norm would be very high promotion rates, e.g. promotion rates of 90 percent to O-6 rather than the 50 percent of today. Longer tenure and higher remuneration for those selected and who join the 'career force' should encourage people to stay for a full career—a career that would end at about forty years of service. Compensation packages need to be structured to motivate the best to stay and encourage those with limited potential for future service to leave. Limited competitive selection might be used to reinforce the compensation system—the stick—but challenging jobs and higher pay should be the prime way to motivate members of the career force—the carrot. Those who are not given, or do not take, the opportunity to join the career force, will receive severance pay and an old-age annuity at the end of their working lives.

Retirement reform is one change among many that would enhance force management effectiveness. I have emphasized retirement reform because the cost of the current system is so high; a flexible retirement system would be such a great asset for force managers; and it would meet the varied needs of service men and women.

THE INSENSITIVITY TO PERSONNEL COSTS

The management emphasis on exogenous market forces, the traditional structure of compensation, the bitter lesson of the pay freezes in the late 1970s, and the heavy emphasis on meeting recruiting and retention goals have made cost control a secondary concern in force management. Even though military compensation costs account for over a quarter of the defense budget and increased at an annual average of 3.5 percent from fiscal year 2000 to fiscal year 2004, they tend to be managed at the margin, when at all.

This was not true at the beginning of the AVF. The first chapter of the Gates Commission's report is devoted to whether a volunteer system would be affordable. It is not the case in the private sector either, where corporations scrutinize personnel costs each month and manage them tightly. Nor is it the case for other elements of the DOD budget, such as the modernization programs, where enormous energy is spent on cost controls, albeit not always effectively.

The continuing emphasis on the transformation of the military forces, along with the ever increasing costs of current operations, should make controlling the personnel budget a high priority. The administration's military transformation is intended to make fundamental changes in defense organizations, doctrine, operations, and capabilities to meet new and changing threats, and that costs money. Furthermore, the administration has made it clear that these transformation goals pertain to human resource management as well.[3]

The lack of cost consciousness is apparent in persistently high first-term attrition. This attrition has been a problem since 1973, when the recruit-training establishment realized that it no longer needed to tolerate poor performers. The rate of attrition for all new enlistees in their first six months of service has hovered around 15 percent from 1995 through 1999. At the 12-month mark it has been around 18 percent. (In the last two years the rates have come down somewhat.) The nonprior service entry cohort for those years averaged 180,000 per year, so the losses numbered about 27,000 at the six-month mark and a total of about 34,200 by the end of the first year, despite the large investment in the recruitment and training of those who left (U.S. Department of Defense 2003). This is not only expensive, but also reflects an institutional failure in either recruit selection or initial training, or both, to identify, motivate, and train new entrants so that they can make a contribution to the force. More importantly, high attrition reflects a failure on DOD's part to fulfill the expectations of these young people who signed up because they believed in the promise of military service.

Over the years, this lack of concern for controlling personnel costs has allowed unseemly "bidding wars" among political factions vying for the support of various recipients. Questionable increases in health and retirement benefits and poorly managed pay increases have built additional costs into the DOD budget over the years. Too many of these benefits are payable at the end of active service, thus limiting their contribution to force management. The most recent example was the provision in the fiscal year 2003 budget that ensures medical care (TRICARE) for life for all retired active duty members 65 and over (and their spouses or survivors) who are eligible for Medicare. The estimated cost of this benefit is $5 billion for fiscal year 2004, with substantial growth in cost projected thereafter.

Cost control problems extend to DOD's quality-of-life programs. The fundamental integrity of the professional military rests on mutual obligations. The force will perform above expectations, and the American people, through DOD, will assure that they are treated with the dignity and respect that they deserve. This is an important compact, but it does not mean continually bidding up perquisites or ignoring cost constraints. It does mean that these programs should be subject to a structured approach that focuses on the results to be achieved and the most effective ways to achieve them.

FUTURE FORCE MANAGEMENT

The AVF began as a concept to solve a set of problems for both the U.S. military and its members. No one knew, at the beginning, whether the massive conversion to a volunteer military manpower system would work. The argument was that the underlying principles were sound, implementation and sustainment appeared feasible, and sufficient management tools were available. But there were many unknowns including the actual propensity of people to enlist and reenlist and the true cost of the new system. Perhaps the most important unknown was whether the DOD would be able to supply strong, systematic, continual, and visible support to this uniquely new system.

This brief program review argues that the necessary adjustments have been made over time to meet the changing market and the changing needs of the department. But the adjustments have been far from optimal. The management of the program has been hampered by

- a strong supply bias that emphasizes adjusting to perceived exogenous factors that affect program performance at the expense of a strong program management orientation

- a willingness to work around and adjust to an outmoded system of compensation incentives that inhibits the adoption of more effective force management tools

- an insensitivity to personnel costs, i.e., program efficiency, in managing the overall system

The major challenge today is to create a flexible, responsive personnel system that can adjust to future, unknown needs in the spirit of DOD's general emphasis on military transformation. This means creating a personnel resource management strategy more broadly based than the traditional one, with its emphasis on recruiting and retention. The strategy will have to be implemented through a set of flexible force management tools. The need for such an approach is clearly recognized. The Defense Science Board's report on human resource strategy calls for "a strategic human resources plan encompassing all elements of the total force" and the identification of "the tools necessary to size and shape the force — to influence the quality, commitment, skills, training, and quality of life of the workforce" (U.S. Department of Defense 2000, ix).

This goal is achievable, but not without both correcting the chronic structural difficulties of the current program and fashioning innovations that address new requirements.

In conclusion, those of us who have participated in the creation and sustainment of the AVF over the years can be very proud of what has been accomplished. The future looks challenging but offers a great opportunity to improve upon what has been accomplished thus far.

NOTES

1. The TRIAD was a three-prong increase to military compensation which included: (1) across-the-board pay increases of 4.8 and 3.7 percent, respectively, in fiscal years 2000 and 2001, together with an increase for the next five years that is 0.5 percent greater than the average private sector raises as measured by the Bureau of Labor Statistics' Employment Cost Index; (2) pay raises targeted to particular pay grades and years-of-service cells; and (3) repeal of the Military Retirement Reform Act of 1986, restoring (increasing) military retirement benefits to amounts designated by the pre-1986 formula.

2. The pay increase enacted in the fiscal year 2004 budget is targeted. The average increase is 4.15 percent and the minimum increase is 3.7 percent. People in enlisted grades E-5 through E-9 receive a larger increase (from 4.6 percent up to 6.25 percent) to bring them closer to the overall goal of all grades being at the 70th percentile of earnings for their civilian (comparably educated) peers. Officers, in contrast, will receive the minimum (3.7 percent) because they are already approximately at the 70th percentile of comparable civilian earnings.

3. For a discussion of the administration's human resource goals, see Chu 2003.

REFERENCES

Asch, Beth J., and John T. Warner. 1996. Should the military retirement system be reformed? In *Professionals on the front line: Two decades of the all-volunteer force.* Edited by J. Eric Fredland, Curtis L. Gilroy, Roger D. Little, and W. S. Sellman. Washington, D.C.: Brassey's.

Asch, Beth, James Hosek, Jeremy Arkes, C. Christine Fair, Jennifer Sharp, and Mark Totten. 2002. *Military recruiting and retention after the fiscal year 2000 military pay legislation.* Santa Monica, Calif.: RAND Corporation.

Chu, David S. C. 2003. Prepared Statement of David S. C. Chu, Under Secretary of Defense for Personnel and Readiness, before the Military Personnel Subcommittee, Senate Armed Services Committee, March 11.

Chu, David S. C., and John P. White. 2000. Ensuring quality people in defense. In *Keeping the edge: Managing defense for the future.* Edited by Ashton B. Carter and John P. White. Cambridge, Mass.: MIT Press.

Gates, Thomas S. 1970. *Report of the President's Commission on an All-Volunteer Armed Force.* Washington D.C.: U.S. Government Printing Office.

Nixon, Richard M. 1980. *The real war.* New York: Warner Books Inc.

Rostker, Bernard. 2002. *Time for a change: Developing a new officer military personnel system for the 21st century.* Santa Monica, Calif.: RAND Corporation.

U.S. Department of Defense. 1996. *Military compensation background papers.* Fifth Edition. Washington, D.C.: U.S. Government Printing Office.

———. 2000. *Report of the Defense Science Board Task Force on Human Resources Strategy.* Washington, D.C.: Office of the Under Secretary of Defense (Acquisition, Technology, and Logistics).

———. 2002. Report of the Ninth Quadrennial Review of Military Compensation. Washington, D.C.: Office of the Under Secretary of Defense (Personnel and Readiness).

———. 2003. Selected recruiting tables. Arlington, Va.: Defense Manpower Data Center.

Zwick, C. 1978. *Report of the President's Commission on Military Compensation.* Washington, D.C.: U.S. Government Printing Office.

★ ★ ★ ★ ★ ★ ★ ★ ★ ★ ★

COMMENTARY
NO MORE GREETINGS

Walter Y. Oi

*"Freedom of action is granted to the individual, not because it gives
him greater satisfaction, but if allowed to go on his own way,
he will, on the average, serve the rest of us better than
under any orders we know how to give."*[1]

The first peacetime draft was enacted in 1948. For a quarter of a century, the armed services relied on conscription and the threat of conscription to recruit young men. On July 1, 1973, Secretary of Defense Melvin Laird presided over the beginning of the all-volunteer force. I begin my commentary with a brief review of the forces that persuaded Congress to terminate the Universal Military Training and Service Act. The members of the President's Commission on an All-Volunteer Force (the Gates Commission) unanimously endorsed the recommendation to end conscription. They reached this conclusion because the draft was unnecessary, inequitable, and inefficient. Freedom of choice was superior to coercion as a way to attract and retain personnel for the nation's defense.

Bernard Rostker asserts that the members of the Gates Commission did not understand the reasons why they reached their recommendation. He is wrong in this assertion, an error that I discuss in the second section of this paper. When an army can obtain low-paid draftees, wars are waged in a different way than with a professional force that must compete in the marketplace for high-quality recruits. The typical soldier today, who has voluntarily chosen to serve, is brighter and better trained than his or her counterpart 40 or 50 years ago—developments that are examined in the final two sections. A free society has embraced a method of manpower procurement in which individuals serve out of choice, not coercion.

★

TO THE LAUNCH PAD

Greetings from the Selective Service Board signaled that your friends and neighbors had conscripted you to serve in the armed forces of the United States. The draft authority under the Universal Military Training and Service Act of 1951 came up before Congress in 1963 for its third renewal. Tom Curtis (Republican from Missouri) voiced his opposition and argued that the draft was not needed for the nation's defense.

A major military manpower policy study was undertaken by the Department of Defense in 1964, I suspect to head off Congress from conducting its own study of the draft. I directed the economic analysis section of this Pentagon draft study, which was completed in June 1965; but hostilities in Vietnam evidently persuaded Secretary of Defense Robert McNamara to shelve the report until August 1966.[2] Opposition to the draft and to the war swelled on college campuses. President Lyndon Johnson asked Burke Marshall to direct a presidential commission whose report, *In Pursuit of Equity: Who Serves When Not All Serve?*, was the basis for the lottery draft (National Advisory Committee 1967).

In the meantime, Professor Sol Tax organized a conference on the draft, which convened in December 1966 at the University of Chicago. Four members of Congress were present: Robert Kastenmeier, Edward Kennedy, Maureen Neuberger, and Donald Rumsfeld. Milton Friedman (1967) appealed to the libertarian principles of freedom and efficiency in developing an eloquent case against conscription.[3] Friedman's article persuaded Martin Anderson to prepare a position paper for Richard Nixon, who was planning to run for the presidency. Four months later, an article entitled "Nixon Backs Eventual End of Draft," appeared in the November 18, 1967, issue of the *New York Times* (Semple 1967, 21). Nixon amplified the reasons for his opposition to the draft in a campaign speech less than a month before the election (Nixon 1968).

The next step was made by W. Allen Wallis, president of the University of Rochester, who assembled a small team to prepare a plan for ending the draft (Oi 1996). Martin Anderson placed the draft on the Nixon policy agenda, and together with Arthur Burns moved it into a prominent position. They persuaded President Nixon to establish a presidential commission, and a reluctant Thomas Gates (a former secretary of defense) agreed to serve as the chair. William H. Meckling, the executive director, guided the commission and the staff to deliver a completed report to President Nixon on February 20, 1970. The report of the Gates Commission became the launch pad leading to the end of peacetime conscription on July 1, 1973.

WERE WE "RIGHT FOR THE WRONG REASON"?
I DON'T THINK SO.

In chapter 3, Bernard Rostker wrote, "I humbly suggest that they [the Gates Commission] made the right recommendation for a reason that they did not fully understand." Chapter 3 of the commission report emphasized the fact that conscription imposed a hidden tax on those who were coerced to serve. Rostker asserts that the "cost" to the population at risk of being drafted was immaterial to the decision reached by the Gates Commission. I find this to be a remarkable and unacceptable assertion on two grounds. How can one know how each commission member reached his or her decision? Rostker did not attend the commission meetings; I did, and believe that the cost argument discussed in the report of the commission carried a lot of weight in the thinking of commission members.

Rostker embraces an opinion voiced by the erstwhile chairman of the Senate Armed Services Committee, Sam Nunn, who stated, "The concept is a clear result of the Vietnam War because it caused the President and Congress to yield to the tremendous pressure to end the draft at almost any price." What Senator Nunn and Mr. Rostker fail to recognize is that the cost of the draft rose sharply when the shooting started. As the cost of the draft climbed, so also did the pressure to end it. The Rostker chapter tosses in an almost extraneous thought: "the problem with the draft was not what it did to society in the form of lost social welfare, but what it did to the military." If the draft was a problem, the military could have asked Congress to end the draft; it did not, suggesting that until compelled to drop it, the military was willing to go along with a coercive system of recruitment until a feasible alternative was spelled out. The Gates Commission supplied this superior alternative.

Mr. Rostker has a narrow concept of "cost." He cites two studies which found that, under certain assumed conditions, a draft could reduce the "social cost" of acquiring and retaining military personnel. But these studies presume that the "social cost" can be calculated from the supply prices of those who serve in the armed forces, a presumption that I also made in my 1967 article.[4] Lawrence Sjaasted and Ronald Hansen (1972) were among the first economists to recognize that the "full social cost" must include the cost of collecting the draft tax, which must include the sometimes substantial costs incurred by many who never put on a uniform. Some youths became fathers to "earn" an exemption, others stayed in college to obtain deferments, and many fled to Canada and Europe.[5] Sjaasted and Hansen reported that the "full social cost" of conscription, which includes the cost of the taxes imposed on those who were coerced to serve, plus the costs incurred by those who evaded and avoided their draft boards, far exceeded the "full social cost" of any other tax levied by the government. The studies showing that conscription could reduce the "cost" of staffing the armed services ignored the costs of collecting the draft tax. If these studies used the right measure of "cost," including the costs of collecting and avoiding the tax, the conclusion would have been reversed. The full social cost is a lower bound estimate of the price of freedom.

The recommendations of the Gates Commission were not confined to what Rostker calls a simple "social welfare" approach. The commission report showed that the nation's defense could be secured without a draft. Pay increases were needed not only to attract qualified individuals in a competitive labor market but also to mitigate the financial penalty placed on first-term enlisted personnel. Notice that I call it a financial penalty rather than a tax because it was imposed on everyone, even the true volunteers. The Gates Commission outlined the steps that had to be taken to staff the reserve forces and the medical corps, to eliminate wasteful personnel practices, to explore efficiency-enhancing civilian substitutions, and to improve the quality of military service life. We showed that the all-volunteer force could work, that it was efficient, and that it was equitable. Did we come up with the right recommendation for the wrong reason? I don't think so. Freedom of choice here, as elsewhere, is surely worthwhile.

PRODUCING NATIONAL DEFENSE

The nature of conflict and the technology of warfare surely influence the way in which troops are recruited, trained, and retained. When the Army could obtain low-cost labor in large numbers, the draftees were brought in for short tours of duty, of two years or less. Most were assigned to the ground combat forces. Upon termination of the draft authority, the Army chose to produce defense capability by embracing a high-quality personnel policy espoused by General Maxwell Thurman (1996).[6] If a majority of recruits had high school degrees and were drawn from the top half of the aptitude distribution, studies indicated that the size of the training bases required for a given end strength could be reduced by 27 percent. But this meant maintaining recruiting effort and pay at high levels.

The AVF is a fragile institution whose survival was threatened in its first six years by two events mentioned in the paper by John White (chapter 4, this volume). First, in its fight against inflation, the Carter administration failed to keep military pay in line with civilian wages. Second, the problem was aggravated by a misnorming of the Armed Services Vocational Aptitude Battery (ASVAB) and, in turn, the Armed Forces Qualification Test (AFQT). In line with its high-quality personnel policy, the Army's recruiters in 1979 were told that only 5 to 6 percent of the total intake could be filled with aptitude category IV recruits (having AFQT scores of 21 to 30). When a flaw in scoring the test was discovered, the Army learned that the actual intake contained 26 to 30 percent category IV recruits. The misnorming of the ASVAB was reported by Sims (1978).[7] Attrition rates are higher, and retention rates lower, for low-quality recruits, which raise the costs of staffing positions in the active duty forces. The sophistication of the equipment and the rapid speed of technical advance make it essential that we retain the high-quality personnel policies adopted by the all-volunteer force.

THE MILITARY SPECIALIST

The Army commanded by General Dwight D. Eisenhower bore little resemblance to the Army headed by Black Jack Pershing. In Eisenhower's Army, relatively fewer soldiers in the ground combat units were supported by a larger support tail. Harold Wool (1970) emphasized the importance and the need of recruiting and training soldiers to become military specialists who can operate and maintain sophisticated weapon systems—a need that was created by the advance in military technology. The structure of the Army has evolved over time with changes in technology calling for higher skills and a more complicated human resource management system. Attrition rates in the all-volunteer force are higher than those under conscription, due partly to a stricter training regime and partly to a policy of releasing individuals who want to leave. Some

13.2 percent of Marine Corps recruits failed to complete boot camp in 1980 during the misnorming period. This rate fell to 11.2 percent in 1991 when the Marines were accepting only high-quality recruits. John White says that these attrition rates are "too high" and could be reduced by better recruit selection or better training procedures. An optimal attrition rate is surely not equal to zero. The Marine Corps and the other services must balance the cost of assessing higher-quality recruits against the cost of changing their training procedures.

In my closing remarks, I offer three possibly heretical proposals.

COMPENSATION

In 1964, I had the privilege to work with Lieutenant Colonel Gorman Smith, who was instrumental in introducing the variable reenlistment bonus. The British call these bonuses "reengagement bonuses." They dislike them because payment in advance reduces the incentive effects of pay. A reenlistment is a payment to persuade a soldier to be present; it does not reward an individual for a job well done. Wages in the private sector are paid at the end of a pay period, rarely are they paid in advance. A bonus in the private sector is an ex post payment for outstanding performance. In 1963, the military had proficiency pay, but it was on its way out. There was an administrative problem in assigning people into pro pay categories—a Lake Woebegone effect, where everyone was above average. A review of the fitness reports for officers reveals a similar bias. Some if not most of the monies now distributed through selective reenlistment bonuses could be reallocated to ex post incentive pay.

PROMOTION

In the British and Canadian Armed Forces, one can occasionally find a corporal, the counterpart of an E-3, who has 18 years of service. The rationale is that a corporal is fully qualified to drive a car for the general. Not everyone in a professional force needs to be a leader. "Up-or-out" rules are of questionable value in a professional force.

CAREER LENGTHS

The vesting of military pensions at the 20-year point is a questionable policy, a point made by John White (chapter 4, this volume). The optimal career length surely ought to be a function of the military specialty; it should be longer for a computer analyst and shorter for a fighter pilot. The sailors who staff the destroyers, submarines, and aircraft carriers confront different working conditions than the crews that work on the supply ships. I heard that at one time, the Swedish armed forces retained contract pilots who served for 10 years. In the British Navy, the supply ships were manned by civil servants. I wholeheartedly endorse White's proposal to introduce differential vesting points depending on the military specialty.

A FREE SOCIETY

On July 1, 1973, Secretary of Defense Melvin Laird presided over the end of the peacetime draft. The last conscript was discharged at Fort Polk, Louisiana, in September 1975. Youths no longer were subjected to the anxiety of waiting to see if they would receive "greetings" from their friendly Selective Service Board. The Marshall Commission, in their report *In Pursuit of Equity: Who Serves When Not All Serve?*, recommended a lottery which supposedly reduced the inequity of involuntary servitude. Young men watched the newspapers to see if they drew a low lottery number. If they did, some took actions to evade the draft.

There is no such thing as a fair and equitable draft. The Gates Commission realized this. The men and women who join the armed forces today do so out of choice, not compulsion. When interviewed by the media, the uniformed personnel serving in Afghanistan and Iraq express a pride and dignity for their role in securing the nation's defense. They obviously believe that their work is important, and they are doing something that is clearly worth their while.

I am pleased to have worked with William H. Meckling, the executive director of the President's commission, my colleague Harry Gilman, and the 15 members of the Gates Commission. While Meckling did most of the writing, we helped in preparing the report that evidently carried some weight in the decision to abolish the draft.

NOTES

1. Phillips 1945, 255.

2. The Pentagon draft study was organized and supervised by William Gorham, a deputy assistant secretary of defense at the time, and Harold Wool. Although the study was never released in its entirety, much of it was contained in testimony by Morris (1966) and Rumsfeld (1967), the former including the analytic findings later published in Oi (1967a). For a more complete discussion surrounding the study, see Oi 1996 and Rostker forthcoming.

3. Friedman introduced the desirability of an all-volunteer force in *Capitalism and Freedom* (1963), which he amplified in his paper for the 1966 Chicago conference (Friedman 1967, 200–207). His description of that conference appears in the autobiography by Milton and Rose Friedman (1998, 377–78).

4. See Oi 1967b, a comment on an article in *Playboy* by Thomas Curtis (January 24, 1967). My comment appears in the *Congressional Record*.

5. Only a few occupations, such as the ministry, were exempted from the postwar peacetime draft. Elected officials were, I believe, always excused from conscription, even during the Revolutionary War.

6. This point is emphasized by Meece 2002.

7. Also see Sims and Truss 1980.

REFERENCES

Friedman, Milton. 1967. Why not a volunteer army? In *The draft: A handbook of facts and alternatives*. Edited by Sol Tax. Chicago: University of Chicago Press.

Friedman, Milton, and Rose Friedman. 1998. *Two lucky people*. Chicago: University of Chicago Press.

Meece, Michael J. 2002. The army officer corps in the all volunteer force. *Contemporary Economic Policy* April: 101–10.

Morris, Thomas. 1966. *Summary of the Department of Defense report on the study of the draft.* Prepared for the House Committee on Armed Services. Washington, D.C.: U.S. Government Printing Office.

National Advisory Committee on Selective Service. 1967. *In pursuit of equity: Who serves when not all serve?* Washington, D.C.: U.S. Government Printing Office.

Nixon, Richard M. 1968. *The all-volunteer force.* CBS radio address, October 18. Reproduced in Martin Anderson, *The military draft* (Stanford, Calif.: The Hoover Institution Press, 1982) 603–9.

Oi, Walter Y. 1967a. The economic cost of the draft. *American Economic Review* 57(2): 39–62.

———. 1967b. The hidden tax of the draft. *Congressional Record.* Vol. 113, March 13, A1236–7.

———. 1996. Historical perspectives on the all-volunteer force: The Rochester connection. In *Professionals on the front line: Two decades of the all-volunteer force.* Edited by J. Eric Fredland, Curtis L. Gilroy, Roger D. Little, and W. S. Sellman, 37–54. Washington, D.C.: Brassey's.

Phillips, H. B. 1945. On the nature of progress. *American Scientist* 33: 255.

Rostker, Bernard. Forthcoming. *An analytic history of the all-volunteer force.* Santa Monica, Calif.: RAND Corporation.

Rumsfeld, Donald H. 1967. Statement of Hon. Donald Rumsfeld, U.S. House of Representatives, on amending and extending the draft law and related authorities. Committee on Armed Services.

Semple, Robert B. 1967. Nixon backs eventual end of draft. *New York Times*, November 18: 21.

Sims, William H. 1978. *An analysis of the normalization and verification of the Armed Services Vocational Aptitude Battery, ASVAB.* Report 1115. April. Alexandria, Va.: Center for Naval Analyses.

Sims, William H., and Ann R. Truss. 1980. *A re-examination of the normalization of the ASVAB.* Report 1152. April. Alexandria, Va.: Center for Naval Analyses.

Sjaasted, Lawrence, and Ronald W. Hansen. 1972. Distributive effects of conscription: Implicit taxes and transfers under the draft system. In *Redistribution to the rich and the poor.* Edited by Kenneth Boulding and Martin Pfaff, 285–308. Belmont, Calif.: Wadsworth.

Thurman, Maxwell R. 1996. On being all you can be: A recruiting perspective. In *Professionals on the front line: Two decades of the all-volunteer force.* Edited by J. Eric Fredland, Curtis L. Gilroy, Roger D. Little, and W. S. Sellman, 55–63. Washington, D.C.: Brassey's.

Wool, Harold. 1970. *The military specialist.* Baltimore, Md.: The John Hopkins University Press.

★ ★ ★ ★ ★ ★ ★ ★ ★ ★ ★ ★

PART II

SUSTAINING THE FORCE: RECRUITING AND RETENTION

★ ★ ★ ★ ★ ★ ★ ★ ★ ★ ★

INTRODUCTION

Christopher Jehn

Effective recruiting and retention is extraordinarily important, indeed essential, for sustaining the all-volunteer force. If the Department of Defense is unsuccessful in attracting and retaining quality people, other successes are unimportant. The department can better achieve the appropriate mix of active and reserve forces. The military compensation system can be reformed. The services can better understand what levels of quality they need. But success in all of these areas matters little if the services are unable to recruit and retain the men and women needed to staff the all-volunteer force.

Not only are recruiting and retention important, but sustained success is difficult to achieve. The past 30 years provide ample evidence of this constant challenge. After the end of conscription in 1973, the department took nearly a decade to design and implement successful recruiting and retention programs. Since then, each of the services has experienced at least one crisis in recruiting or retention. These crises have often required new thinking and implementation of new approaches to regain success. Yet just as often, the services have simply forgotten the lessons of the past and have been reminded of how easy it is to make wrong decisions with regard to recruiting and retention programs. Regrettably, there will probably be occasions in the future when the services will get it wrong again and will need to rethink their approach. Consider the challenge.

Each year the department must recruit and retain enough personnel to replace those who leave and to meet desired force levels. In fiscal year 2003, all the services met their active duty recruiting goals for both quantity and quality. Retention rates were at or above target levels. But that success was hardly automatic. A relatively high unemployment rate in 2003 and increased recruiting resources contributed to recruiting success. With the high operations tempo associated with the global war on terrorism and likely improvement in the economy, recruiting in 2004 and 2005 may be more challenging. These circumstances mean that the department must maintain focus and spend enough to avoid a repeat of the difficult recruiting experience of the late 1990s, when attention and recruiting budgets were inadequate in the face of a strong civilian labor market. Retention rates must also remain at levels sufficient to sustain the force. So budgets for selective reenlistment bonuses must be adequate and other management tools must be available and used.

Understanding the issues that influence successful recruiting and retention is the subject of part 2 of this volume. Success requires that the department thoroughly understand its demand for manpower and how to conserve manpower resources wherever possible. Success also requires that the department understand how external factors such as economic conditions and demographic changes, as well as internal factors such as compensation and personnel policies, affect recruiting and retention. At the same time, the services must be careful stewards of their share of the federal budget, spending no more than is necessary to sustain a quality force, lest the costs of recruiting and retaining people starve the budgets for developing, buying, and maintaining the equipment and facilities also essential to a quality military.

The three papers in this section review what the manpower and personnel policy community has learned about the effects of both external and internal factors on meeting manpower requirements. The arguments and analysis in these papers remind us of how difficult it is to "get recruiting right" and how demanding it is to ensure recruiting and retention success without wasting the taxpayers' money. The papers discuss options for compensation and personnel policies, the importance of personnel aptitude in setting enlistment standards, and the demographic changes the department must confront in coming years. Collectively, they provide a useful foundation for the department's continual review of its manpower, personnel, and compensation policies.

Today's military is as strong a military as this country has ever enjoyed, possibly the strongest military the world has ever seen. I believe this force is what it is because it is made up of men and women who joined voluntarily — who serve their country by choice. It is hard to imagine that an organization as large, as complex, and with as challenging and important a mission as the U.S. military, could function in any other way; that it could somehow be better if a substantial fraction of its members did not want to be there, were conscripted, or otherwise forced to serve against their will. Yet despite the obvious necessity, inevitability even, of a volunteer military, it has not been easy to achieve. Thus the success of our all-volunteer force — the ability of the military services to recruit and retain a high-quality force over the past three decades — is especially worthy of celebration. Let us all work hard to ensure the celebration continues indefinitely.

CHAPTER 5

SUSTAINING THE FORCE IN AN ERA OF TRANSFORMATION

PAUL F. HOGAN
CURTIS J. SIMON
JOHN T. WARNER

INTRODUCTION

In the 30 years since the inception of the all-volunteer force (AVF), the services, Department of Defense (DOD), and researchers have learned much about successfully sustaining the force. As noted by Stanley Resor, Secretary of the Army at the time, and AVF skeptic, success must be measured not only in terms of meeting numerical recruiting and retention goals — the focus of the early AVF — but, first and foremost, by "the kind of fighting capability [the AVF] creates to carry out our foreign policy and support our national interest."[1] If judged by its performance in Afghanistan, two Gulf conflicts, and other missions, it appears that the AVF has met the crucial test. As suggested by the title of a book commemorating the 20th anniversary of the AVF, *Professionals on the Front Line: Two Decades of the All-Volunteer Force*, the U.S. military has succeeded in evolving into not only a volunteer force, but a highly professional one as well.

The evolution of this professional force from its early days to the present has not occurred without some setbacks.[2] As James Hosek (1996, 123–24) wrote in the 20th anniversary book, "In the 1970s, as the U.S. armed forces were learning how to manage the volunteer force, they also learned that it was within their capacity to destroy it through mismanagement. In the 1980s, at the other extreme, we learned that the volunteer force could be managed to magnificent success." The recruiting outlook looked even rosier as the next decade opened with a period of military downsizing. However, in fiscal year (FY) 1994, all four services began to experience recruiting difficulties that persisted throughout the 1990s, difficulties that strongly challenged the notion that AVF management problems had been solved for good. Unprecedented economic growth, the lowest unemployment rate in 30 years, and historically high numbers of high school graduates bound for college combined to produce cumulative recruiting shortfalls.[3] A technology boom led to retention problems in high-tech skills in the late 1990s

★

and further demonstrated the lesson of the 1970s, that a booming civilian economy can wreak havoc on policies designed for normal or recessionary times. By the end of the decade, however, the services had adjusted to these unusual circumstances and met their goals at reasonable taxpayer cost, thus reinforcing the successes of the 1980s.

This paper provides an overview of the lessons learned over 30 years of the AVF and how those lessons can be used to sustain the AVF in the future. These lessons can help shape future policies relating to the changing role of reserve forces, civilianization of military jobs, and privatization. In our view, to be successful, the various stakeholders charged with responsibility for nurturing the AVF must

- understand the demand for and supply of personnel and the factors that affect them

- shape attitudes about the military as an institution and attitudes about military service among military members and the public at large

- effectively use compensation and personnel policies to attract, motivate, sort, retain, and separate personnel

- appropriately size the active force, the reserve forces, and the civilian work forces

The following sections of the paper address these various topics.

PERSONNEL DEMAND

The military personnel system has a hierarchical rank structure. There is little or no lateral entry; rather, the military fills billets at various levels by recruiting youth at the bottom, training them in various occupations, and promoting them to more-senior positions. This means that the senior leaders of 2030 must be in the pipeline today. The primary criterion for promotion to junior ranks is the acquisition of skill, while for the senior ranks it is performance on the job. Promotions to senior ranks can be characterized as tournaments in which a certain fraction of personnel are selected for advancement based on their relative performance. Because the rank structure is hierarchical, the fraction selected, and hence the probability of promotion, declines with rank, and competition becomes increasingly keen at higher levels.

The military thus has a demand for entry-level personnel and a demand for personnel to fill the more-senior positions. Entry-level demand, usually called "accession requirements," is the difference between overall desired force size (end strength) and flows out of the force due to retirement and pre-retirement separations.

The overall desired force size and the demand for personnel derive ultimately from the military mission as defined by the national defense strategy and DOD planning guidance. Given this mission, force size and the shape of the hierarchy are a function of a number of variables, including the state of military technology, the experience levels of the personnel in the force, and their ability. Because various configurations of personnel are capable of performing a given mission, the demand for personnel is derived by identifying the least-cost combination of personnel and technology that can accomplish that mission. This determination includes choosing the rank and experience structure of the force as well as the quality of the force as measured by the Armed Forces Qualification Test (AFQT) and educational attainment. Because DOD's mission is fulfilled by the totality of active forces, reserve forces, federal civilian employees, and civilian contractors, it is important to understand substitutability among all four categories of personnel.

The size of the force and the demand for U.S. personnel also derive indirectly from the level and type of aid that is supplied by allies in NATO and elsewhere. Recent difficulties in NATO with allies such as France and Germany point to the challenges faced. Moreover, as the paper by Martha Farnsworth Riche and Aline Quester (chapter 7, this volume) indicates, the demographics of U.S. allies in western Europe suggest that there may not be large numbers of allied troops in the future, in any case. The availability of ally forces affects not only necessary U.S. force size, but force function. For example, many U.S. allies' military forces specialize in peace-keeping and policing tasks. To the extent that the United States cannot rely on those allies for combat, training of U.S. active and reserve forces must be adjusted.

RANK AND EXPERIENCE

A major change in the force over the history of the AVF has been in the distribution of personnel by rank and experience (table 1). The table shows, since the start of the AVF, steep reductions in the percentage of enlisted personnel in the bottom three grades—an 18 percent reduction in pay grades E1–E3—as well as a 23 percent reduction in first-term (year of service 0–4) personnel.[4] The enlisted turnover rate fell from 21 percent in FY 1974 to 15 percent in FY 1999, and the average age of the enlisted force rose from 25.0 to 27.5 years.[5]

The growth in rank, experience, and age of the force, and the associated reduction in turnover, resulted in higher productivity, if the studies reviewed in Warner and Asch (1995) are any indication. Some studies estimate that careerists (defined here as personnel with more than four years of service) are *at least* 1.5 times more productive than service members in their first term. Moreover, the productivity advantage of careerists rises with the complexity of the skill and the steepness of the learning curve in the skill. Because increases in career content and experience lead to increased readiness, experience can substitute for overall force size: a smaller, more career-intensive force can deliver the same readiness as a larger force of less-experienced personnel.

It takes fewer recruiting resources to recruit a smaller size force, other things the same. However, to the extent that a career force demands higher levels of ability and education, recruiting costs are higher. Similarly, some components of personnel cost are smaller with reduced force size (paying fewer people), but others are higher (paying for more highly skilled personnel). Because many components of labor cost do not differ much between skilled and unskilled personnel (medical care, basic training costs), a smaller, more highly skilled force will tend to be cheaper overall than a larger, less-skilled force.

TABLE 1. RANK AND EXPERIENCE DISTRIBUTION OF THE DOD
ENLISTED FORCE, FY 1974 AND FY 1999
(PERCENTAGE OF THE ENLISTED FORCE)

RANK	YEARS OF SERVICE				
	FY 1974				
	0–4	5–9	11–20	21–30	Total
E7–E9	0.0	0.0	5.7	3.9	9.6
E4–E6	21.4	16.0	14.2	0.2	51.9
E1–E3	37.8	0.8	0.0	0.0	38.5
Total	59.2	16.8	19.9	4.1	100.0
	FY 1999				
	0–4	5–9	11–20	21–30	Total
E7–E9	0.0	0.0	7.8	3.7	11.6
E4–E6	15.0	22.2	19.7	0.1	57.0
E1–E3	30.9	0.5	0.0	0.0	31.4
Total	45.9	22.7	27.5	3.9	100.0

Source: Data provided by Defense Manpower Data Center.

TECHNOLOGY

Technology affects the degree to which personnel of one type can substitute for personnel of other types, as well as the ability of military planners to substitute capital for labor. As the recent conflict with Iraq has demonstrated, high levels of technology embodied in military equipment such as laser-guided bombs and GPS-guided cruise missiles reduce both the capital and labor required to accomplish a given mission; but operation, maintenance, and repair of such equipment tends to require more-experienced and higher-quality personnel.[6]

Changes in technology have resulted in a significant decline in the number of enlisted personnel per officer. At the start of the AVF, the Army had about six enlisted personnel per officer; now it has about five. The number of enlisted personnel per officer in the Navy has declined from about seven to about six, and in the Air Force from about five to about four.

RECRUIT AND TOTAL FORCE QUALITY

A major concern of AVF skeptics was that the force would consist of less-educated, less-able personnel. Such concerns appeared to be justified when measures of recruit ability plummeted during the early AVF period, a period which seemed to merit the claim that "half the Army reads comic books, the other half just looks at the pictures." Those early difficulties were traced back to the now well-known misnorming episode that accompanied the implementation of a new version of the Armed Services Vocational Aptitude Battery (of which the AFQT is a subset), and which resulted in recruits being admitted who otherwise should not have been. Since the early 1980s, recruit quality as measured by average AFQT score has more than recovered (table 2).

TABLE 2. APTITUDE DISTRIBUTION OF ACCESSIONS,
VARIOUS YEARS (PERCENT)

YEAR	I (93–100)[a]	II (65–92)	III			IV (10–30)	V (<10)	AVG. AFQT[b]
			ALL III (31–64)	IIIA (50–64)	IIIB (31–49)			
1980 (male youth benchmark)	5	35	29			23	8	52
1952	6	22	32			39	0	49
1957	8	25	43			24	0	54
1968	6	32	38			25	0	55
1973	4	31	52	24	28	13		56
1978[c]	5	23	43	16	28	29		51
1983	6	31	52	21	32	11		57
1988	4	36	55	26	28	5		59
1993	4	38	56	29	28	1		61
1998	4	35	60	29	31	1		59

Source: Aptitude frequencies for 1980 male youth, 1952, 1957, and 1968 are from U.S. Department of Defense 1982. Data for 1973–1993 are from U.S. Department of Defense 1998. Fiscal year 1998 data were provided by the Defense Manpower Data Center.

a. Numbers in parentheses are AFQT percentile ranges.

b. AFQT averages for 1988, 1993, and 1998 computed from raw enlistment contract records supplied by the Defense Manpower Data Center. Means for earlier years were estimated as sums of values representing within-aptitude group average AFQT scores multiplied by percent of enlistees in the group. Within-aptitude AFQT averages were constructed from Army enlistment data for 1987–1998. Estimated averages were constructed for years 1988, 1993, and 1998 and in all three cases were within one percentage point of the actual average.

c. 1978 data corrected for misnorming.

Educational attainment, another common measure of force quality, has also improved remarkably since the inception of the AVF. In 1973, less than two thirds of enlistees had high school diplomas. Since 1984, diploma graduates have constituted 90 percent or more of DOD accessions, and since 1991, at least 90 percent of *each* service's recruits have had high school diplomas. Recruits' educational attainment is strongly correlated with the likelihood that individuals complete their initial term of enlistment. The critical factor is possession of a high school diploma rather than an alternative credential such as a General Educational Development (GED) certificate. Over the 1988–1998 period, 23 percent of DOD enlisted recruits possessing a high school diploma failed to complete the first two years of service. About 40 percent of recruits who held GED and other high school equivalency certificates failed to complete the first two years of service.

Asch, Hosek, and Warner (2001) document a substantial increase in the educational attainment of the enlisted force. In particular, there has been a significant increase in the fraction of senior enlisted personnel who report having some college education or even a college degree.

The quality, and consequently, the productivity of personnel must of course be considered when assessing the overall demand for personnel. The body of evidence reviewed by Gilroy and Sellman (1996) suggests that higher-quality personnel are more productive. For example, Fernandez (1992) studied the repair times of Army radiomen, and Orvis, Childress, and Polich (1992) studied performance of Patriot missile system operators. Both studies found that higher aptitude leads to better performance.

Another important trend in the last decade has been the rise in the number of women in service as a fraction of the force. Women now constitute about 14 percent of both the enlisted and officer forces and have occupations that were not available to them even 10 years ago, such as bridge crewmember in the Army, fire controlman in the Navy, special operations pilot in the Air Force, and air support operator in the Marine Corps (Harrell et al. 2002).

THE RELATIONSHIP BETWEEN RANK AND PERSONNEL QUALITY

The military is a hierarchical organization: those further up control more resources and hence make more important decisions than those at the bottom. The capacity of the personnel system to identify and "percolate" the best-qualified personnel to the upper ranks is critical for military readiness and warfighting capability.[7] Quality, although correlated with observable traits such as AFQT scores and education, cannot be perfectly measured. Because quality only reveals itself over time, it is not possible to automatically select the best person for assignment to the top (most important) billet. The top billet and all other billets are filled in a series of promotion tournaments that successively winnow the contestant pool. Promotion through a series of promotion gates not only provides valuable training and preparation, but also helps reveal the productivity of those destined for the top.

If compensation and personnel policies are improperly structured, the military runs the risk that the best people will leave early and higher-level positions will be filled with less-qualified retainees—a problem called "adverse selection." Sustaining the force requires that policies be designed to give an incentive for more-qualified personnel to remain in the military and be promoted to the top. A later section of this chapter on compensation and personnel policies discusses these issues in more detail.

PERSONNEL SUPPLY

The military draws its personnel from the population at large. Success in meeting the demand for personnel requires that one understands the range and empirical relevance of the various factors that affect decisions to enter and remain in the military. Theoretically, the decision to join or remain in the military is based on a comparison of the value of joining (or staying) with the value of not joining (or leaving). Individuals join (or stay) when the value of doing so exceeds the opportunity cost, i.e., the value of the forgone civilian option. Decisions are influenced by both economic and noneconomic factors. Economic factors include the level of military pay and benefits relative to civilian-sector pay and benefits, and the state of the civilian job market as measured by the civilian unemployment rate. Noneconomic factors include attitudes about the roles and missions of the military, about patriotism and service to the country, and about risk, as well as the perceived conditions of life (both family life and work life) in the two sectors.

THE ECONOMIC FACTORS: PAY AND UNEMPLOYMENT

Studies have demonstrated time and again the sensitivity of enlistment and reenlistment rates to economic factors.[8] The sensitivity is evident in figure 1, below, which plots high-quality enlistments (high school graduates who score 50 or more on the AFQT) as a percentage of total enlistments, along with relative military pay and unemployment. Each series is normalized to have a value of 1.0 in 1974 so that the scale measures proportionate deviations from 1974 values.

FIGURE 1. HIGH-QUALITY ACCESSIONS (%), CIVILIAN UNEMPLOYMENT RATE, AND RELATIVE PAY AT ENTRY

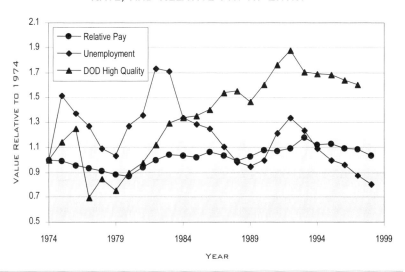

Source: Warner and Asch 2001.
Note: Each series is normalized to 1.0 in 1974.

The sensitivity of enlistment and reenlistment to the state of the civilian economy requires that the civilian market be continuously monitored. There were instances during the last 30 years when failure to do so had deleterious conse-

SUSTAINING THE FORCE IN AN ERA OF TRANSFORMATION

quences. Just three years into the AVF, Congress removed GI bill benefits at a time when relative military pay and the civilian unemployment rate were both declining. The result was a serious decline in both recruit quality and enlisted retention in the late 1970s. Recruit quality soared during downsizing in the early 1990s, which was a period of smaller recruiting goals and still substantial (if declining) recruiting resources, combined with rising unemployment and a lengthy, albeit shallow, economic recession. Perhaps the years of relatively easy recruiting in the early 1990s caught the services unaware and hence unprepared to deal with the economic and technological boom of the late 1990s, a period of historically low unemployment. The civilian economy was so strong that concern arose that the tastes of youth had so shifted against the military that supply relationships of the 1980s were no longer valid. Fortunately, such concerns turned out to be largely misplaced (Warner, Simon, and Payne 2001). Instead, the late 1990s and early 2000s was a period of relearning old lessons: recruiting recovered as the services responded with higher military pay, larger recruiter forces, higher advertising budgets, and increased availability of enlistment incentives.

OTHER DETERMINANTS OF SUPPLY

Personnel supply can change due to a number of external and internal factors other than pay and unemployment. The volume of recruiting efforts, as measured by recruiters and advertising, can also affect rates of enlistment.

EXTERNAL FACTORS

A skeptic examining figure 1 might be hard pressed to identify any military recruiting difficulties whatsoever. Despite the dip that began in FY 1993–1994, the percentage of high-quality accessions has risen secularly since the early 1980s. High-quality accessions now constitute about 60 percent of total enlistments, a 60 percent improvement over FY 1974. This quality improvement is due in part to a one-third decline in accessions, from about three hundred thousand per year in the mid-1980s to two hundred thousand today.

Despite the improvement in recruit quality, recruiting became more difficult during the 1990s. One factor related to the increased difficulty of recruiting was a rise in the percentage of high school seniors entering college in the year after graduation. This percentage has increased from about 48 percent in 1980 to 63 percent today. This increase can be traced to a rising disparity in earnings between high school and college graduates and has presumably been influenced by more-generous financing of higher education (especially for minority students). The increasing attractiveness of college degrees threatens to degrade the attractiveness of serving in the military as an enlisted person, where the pay and working conditions are designed to be competitive with those offered to high school graduates.

A second external factor affecting personnel supply is the waning influence of veterans on enlistment decisions. Adults who have served in the military are a potentially important source of influence on youths' decision to enlist in the military. Veterans have been declining as a fraction of the population for many years, partly as the World War II and Korean War veterans pass on, and partly because the downsizing of the early 1990s reduced the size of the force by about a third. Warner, Simon, and Payne (2001, 43) found the presence of veterans in the population to be a strong predictor of military enlistment. Veterans declined as a percentage of the male population over the age of 35 from 39 to 25 percent between 1987 and 1997. This decline was estimated to have caused a DOD-wide decline in enlistment of about 19 percent.

A third possible factor is the lack of clarity in the military mission that followed the end of the cold war. The downsizing of the armed forces that occurred in the early 1990s; the reduced recruiting and, especially, advertising resources during this period; and, in particular, the temporary vacuum created by the end of the Soviet Union as a major threat to Western democracy most likely raised questions regarding the raison d'être of our active duty military forces in the eyes of recruit-age youth. Presumably, these questions were answered, at least in part, on September 11, 2001.

A fourth external factor that will impact future recruiting is the rising proportion of Hispanics in the U.S. population, which has recently surpassed that of blacks. Hispanics now constitute about 14 percent of the population. This trend would seem to make military recruiting easier because Hispanic youth have a higher propensity to enlist than whites or blacks, other things the same (Warner, Simon, and Payne 2001, 23). However, Hispanics tend to score less well on aptitude tests and are less likely to have the education credentials necessary for entry into military service. Making Hispanics and other groups with a high propensity for enlistment more aware of the services' educational entry standards and of the need to earn a high school degree may help enlistment in the future.

INTERNAL FACTORS

Youths' perceptions about the U.S. military's roles and missions, their perceptions of the risks associated with military service, and their willingness to participate in the military life (e.g., accept regimentation) affect enlistment supply, as do other conditions of military life. There is little evidence that youths' perceptions have changed over time. However, the role of the U.S. military in world affairs has, and it continues to evolve. This changing role may have contributed to a decline in enlistment supply in the 1990s, and it may become an increasingly important influencer of enlistment as the role of the military continues to change.[9]

Unlike initial enlistment, retention decisions of both enlisted and officer personnel are based on actual in-service experiences. The conditions of personal (family) life and work life in service play an important role in retention decisions. According to conventional wisdom, work conditions peculiar to the military negatively affect an individual's view of military life. Intense training, long work hours, frequent permanent change of station (PCS) moves, and frequent unit deployments for uncertain periods of time on potentially unpleasant assignments (e.g., assignment to hostile fire areas) are among the factors that place strains on the personal lives of military personnel. High operational tempos, preparations for inspections, and the inspections themselves are among those factors that increase stress on the job. On the other hand, stimulating and challenging jobs, and a sense of accomplishment from participating in work of national importance are positive factors that can offset these negative aspects of military life.

Tabulations from the 1999 DOD Active Duty Personnel Survey by Gaines et al. (2000) indicate that, overall, personnel are satisfied with the conditions of military life. About 49 percent of personnel in this survey reported being very satisfied or satisfied with the military way of life and another 22 percent reported being neither satisfied nor dissatisfied (table 51). Furthermore, 40 percent of both officers and enlisted personnel reported conditions to be better than expected at entry while another 31 percent reported conditions were about what they had expected at entry (table 46). As to be expected, rates of dissatisfaction decline as rank and experience increase. Such a decline no doubt reflects the improvements in jobs and working conditions as rank and experience increase. But the improvements also result in part from the earlier departures of personnel who are dissatisfied. While dissatisfaction rates are not terribly high overall, the fact that 28 percent of personnel overall, and larger percentages of junior personnel, report being dissatisfied is cause for concern and points to the need for commanders and personnel managers at all levels to strive to improve the lives and working conditions of the personnel for whom they are responsible.

RECRUITING RESOURCES AND ENLISTMENT SUPPLY

The resources devoted to the recruiting effort—namely the size of the recruiter force and advertising outlays—are important determinants of military enlistments. (See Warner, Simon, and Payne 2001, for a review.) The recruiter forces of the Army and Navy increased in the 1980s, declined during the drawdown of the early 1990s, and rose after FY 1994, ceasing to do so by around FY 1998 in the Army, and FY 1999 in the Navy. By contrast, the number of Air Force recruiters fell steadily between FY 1987 and FY 1997, while the number of Marine recruiters rose between FY 1981 and FY 1986, and held relatively steady thereafter.

Estimates by Warner, Simon, and Payne (2001) indicate that a 10 percent increase in the size of the recruiter force raises high-quality enlistments by about 5 percent. However, the effectiveness of a recruiter force of a given size depends on other factors, including the state of the civilian economy and the other external and internal factors discussed above, as well as other recruiting tools, such as the availability of enlistment incentives as well as the level of advertising. The services found it necessary to increase the size of their recruiter forces after the downsizing period of the 1990s. Because new recruiters are less productive than their more-experienced counterparts (Asch 1990), quick ramp-ups take time to manifest their maximum effectiveness. Some eye must be kept on the inevitable ups and downs of the business cycle when making decisions about the size of the recruiter force.

Perhaps the most difficult policy issue surrounds advertising. Advertising budgets have exhibited several large swings over the course of the AVF. During the period 1979–1986, advertising budgets grew 35 percent in real terms. They declined by 65 percent between 1986 and 1993, but grew by about 350 percent over the decade from 1993 to 2003. The studies reviewed in Warner, Simon, and Payne (2001) indicate that advertising has a significant positive effect on enlistment and that it is a cost-effective recruiting resource. But advertising may affect recruiting with long and variable lags, and the timing of its effects is still imperfectly understood. Furthermore, advertising may be ineffective when done on a small scale (as during periods of downsizing), and its benefit per dollar of investment may diminish sharply when done on a very large scale (as in the 1999–2003 period). Dertouzos and Garber (2003) have made an important start in addressing issues related to advertising, but more research is needed.

SHAPING ATTITUDES IN THE EXTERNAL AND INTERNAL ENVIRONMENTS

In the wake of increased challenges to the management of the military and civilian work forces, in 1998 Secretary of Defense William Cohen appointed a Defense Science Board (DSB) Task Force on Human Resources Strategy, co-chaired by retired Air Force General Larry Welch and Dr. John Foster, to study human resource issues within DOD. Upon his confirmation, Secretary of Defense Donald Rumsfeld formed the Military Morale and Quality of Life (QoL) panel, chaired by retired Navy Admiral David Jeremiah. Both study groups recommended that DOD do more to inform the American public about the value and importance of public service.

EXTERNAL ENVIRONMENT

Success in recruiting and retention is easier when military service is more highly valued and respected by the public at large. By most accounts, the U.S. military is one of the most highly respected institutions in America, and in fact was ranked number one in Gallup polls throughout the 1990s (*Christian Science Monitor* 2000). Although traditional advertising plays an important role in shaping public attitudes about military service, both the DSB and QoL panel suggested that advertising, by itself, is insufficient, and that more should be done to engage the American public about the importance and "nobility" of public (including military) service. Leadership at the highest levels tends to wax during periods of crisis, such as during Operation Iraqi Freedom, but wane during periods of relative calm. The DSB proposed that outreach on a continuing basis to the American public is the responsibility of the national leadership, "beginning with the President and executive branch and including the Congress" (U.S. Department of Defense 2000, 10).

One role of leadership is to clarify the military's mission. The U.S. military has undertaken increasing numbers of less-traditional missions in recent times, missions not as easily articulated as countering the cold war threat from the Soviet Union. For this reason, these missions need to be better and more regularly communicated by leadership at the highest levels if they are to be accepted by the public at large and motivate the nation's youth to seek military service.

The DSB also recommended changes in the advertising message and the audience to which the advertising is targeted. The nation's youth are the primary target of military advertising, for it is their decision whether or not to join. However, the tastes of youth for military service are heavily influenced by their parents and other adults over very long periods of time. For this reason, the DSB recommended that the DOD undertake a public information campaign that is targeted not just at youth, but at parents and other youth influencers (school teachers, counselors, etc.). Such advertising would stress themes of patriotism, duty, and service to country rather than the traditional themes found in military advertising (high-tech skill acquisition, educational benefits, adventure, etc.). It would complement, not supplant, service-specific advertising. This theme was echoed in a recent report by the National Research Council (2002) and in an audit of the military's recruit advertising program (Bozell et al. 2002).

The DSB believes that DOD could do more to engage the American public, at relatively low cost, through other citizenship and education programs. Programs deserving of expansion might include the Junior Reserve Officer Training Corps (JROTC) programs in high schools, the JROTC Career Academy program, and the National Guard ChalleNGe program. It also recommended that the active and reserve forces place more emphasis on community outreach programs such as sending speakers to high schools, colleges, and civic groups.

These recommendations have been taken to heart. On June 24, 2003, Under Secretary of Defense for Personnel and Readiness David Chu announced a new advertising campaign designed to reconnect DOD with the American public so as to encourage adults to be more inclined to advocate military service to the young. Print advertisements ran in national magazines throughout the summer of 2004 featuring veterans from the various military branches. The ads focused on the qualities the individuals gained as members of the armed services and how these characteristics benefit them in their civilian lives.

INTERNAL ENVIRONMENT

High morale and esprit de corps are essential ingredients in enlisting, training, and retaining an effective fighting force. These ingredients are affected by several key factors identified by the DSB and QoL panel.

The first factor is that each individual in the organization should have a clear understanding and acceptance of the mission. Morale and esprit de corps are higher, the more clearly personnel understand their roles and the importance of the missions to which they have been assigned.

Second, individuals must feel valued and believe that they are contributing to the mission. Individuals filling "make-work" positions that contribute little to the mission are not likely to be very motivated. Each job must have value and each person in service must feel valued. Billets must be continually reviewed and their existence justified.

Third is the integrity of leadership. The QoL panel recommended continual review of integrity throughout the chain of command and insistence on high standards from senior uniformed and civilian leaders on down. An important aspect of integrity is making and keeping realistic commitments. The QoL panel heard anecdotes about how deployment schedules had been announced and later changed. Frequent reneging on announced deployment schedules, as well as deployment involving higher-than-expected operational tempo, can be damaging to morale and esprit de corps. News reports indicate that this scenario is beginning to be repeated with personnel now stationed in Iraq; it should be (and is) an area of concern.

Fourth is the command climate. Military officers rotate frequently, and often occupy command billets for only 18 months to 2 years. The QoL panel concluded that high rates of turnover among commanders and senior staff officers contribute to an atmosphere of turbulence and instability in military organizations. In key policy jobs, rapid turnover impedes the sustained effort often required to achieve significant policy change. The panel suggested that the command climate is improved when senior military leaders have sufficient time in command to execute a vision. Longer command tours would allow more time for mentoring of junior officers. There is some evidence from the Navy that the readiness condition of ships is lower the more frequent are changes in ships' commanding officers (Beland and Quester 1991). The main obstacle to longer tour-lengths is the desire to provide command opportunities for a larger pool of officers.

Fifth is the condition of the work environment. A negative element of the work environment is the increasing age of DOD's vast array of installations and infrastructure and the fact that DOD has not kept pace with needs for improvements, maintenance, and repair. The QoL panel reported that the deteriorating condition of DOD's infrastructure stretches work schedules and reduces the ability of personnel to do their jobs effectively, with adverse consequences for morale and quality of work.

The panel recommended that DOD modernize its infrastructure, transform its business practices, and improve the quality of life in the workplace. Excess facilities and installations need to be closed or eliminated and infrastructure improvements targeted to a smaller number of larger facilities. In addition to improving morale and quality of work, such changes would reduce overhead costs, reduce the number of personnel needed for support activities, and reduce the frequency of PCS moves. More-modern business practices might also permit a reduction in the number of personnel involved in support activities. Quality of life in the workplace could be further improved by reducing or eliminating excess requirements such as superfluous paperwork, reports, and inspections.[10]

A final factor is improvement in the quality of personal military life. By the end of the fourth year of service, over half of the officer force and 40 percent of the enlisted force is married. By the 10th year of service over 80 percent of both groups is married. Policies aimed at improving the quality of personal life in the military involve improving the quality of family life. DOD has a myriad of policy levers it can use to affect the quality of family life. Many of these levers involve cash or in-kind compensation (e.g., housing and medical benefits). Noncompensation policy levers include the number and location of military bases, the frequency of PCS moves, the frequency and duration of deployments, the support offered to families affected by deployments, and employment opportunities for spouses.

It is generally recognized that the United States operates too many military installations and that another round of base closings is needed. An important aspect of long-run improvement in the quality of life is the judicious choice of which bases to close and which to improve and expand. Concentrating forces at a smaller number of bases could lead to a number of quality-of-life improvements.

USING COMPENSATION AND PERSONNEL POLICIES TO SUSTAIN THE FORCE

At the core of force management are DOD's compensation and personnel policies. Sustaining the AVF requires a level and mix of compensation that—together with complementary personnel policies—will provide a force able to perform the missions specified in DOD planning guidance. There are various levels and mixes of compensation that will accomplish this objective. Theoretically, there exists a level and mix of compensation that will accomplish this objective most efficiently, i.e., at least cost. The least-cost level and mix of compensation depends on DOD's success in shaping internal and external attitudes about the military. If better success in shaping attitudes translates into improvements in recruiting, retention, and other measures of effectiveness, then the compensation required to sustain the force will decline.

A factor that limits the feasible range of compensation and personnel policies is that the U.S. military is a monopsonist. This means that, holding constant working conditions and personnel policies, the military must increase some element of compensation in order to attract more recruits and retain more personnel already in service. Conversely, the recruiting pool will not evaporate, and not everyone currently in the force will leave, if some element of compensation is reduced. The monopsony problem is that pay increases aimed at attracting more people must be given to personnel who would have joined or stayed without the increase. The marginal cost of personnel (the cost of an additional person) equals the compensation of the additional person plus the increase that must be granted to everyone else.[11] Implications of the fact that the military is a monopsonist are explored in the following discussion.

Below, we briefly review the overall structure of military compensation. We also suggest some areas where we believe that a good system might be made better to sustain the AVF in the future. Our suggestions emphasize increasing the flexibility of the current system, providing stronger linkages between compensation and performance, and continuing to rely on the choice of members in staffing allocation after they have chosen to enter.

OVERVIEW OF MILITARY COMPENSATION

It is useful to briefly review the elements of compensation. Regular military compensation (RMC) consists of basic pay, allowances for housing and subsistence, and a tax advantage owing to the nontaxability of the allowances. Based on the pay rates that went into effect in January 2003, the RMC of the 2003 force will total about $63 billion, an average of $45,470 per person on active duty.[12] Other components of active force compensation include an accrual charge for the future retirement liability of those currently on active duty as well as a myriad of special and incentive pays such as enlistment and reenlistment bonuses, sea pay, hostile fire/imminent danger pay, and aviation career incentive pay. The data in table 3 do not reflect certain other benefits such as veterans' educational benefits or the health care benefits of the active force members and their families.

Two features of military compensation are evident from the data in table 3. The first is a heavy reliance on the pay and allowances received by all personnel. Special and incentive pays, in fact, constitute less than 10 percent of basic pay outlays. The second feature is the heavy reliance on deferred compensation in the form of retirement benefits for those who complete 20 or more years of service. Over the AVF period, there has been little fundamental change in the distribution of compensation among the various components in table 3.

TABLE 3. ACTIVE FORCE COMPENSATION IN FY 2003

	TOTAL (BILLIONS)	PER CAPITA
Basic pay	$39.68	$28,513
Basic allowance for housing (BAH)	15.85	11,390
Basic allowance for subsistence (BAS)	3.85	2,770
Tax advantage	3.89	2,797
Total regular military compensation (RMC)	63.28	45,470
Special and incentive (S&I) pays	3.42	2,460
Other allowances	1.52	1,091
Retired pay accrual	10.67	7,670
Total compensation	78.90	56,691

Source: Items of RMC calculated from U.S. Department of Defense 2003a. Other items calculated from data in U.S. Department of Defense 2003b.

It is useful to mention a fundamental improvement to RMC that occurred in the mid-1990s. Prior to the mid-1990s, housing allowances were established in different geographic areas based on actual out-of-pocket outlays for housing.[13] Because personnel in high-cost areas would skimp on housing and personnel in low-cost areas would overconsume housing, the geographic variation in allowances understated the true extent of geographic variation in housing costs and caused hardships for personnel located in high-cost areas. Due to this problem, DOD switched to a system based on local-area housing costs rather than out-of-pocket outlays by military members. As a result, BAH rates are now more reflective of local housing costs and reduce the inequities that arise due to assignment to different geographic areas.

ALTERNATIVE POLICIES

BASIC PAY AND TARGETED PAYS

The basic pay table is the core of military compensation, common to all in the sense that compensation is purely a function of rank and years of service. However, military personnel eventually receive different training, enter different military occupations, and pursue different career paths. Because of differences in conditions of service in the various occupations, shortages will tend to occur in arduous occupations, and surpluses in those less so, when pay is based on this common pay table. Moreover, training and experience increase some personnel's civilian market value more in some occupations than in others, again generating shortages or surpluses, depending on the state of the civilian labor market.

Compensation must be sufficient to attract sufficient numbers of new recruits into—and retain sufficient numbers of experienced personnel in—varied occupations with a wide variety of working conditions, including different locations. Compensation is not the only tool available: promotion rates can be adjusted to alleviate shortages or surpluses as well. However, adjusting promotion rates is not a panacea, for the primary function of promotion is to certify competency and reward performance, a function that may be weakened if it also must shoulder the burden of adjusting supplies to meet demands.

Imbalances in manpower supplies and demands can be usefully classified according to whether they are temporary or permanent and whether they are overall, rank-specific, or occupation-specific. Different types of imbalances call for different compensation policies. There are three basic strategies: across-the-board changes in the overall level of pay in the common pay table; changes within the pay table that are skewed toward certain ranks or experience levels; and changes that leave the basic pay table unchanged but are targeted to specific skills, duties, ranks, or experience cohorts.

Across-the-board increases in basic compensation paid to new recruits are often proposed to make enlistment more attractive. Because the military is a monopsonist, such increases are expensive, and can result in payment of economic rents above the minimum necessary to induce recruits to join. The marginal cost of attracting new recruits through across-the-board pay hikes is much higher than the average cost of those recruits because such hikes are received by recruits who were willing to serve at the original, lower wage. This extra money paid to recruits who do not require the incentive is the economic rent. In fact, some studies calculate the marginal cost of a high-quality recruit obtained by a pay raise to be over $75,000 *per year* during the initial enlistment. Studies have found that expanding initial enlistment incentives, such as the enlistment bonus, college funds, and the Loan Repayment Program, offer a lower-cost solution to recruiting problems (Warner, Simon, and Payne 2001). Increasing enlistment incentives was a particularly attractive way to address recruiting shortfalls in the late 1990s, shortfalls that were relatively small overall.

An important question is whether there is sufficient flexibility to adjust to differences in supply and demand across occupational specialties within the context of a common pay table. Until now, shortages that are specific to certain skills and duty conditions have been addressed by offering enhanced enlistment or reenlistment incentives in those skills, called special and incentive pays. Such pays are both flexible and efficient: flexible, because they are easily increased, decreased, or eliminated as conditions warrant; efficient, because they avoid payment of economic rents to other personnel.

Some have argued that separate pay tables by occupation are needed to achieve this flexibility. Such a system, though, could make the system less, not more flexible, for several reasons. First, historically, once compensation has been set in the basic pay table, it has never been reduced (in nominal terms). Second, managers of occupation-specific pay tables may tend to focus not on supplies and demands, but on comparisons with presumed civilian occupation counterparts, the tracking of which may add to management complexity and cost. Finally, efficient management necessarily involves difficult trade-offs that may become even more so if the managers responsible become advocates for their occupation's pay table.

Increasing the proportion of special and incentive pays in total compensation—such pays constitute less than 10 percent of basic pay, and only 4–6 percent of total military compensation—could both reduce personnel costs and give careerists a greater incentive to work hard.[14] Overall pay hikes for careerists, like hikes in basic pay for new recruits, transfer economic rents to personnel who would have stayed without the hikes.[15] Critics of targeted pays argue that such pays run the danger of eroding morale and esprit de corps and, because much military activity is team-oriented, reducing unit cohesion. Taken to its extreme, this argument would recommend "full equity" in compensation, in which personnel are rewarded based on rank and experience—presumably, a measure of their military value.

In fact, DOD pay policy combines aspects of the "full equity" and "rent extraction" views of compensation. Full equity would require compensating all personnel at the marginal recruit's most valuable outside market opportunity, and would not only be expensive, but would result in a surplus of personnel in many skills. On the other hand, rent extraction is efficient only in a narrow sense: if all rents were extracted fully, military personnel would, by definition, be indifferent between retaining their jobs and separating from the military, and would certainly not be concerned about performance and promotion.

What is the right solution? Each tool fits a particular problem. Across-the-board pay hikes are warranted when shortages are encountered across-the-board. For example, the retention problems of the late 1990s were not across-the-board, but were more pronounced in the Navy and Air Force than in the Army and the Marine Corps and, within services, more apparent in the high-tech military skills than in the low-tech skills, a result of the boom in salaries of civilians employed in technology-related jobs. Because the retention problems were localized, they were handled through judicious expansion of selective reenlistment bonuses targeted toward high-tech skills, thus solving the retention problem at far lower cost than across-the-board pay hikes, which would have paid economic rents to personnel in "soft" skills.

Figure 2 shows DOD enlisted continuation rates for fiscal years 1987, 1999, and 2002.[16] FY 1999 retention beyond the fourth year of service (YOS) fell below FY 1987 levels.[17] How did DOD address the problem? There existed any number of options, including across-the-board pay hikes, pay hikes targeted to specific ranks and experience groups, and expanded use of bonuses and other special and incentive pays. The issue was addressed by the Ninth Quadrennial Review of Military Compensation (QRMC). It noted that lifetime earnings of male enlisted personnel hovered around the 70th percentile of lifetime earnings of civilian high school graduates (U.S. Department of Defense 2002b, fig. 2.5), but at around only the 50th percentile of earnings of males with some college education (U.S. Department of Defense 2002b, fig. 2.6). Moreover, midcareer military RMC (YOS 10–20) grew at a slower rate than earnings even among civilian high school graduates. Because the percentage of the enlisted force reporting having at least some college education had grown, the QRMC concluded that enlisted compensation was out of step with the civilian market for the types of personnel the services want to attract and retain.[18]

FIGURE 2. DOD ENLISTED CONTINUATION RATES, SELECTED YEARS

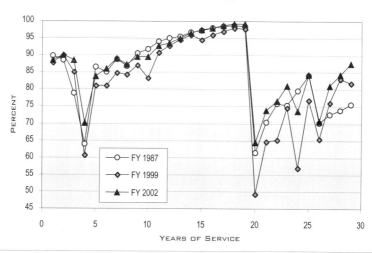

Source: Data provided by Defense Manpower Data Center.

Incorporating the QRMC's findings, DOD implemented pay raises in January 2002 and 2003. These pay increases were targeted to shore up retention and provide other incentives to careerists. Between FY 2001 and FY 2003, enlisted basic pay increases ranged from 10 percent for E-1s to 17 percent for E-9s, raising pay relative to FY 1999 by between 21 percent and 28 percent. These pay increases, coupled with a rise in civilian unemployment that began in 2001, raised both enlisted and officer retention rates. By FY 2002, enlisted continuation had returned to FY 1987 levels (figure 2). In fact, FY 2002 continuation rates for the first six years of service exceeded FY 1987 rates, partly a result of higher first-term reenlistment and partly a result of a trend toward longer terms of enlistment.

Targeting the pay raises toward the upper ranks had another purpose. According to some previous analyses of military compensation (e.g., Asch and Warner 2001), inter-rank pay spreads that are too small will provide inadequate incentives to stay, work hard, and seek promotion.[19] Compared with across-the-board raises, skewed pay hikes that increase inter-rank pay spreads provide more incentive for personnel to stay, work hard, and seek promotion. A flat pay system is least attractive to the most able personnel, who have the best civilian-sector opportunities. Targeted raises tend to provide greater rewards to the more-able personnel, the ones the military most wants to stay and seek advancement.

Skewed pay increases, of course, provide smaller increases for junior personnel and tend to reduce the compensation received during an initial enlistment (compared to across-the-board pay hikes). Since more than half of enlistees leave at the end of the initial enlistment, and therefore never benefit from a targeted increase that restructures the pay table, targeted increases make initial enlistment less attractive than do across-the-board increases.[20]

Assignment Pay Differentials and Flexibility

Although the services have successfully carried out their mission with an AVF, the allocation of assignments within the force remains largely involuntary. Because the services recognize that some assignments are less desirable than others, an implicit policy of "sharing the pain" exists in which desirable assignments follow less desirable ones in an effort to preserve equity. Individual members, however, have different tastes and circumstances. An assignment to Alaska may be a vacation for personnel who hunt and fish, but vacation hell for those who yearn for warmer climes. Even an ostensible dream assignment like Hawaii could burden a member whose spouse is employed and whose children are in high school.

Assigning members based on their preferences can improve retention and morale and can potentially reduce cost. For particularly disagreeable assignments, financial incentives can be offered. A question that arises, of course, is how this can be achieved. The Navy's recent innovation of "assignment incentive pay," where a dollar-denominated compensating differential for certain assignments is determined by auction, is a promising example. In this system, incentives by design, are set not according to arbitrary assessments of harshness of location or arduousness of duty, but so as to equilibrate the supply of personnel willing to accept a particular assignment with the demand for personnel at the location. In this system, not only are members given the flexibility to choose their preferred assignments, but DOD can be confident that the missions are being filled at the lowest possible cost.

Structuring Compensation to Enhance Performance

The capacity to stimulate effort through the compensation system is limited by the measurement of productivity or performance. In those occupations where performance or productivity is directly and objectively measurable, compensation should, at least in part, be tied to performance. For example, since recruiter productivity is measurable, tying recruiters' special duty assignment pay to performance could enhance productivity. Other areas where special and incentive pays could tie compensation directly to performance could also be explored.

In many, if not most, military occupations, measuring performance or productivity is difficult. Promotion is the major reward for performance in the military, for it is mainly through promotion that personnel can earn higher levels of compensation. Enlisted promotions through grade E-3 are "standards-based," while beyond E-3, they are more or less competitive. Promotions to grades E-8 and E-9 are centralized in all the services, and are highly competitive.

Promotions beyond E-3 tend to be "vacancy-driven" in all of the services.[21] This means that occupations with lower retention will typically have faster promotion rates. This feature is desirable in the sense that the system responds automatically to imbalances in supply and demand. However, although most of those promoted during periods of rapid promotion would eventually be promoted during slower times, the vacancy-driven nature of the current system weakens the link between service members' actions and their promotion. This weakened connection in turn weakens promotion as an incentive device.[22]

The Defense Officer Personnel Management Act (DOPMA) limits the fraction of officers who can occupy grades O-4 through O-6.[23] Currently, officers compete for promotion within year-groups and competitive categories, usually military occupation groups. The individual services have some discretion in setting promotion flow points — the modal year of service at which an officer is selected to the next higher grade — and opportunity for selection. Even so, modal promotion points to each grade are within roughly the same two-year window for each service. DOPMA also limits the tenure of officers within each grade. In the absence of a waiver by a selective retention board, O-3 and O-4 officers must leave service if they are twice passed over for promotion, and O-5 officers and above have specific tenure limits. These constraints limit the admissible promotion flow points, and give an "up-or-out" flavor to the system. This up-or-out feature enhances motivation, particularly within officer ranks, because personnel do not become eligible for retirement benefits until their 20th year of service. Among enlisted personnel, high tenure limits are set, so that most members who achieve E-5 and perform satisfactorily may remain until retirement.

The personnel system must accomplish three tasks. First, positions must be filled with qualified personnel. Second, personnel must acquire the experience and skill that are necessary to perform well at the next level. Finally, superiors must observe performance and determine whether a service member has the potential to succeed at higher levels of responsibility. The current system tends to separate service members who are competent in their current positions but who, *in comparison with their contemporaries*, do not exhibit as much potential to assume higher levels of responsibility or command. Termination of such individuals results in a loss of valuable experience and skill.

Current policy and law provide some flexibility to waive the up-or-out provision in some cases. However, additional flexibility to alter the rank distribution might be desirable. Because DOPMA constrains the number of O-4 through O-6 officer positions, retaining noncompetitive, yet fully competent, officers in these grades results in fewer positions for those officers who remain competitive. Reducing the number of competitive positions reduces the probabilities of promotion for those lower down, thus negatively affecting motivation to perform well. Additional billets in the O-4 to O-6 ranks would enable retention of personnel for the skills they possess in their current ranks while maintaining promotion opportunities for those destined for higher ranks.

In addition to promotion, personnel are rewarded through lock-step time-in-service (TIS) increases in basic pay. For example, an E-6 with 10 years of service earns about 25 percent more in basic pay than an E-6 with 2 years of service. The automatic connection between pay and TIS has been a source of much past discussion. Some critics believe that TIS-based pay hikes dampen the connection between performance and reward. One result of TIS-based pay is that early promotees receive smaller promotion increases than late promotees.

Linking *within-rank* pay to performance rather than longevity would build better performance incentives into the compensation system and would reduce the need to use promotions as the primary mechanism for providing financial rewards for personnel. An often-discussed means of doing so would be to link pay to time in grade (TIG) rather than TIS. TIG-based increases would give early promotees a permanent earnings advantage over slow promotees. In the past, the Navy, with its higher turnover and faster promotions, has been a proponent of TIG-based pay. Not surprisingly, the Air Force, with its lower turnover and slower promotions, has opposed it. An alternative approach, popular in the private sector, is pay banding, which establishes a range of pay for each rank and places individuals within the band based on supervisor ratings. Pay banding experiments with federal civilian scientists and engineers show promise (Morrow 1999). Efficient implementation could be bureaucratically complex, however, particularly when it is necessary to compare individuals who are evaluated by different supervisors.

The Retirement System: Managing Exits from the Force

The military retirement system differs from its civilian counterparts in a number of ways. First, members are vested only after completing 20 years of service, at which time their benefits are 100 percent vested—a system called "cliff vesting." Second, vested members are eligible for an immediate annuity upon separation. Third, the annuity is relatively generous, equal to about 50 percent of the member's basic pay. Although the generosity of the retirement system plays a limited role in members' initial decisions to enlist—youth tend to discount the future at high rates, and only a fraction of all enlistees plan to stay until retirement—it is evident from figure 2 that the system has large effects on retention behavior beyond six or eight years of service.[24] It both pulls those in the mid-career range to the 20-year point and pushes out those who become vested. The push effect—inducing voluntary separations of senior personnel—is the distinctive purpose of the retirement system (Asch and Warner 2001).

The retirement system is the linchpin of the compensation and personnel systems and shapes a wide range of personnel policies. Promotion points and up-or-out points are built around the 20-year system. In some cases, the results are desirable. Individual career paths and aggregate personnel flows are more predictable than they would be in a more flexible system. In other cases, though, the results are costly. One cost is that the services feel compelled to retain nonpromotable personnel in the midcareer range to the 20-year point.[25] The system is also limited in its ability to respond to shifts in demand (as was evident during downsizing), technological change, and other factors. Another result of the system is similar patterns of retention and experience across the spectrum of military occupations. It is a one-size-fits-all system.

According to the Defense Science Board, the military retirement system does not adequately fulfill the two distinct purposes of a retirement system: (1) helping individuals accumulate for old age and (2) managing the force by separating personnel on good terms at the appropriate time. While the second purpose of the system is the more important one, many observers feel that more should be done to serve the first purpose. The vast majority of personnel (75 percent of officers and more than 85 percent of enlisted personnel) separate prior to the 20-year mark and receive no retirement benefits. To mitigate this shortcoming, the DSB recommended earlier vesting of retirement benefits. One way to accomplish this would be for DOD to contribute into the "thrift savings plan" that was recently authorized for military personnel. A government contribution, perhaps on the order of 3–7 percent of basic pay, could become vested after completion of six years of service, by which time most personnel will have completed their initial term of service. Such a vesting provision would provide an incentive to members to complete, successfully, the initial term of service, and provide an incentive for first-term reenlistment.

Inducing separation on good terms requires a system of separation payments to induce eligible recipients to leave at the appropriate time. Such payments could take the form of lump-sum cash payments, which would appeal more to younger personnel, or annuity payments, which would be more appealing to older personnel. The years of service at which eligibility for separation payments start could deviate from the currently required 20 years depending on the desired experience distribution of the force. Separation points could be set differently for those occupations in which people are needed primarily for the individual skills they possess (e.g., doctors, nurses, and lawyers) than in combat-oriented areas (e.g., unrestricted line officers), where selection for command and maintaining flows through the military hierarchy are more important.[26] Care must be taken in the construction of separation incentives to ensure that the retention of those whom it is desirable to retain is not discouraged.

Earlier vesting and explicit recognition of the distinct purposes of the retirement system would permit more-innovative force management. In fact, they are necessary if the potentially productive changes in career patterns that have been discussed are to be implemented.

IN-KIND BENEFITS AND THE DIFFERENTIAL TREATMENT OF MARRIED AND SINGLE PERSONNEL

A substantial fraction of military compensation comes in the form of in-kind benefits, including medical care, housing, and a myriad of other services that are provided to military families. By some estimates, in-kind benefits amount to as much as half of outlays for basic pay. A full analysis of in-kind benefits is beyond the scope of this paper. However, it is worth reinforcing the recommendations of the DSB task force and the QoL panel regarding two issues: military housing and the differential treatment of married versus single personnel.

About half of the force lives in government quarters and draws the housing allowance in-kind. About 300,000 military housing units are supplied and maintained by DOD, the cost of which is buried in various parts of the DOD budget. About 60 percent of the current stock of housing has been judged to be substandard; at the current rate of investment the stock will not be fully upgraded until about 2014. Even more problematic is that the cost of DOD-supplied housing is much higher than the cost of comparable housing supplied by the private sector. Internal DOD cost estimates using 1997 data indicate that housing an E-6 family on base costs about $15,000 on average while off-base housing costs about $10,600.

DOD recognizes that one key to reducing the high cost of government-provided housing is to reduce excess infrastructure and, in particular, to consolidate bases, which would free resources for DOD to upgrade housing at the bases remaining. Another key to reducing high housing costs is to determine whether the private sector can upgrade, operate, and maintain housing at lower cost. Demonstration projects at Lackland Air Force Base and elsewhere suggest that private firms can indeed provide better housing at reduced costs.[27]

The extent of in-kind benefits in the military derives from an era when many military facilities were located in remote areas and there was no opportunity to pay personnel in cash and let them purchase such benefits in the private market as they saw fit. Because married personnel "needed" more housing, they were afforded better on-post housing. As opportunities to live in housing off post increased, cash housing allowances were made available in lieu of on-base housing. Just as single personnel were given less on-base housing, they were given less cash for off-base housing. As a result, today's pay and allowances system compensates married personnel significantly more than single personnel. Based on FY 2003 pay rates, single personnel living off post receive $2,250 less per year than their married counterparts. Furthermore, while the BAH that married personnel forgo in order to live in government-provided housing may be in line with the value of the housing, the BAH that single personnel forgo far exceeds the value of that housing. Single E-1s living in the barracks or aboard ship are in effect charged $670 per month for the privilege of occupying (and, in many cases, sharing) that space. The excess rent charged to single personnel for government quarters and the loss of freedom that life in such quarters often entails create a strong desire for single personnel to leave post as soon as possible.

Fully equitable treatment of single personnel would eliminate the cash BAH differential for those living off base and rebate the excess rent charged to single personnel living on base. Calculations by the authors indicate that the former change would cost about $440 million annually. Assuming that about half of the BAH forgone by singles living on base or on ship is excess rent, rebating excess rent would cost about $1.7 billion per year.

The cost of such changes, not surprisingly, has impeded reform of the allowance system. However, favoritism toward married personnel may result in higher indirect costs that might be reduced if single personnel were treated on a par with married personnel. One cost derives from the fact that the differential increases the incentive for single personnel to marry — a form of adverse selection. Such marriages might be less happy, stable, or durable than those not thus motivated, and may lead to higher indirect costs in the form of reduced job performance. In addition, married personnel are more costly not just because they receive larger housing allowances, but because they receive family separation allowances when members are deployed, impose larger PCS costs, and consume greater amounts of medical care, day care, and educational resources for dependent children. Because retention rates are lower for single personnel than married personnel (Hosek and Totten 2002) — another form of adverse selection — the military tends to keep relatively more-costly personnel.

SIZING THE ACTIVE
AND RESERVE FORCES

In April 2003, there were 866,345 individuals in the selected reserve, or nearly 6 reservists for every 10 active duty soldiers (U.S. Department of Defense 2003d). These reservists have been activated with increasing frequency. The military activated as many as 80,000 reserve component personnel right after September 11, and activated 200,000 reserve personnel for Operation Iraqi Freedom (Kozaryn 2003). Between 1986 and 2002, the military's use of the nation's 1.2 million reserve and National Guard personnel increased from 800,000 duty-days annually to 46.8 million.

Two key considerations governing the size of the active-reserve force mix are relative cost and readiness.[28] Historically, reserve forces have been sized to meet transitory fluctuations in demand. When integrated properly with the regular force, reserves can provide essentially the same level of military productivity, but without the cost of paying them on a full-time basis. Because reservists are able to enjoy the benefits of civilian life for a large proportion of their time, costs to the military of providing a given level of readiness are reduced.

Current military planning foresees even greater usage of reserve personnel. According to David Chu, Under Secretary of Defense for Personnel and Readiness, the Defense Transformation for the 21st Century Act promises to shift the paradigm for how reserve forces are viewed. It will create a "continuum of service" between the current reserve duty of 38 days per year and full-time active duty of 365 days per year, as well as make it easier for individuals to shift between the active and reserve components (U.S. Department of Defense 2003c).

One advantage of such a continuum of service is that the military may potentially be able to take greater advantage of individuals whose civilian jobs provide militarily useful training and technological skills.[29] The military can, and does, enhance efficiency by targeting such individuals with special pays.

Currently, reservists of a given rank and time in grade receive equal pay for equal days of active duty work. However, it may be unrealistic to expect reservists to value a day of foregone civilian time the same on a deployment of 4 weeks as on a deployment of 20 weeks. This is especially true of reservists who incur a cut in pay during deployment. Although forward-looking individuals should, in principle, take into account such factors when deciding on whether to enlist in the reserves, forecasting likely deployments three or six years in the future may be almost impossible. If such deployment differentials persist, they may come to be perceived as "equal pay for unequal work." It may be worth considering paying bonuses to reservists who face unusually long deployments.

Currently, many reservists are operating at an unusually high operational tempo. This may not be sustainable in the future, at least without clearly communicating to the reservists what to expect. It may also be necessary to redistribute work loads. As Deputy Defense Secretary Paul Wolfowitz said, in an interview upon his return from a trip to Iraq, about the Air National Guard crew from Nashville, Tennessee, that flew him in part of that country, "They have a joke among themselves that they have a departure date: it's six weeks from now, whenever 'now' is. Well, that is not acceptable."[30] Reducing uncertainty is an important priority.

Deployment of reserve forces places stress on the civilian employer as well as the employee. Current thought emphasizes appealing to the patriotism of employers, as well as making them more aware of the contributions of reservist employees to society, but does little to address the issue of cost. Such appeals may, in the end, be as successful as such appeals were to secure the cooperation of draftees during the draft era, particularly if plans go ahead to make increased use of reserves in the future.[31]

Recently, some critics have questioned the degree to which the forces represent the larger population, and, in particular, whether sufficient numbers of college-bound and college-educated youth are choosing to serve in the military. This concern motivated Senators Evan Bayh (Democrat from Indiana) and John McCain (Republican from Arizona) to propose a short enlistment option targeted toward such youth. Their proposal culminated in the National Call to Service program, which DOD will begin to implement in FY 2004. This program will involve a short active duty enlistment (a training period plus 15 months of post-training service) followed by 24 months of participation in the selected reserve, plus an additional period in the individual ready reserve. A range of incentives to attract high-quality youth will be offered. There are, of course, questions regarding how this program will affect recruiting for longer-term enlistments and whether it is cost effective.[32] Given the initial scale of the program, to consist of about 2,500 recruits, its impact will be minimal.

A proposal for a much larger program — to enlist 100,000 accessions annually as "citizen-soldiers" — is another matter. (See Magee and Nider 2003 for a discussion of such a program.) To proponents who envision a large scale for the program, the real target of the program is students at "elite" colleges and universities. It is unlikely that the incentives available would be sufficient to attract such individuals. Furthermore, benefits aimed at such students (and not available to other recruits) at the levels necessary to entice 100,000 of them into service would, in our opinion, raise serious equity and efficiency problems.

Independent of the Call to Service initiative, the participation of college students in the selected reserve programs could be increased by better matching of training periods with college terms. Currently, reserve enlistees serve a minimum of 38 days per year. Such a commitment, and longer ones, could be served during summer months, thus synchronizing military and college schedules. Consideration would have to be given to the fact that activation of these summer reservists might interrupt their college education. College students' incentives to participate in the reserves could be enhanced if they could earn college credit for their participation. Although this gets into the tricky issue of college curricula, there are some natural fits, such as credit for physical education and leadership courses.

Finally, the Call to Service program raises the question of whether it is possible to expand the opportunity to serve in the military more broadly. The services mainly access and train young people. Some become linguists, for example, but there are many older people in the population who possess linguistic skills. There is currently very limited opportunity for lateral entry into the military. Whether the military could accommodate more lateral entrants, and whether it should, are open questions.

SIZING THE MILITARY AND NONMILITARY WORK FORCES

The DSB and QoL panels both recommended that DOD civilianize all positions that do not have an essentially military function. Under Secretary Chu recently stated that 320,000 jobs currently done by military personnel could be civilianized. The optimal sizes of the military and nonmilitary work forces are partly a function of relative costs, but are also functions of which tasks are best kept within the military hierarchy. There are several reasons to keep certain tasks within the military. First, some tasks must be kept within the command and control of military leaders. Second, one purpose of the military hierarchy is to channel better-performing individuals into higher ranks. Some nonmilitary tasks may provide on-the-job training or reveal leadership qualities that are valuable in higher-ranking military positions. Third, the military hierarchy provides a competition for higher-ranking slots in order to motivate those lower down.

Civilianization might reduce costs. One reason is that civilians would not be required to undergo basic military training. Another is that individuals might be more willing to work for DOD as civilians than as military personnel, implying a lower supply price for their labor. And if individuals are more willing to work as civilians than as military personnel, hiring costs could also diminish.

However, civilianization is not a panacea, particularly because current work rules (e.g., title 5) that govern civilian governmental employees impose such high costs that military planners find it less costly to use military personnel to do jobs that might otherwise be more cost-effectively done by civilians. For example, current hiring practices make it difficult for DOD to compete in the civilian marketplace. One reason is that the hiring process is so long that qualified job applicants often receive civilian offers long before DOD is ready to make an offer. A second reason is that federal civil service pay scales in different civil service grades are based largely on educational requirements for the jobs and not market conditions in different occupations. For example, economists and psychologists with similar degrees and in the same grade are paid the same even though those two skills might be rewarded differently in the nonfederal market. Of course, the failure to base rates of pay on what other sectors are paying means that applicants will be plentiful for some federal jobs and scarce for other federal jobs.

Third, when civil service job duties change, current rules require that the job be reopened to competition, even if the supervisor is satisfied with the performance of the individual in the position. This has the peculiar side effect of possibly causing individuals with a good performance rating to lose their jobs if their responsibilities are increased. Fourth, current rules require that DOD bargain with unions on a local basis instead of on a national basis. Good-government studies such as that of the Volcker Commission suggest more agency-specific personnel practices and more performance-related pay (Volcker 1989). Recently (on April 10, 2003), the Department of Defense tabled a proposal for the so-called "National Security Personnel System," which would allow these areas, and others, to be addressed.

CONCLUSIONS

The AVF has shown great resiliency over its 30-year history. Its capabilities have surprised even its most ardent proponents. Indeed, we believe that the potency of today's military, and its ability to apply force while minimizing losses to itself and to noncombatants, is a direct outgrowth of the AVF. The United States is in the enviable position of being able to tell the world that those who serve in the world's best military are there by choice, not compulsion.

Sustaining the force in the future will remain a challenge. Worldwide commitments are stretching the force thin, and budget pressures may limit resources available for recruiting and retention. The experience of the late 1990s showed that continued success requires constant monitoring and management as well as innovative programs to attract and retain qualified personnel. Despite the post-2000 turnaround in recruiting, recent studies indicate the existence of a secular decline in propensity to enlist that is linked to rising college attendance and waning numbers of veteran influencers. Another challenge for the DOD will be to help the fastest growing segments of the youth population meet enlistment standards.

This paper has identified a number of actions that we believe are important for sustaining the force in the face of these challenges. Recommendations include the following:

- Clearly explain the military mission to the American public, including to military members themselves.

- Appropriately size the recruiting establishment and the level of advertising for recruiting today and in the future, recognizing that sharp resource swings have lasting effects.

- Recognize that youth entering military service today face a choice between college and military service, and adopt innovative policies to allow them to pursue both.

- Improve the internal environment for military members and their families while meeting the demands of military readiness. Allow voluntary choice where possible, and care for personnel where it is not.

- Ensure that compensation remains sufficient to attract and retain personnel with the aptitudes and skills necessary to perform in the military environment.

- Differentiate between problems that are across-the-board and those that are localized, and between problems that are temporary and those that are permanent. Utilize the proper compensation tool for the particular problem.

- Consider that transformation of military careers will require modifying incentives to stay, work, and leave.

NOTES

1. Remark by Stanley Resor, quoted by Maxwell R. Thurman (1996, 55).

2. See Hosek 1996, especially page 122, for a brief discussion of pre-1996 problems. See Warner and Asch 2001, especially pages 182–85, for a discussion of these, as well as more recent difficulties.

3. Warner, Simon, and Payne (2001) estimated that these factors alone could account for a DOD-wide recruiting decline of 25,000 per year.

4. The data for table 1 were provided by the U.S. Department of Defense, Defense Manpower Data Center (DMDC). Unless otherwise stated, all figures in this paper are based on data provided by DMDC.

5. Walter Oi (1967) predicted, correctly, a 30-percent reduction in enlisted turnover with a volunteer force.

6. Sometimes, though, technological improvements built into new equipment reduce skill requirements. For example, the Abrams tank was designed to reduce the number of calculations made by gunners to operate the gun. To take another example, much equipment is now "plug-and-play," thereby reducing the tasks required of maintenance personnel in the field.

7. Interested readers are referred to Rosen (1992) for further discussion of the relationship between quality and productivity in the military hierarchy.

8. See Warner and Asch 1995 and Warner, Simon, and Payne 2001 for a summary of such studies. We do not downplay the importance of noneconomic factors such as the taste for military life, which are discussed at some length later in this chapter. However, Asch and Warner (2001) point out that the more similarly individuals value the noneconomic aspects of those decisions, the more sensitive enlistment and retention decisions will be to the economic factors.

9. In 1998 one of the authors asked the students in his Clemson University class whether they had considered military service prior to entering college. Several mentioned low pay, their distaste for military regimentation, and the risks associated with military service. Several others remarked that in the absence of a Soviet threat, there was no longer any compelling reason to serve. They saw little reason to join the military in order to become peace-keepers in Bosnia.

10. Of course, inspections and paperwork have a purpose—improving readiness—so it may seem facile to recommend reducing or eliminating them. The point is to continually review these activities and eliminate practices that no longer serve a positive purpose.

11. This marginal cost calculation includes "rent"—the amount paid to some members above that which is necessary to keep them in military service. This "rent" is, from a social cost viewpoint, not the same as a cost that directs real resources to a different endeavor. Hence, in comparing two or more ways of achieving the same outcome that have approximately the same marginal cost when rents are included, the option with the lower marginal cost when rents are omitted is preferred from the perspective of the economy as a whole.

12. About half of the force draws the basic allowance for housing (BAH) in cash, while the other half draws the housing allowance in kind; the numbers for BAH in table 3 value in-kind housing based on the BAH payments personnel forgo to receive it. The costs to DOD of supplying in-kind housing that are above and beyond forgone BAH payments are not reflected in the numbers in table 3.

13. Housing allowances make up about 25 percent of RMC on average, but the percentage is larger for personnel in lower ranks. The share of housing in RMC at different ranks is based on budget studies showing how much civilians at different income levels spend on housing.

14. See figure 1-4 of U.S. Department of Defense 2002b. Total military compensation includes allowances and retirement pay.

15. Note, however, that if there are two or more ways of achieving a given enlistment or retention goal that have approximately the same marginal costs inclusive of rents, the alternative for which the marginal cost exclusive of rents is lower should be chosen, from the perspective of the economy as a whole.

16. FY 1987 was chosen as a base because it represents a "steady-state" period during which the services were quite happy with their retention rates.

17. Analysis for the QRMC by Asch, Hosek, and Warner (2001) indicated that if FY 1999 retention rates had remained constant at 1999 levels, only the Marine Corps could have maintained its career force at FY 1999 levels.

18. Analyses of officer pay concluded that (1) over time, officer pay had lagged behind the earnings of college graduates even more than the pay of enlisted personnel had lagged behind the earnings of high school graduates and (2) career earnings growth was slower for officers than civilian college graduates.

19. The flat system of inter-rank spreads was partly a legacy of the end of the draft, when pay in the junior ranks was raised dramatically relative to pay in the more senior ranks. Asch and Warner (2001) offer a theoretical reason for the relative flatness of the military compensation system based on the lateral entry constraint.

20. During the Ninth Quadrennial Review of Military Compensation deliberations, the Marine Corps opposed targeted raises for this very reason. Reenlistment rates and the career content of its force are so much lower in the Marine Corps that across-the-board raises would be more beneficial to Marine Corps personnel than personnel in the other services. The other services strongly supported targeted raises.

21. The Air Force is arguably the least vacancy-driven in that it attempts to maintain constant promotion opportunities over time; the Navy is arguably the most vacancy-driven.

22. To see this, consider a promotion candidate who is close to the margin for promotion. Other things being equal, the candidate can increase the probability of promotion by exerting additional effort to improve performance in the two-year period before selection. However, the candidate realizes that if vacancies are low during the selection period due to high retention, this additional effort will have no effect. Similarly, if vacancies are high during the selection period because of low retention, the candidate will be selected even if no additional effort were exerted. Hence, the candidate rationally chooses not to exert additional effort. The uncertainty in the promotion rates has lessened the ability of the promotion system to enhance effort and performance.

23. DOPMA was enacted into law on September 15, 1981.

24. Warner and Pleeter (2001) estimate a real personal discount rate for first-term military members of about 18 percent.

25. Involuntary separation, while an option, may be perceived as opportunistic; this could reduce the overall attractiveness of military service to youth.

26. Doctors and nurses are needed for the skills they possess, not their command potential. We see no reason why positions for them should be required to fit a hierarchical rank structure, why doctors and nurses should be subject to up-or-out rules, or why they should be encouraged to separate in their early- to mid-40s by a 20-year retirement system. The same could be said of many other military billets.

27. See Pint and Hart 2001 for additional discussion.

28. RAND has issued a report on the determination of the optimal reserve-active mix (Robbert, Cook, and Williams 1999) that emphasizes issues other than relative cost and readiness.

29. See chapter 4 of U.S. Department of Defense 2002a.

30. http://www.dod.mil/transcripts/2003/tr20030723depsecdef0441.html.

31. A number of awards and recognitions are available, including the "My Boss is a Patriot" certificate of appreciation, the local Employer Support of the Guard and Reserve (ESGR) Committee Chair's Award, the PRO PATRIA award, and Employer Support Freedom awards.

32. The program is reminiscent of the Army's 2+2+4 experiment of the late 1980s (2 years of active duty, 2 years of selected reserve duty, and 4 years of individual ready reserve duty). Buddin (1991) found that this program expanded Army enlistments by about 7 percent overall and did not detract from longer-term enlistments.

REFERENCES

Asch, Beth J. 1990. Do incentives matter? The case of Navy recruiters. *Industrial and Labor Relations Review* 43(3) (special issue): 89S–106S.

Asch, Beth J., James R. Hosek, and John T. Warner. 2001. *On restructuring enlisted pay: Analysis in support of the 9th Quadrennial Review of Military Compensation.* AB-468-OSD. Santa Monica, Calif.: RAND Corporation.

Asch, Beth J., and John T. Warner. 2001. Compensation and personnel management in hierarchical organizations: Theory and application to the U.S. military. *Journal of Labor Economics* 19(3): 523–62.

personal discount rate: *...
nomic Review* 91(1): 33-5...

h M. Payne. 2001. *Enlis...
t other enlistment incen...
se Manpower Data C...

*ent: Evidence from th...
*on, S.C.

the all-volunteer force
sured enlistment from
oportionate number of
s and skills (the defini-
F era has been how to
t a sufficient number of

quality over the past 30
cord highs in the early
oth internal and external
ditures are among those
e level of recruiting and
level of quality.

first describe manpower
s, and provide the ration-
enlisted forces. We then
or maintaining quality in
pulation. Finally, we dis-
y: alternative high school
Armed Forces Qualifying

TIONALE
lity recruit: scores on th...
is a composite score com...

Beland, Russell, and Aline Quester. 1991. The effects of manning and crew stability on the material condition of ships. *Interfaces* 21: 111–20.

Bozell/Eskew, Murphy, Pintak, Gautier, Hudome. 2002. *A report on the audit of the armed services recruitment advertising.* Santa Monica, Calif.: RAND Corporation.

Buddin, Richard J. 1991. *Enlistment effects of the 2+2+4 experiment.* R-4097-A. Santa Monica, Calif.: RAND Corporation.

Christian Science Monitor. 2000. Annual Gallup poll rates U.S. institutions. July 13.

Dertouzos, James N., and Steven Garber. 2003. *Is military advertising effective? An estimation methodology and applications to recruiting in the 1980s and 90s.* Santa Monica, Calif.: RAND Corporation.

Fernandez, Judy. 1992. Soldier quality job performance in team tasks. *Social Science Quarterly* 73(2): 253–65.

Gaines, Christine, Mary Ann Deak, Cyntia Helba, and Laverne Wright. 2000. *Tabulations of responses from the 1999 Survey of Active Duty Personnel: Volume 1 assignments, careers, and military life.* DMDC Report No. 2000-06. Arlington, Va.: Defense Manpower Data Center.

Gilroy, Curtis L., and W. S. Sellman. 1996. Recruiting and sustaining a quality army: A review of the evidence. In *Future soldiers and the quality imperative.* Edited by R. L. Phillips and M. R. Thurman. Washington, D.C.: U.S. Government Printing Office.

Harrell, Margaret C., Megan K. Beckett, Chiaying S. Chen, and Jerry M. Sollinger. 2002. *The status of gender integration in the military: Analysis of selected occupations.* MR-1380-OSD. Santa Monica, Calif.: RAND Corporation.

Hosek, James R. 1996. Commentary. In *Professionals on the front line: Two decades of the all-volunteer force.* Edited by J. Eric Fredland, Curtis Gilroy, Roger D. Little, and W. S. Sellman. Washington, D.C.: Brassey's.

Hosek, James R., and Michael G. Mattock. 2003. *Learning about quality: How the quality of military personnel is revealed over time.* MR-1593-OSD. Santa Monica, Calif.: RAND Corporation.

Hosek, James R., and Mark Totten. 2002. *Serving away from home: How deployments affect reenlistment.* MU-1594. Santa Monica, Calif.: RAND Corporation.

Kozaryn, Linda D. 2003. Rumsfeld, Myers thank employers of guard and reserve members, *DefenseLINK* http://www.defenselink.mil/news/ Jul2003/ n07182003_200307186.html.

Magee, Marc, and Steven J. Nider. 2003. *Uncle Sam wants you . . . for 18 months: Benchmarks for a successful citizen soldier program.* Washington, D.C.: Progressive Policy Institute.

Morrow, Walter. 1999. *Hiring and retaining scientists and engineers in DOD: A briefing to the Defense Science Board task force on human resources strategy.* Cambridge, Mass.: MIT/ Lincoln Laboratories.

National Research Council. 2002. *Attitudes, aptitudes, and aspirations of American youth: Implications for military recruitment.* Washington, D.C.: National Academies Press.

Pint, Ellen, and Rachel Hart. 2001. *Public-private partnerships: Proceedings of the U.S.-U.K. conference on military installation assets, operations, and services.* Santa Monica, Calif.: RAND Corporation.

Oi, Walter Y. 1967. The economic cost of the draft. *American Economic Review* 57(2): 39–62.

Orvis, Bruce R., Michael T. Childress, and J. Michael Polich. 199
    quality on the performance of Patriot Air Defense System operato
    RAND Corporation.

Robbert, Albert A., Cynthia R. Cook, and William A. Williams.
    mining the air force active/reserve mix. MR-1091-AF. Santa M
    Corporation.

Rosen, Sherwin. 1992. The military as an internal labor marke
    ductivity, and incentive problems. *Social Science Quarterly*

Simon, Curtis J., and John T. Warner. 2003. *What difference doe
    enlistment and the Air Force enhanced initial enlistment bonu*
    Economics, Clemson University, Clemson, S.C.

Thie, Harry J., Margaret C. Harrell, Clifford M. Graf, and Jer
    General and flag officer careers: Consequences of increased te
    Monica, Calif.: RAND Corporation.

Thurman, Maxwell R. 1996. On being all you can be: A recr
    Professionals on the front line: Two decades of the all-volunt
    Fredland, Curtis Gilroy, Roger D. Little, and W. S. Sell
    Brassey's.

U.S. Department of Defense. 1982. *Profile of American youtl*
    the Assistant Secretary of Defense (Manpower, Reser'

———. 1998. *Population representation in the military servic*
    Office of the Assistant Secretary of Defense (Force M

———. 2000. *Report of the Defense Science Board Task Forc*
    Washington, D.C.: Office of the Under Secretary of I
    Technology, and Logistics).

———. 2002a. *Annual Report to the President and the Con*

———. 2002b. *Report of the Ninth Quadrennial Review of*
    Washington, D.C.: Office of the Under Secretary of
    Readiness).

———. 2003a. *Selected military compensation tables.* Was
    Under Secretary of Defense (Personnel and Readi)
    Compensation.

———. 2003b. *Defense budget materials FY 2003.* http:/
    comptroller/defbudget/FY2003.

———. 2003c. *Under Secretary Chu briefing on the nati*
    http://www.defenselink.mil/transcripts/2003/

———. 2003d. *Total force report.* Arlington, Va.: Defe:

———. Various years. *Selected military compensation t*
    Under Secretary of Defense (Personnel and Reac

Volcker, Paul A. 1989. *Leadership for America: Rebuil*
    the National Commission on the Public Sector

Warner, John T., and Beth J. Asch. 1995. The econc
    Handbook of Defense Economics, vol. 1. Edited b
    348–98. New York: Elsevier.

———. 2001. The record and prospects of the all-
    States. *Journal of Economic Perspectives* 15(2): 1

CHAPTER 6

MANPOWER QUALITY IN THE ALL-VOLUNTEER FORCE

DAVID J. ARMOR
PAUL R. SACKETT

INTRODUCTION

The issue of manpower quality has been intertwined with
(AVF) since its creation in 1973. Conscription generally e
a broad cross section of American youth, including a pr
high school graduates who had above-average aptitude
tion of high quality). A major policy concern in the AV
maintain that cross section and, especially, how to attrac
high-quality recruits.

Indeed, there have been substantial variations in recruit
years, from unprecedented lows in the late 1970s to re
1990s. These swings are caused by a variety of factors, b
to the military. Because recruiting and advertising exper
factors, the quality swings have sparked debates over t
advertising expenditures needed to maintain a specified

This paper addresses several issues in this debate. We
quality standards, a component of enlistment standard
ale for maintaining minimum levels of quality in the
review trends in manpower quality and the prospects
light of education and aptitude trends in the youth pc
cuss two current issues in the definition of high quali
graduation definitions and the issue of renorming the
Test (AFQT).

QUALITY STANDARDS: DEFINITION AND RA

The services use two attributes to define a high-qu
AFQT and high school graduation status. The AFQ

Beland, Russell, and Aline Quester. 1991. The effects of manning and crew stability on the material condition of ships. *Interfaces* 21: 111–20.

Bozell/Eskew, Murphy, Pintak, Gautier, Hudome. 2002. *A report on the audit of the armed services recruitment advertising.* Santa Monica, Calif.: RAND Corporation.

Buddin, Richard J. 1991. *Enlistment effects of the 2+2+4 experiment.* R-4097-A. Santa Monica, Calif.: RAND Corporation.

Christian Science Monitor. 2000. Annual Gallup poll rates U.S. institutions. July 13.

Dertouzos, James N., and Steven Garber. 2003. *Is military advertising effective? An estimation methodology and applications to recruiting in the 1980s and 90s.* Santa Monica, Calif.: RAND Corporation.

Fernandez, Judy. 1992. Soldier quality job performance in team tasks. *Social Science Quarterly* 73(2): 253–65.

Gaines, Christine, Mary Ann Deak, Cyntia Helba, and Laverne Wright. 2000. *Tabulations of responses from the 1999 Survey of Active Duty Personnel: Volume 1 assignments, careers, and military life.* DMDC Report No. 2000-06. Arlington, Va.: Defense Manpower Data Center.

Gilroy, Curtis L., and W. S. Sellman. 1996. Recruiting and sustaining a quality army: A review of the evidence. In *Future soldiers and the quality imperative.* Edited by R. L. Phillips and M. R. Thurman. Washington, D.C.: U.S. Government Printing Office.

Harrell, Margaret C., Megan K. Beckett, Chiaying S. Chen, and Jerry M. Sollinger. 2002. *The status of gender integration in the military: Analysis of selected occupations.* MR-1380-OSD. Santa Monica, Calif.: RAND Corporation.

Hosek, James R. 1996. Commentary. In *Professionals on the front line: Two decades of the all-volunteer force.* Edited by J. Eric Fredland, Curtis Gilroy, Roger D. Little, and W. S. Sellman. Washington, D.C.: Brassey's.

Hosek, James R., and Michael G. Mattock. 2003. *Learning about quality: How the quality of military personnel is revealed over time.* MR-1593-OSD. Santa Monica, Calif.: RAND Corporation.

Hosek, James R., and Mark Totten. 2002. *Serving away from home: How deployments affect reenlistment.* MU-1594. Santa Monica, Calif.: RAND Corporation.

Kozaryn, Linda D. 2003. Rumsfeld, Myers thank employers of guard and reserve members, *DefenseLINK* http://www.defenselink.mil/news/ Jul2003/ n07182003_200307186.html.

Magee, Marc, and Steven J. Nider. 2003. *Uncle Sam wants you . . . for 18 months: Benchmarks for a successful citizen soldier program.* Washington, D.C.: Progressive Policy Institute.

Morrow, Walter. 1999. *Hiring and retaining scientists and engineers in DOD: A briefing to the Defense Science Board task force on human resources strategy.* Cambridge, Mass.: MIT/Lincoln Laboratories.

National Research Council. 2002. *Attitudes, aptitudes, and aspirations of American youth: Implications for military recruitment.* Washington, D.C.: National Academies Press.

Pint, Ellen, and Rachel Hart. 2001. *Public-private partnerships: Proceedings of the U.S.-U.K. conference on military installation assets, operations, and services.* Santa Monica, Calif.: RAND Corporation.

Oi, Walter Y. 1967. The economic cost of the draft. *American Economic Review* 57(2): 39–62.

Orvis, Bruce R., Michael T. Childress, and J. Michael Polich. 1992. *The effect of personnel quality on the performance of Patriot Air Defense System operators.* Santa Monica, Calif.: RAND Corporation.

Robbert, Albert A., Cynthia R. Cook, and William A. Williams. 1999. *Principles for determining the air force active/reserve mix.* MR-1091-AF. Santa Monica, Calif.: RAND Corporation.

Rosen, Sherwin. 1992. The military as an internal labor market: some allocation, productivity, and incentive problems. *Social Science Quarterly* 73(2): 227–37.

Simon, Curtis J., and John T. Warner. 2003. *What difference does a year make? Term of enlistment and the Air Force enhanced initial enlistment bonus program.* Department of Economics, Clemson University, Clemson, S.C.

Thie, Harry J., Margaret C. Harrell, Clifford M. Graf, and Jerry M. Sollinger. 2001. *General and flag officer careers: Consequences of increased tenure.* MR-868-OSD. Santa Monica, Calif.: RAND Corporation.

Thurman, Maxwell R. 1996. On being all you can be: A recruiting perspective. In *Professionals on the front line: Two decades of the all-volunteer force.* Edited by J. Eric Fredland, Curtis Gilroy, Roger D. Little, and W. S. Sellman. Washington, D.C.: Brassey's.

U.S. Department of Defense. 1982. *Profile of American youth.* Washington, D.C.: Office of the Assistant Secretary of Defense (Manpower, Reserve Affairs, and Logistics).

———. 1998. *Population representation in the military services (FY 97).* Washington, D.C.: Office of the Assistant Secretary of Defense (Force Management Policy).

———. 2000. *Report of the Defense Science Board Task Force on Human Resources Strategy.* Washington, D.C.: Office of the Under Secretary of Defense (Acquisition, Technology, and Logistics).

———. 2002a. *Annual Report to the President and the Congress.* Washington, D.C.

———. 2002b. *Report of the Ninth Quadrennial Review of Military Compensation.* Washington, D.C.: Office of the Under Secretary of Defense (Personnel and Readiness).

———. 2003a. *Selected military compensation tables.* Washington, D.C.: Office of the Under Secretary of Defense (Personnel and Readiness), Directorate of Compensation.

———. 2003b. *Defense budget materials FY 2003.* http://www.dod.mil/comptroller/defbudget/FY2003.

———. 2003c. *Under Secretary Chu briefing on the national security personnel system.* http://www.defenselink.mil/transcripts/2003/tr20030610-0268.html.

———. 2003d. *Total force report.* Arlington, Va.: Defense Manpower Data Center. (April).

———. Various years. *Selected military compensation tables.* Washington D.C.: Office of the Under Secretary of Defense (Personnel and Readiness), Directorate of Compensation.

Volcker, Paul A. 1989. *Leadership for America: Rebuilding the public sector.* The Report of the National Commission on the Public Sector. Washington, D.C.

Warner, John T., and Beth J. Asch. 1995. The economics of military manpower. In *Handbook of Defense Economics,* vol. 1. Edited by Keith Hartley and Todd Sandler. 348–98. New York: Elsevier.

———. 2001. The record and prospects of the all-volunteer military in the United States. *Journal of Economic Perspectives* 15(2): 169–92.

Warner, John T., and Saul Pleeter. 2001. The personal discount rate: Evidence from military downsizing programs. *American Economic Review* 91(1): 33–53.

Warner, John T., Curtis J. Simon, and Deborah M. Payne. 2001. *Enlistment supply in the 1990s: A study of the Navy College Fund and other enlistment incentive programs.* DMDC report no. 2000-015. Arlington, Va.: Defense Manpower Data Center.

———. 2002. *Propensity, application, and enlistment: Evidence from the Youth Attitude Tracking Study.* Clemson University, Clemson, S.C.

CHAPTER 6

MANPOWER QUALITY IN THE ALL-VOLUNTEER FORCE

David J. Armor
Paul R. Sackett

INTRODUCTION

The issue of manpower quality has been intertwined with the all-volunteer force (AVF) since its creation in 1973. Conscription generally ensured enlistment from a broad cross section of American youth, including a proportionate number of high school graduates who had above-average aptitudes and skills (the definition of high quality). A major policy concern in the AVF era has been how to maintain that cross section and, especially, how to attract a sufficient number of high-quality recruits.

Indeed, there have been substantial variations in recruit quality over the past 30 years, from unprecedented lows in the late 1970s to record highs in the early 1990s. These swings are caused by a variety of factors, both internal and external to the military. Because recruiting and advertising expenditures are among those factors, the quality swings have sparked debates over the level of recruiting and advertising expenditures needed to maintain a specified level of quality.

This paper addresses several issues in this debate. We first describe manpower quality standards, a component of enlistment standards, and provide the rationale for maintaining minimum levels of quality in the enlisted forces. We then review trends in manpower quality and the prospects for maintaining quality in light of education and aptitude trends in the youth population. Finally, we discuss two current issues in the definition of high quality: alternative high school graduation definitions and the issue of renorming the Armed Forces Qualifying Test (AFQT).

QUALITY STANDARDS: DEFINITION AND RATIONALE

The services use two attributes to define a high-quality recruit: scores on the AFQT and high school graduation status. The AFQT is a composite score comprising four subtests from the Armed Services Vocational Aptitude Battery (ASVAB) that measure quantitative and verbal skills and aptitudes. While AFQT scores are central to initial entry to the services, other ASVAB composites are used to determine qualifications for assignment to various occupational specialties. Scores on the AFQT are collapsed into a set of categories, as shown in table 1.

TABLE 1. CATEGORIES FOR ARMED FORCES
QUALIFYING TEST SCORES

AFQT CATEGORY	AFQT PERCENTILE
I	93–99
II	65–92
IIIA	50–64
IIIB	31–49
IV	10–30
V	1–9

Congress mandates that individuals in category V are not eligible for service, and that no more that 20 percent of recruits in any service can be drawn from category IV. Department of Defense guidance recommends that at least 60 percent of new recruits come from aptitude categories I–IIIA, and that no more than 4 percent be from category IV. Statutes also mandate that all category IV recruits must be high school graduates. The Department of Defense defines a high-quality recruit as a high school diploma holder in the top 50 percent of the AFQT distribution (i.e., in categories I, II, or IIIA). Department guidance also indicates that no more than 10 percent of nonprior service accessions can lack a high school diploma.

It is important to note that "quality" reflects value judgments on the part of an organization. Quality is not something etched in stone: each organization decides what features of individuals it values. Using an example from the civilian world, research in the supermarket industry on selection systems for the position of cashier finds that some chains define quality in terms of checkout speed, others define it in terms of customer service, and yet others define it in terms of honesty (not stealing). Each of these three types of supermarkets thus uses a different set of criteria for screening prospective employees (Sackett, Zedeck, and Fogli 1988).

It is worthwhile to consider the implications of using AFQT scores and high school diploma status to define quality. A common distinction made is between measures of typical performance and measures of maximal performance. Maximal performance is a measure of what one "can do"; typical performance is a measure of what one "will do." AFQT is meant to predict maximal performance and thus identify individuals who are capable of performing job tasks well; other mechanisms, such as indoctrination in training, military leadership, and team support are intended to ensure that the capable recruit performs up to potential.

The high school diploma requirement is not used to predict the level of performance, but rather to predict attrition. The relationship between diploma status and attrition is addressed later in the chapter.

AFQT AND TRAINING PERFORMANCE

The initial goal of the AFQT was to predict success in training (Eitelberg, Laurence, and Waters 1984). The evaluation strategy that was used to determine the predictive value of the AFQT is the mainstay of testing research: obtain test scores for a group of applicants, put the applicants into a training setting, obtain measures of training performance, and then examine the relationship between test scores and training scores.

While the relationship between test scores and training grades is commonly measured by a correlation coefficient, the relationship is better visualized by plotting test scores against training performance, as shown in figure 1. This figure summarizes a National Research Council (NRC) committee review of 178 military studies using AFQT to predict training performance (Hartigan and Wigdor 1989).

FIGURE 1. AFQT AND MILITARY TRAINING PERFORMANCE

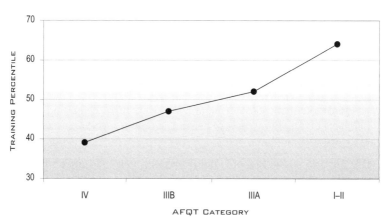

The figure clearly shows a pattern of continuously increasing performance as test scores increase. Note the relatively small difference between categories IIIA and IIIB. These categories include individuals just above the AFQT average (IIIA) and just below it (IIIB). Given that scores on the AFQT follow a bell-shaped distribution, large numbers of individuals are bunched around the average, resulting in this limited difference between categories IIIA and IIIB.

Figure 2 shows a similar relationship using data from the civilian sector. The most widely studied test for civilian personnel selection is the Department of Labor's General Aptitude Test Battery (GATB), which is similar to the ASVAB. An NRC committee integrated the results of hundreds of validity studies using the GATB's general-verbal-numerical composite, which is roughly comparable to the AFQT, to predict training performance (Hartigan and Wigdor 1989). The predictive power of GATB was found to be exactly that of the AFQT. This is an important finding, as it helps validate the use of aptitude tests for personnel decisions. (For comparison purposes, scores in figure 2 are presented for percentile ranges corresponding to AFQT categories, though such score categories are not used operationally with the GATB.)

FIGURE 2. GATB AND CIVILIAN TRAINING PERFORMANCE

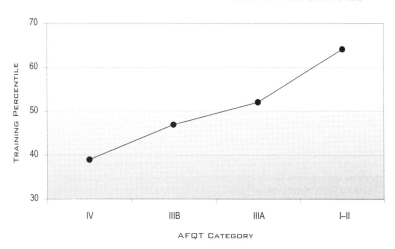

AFQT AND JOB PERFORMANCE

A key question in justifying the AFQT for screening is whether it predicts broader measures of human performance, especially on-the-job performance. The use of the AFQT came under congressional scrutiny in 1980 after it was discovered that a misnorming of the ASVAB had resulted in enlisting a far larger number of category IV recruits than intended.[1] One result was an extraordinary research effort, known as the Joint Services Job Performance Measurement (JPM) Project.

Early efforts to examine relationships between AFQT and job performance produced mixed results, with some studies suggesting that the two were not related. The point of central importance is that the quality of job-performance measures is the Achilles' heel of attempts to examine test-performance relationships. With a poor-quality performance measure, a truly effective test can wrongly be seen as an ineffective screening device. Hence it was quickly recognized that efforts to document AFQT-job performance relationships hinged on developing sound performance measures.

The centerpiece of the JPM Project was the decision to focus on an approach to measuring performance referred to as "hands-on performance testing" (HOPT). A National Research Council committee reviewed the range of approaches to the measurement of performance, and recommended the HOPT approach (Wigdor and Green 1991). In this approach, a sampling of the most critical job tasks are identified, and job incumbents perform these tasks while being observed and evaluated by a trained expert in the job in question. The observation period is roughly half a day for each incumbent, making this an extraordinarily expensive way of gathering performance data (particularly in contrast with commonly used supervisor-ratings approaches). Thus an approach such as this is rarely used, and its use makes the JPM Project one of the most important research projects in the history of the field of personnel testing. Each service developed hands-on performance tests for a sample of important occupational specialties.

It is important to note that the HOPT approach focuses on the "can do," rather than the "will do" aspects of performance. The assumption is that incumbents will give their best effort when being observed during HOPT. That an incumbent can perform a task correctly when observed is no guarantee that the same level of performance will be exhibited on a day-to-day basis without similar close observation. This type of measure is consistent with the military's perspective on quality, as discussed earlier: the goal of testing as part of a recruiting and selection system is to identify individuals who are capable of performing job tasks well.

Figure 3 shows in graphic form the relationship between ASVAB composite scores and performance on the hands-on performance tests. For presentation purposes, results are shown for test score ranges corresponding to AFQT categories. HOPT scores are expressed as the percentage of job task steps performed correctly. The figure clearly shows that ASVAB composites are related to success in performing important job tasks.

FIGURE 3. APTITUDE AS A PREDICTOR OF HANDS-ON PERFORMANCE

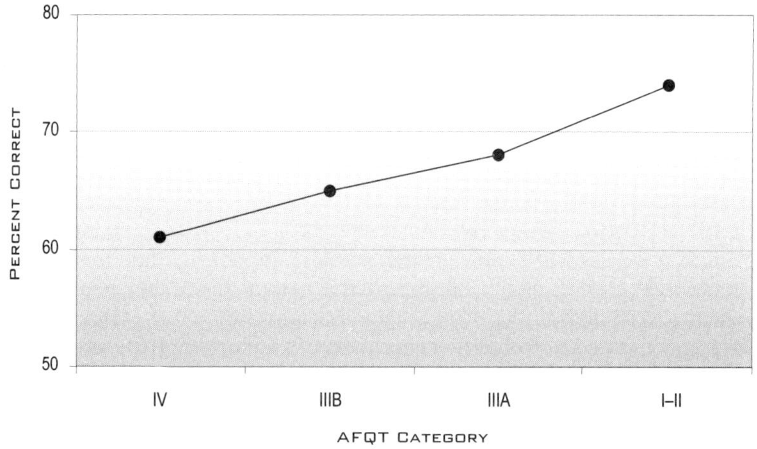

Several additional observations are in order. First, note the close correspondence between this pattern of findings and the findings shown earlier for the prediction of training performance. Test scores predict job and training performance in a similar manner. Higher scores are linked to higher performance throughout the test score range. Second, just as findings in the prediction of training performance correspond almost exactly with findings in the civilian labor market, the Department of Labor's GATB predicts civilian job performance almost exactly as well as ASVAB predicts HOPT performance (Hunter and Hunter 1984).

Research with HOPT refutes the theory that experience allows lower-aptitude individuals to catch up to those with higher aptitudes; that is, that experience can be substituted for aptitude. Armor and Roll (1994) showed AFQT-HOPT relationships broken down by year of service (see figure 4). The figure shows that those with higher aptitudes continue to outperform those with lower aptitudes throughout the first term of service. It is certainly the case that performance improves with experience; however, this holds true for both high- and low-aptitude individuals. The implicit belief of those holding the "catch-up" theory is that only low-scoring individuals benefit from experience; in fact, both low- and high-scorers benefit from experience.

FIGURE 4. JOB PERFORMANCE AND AFQT BY TIME IN SERVICE

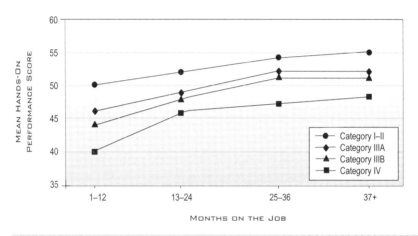

Source: Reprinted with permission of the National Academy of Science from Armor and Roll, 1994, fig. 2.

It should also be noted that the performance difference between category IIIA and IIIB is quite small and diminishes with experience to just one or two percentage points. This point is important to remember when the services experience recruiting difficulties such as those of the late 1990s. The replacement of a modest number of IIIA applicants with IIIB applicants is not likely to significantly reduce overall military effectiveness.

HOW MUCH IS ENOUGH?

The fact that aptitude test scores are related linearly to both training performance and job performance does not tell us how to use test scores operationally to set enlistment standards. That is, the relationship does not yield particular "cutoff" scores for deciding whether prospective recruits should be enlisted into military service or made eligible for specific jobs.

If cost were of no concern, and if there were an unlimited supply of high-aptitude recruits, then the "more is better" message resulting from aptitude-performance relationships would lead to setting extremely high qualifying scores, both for entry to military service and for occupational assignment. The reality, though, is that the cost of recruiting a category I–IIIA high school diploma graduate is substantially greater than the cost of recruiting one with lower scores, so a force with a higher proportion of high-quality enlistees is more costly. The question becomes how much the military is willing to pay for a force with a given level of quality (and hence performance).

Consideration of this question was facilitated by the development of a cost-performance trade-off model, as described in Green and Mavor (1994). Conceptually, the goal of the model is to achieve a specified level of performance at the minimum cost. The output of the model is the number of recruits at each aptitude level for each occupational area that would result in meeting a performance constraint at the lowest cost.

The model uses the hands-on performance tests for the measure of job performance. It conceptualizes total performance as the sum of individual performance. For example, one can obtain 150 units of performance from two recruits, each with a HOPT score of 75, or from one recruit with a HOPT score of 60 and one with a HOPT score of 90. This basic example gets more elaborate as the model incorporates research findings on performance over time. Occupation is yet another key variable: a recruit expected to score 75 in the first year in "job A" might be expected, on the basis of JPM findings, to score 65 in "job B." Projected rates of turnover, based on educational attainment, are also added to the model.

It is important to note that the cost-performance trade-off model still does not offer a definitive answer to the question of "how much is enough." In fact, the model requires that one specify in advance the aggregate level of performance one wishes to achieve; the model then estimates the most cost-effective way of achieving this performance level. The absolute level of required performance remains a matter of judgment. To establish the current Department of Defense recruiting guidance (to draw at least 60 percent of new recruits from categories I–IIIA and no more than 4 percent from category IV), the absolute level of performance used was that of the Desert Shield/Desert Storm force (Sellman 1997).

HIGH SCHOOL COMPLETION AND ATTRITION

The second component of enlistment standards, high school diploma status, is used to predict not job performance but rather whether an enlistee will complete a full term of service. As such, it is not so much a measure of "can do" but "will do." The relationship between high school completion and attrition is well documented. Table 2 shows 24-month enlisted attrition rates by education. Nongraduates have an attrition rate roughly twice as high as that of graduates.

Of particular interest are categories reflecting nontraditional education credentials, such as General Educational Development (GED) certificate holders. Note that GED holders have attrition rates similar to nongraduates; enlistees with adult education certificates or high school certificates of completion have somewhat lower rates of attrition than those with GEDs, but the rates are still much higher than for diploma graduates.

TABLE 2. 24-MONTH ENLISTED ATTRITION RATES BY EDUCATION, 1988–1998

EDUCATION	NUMBER IN FORCE	24-MONTH ATTRITION (%)
High school diploma graduate	2,027,546	23.4
College	95,628	25.5
Adult education	32,330	36.8
High school GED	73,371	41.2
High school certificate of completion	6,798	35.4
Other equivalent	1,149	34.5
Non–high school graduate	26,440	43.7
Total Department of Defense (less missing data)	2,263,262	24.5

Source: Reprinted with permission of the National Academy of Science from Sackett and Mavor 2003, table 4-1.

Military manpower research has shown, generally, that educational attainment is not a proxy measure of aptitude. Completing a traditional high school degree is perhaps best viewed as an indicator of an individual's ability and willingness to work within the constraints of a social system that imposes schedules, rules, and discipline—a system that requires such things as daily attendance, being in an assigned place at an assigned time, and completing assignments as required. Individuals who opt out of such a system have a higher likelihood of similarly opting out of a commitment to a tour of duty.

The issue of alternative high school credentials becomes increasingly important as alternatives to a traditional high school education increase. This issue is discussed in greater detail below.

TRENDS IN QUALITY: PAST AND FUTURE

Trends in manpower quality are influenced by a complex mix of factors, some deriving from military policies and others deriving from changes in society at large. Changes in military policies and programs, that make a military career appear more attractive than civilian options, can increase the supply of high-quality recruits. (More precisely, they lower the marginal cost of recruiting high-quality youth.) In contrast, trends in the civilian sector that make civilian careers appear more attractive than the military option, such as declining unemployment or changes in youth attitudes, can lower the supply of high-quality recruits.

In assessing the outlook for recruit quality in the future, we clearly cannot predict all relevant changes that might occur in society or even in military policy. But two kinds of more-available information can improve our assessment. First, we can try to understand the extent to which military policies have influenced past trends, in order to identify policies that will increase the supply of manpower quality in the future. Second, we can utilize information about current trends in the youth population, including trends in the size of youth cohorts, in their aptitude and education levels, and in their propensity for military service. This section will examine both sets of information.

EXPLAINING QUALITY TRENDS IN THE AVF

During the early years of the AVF, initial fears that the AVF would not attract a broad cross section of American youth, especially higher-quality youth, appeared unwarranted. Contrary to forecasts from some quarters, over the first six or seven years of the AVF, quality indicators did not decline. Indeed, a major evaluation undertaken by RAND in 1977 was very positive, stating that "the military services can attract a socially-representative mix of the desired quantity and quality of new recruits . . . at a cost substantially lower than commonly assumed" (Cooper 1977, vi). The RAND report also found that the quality of new recruits actually increased after the AVF was established.

This rosy picture changed dramatically in 1980, however, when it was discovered that AFQT scores were erroneous due to a norming, or calibration, problem that had occurred in 1976. When the scores were corrected in 1980, it turned out that, in fact, manpower quality levels had declined to 20-year lows, with the Army being affected the most. At the end of the draft era all services had been recruiting approximately 55–56 percent category I–IIIA recruits (males only); the Army was only a few points behind. After the AFQT scores were corrected, new data revealed a steady decline in quality indicators beginning in 1976, and by 1980 the percent of category I–IIIA recruits had fallen to 44 percent for all services and to only 29 percent in the Army. In 1979 the Army had actually enlisted 50 percent category IV recruits (Eitelberg, Laurence, and Waters 1984).

This discovery shocked military planners and policy leaders, because up until that time they had come to believe that the AVF was succeeding with only modest changes in manpower budgets and programs. After the true levels of manpower quality were discovered in 1980, it was clear that major—and costly—changes would have to be made in military manpower programs in order to return quality levels to what they had been prior to the AVF.

The changes in manpower policies and programs that took place after 1980 were unprecedented. Basic military pay was increased to make military jobs more comparable to civilian occupations; enlistment bonuses and education incentives were expanded; and funding for advertising and recruiting programs was increased substantially. Advertising expenditures for the Army, in particular, doubled between 1980 and 1987 (Sackett and Mavor 2003, fig. 8-1).

Figure 5 shows the trends in AFQT categories across all services from 1980 to 2001 for active duty enlisted accessions. The changes in military policies, and especially the increased expenditures for manpower programs during the early 1980s, had the desired effects, perhaps even sooner than expected. The percentage of categories I–IIIA recruits reached pre-AVF levels by 1983, and the percentage continued to rise until 1987. These gains in quality are all the more impressive because the requirements for nonprior service accessions remained relatively constant (at about three hundred thousand) during this time period, and the size of the relevant youth cohort was decreasing slightly (U.S. Department of Defense 2000, fig. 1-1).

FIGURE 5. TRENDS IN APTITUDES FOR MILITARY RECRUITS, 1980–2001

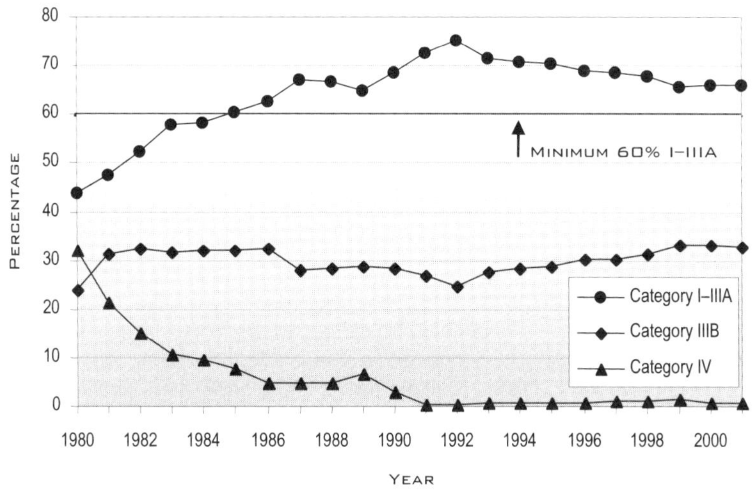

Source: U.S. Department of Defense 2003.

After a brief hiatus, the percentage of high-aptitude recruits began increasing again in 1989, and it reached an all-time high of 75 percent in 1992. Equally impressive was the decline in the percentage of recruits in the lowest aptitude group, category IV, between 1980 and 1992, dropping from over 30 percent in 1980 to less than 1 percent by 1991. It must be noted that in 1988, and again in 1990, accession requirements declined due to force structure changes necessitated by the end of the cold war. Accession requirements fell to two hundred thousand in 1991, so some of this increased level of quality was caused by a lower demand for new recruits.

After reaching the all-time high in 1992, the percentage of high-aptitude recruits began declining steadily until 1999, when it finally flattened out. For all services combined, since 1985 the high-quality rate has not fallen below the 60 percent minimum set by the Defense Planning Guidance report, although the Army came very close to that level in 1999, with 62 percent category I–IIIA recruits. The Army returned to 65 percent in 2000 and 64 percent in 2001.

Like the earlier increases, the decline in recruit quality has been influenced by numerous factors. We can rule out two potential explanations: requirements and demography. Between 1992 and 1999, nonprior service accession requirements actually declined slightly to 180,000. Moreover, the size of the relevant youth population was fairly stable during the first few years of this period and then increased modestly; altogether, the number of American youth aged 18 to 21 increased by 12 percent over this eight-year period (U.S. Department of Defense 2000, fig. 1-1).

The decline in high-quality enlistments was accompanied by a decline in the propensity of youth to enlist in the military (that is the percentage of youth who are definitely planning to enlist) which, according to the Youth Attitude Tracking Study (YATS), began occurring right after Operation Desert Storm in Iraq (Armor 1996). The drop was especially steep for black youth. Of course, a change in propensity also requires explanation, and we believe that part of the reason was a shift in youth attitudes about duty to country and increasing interest in attending college immediately after high school (Sackett and Mavor 2003, chapter 6).

These attitudinal shifts were accompanied by two other societal changes, as documented by Hogan, Simon, and Warner (chapter 5, this volume): a decline in military pay relative to civilian pay, coupled with a decline in civilian unemployment. If that was not enough, military expenditures for recruiting and advertising declined in the late 1980s, and these reductions may also have contributed to declines in propensity to enlist. Advertising budgets were cut by half between 1987 and 1993, and while those budgets were restored and even exceeded by 1998, there is probably a lag before the increased advertising expenditures affect behavior. Indeed, the decrease in numbers of high-aptitude recruits finally leveled off in 1999, perhaps due to these increases in recruiting and advertising budgets during the late 1990s.

What about trends in recruit education levels? Figure 6 shows the trends in education levels between 1980 and 2001 for active duty enlisted accessions. The swings in education levels have been less drastic, but they tend to parallel the increases and declines in aptitude levels. There was a substantial increase in the percent of high school diploma graduates (tier 1) between 1980 and 1984, from 78 percent to 95 percent, and it remained well above 90 percent until 1996.[2] Thereafter the percentage of high school graduates began declining until 1999, when it dropped below the level set in the Defense Planning Guidance report for the first time since 1982. In 2001 the rate returned to 90 percent across all services, although it remained at 85 percent for the Army due to a special program called GED Plus which allows the Army to take in up to 5 percent of its recruits with GEDs without counting against quality requirements.

It is interesting to note that the percentage of non–high school diploma graduates in the AVF has remained at or below 1 percent since 1998. The declining level of high school graduates was matched by an increase in those with alternative high school credentials. These include GEDs, certificates of completion, and adult education (the first two are considered tier 2 but the last is considered tier 1). The services may have less difficulty maintaining the high school graduation standard in the future simply because high school graduation rates have climbed steadily for white and black youth for the past 20 years or so (see figure 7). The relatively large proportion of high school dropouts remains a substantial

FIGURE 6. TRENDS IN EDUCATION FOR MILITARY RECRUITS,
1980–2001

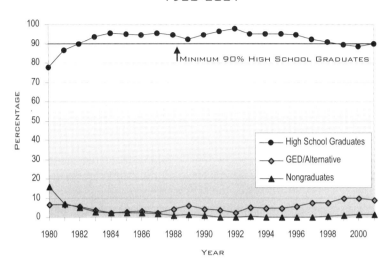

Source: U.S. Department of Defense 2003.

FIGURE 7. TRENDS IN HIGH SCHOOL GRADUATION RATES BY RACE
(PERSONS AGED 25–29)

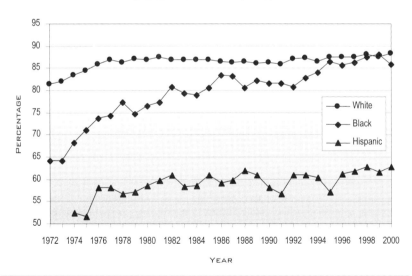

Source: Sackett and Mavor 2003, fig. 4-11.

problem among Hispanic youth, who comprise an increasing proportion of American youth (Sackett and Mavor 2003, 87). Thus, full representation of Hispanic youth may be a continuing challenge for military recruiters.

However, high school graduation rates may not remain as high as they are now, as more and more states are implementing exit exams as a requirement for graduation. Those students who do not pass the exam do not get diplomas, receiving certificates of completion instead. Depending on the eventual academic standards reflected by high school exit exams, we could see a decrease in diploma graduates. We will discuss this issue in the last section of this chapter.

TRENDS IN YOUTH CHARACTERISTICS

What does all of this information say about the prospects for future quality? We can help answer this question by considering several trends in the youth population at large. We will consider demographic trends, trends in education levels and college attendance, and trends in aptitudes. Most of these findings are taken from a recent study by the National Research Council (Sackett and Mavor 2003).

Demographic projections of the size of the youth population are quite reliable because they are based on births that have already occurred. The 18-year-old population in the United States will generally increase from its current level of 4.0 million until the year 2010, when it will reach a maximum of 4.4 million (Sackett and Mavor 2003, 54). Thereafter, the number of 18-year-olds will decline to about 4.1 million, where it will remain until 2020. Assuming that accession targets remain where they are today, demographic trends alone are favorable for maintaining current quality levels.

Regarding education levels, figure 7 shows high school graduation rates for persons aged 25–29 from 1972 to 2000. Graduation rates for whites have remained between 86 and 88 percent since 1977, and the rates for blacks have risen markedly to nearly match the white rate starting in 1995. For these two groups, then, the current and near-future supply of high school diploma graduates appears fully adequate for existing recruiting requirements. The issue of exit exams, however, could have adverse impacts on these positive trends. Hispanics continue to have relatively low high school graduation rates compared to whites and blacks (just over 60 percent), so recruiting a representative proportion of qualified Hispanic youth will continue to be a challenge for the military.

The other relevant education issue concerns the trends in college attendance. The proportion of recent high school graduates who attend college has increased dramatically since the advent of the AVF. Less than half of recent high school graduates attended college in 1973, but that rate rose to two thirds by 1998 (Sackett and Mavor 2003, 48). There was a modest decline to about 62 percent by 2000, but youth surveys suggest that these high levels of college attendance will remain for the foreseeable future. For example, in 1976 the proportion of high school seniors who said they would *definitely* graduate from a four-year college was 30 percent for both genders; in 1996 that rate had risen to 50 percent for males and 60 percent for females (Sackett and Mavor 2003, 158). The one bright spot for military recruiting is that the proportion planning to graduate from college remained relatively flat between 1996 and 2001, which suggests that college attendance rates may level off at their current (relatively high) levels.

Finally, we turn to trends in youth aptitudes. For the purpose of predicting the future supply of high-aptitude youth, results from the National Assessment of Educational Progress (NAEP) are very useful. NAEP assesses reading, math, and science achievement of school children ages 9, 13, and 17. By examining achievement trends for 9-year-olds, we can get some idea of the aptitudes and cognitive skills of cohorts that will be graduating from high school about a decade later.

Figure 8 shows the trends in NAEP scores for 9-year-olds scoring at the 50th percentile, which is the cutoff point for defining high-quality aptitudes. Reading scores have remained relatively flat for the past 30 years, but scores in math and science (important for technical occupations) rose substantially between 1982 and 1990, and they have remained at the higher levels until at least 1999. The rise was about 10 points on the NAEP scale, which is about one third of a standard deviation. This suggests that the 1999–2008 18-year-old cohorts will have higher cognitive skills than cohorts in the prior decade, a favorable result for the supply of high-quality recruits over the next 10 years or so.

FIGURE 8. TRENDS FOR NAEP SCORES
AT THE 50TH PERCENTILE, AGE 9

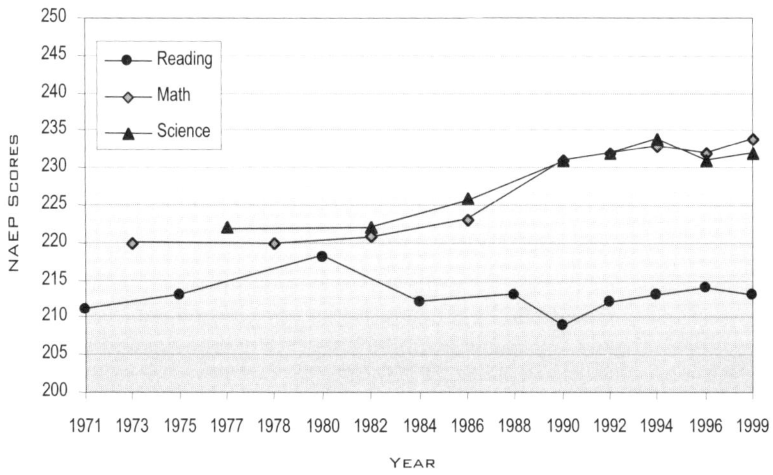

Source: Sackett and Mavor 2003, fig. 4-15.

We can now summarize the outlook for maintaining the current levels of high-quality manpower. On the potential supply side, the projected trends in the number of youth, high school graduation rates, and aptitudes suggest there are sufficient numbers of high-quality youth in the population at large, and those numbers should remain adequate for at least the next 10 years. On the other hand, trends in college education and the declining propensity to join the military portend a continuing challenge to motivate youth to consider the military option. Military pay and benefits will have to keep pace with the civilian sector, and recruiting and advertising budgets must be maintained at reasonable levels in order to get the message out that the military is a viable option for those who eventually plan to attend college. In particular, the National Research Council report recommends that the military continue its efforts to attract college-bound youth (and those students who leave college temporarily, termed "stop-outs") and to direct advertising efforts to promote values related to a military career, such as duty to country, self-sacrifice, and opportunity for adventure (Sackett and Mavor 2003, chapter 9).

CHANGING QUALITY INDICATORS

There are two important developments in quality indicators that require further attention and policy decisions in the near future. One is the increasing number of alternative education credentials, and the other is the increase in aptitude scores, which has raised the prospect of renorming the AFQT. Both of these developments have the potential for changing the supply of high-quality youth.

ALTERNATIVE HIGH SCHOOL CREDENTIALS

There are several trends in secondary school education that might affect both the number and the interpretation of high school diploma graduates. These include the trends in charter schools, home schooling, and high school exit examinations.

Charter schools are increasing in popularity, especially in such states as Arizona, Florida, Massachusetts, Michigan, and Minnesota. Home schooling is also increasing throughout the country. It is unclear at this point what impact these trends might have on high school diploma rates; at this point the impact is small because only a small fraction of secondary students are utilizing these options. The impact could become more important if use of either of these options expands significantly in the future.

The situation is somewhat different for exit examinations, because a majority of the states have adopted them, and more may adopt them as a result of the No Child Left Behind Act. The potential impact here is on the usefulness of the high school diploma as a predictor of attrition. In states with exit exams, students who would have received a diploma might not receive one if they fail the exam; they would be awarded a certificate of completion instead. Thus exit exams have the potential to change the meaning of high school diploma status.

Before making any permanent changes to the classification of different high school credentials, we believe the military should conduct research on the attrition patterns of recruits with alternative educational credentials, especially those with certificates of completion and those attending charter schools. Data on the attrition rates of enlistees with different types of credentials or attending different types of high schools should be gathered and analyzed (by state if possible).

It might be necessary to establish clear definitions for alternative credentials and then conduct prospective research on a sample of states with and without alternative high school credentials. The research should attempt to assess attrition rates for enlistees with diplomas, certificates of completion, or other high school backgrounds including attendance at charter schools and home schooling. The data should be gathered by state so that attrition rates can be compared in states with and without exit exams. This type of research could help establish whether the classification of various education outcomes (e.g., tiers 1 to 3) should be modified.

RENORMING THE AFQT

The increases in math and science scores documented in the NAEP tests (figure 8) are similarly reflected by changes in AFQT scores between 1980 and 1997. Since the current AFQT norms were established in 1980, the Department of Defense commissioned a renorming study for the entire ASVAB in 1997. David Segall (forthcoming) found that raw scores had increased for AFQT composites and for certain other composites used for job selection. These increases reflect a general gain in cognitive skills in the youth population.

Because of the increase in raw scores, the percentage of youth scoring in category I–IIIA has actually increased beyond 50 percent when 1980 norms are used to establish percentile scores. That is to say, category I–IIIA no longer means the upper half of the current youth population; it means something closer to the upper 55 percent. In order for category I–IIIA to retain its current meaning of upper half, 1997 norms would have to be used to establish percentile scores. When this is done, a significant proportion of youth who are now classified as category IIIA (by 1980 norms) will be reclassified as IIIB (by 1997 norms), and a similar proportion will be reclassified from category IIIB to IV.

Table 3 shows how renorming of AFQT scores using the 1997 results will affect the supply of youth in various aptitude categories. There is little change for those scoring at the upper end, in categories I and II, which currently make up about 36 percent of all enlistees (34 percent for the Army). However, about 4 percent of high-aptitude applicants (category IIIA) will be shifted into category IIIB, and about 5 percent of category IIIB applicants will be shifted into category IV.

TABLE 3. PERCENTAGE OF 2002 APPLICANTS WHO SCORE ABOVE VARIOUS AFQT CUTOFF SCORES USING 1980 VS. 1997 NORMS

CUTOFF SCORE	1980 NORMS	1997 NORMS
65th percentile (category I –II)	36	35
50th percentile (category I –IIIA)	59	55
31st percentile (category I –IIIB)	84	79

Source: Adapted from Segall forthcoming, table 4.2, 39.

In order to retain the long-standing meaning of category I–IIIA, the Department of Defense is planning to recalibrate ASVAB scores using 1997 norms. Renorming will create a de facto increase in quality standards compared to the

MANPOWER QUALITY IN THE ALL-VOLUNTEER FORCE

existing 1980 norms. If the 1997 norms are applied to the 2002 applicant pool, according to the data in table 3, there would be a shift of about 15,000 applicants from category IIIA to IIIB (there were 380,000 active component applicants in 2002). There would also be a shift of about the same number of category IIIB applicants into category IV. Therefore, application of 1997 norms will decrease the supply of high-quality recruits, and in the future it might be somewhat more difficult to meet department guidance of 60 percent category I–IIIA recruits, depending on the recruiting climate.

Nonetheless, the increases in AFQT and NAEP scores in the last two decades mean that the cognitive skills of youth have increased in the society as a whole, and if the Department of Defense wants categories I–IIIA to keep its traditional meaning of "above average," then the change in norms is necessary—because at this time it does not have that meaning. Those who argue that military jobs are becoming increasingly technical and more complex would support this change, because under the 1980 norms the aptitude of some category IIIA recruits is actually below the average of all youth in the nation.

Even after renorming the ASVAB, there are still some policy options to consider. For many military jobs, where there has been no significant technical change in job skills, the 1980 norms may be fully adequate for the purpose of selection. We support one option being considered by the Department of Defense to ameliorate the effect of raising aptitude standards, which is to consider modifying the current Defense Planning Guidance report. For example, the current guidance of 60 percent category I–IIIA might be lowered, perhaps to 55 percent, in recognition that there are some jobs that have not changed very much and in which category IIIB recruits can attain satisfactory performance. Indeed, the performance difference between categories IIIA and IIIB, as shown in figure 4, is quite small compared to the performance difference between categories IIIB and IV.

Before any changes are made to quality targets, of course, we would recommend a careful assessment of the current recruiting climate. Recruiting resources were increased substantially between 1999 and 2002 and, coupled with higher unemployment rates, quality levels have been improving since 2000. In fact, it appears that 2003 quality indicators for active enlisted accessions—95 percent high school diploma graduates and 75 percent scoring in the upper half of the AFQT—have climbed to their highest levels since the mid-1990s. Given these developments, we support the department's plans to use the cost-performance trade-off model for enlistment standards to test the impact of new norms and to enquire about the viability of existing defense planning guidance with respect to quality standards.

CONCLUSIONS

Contrary to predictions of early critics of the AVF, the last 30 years have shown that high levels of manpower quality can be maintained in a volunteer environment. We believe that the current levels of quality are well validated by research findings showing that aptitudes and education predict job performance and retention, and therefore ultimately influence force effectiveness.

We also recognize that maintaining a certain level of manpower quality cannot be done cheaply, particularly in this era of high college attendance and declines in youth attitudes favorable to a military career. Military compensation must keep up with compensation in the civilian sector, bonuses and education benefits are still important, and there must be sufficient resources for skilled, motivated recruiters and for good advertising campaigns that have the potential to shape favorable youth attitudes.

On the positive side, we are encouraged by trends in the broader society that show increasing numbers of youth, no declines and some increases in youth aptitudes, and high levels of high school graduation for all groups except Hispanics. At least we can say that the potential supply of quality youth exists; it remains for the Department of Defense to motivate a sufficient number of high-quality youth to consider and to choose the military option.

Finally, there are two developments on the horizon that might affect the supply of high-quality youth, and they must be carefully monitored and evaluated. First, the expansion of alternative high school credentials is a matter of concern because it affects the meaning of high school graduation, and we recommend research to assess the impact of alternative high school credentials on attrition rates.

Second, renorming of the ASVAB and the AFQT will have the immediate effect of raising enlistment standards by a modest degree. Maintaining the goal of 60 percent category I–IIIA may require more recruiting and advertising resources, depending on future recruiting environments. Accordingly, the existing cost-performance trade-off model should be re-evaluated to investigate and validate future enlistment standards that might be affected by renorming and changes in other factors that affect recruiting.

NOTES

1. When standardizing the AFQT, scores at the lower end were set too high. When the error was corrected, scores were moved downward. As a result, substantial numbers of category IIIB recruits were reclassified as category IV.

2. Tier 1 refers to a high school graduate (possessing a high school diploma, having completed two years of college, or having been awarded an adult education diploma); tier 2 refers to alternative credential holders (possessing a test-based equivalency diploma [such as a GED], a high school certificate of attendance, a correspondence school diploma, or an occupational program certificate); tier 3 refers to all non–high school graduates.

REFERENCES

Armor, D. J. 1996. Race and gender in the U.S. military. *Armed Forces and Society* 23: 7–27.

Armor, David J., and Charles R. Roll Jr. 1994. Military manpower quality. In *Modeling cost and performance for military enlistment.* Edited by Bert F. Green and Anne S. Mavor, 13–34. Washington, D.C.: National Academies Press.

Cooper, Richard V. L. 1977. *Military manpower and the all-volunteer force.* R-1450-ARPA. Santa Monica, Calif.: RAND Corporation.

Eitelberg, Mark J., Janice H. Laurence, and Brian K. Waters. 1984. *Screening for service: Aptitude and education criteria for military entry.* Alexandria, Va.: Human Resources Research Organization.

Green, Bert F., and Anne S. Mavor, eds. 1994. *Modeling cost performance for military enlistment.* Washington, D.C.: National Academies Press.

Hartigan, J., and Alexandra Wigdor, eds. 1989. *Fairness in employment testing: Validity generalization, minority issues, and the General Aptitude Test Battery.* Washington, D.C.: National Academies Press.

Hunter, J. E., and R. F. Hunter. 1984. Validity and utility of alternative predictors of job performance. *Psychological Bulletin* 96: 72–98.

Sackett, Paul, and Anne Mavor. 2003. *Attitudes, aptitudes, and aspirations of American youth.: Implications for military recruitment.* Washington, D.C.: National Academies Press.

Sackett, Paul R., S. Zedeck, and L. Fogli. 1988. Relations between measures of typical and maximum performance. *Journal of Applied Psychology* 73: 482–86.

Segall, Daniel O. Forthcoming. *Development and evaluation of the 1997 ASVAB score scale.* Arlington, Va.: Defense Manpower Data Center.

Sellman, W. S. 1997. Public policy implications for military entrance standards. Keynote address to the 39th annual conference of the International Military Testing Association. Sydney, Australia.

U.S. Department of Defense. 2000. *Population representation in the military services, FY99.* Washington D.C.: Office of the Assistant Secretary of Defense (Force Management and Personnel).

———. 2003. Special tabulations. Arlington, VA.: Defense Manpower Data Center.

Wigdor, Alexandra, and Bert F. Green. 1991. *Performance assessment for the workplace.* Washington, D.C.: National Academies Press.

★ ★ ★ ★ ★ ★ ★ ★ ★ ★ ★

CHAPTER 7

THE EFFECTS OF SOCIOECONOMIC CHANGE ON THE ALL-VOLUNTEER FORCE: PAST, PRESENT, AND FUTURE

MARTHA FARNSWORTH RICHE
ALINE QUESTER

INTRODUCTION

This paper assesses past, present, and likely future trends in population charac-teristics that influence both the supply and the characteristics of potential recruits to the all-volunteer force (AVF), as well as retention of the force. First, we address the relatively stable size of the population within the age range from which the military traditionally recruits, as well as the ongoing decline in its share of the overall population. Since these trends are very different from those present both in nations that are traditional U.S. allies and in less-developed countries, we situate U.S. trends within the global context. Second, we discuss several changes in the typical American life course, and in economic opportuni-ties across the life course, that determine the context in which individuals make the choice to join the AVF and to stay in it. Finally, we assess the likelihood, and nature, of continuing divergences between the makeup of the AVF and of the population as a whole.

TRENDS IN THE SUPPLY OF POTENTIAL RECRUITS

The size and population share of young adults, relative to the population as a whole, are changing both in the United States and worldwide.[1] However, these trends are poorly understood. Thanks to confusing (and confused) reporting in the media, the average American thinks the U.S. youth population is declining in size. The youth population is declining in some of the countries that are tra-ditional U.S. allies, but it is not declining here.

THE UNITED STATES

The number of people in the traditional target age-group for advertising and then recruitment to the armed forces — that is, the number of people between the ages of 15 and 19 — is growing slowly in the United States in absolute numbers, while becoming proportionately smaller as a share of the total population. Between 2000 and 2025, the number of Americans aged 15–19 is projected to increase by 11 percent (U.S. Census Bureau 2003a). This increase is smaller than the increase that military recruiters saw before the advent of the AVF, or in its first decade, when the numbers of young people were swelling as a result of the post–World War II baby boom (figure 1). However, at that time the military still focused on recruiting from the male population, while the AVF has actively recruited females as well as males. Broadening the target population yields a significantly larger current and future potential recruit pool than the pre-AVF pool. That said, very slow growth in the population of 15–19-year-olds is the new demographic reality for military recruiters.

FIGURE 1. SIZE OF THE 15–19-YEAR-OLD COHORT, 1950–2025 (HISTORICAL AND PROJECTED)

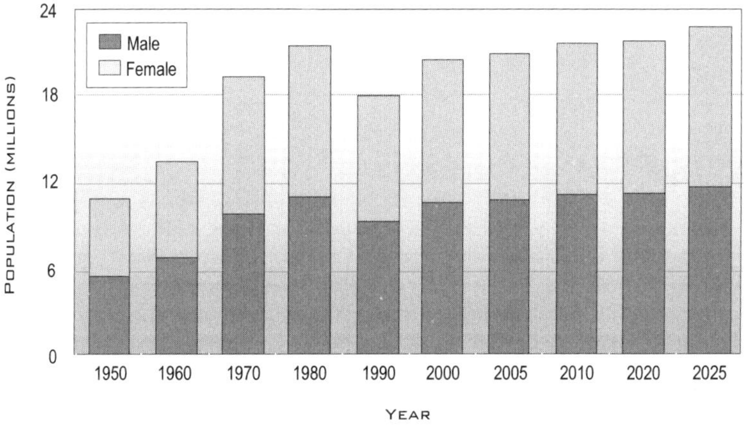

Source: U.S. Census Bureau 2003a.
Note: The left side of the chart (past) is in ten-year increments; the right side of the chart (future) is in five-year increments.

This slow growth in the youth population is occurring in the context of significant overall U.S. population growth (figure 2). What mechanisms explain these trends? People who are not specialists tend to confuse the birth rate (the number of births relative to the size of the total population) with the fertility rate (the number of births relative to the number of women of childbearing age). The birth rate is naturally declining in the United States even though fertility rates remain relatively stable. With population growth primarily concentrated among people beyond the childbearing and child-rearing years, the denominator in the birth rate grows much faster than the numerator.

The new demographic reality is that our population now grows largely due to the other two sources of population change: mortality and migration. Older age-groups are growing rapidly, primarily due to longer life expectancy but also to ongoing immigration, while fertility rates hover just below the "replacement rate" of two children per woman.

FIGURE 2. SIZE OF THE U.S. POPULATION, 1950–2025 (HISTORICAL AND PROJECTED)

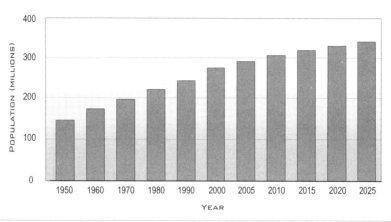

Source: U.S. Census Bureau 2003a.
Note: The left side of the chart (past) is in ten-year increments; the right side of the chart (future) is in five-year increments.

As a result, the 15–19 age-group will account for 6.4 percent of the population as a whole in 2025, down from 9.3 percent in 1970 (U.S. Census Bureau 2003a). According to these projections, the size of the age-group will continue to decline relatively, but not absolutely, into the future. This relative decline is part of the mental model that military human resource planners should use in assessing future reports about the shifting age composition of the population, and situating target age-groups within it. Thanks to a longer, healthier life expectancy, allied with Americans' continuing preference for the two-child family, the United States is becoming a population that has roughly equal numbers of people in every age-group except the oldest (figure 3).

FIGURE 3. PYRAMIDS TO PILLARS: U.S. POPULATION DISTRIBUTION BY AGE-GROUP AND SEX, 1970 AND 2025 (PROJECTED)

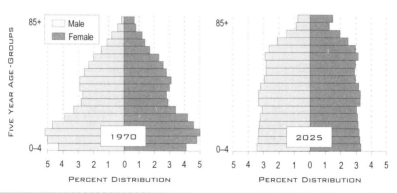

Source: U.S. Census Bureau 2003a.

THE EFFECTS OF SOCIOECONOMIC CHANGE ON THE AVF

Throughout world history, the age picture of any population has been a pyramid, with a wide base representing a large share of babies born, a narrowing midsection in which many died in early childhood and continued to die less rapidly with age, and rising to a pinnacle depicting the few who survived to old age. In this world, children constituted half of the population, and many died before they had children of their own. The few elderly, along with the children, could be cared for by the people in the middle.

The U.S. age picture for 1970 seen in figure 3 was still the traditional population pyramid (though cinched at the middle by the Depression babies, then widened by the baby boom). In contrast, the picture for 2025 is projected to be more of a population "pillar," because each age-group, except the oldest ones, will be roughly the same size. While the bars at the bottom continue to widen slightly, thanks to considerably fewer people dying before reaching old age, the bars toward the top are becoming almost as wide. In 2000, the seven youngest cohorts, ages 0–69, ranged in size from 20.4 million to 43.2 million. This disparity will be nearly erased by 2025, assuming a continuation of current birth, death, and migration patterns (table 1).

TABLE 1. PROJECTIONS OF THE U.S. POPULATION BY AGE: 2025 (MILLIONS)

AGE-GROUP	2000	2025
Under age 10	39.7	46.7
10 to 19	40.9	45.4
20 to 29	38.5	43.6
30 to 39	43.2	46.1
40 to 49	42.8	43.0
50 to 59	31.4	40.3
60 to 69	20.4	40.8
70 to 79	16.3	28.3
80 and older	9.3	15.6

Source: U.S. Census Bureau 2003a.

Unless labor force participation trends change significantly, this trend suggests a similar shift within the U.S. labor force, with growth concentrated among people ages 45 and older. Indeed, during the current decade the median age of the labor force is expected to approach age 41, surpassing the previous record set in 1962, just before the baby boom population entered the working ages (Toosi 2002). The youth labor force is now larger than it has been since the 1970s. But with little growth ahead, recruiting planners will pay increasing attention to the match between their goals and their strategies for reaching them.

Demographic trends are altering population patterns in the rest of the world, but in very different ways than in the United States. In other industrialized countries, fertility rates are lower and immigration tends to be less acceptable, leading to population stagnation in some countries and population decline, especially among youth, in other countries. At the same time, political unrest and war have intensified existing cultural, financial, and public health barriers to family planning in many less-developed countries, leading to explosive growth in youth populations in those countries.

Population decline due to below-replacement fertility is occurring in traditionally countries such as those in the G-7 economic grouping (figure 4).[2] This decline seems likely to be prolonged over decades, and is a new demographic phenomenon. Figure 4 shows that in the G-7 as a whole, the cohorts currently under age 20 are significantly smaller than the cohorts that preceded them. This means that the coming generations of parents will be significantly smaller than current generations. As a result, even a return to replacement-level fertility will not swell the ranks of youth—i.e., potential military recruits—in many of these countries.

FIGURE 4. POPULATION DISTRIBUTION IN G-7 COUNTRIES BY AGE-GROUP AND SEX, 2000 AND 2025 (PROJECTED)

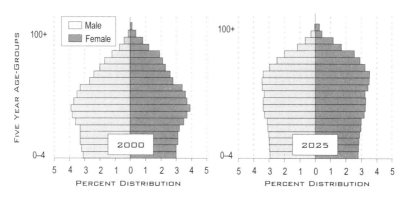

Source: United Nations 2003.
Note: For 2025, Canada is not included for ages 80+ due to the lack of available data.

Obviously, this picture would be more extreme if we were to remove the United States from it, as the U.S. youth population is expected to be relatively stable in numbers, and indeed to grow slightly (figure 5). However, the resulting picture would still mask two quite different outlooks for the supply of military recruits in other industrialized countries. That is, in some countries the youth population is declining noticeably; in others it is roughly stable or declining only slightly.

Nondemographers are focused on the previously unknown path being taken by Germany, Japan, and Italy (in the G-7), and by other, largely Mediterranean countries, such as Spain and Greece. Taking Germany as an example, the distinctly smaller youth population of today in these countries, compared with recent generations of youth, augurs an even smaller youth population a quarter century from now (figure 6). In these countries, which lack the cultural flexibility to be supportive of single parents as well as married ones, fertility rates are very low. This limits the pool of parents to currently married couples, who, primarily because of the direct and indirect costs of child bearing and child rearing, seem to be having only one child.[3] Since these countries are also unwilling to accept many immigrants, they are on a path of population decline. That decline shows up first in the youngest generations, as the supply of future parents shrinks.

FIGURE 5. U.S. POPULATION DISTRIBUTION BY AGE-GROUP AND SEX, 2000 AND 2025 (PROJECTED)

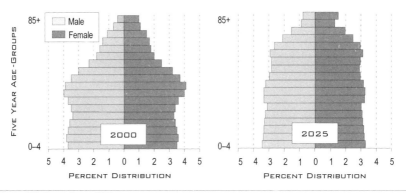

Source: U.S. Census Bureau 2003a.

FIGURE 6. GERMAN POPULATION DISTRIBUTION BY AGE-GROUP AND SEX, 2000 AND 2025 (PROJECTED)

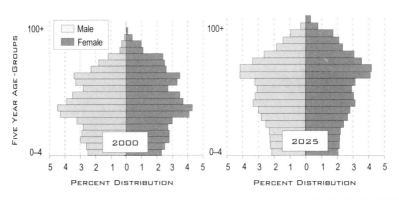

Source: United Nations 2003.

The United Kingdom offers an example of the other population growth pattern occurring in developed countries—a pattern appearing in countries in Northern Europe as well as elsewhere in the English-speaking world. These countries tend to have instituted policies that make it easier for people to have and rear children while providing for themselves in a 21st-century postindustrial economy. The same societal flexibility that supports single as well as married parents also makes immigration more acceptable. The result is a roughly stable or slightly growing population, overall, and of young adults. Indeed, as table 2 suggests, acceptance of a relatively high level of immigration makes the difference between one group of developed countries where the population is projected to continue to grow, and another group where, under current conditions, the population is expected to decline.[4]

TABLE 2. POPULATION OF THE UNITED STATES AND SELECTED
MORE-DEVELOPED COUNTRIES, 2002 AND 2050 (PROJECTED)

	POPULATION (MILLIONS)		
COUNTRY	2002	2050	PERCENT CHANGE
United States	287.7	420.1	46.0
Canada	31.9	41.4	29.8
United Kingdom	59.9	64.0	6.8
France	59.9	61.0	1.8
Spain	40.2	35.6	-11.4
Italy	57.9	50.4	-13.0
Germany	82.4	73.6	-10.7
Poland	38.6	33.8	-12.4
Russia	145.0	118.2	-18.5
Ukraine	48.4	37.7	-22.0
Japan	127.1	99.9	-21.4
Australia	19.5	24.3	24.6

Source: U.S. Census Bureau 2002a.

Meanwhile, current levels of population growth in the developing countries augur a continued and perhaps increasing supply of immigrants to developed countries (figure 7). Currently, 99 percent of the world's population growth is in developing countries. Among developed countries, "only the United States, which has a relatively high birth rate for a developed country, as well as steady immigration, shows robust growth" (Population Reference Bureau 2003).

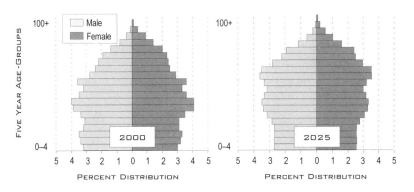

Source: United Nations 2003.

Pakistan and France illustrate the current effects of these divergent growth patterns on the age composition of the population (figure 8). In France, where population size is relatively stable, young people make up a relatively small share of the population. In Pakistan, high fertility rates continue to increase the size of the population by increasing the number of youth.

Table 3 shows the countries with populations of 10 million or more in which a very large share of the population is currently under age 15. By and large, less-developed countries do not have enough economic activity to employ their current generations of working-age people.[5] Indeed, regardless of the degree of economic development, it would be very difficult for any country to absorb such large numbers of youth into the work force.[6] Given the normal reluctance to leave one's family and culture, combined with the unwillingness of most developed countries to accept increased levels of immigration, we can expect most of these young people to seek employment at home.

It is hard to avoid the conclusion that in the developing world, the military faces an oversupply of young people. In the worst of situations, of course, the existence of large numbers of unemployed youth could threaten those countries' stability (or that of other countries).[7] Meanwhile, in the developed world, the supply of young people is either holding steady or diminishing. Consequently, managing the appeal of military service relative to other opportunities for young adults is becoming an increasingly important component of military recruiting around the developed world.

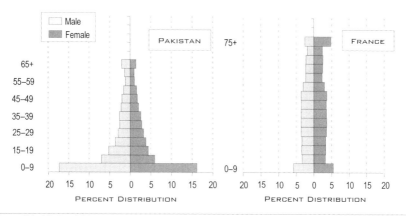

FIGURE 8. POPULATION DISTRIBUTION IN PAKISTAN
AND FRANCE BY AGE-GROUP AND SEX, 2000

Source: United Nations 2003.
Note: The two age-groups under age 10 are combined into a single group due to limitations in the availability of data.

TABLE 3. COUNTRIES WITH VERY LARGE YOUTH POPULATIONS

ASIA	PERCENT UNDER AGE 15	AFRICA	PERCENT UNDER AGE 15
Afghanistan	43	Angola	47
Cambodia	43	Burkina Faso	49
Iraq	47	Cameroon	43
Nepal	41	Congo, DR	43
Pakistan	42	Ethiopia	44
Saudi Arabia	43	Ghana	43
Yemen	48	Ivory Coast	46
		Kenya	44
		Madagascar	45
LATIN AMERICA AND THE CARIBBEAN	PERCENT UNDER AGE 15	Malawi	46
		Mali	47
		Mozambique	45
Guatemala	42	Niger	50
		Nigeria	44
		Senegal	44
		Sudan	45
		Tanzania	45
		Uganda	51
		Zambia	47

Source: Population Reference Bureau 2003.
Note: Table shows countries with populations of 10 million or more where more than 40 percent of the population is under age 15.

TRENDS IN OTHER DEMOGRAPHIC CHARACTERISTICS

Several other demographic trends will affect the characteristics of potential U.S. military recruits, including trends relevant to the recruit's life course and its context.

RACE AND ETHNICITY

Large waves of immigration in the latter decades of the 20th century have increased the racial and ethnic diversity of the U.S. population, making Americans very conscious of the racial and ethnic composition of groups like the police or the military that are both important and visible (figure 9). People who assess such composition need to bear in mind that the nation's minority populations are much younger than the majority population. This is particularly important for groups like the military that have a very youthful age profile.

FIGURE 9. MINORITY SHARE OF U.S. POPULATION, 1975, 2000, AND 2025 (PROJECTED)

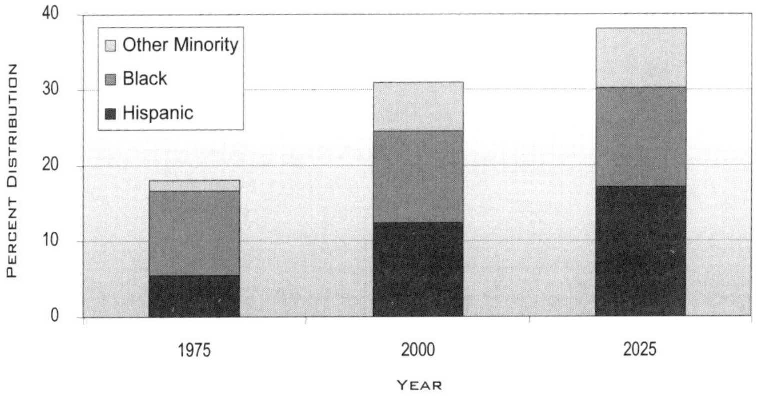

Source: U.S. Census Bureau 2003a.

The median age is a good way to capture these age-based racial and ethnic differences. As of the 2000 census, the median age of the U.S. population was 35, which is the oldest it has ever been (table 4). However, it was nearly 39 for white, non-Hispanics, compared to 26 for Hispanics, 30 for African Americans, 33 for Asian Americans, and 28 for American Indians (U.S. Census Bureau 2001). These differences are the product of differences in migration and fertility, as well as the interaction between them. To the extent that immigrants come from countries where people tend to have large families, as do the Mexican immigrants of recent years, they make their population group relatively younger.

Consequently, the population as a whole is less diverse than the population aged 18 to 44, which includes most military personnel, and considerably less diverse than the age-groups which include most new recruits. (In a later section we address the racial composition of the military compared to that of the population as a whole.) Moreover, projections of current trends suggest that minority populations will continue to be younger in the future. The result will be an increasingly diverse population, one even more diverse than projected before the results of the 2000 census became available.[8]

TABLE 4. U.S. MEDIAN AGE, 2000

RACE	AGE
White, non-Hispanic	38.6
Hispanic	25.8
African American [a]	30.2
Asian	32.7
American Indian/Alaska Native	28.0
Native Hawaiian/Pacific Islander	27.5
Total U.S. population	35.3

Source: U.S. Census Bureau 2001.
a. May include some Hispanics.

The 2000 census was the first to find more people than the annual population estimates had suggested; normally, the census finds fewer people than estimated (the census "undercount"). Aside from a large number of duplicates, the difference was largely among Hispanics, particularly young men. Thus, projections based on current patterns in the nation's racial and Hispanic origin populations suggest that the target age-group for advertising and recruiting, ages 15 to 19, will contain more Hispanics than previously estimated (table 5).

TABLE 5. RACE AND HISPANIC ORIGIN OF THE POPULATION, AGES 15–19, 2025 (PROJECTED)

RACE	PERCENT
White non-Hispanic	55.8
Hispanic	23.8
Black non-Hispanic	15.3
Other, non-Hispanic	5.0

Source: Farnsworth Riche Associates.
Note: See appendix to this paper for immigration assumptions.

To be sure, Hispanic is a designation of ethnic, not racial origin; most official surveys have found that the great majority of Hispanics select "white" when they are asked to choose a racial origin. Thus, it is quite possible that by 2025 a different proportion of youth than projected will report that they are Hispanic. Certainly, patterns of intermarriage, impossible to project with any confidence, could affect how the children and grandchildren of today's Hispanic population choose to classify themselves. And with intermarriage more common among all racial groups, many wonder whether the population is becoming so diverse that racial and Hispanic-origin designations may lose all relevance.

The 2000 census took the first step in the direction of a more nuanced racial and ethnic profile, in that respondents were offered a greater array of categories to choose from than in the past, including the option of more than one race. Table 6 shows the results. Note the category labeled "some other race," which represents the 15 million census respondents who were unable to identify with the five racial categories designated by the Office of Management and Budget. Instead, they checked "other" and wrote in an entry such as Moroccan, South African, Belizean, or a particular Hispanic origin.[9] (Indeed, the majority of "some other race" were Hispanic.) Another 6.8 million checked two or more races. Thus, nearly 8 percent of Americans found even these expanded racial categories too constraining. Tabulations prepared for this paper use a simplified version of the current census categories: white, non-Hispanic; black or African American, non-Hispanic; Hispanic; and other.

TABLE 6. POPULATION BY RACE AND HISPANIC ORIGIN
FOR THE UNITED STATES: 2000

RACE AND HISPANIC OR LATINO	NUMBER	PERCENT OF TOTAL POPULATION
Race		
One race	274,595,678	97.6
White	211,460,626	75.1
Black or African American	34,658,190	12.3
American Indian and Alaska Native	2,475,956	0.9
Asian	10,242,998	3.6
Native Hawaiian and Other Pacific Islander	398,835	0.1
Some other race	15,359,073	5.5
Two or more races	6,826,228	2.4
Total U.S. population	281,421,906	100.0
Hispanic or Latino		
Hispanic or Latino	35,305,818	12.5
Not Hispanic or Latino	246,116,088	87.5
Total U.S. population	281,421,906	100.0

Source: U.S. Census Bureau 2001.

In short, the young population that military recruiters target is more diverse than the population as a whole, and it is projected to become even more diverse. However, it is important for recruiting planners to understand how racial identities are evolving in the U.S. and to monitor new developments that could be relevant to recruiting plans.

CHANGES IN PATTERNS AND LEVELS OF EDUCATIONAL ATTAINMENT

The educational parameters of military accession call for careful thinking about the interaction of trends in educational attainment and in recruiting and retention strategies. The enlisted force and officer corps both have distinct entry points, defined quite strictly by education and somewhat less strictly by age. Enlisted personnel are usually high school diploma graduates, entering around 18 years of age; officers are college graduates, entering at about age 22.[10]

The military's preference for recruits who are high school diploma graduates has been well tested and justified. Currently, military accessions include a significantly higher proportion of high school graduates than does the comparable civilian age-group (U.S. Department of Defense 2003a). In this sense, the increasing proportion of young people who attain this educational level increases the pool of potential recruits, at least to the extent that the share of recruits who hold general educational development (GED) certificates does not increase at the expense of high school diploma graduates.

At the same time, increasing numbers of Americans are pursuing higher education. Given the military's preference for enlistees with high school diplomas, other things equal, this trend would act to reduce the potential pool of youth who are interested in military service. Indeed, the recent National Academy of Sciences panel concluded that the dramatic increase in college enrollment may well be the single most significant factor affecting the recruiting environment (Sackett and Mavor 2003).

However, with many young Americans postponing their investment in higher education while they accumulate experiences that will guide their future educational choices, the military's concentration on very young adults seems to fit current trends. Whether officer or enlisted, many service members do only one tour of duty, then go on to the civilian sector. To the extent that the military offers educational benefits and useful job-related learning, the military becomes one stop on a young adult's increasingly long transition from school to adult career.[11] Thus, the military should continue to monitor the educational patterns of Americans in the context of force requirements, so that it can tailor pay and benefits to attract the people it needs and retain them for as long as it needs.

SECONDARY/ENLISTED LEVEL

In 1974, 82 percent of the population aged 25 to 29—the ages when Americans are expected to have completed their formal education—had completed four or more years of high school. By 2000, the share had risen to 88 percent (U.S. Census Bureau 2000a).[12]

Educational attainment has improved for all population groups, but minority populations continue to lag non-Hispanic whites in high school completion. This lag has hampered the military's strenuous efforts to achieve racial and ethnic population representation while simultaneously recruiting a high-quality force. In 1974 (the first year for which U.S. educational data are available for Hispanics), little more than half (53 percent) of Hispanics aged 25 to 29 had completed four or more years of high school, compared to 68 percent of blacks and 83 percent of whites (U.S. Census Bureau 1975).[13] By 2002, 62 percent of Hispanics had attained this educational level, as had 88 percent of blacks and 93 percent of white non-Hispanics (U.S. Census Bureau 2003c). Thus, given the educational requirements of the all-volunteer force, different attainment levels remain a cause for concern.

Will educational attainment continue to improve? There is some concern that attainment levels have begun to stagnate, i.e., that today's young Americans are no better educated than the next older generation was at the same age, and may even fall behind. However, age changes in enrollment patterns (that are relevant to military recruiting) seem to explain this apparent stagnation and suggest that improvements will continue.

Throughout the 20th century, each successive cohort of the American population attained higher levels of education than its predecessor. As a result, younger, better-educated cohorts have continually replaced older, less-educated cohorts. This pattern is changing, largely because the bulk of the population now has attained the basic, high school level of education required to function in today's economy.[14]

However, the pattern is also changing because education is increasingly spread over the life cycle, and young Americans are taking longer to complete their education, often taking time out to explore alternative careers or to earn money to pay for higher education. Meanwhile, immigration of large numbers of people who lack a high school diploma, particularly Hispanics, works to lower the average educational level of the U.S. population.

Unofficial projections from the Census Bureau indicate that, taking all of these factors into account, the educational attainment of the U.S. population aged 25 and older should in fact continue to improve over the next quarter century (figure 10). Between 2003 and 2028, even under conservative assumptions, the proportion of Americans with a high school education is projected to increase among all population groups—men and women, native and foreign-born, white and black, and Hispanic and non-Hispanic in origin (Day and Bauman 2000). The greatest improvement will be for native-born black and Hispanic males, groups that start from a considerably lower base and have been of particular interest to military recruiters.

Overall, by 2028 the proportion of American adults with a high school education should reach somewhere between 87 and 91 percent.[15] However, compared to the present, there is projected to be little or no improvement for the younger cohorts that military recruiters target, largely due to the impact of immigration.[16] Moreover, federal survey-based data on high school completion include both high school diploma graduates and recipients of GEDs. However, an abundant body of research has led military recruiters to prefer the former at the expense of the latter.

Source: Day and Bauman 2000.

HIGH SCHOOL DIPLOMA VERSUS GED TRENDS

Although comparable data are in short supply, an Urban Institute researcher has divided the numbers of high school diploma graduates in each year since 1870 by the number of 17-year-olds in that year (Chaplin 2002). Using this "degree ratio" method, the proportion of degree graduates rises steadily until 1969, when 77 percent of 17-year-olds graduated from high school. Since 1970, however, the degree ratio has been slipping, down to 70 percent in 2000, as GED recipients made up a larger fraction of teenagers with high school credentials. These estimates are similar to those of Tyler (2003, 369), who estimates that about one in every seven high school "diplomas" currently issued each year is a GED credential.[17]

The GED testing program was originally started by the military to provide returning World War II veterans with the opportunity for high school credentials. With the federal minimum age for GED eligibility now at 16 years, the possibility of substituting a GED for a diploma may be causing some teenagers to drop out of school, decreasing the size of the potential recruit population.[18] This is because the Department of Defense requires that the educational background of at least 90 percent of each service's enlisted accessions be "tier 1," which excludes individuals who obtain their high school credentials through examination (primarily by earning GED certificates).

Tier 1 recruits are primarily high school diploma graduates, but the categorization also includes people with additional schooling. Service rules can be even stricter, with the Air Force recruiting about 98 percent tier 1 and the Marine Corps requiring a minimum of 95 percent tier 1. These minimum educational requirements were established because recruits with other educational credentials had significantly greater attrition rates. Since the military provides considerable up-front training and pays recruits during training, it is not cost effective to access recruits with poor chances for successful completion of their contractual obligations.

As new educational credentials arise, there are questions about their categorization for accession. Generally, new educational backgrounds like home schooling would be grouped with the accession-constrained categories. Unfortunately, the number of accessions in these categories is often too small to systematically evaluate their potential for military service. Currently the CNA Corporation is evaluating a congressionally-authorized pilot program that permits the services to access sufficient numbers of home-schooled youth to evaluate their potential and see if they belong in tier 1. Similar questions will arise with the new tests that are required for high school graduation. Research will be needed to see if youth who complete all requirements for high school graduation except the final "high school graduation test" should be placed in the unconstrained tier 1 category or remain in an accession-constrained educational category.

The Department of Defense also requires that at least 60 percent of each service's accessions score in at least the 50th percentile on the nationally-normed Armed Forces Qualification Test. Thus, with regard to both test scores and educational credentials upon entry, the services demand an unrepresentative (and higher-quality) slice compared to the overall civilian target population of 18 to 24-year-olds. Moreover, even though few enlisted accessions have college credentials when they enter military service, most have intentions, or at least aspirations, to acquire a college education. The Ninth Quadrennial Review of Military Compensation recognized this fact when it stated that "it is no longer appropriate to consider the high school graduate as the standard for pay comparability for much of the enlisted force" (U.S. Department of Defense 2002a, xxiii).

The review suggested that while civilian high school graduates would serve as an appropriate comparison group for personnel in their first term of service, midterm personnel should be compared to civilians with some college education, and senior enlisted personnel should be compared to college graduates. These progressive standards of comparison reflect the continuing educational attainment of service members as they advance in their military careers. They also reflect current trends in the educational attainment of the population as a whole, as education becomes an ongoing part of the average work life.

IMPLICATIONS FOR RECRUITERS

The implications for military recruiters are threefold: two good stories and one more cautionary. First, recruiters can make a working assumption that current levels of high school completion—whether by diploma or GED—are relatively stable. Second, they can assume that a greater share of high school graduates will be interested in furthering their education at some time. Thus, the military can offer benefits that enlistees can apply to this goal once they leave the military, or provide important elements that further their educational qualifications while they are in the military.[19] Third, recruiters can assume that GED holders and youth with other nontraditional educational credentials will make up an increasing share of high school completions, making it more difficult for recruiters to find youth who meet existing enlistment standards.

Clearly more research is needed to determine the educational dimensions of the pool from which the Department of Defense will be recruiting. But if the Department hopes to continue to target high school diploma graduates for recruitment, it may want to exert more effort to encourage young people to stay in school until they obtain their diplomas, especially within populations of interest to the military.[20] Otherwise, it may be difficult to recruit enough young people who meet military enlistment standards over the coming decades.

POSTSECONDARY/OFFICER LEVELS

The proportion of Americans who have completed four or more years of college by ages 25 to 29 has also increased over the 30 years of the all-volunteer force, from 21 percent in 1974 to 29 percent in 2002. The shift in the nation's racial and Hispanic-origin composition masks the dramatic nature of this increase for each large population subgroup. In 2002, 18 percent of blacks aged 25 to 29 had completed four or more years of college, compared to 8 percent in 1974; for Hispanics, completions rose from 5 to 9 percent. (The arrival of large numbers of Hispanics with relatively little education has constrained the increase for the Hispanic population as a whole.) Among blacks, women are slightly more likely than men to have completed college by this age; among Hispanics, completion rates are higher for men (U.S. Census Bureau 2003c).

Americans continue to seek higher education in increasing numbers, and all population groups should see a higher level of postsecondary attainment. Over all age-groups, Day and Bauman (2000) project that between 56 and 63 percent of American adults will have some postsecondary education by 2028, depending on the assumptions used. Looking specifically at younger cohorts, the significant change is that more will attain the level of "some college." Meanwhile, different demographic patterns appear at the bachelor's degree level, where women are generally projected to attain higher levels than men, particularly among native-born minorities. These demographic differences reinforce the suggestion made earlier that special attention could be paid to Hispanic youth.

Since the primary educational requirement for enlistment into the military's commissioned officer corps is a baccalaureate degree, current trends in educational attainment suggest a larger pool of potential officer candidates, especially within minority populations. However, minority populations, especially Hispanics, will still be underrepresented in the baccalaureate population. At the same time, as in the enlisted force, the educational levels of the officer corps have increased over time as officers pursue advanced degrees over the course of their careers. Even now, 40 percent of O-3s, 70 percent of O-4s, and 90 percent of O-6s and above have advanced degrees (U.S. Department of Defense 2002b). Again, this trend is paralleled in the civilian population.

Ongoing demographic and social changes often interact with policy changes, such as the change to an all-volunteer force, in unexpected ways. For instance, an important although perhaps unintended effect of the AVF is that smaller proportions of adults—i.e., the parents, teachers, and other adults who influence a young person's choices—have military experience than in the days of the draft.

The 2000 census found that 12.6 percent of adult Americans are veterans, but the bulk of them are over the age of 65. Over a quarter of Americans (27.6 percent) over the age of 65 are veterans, compared with less than one tenth (9.6 percent) of Americans aged 18–64. According to Under Secretary of Defense for Personnel and Readiness David S. C. Chu, "Studies have shown that adults with military experience are more likely to recommend military service to high school students, but an ever growing number of Americans never have served in uniform" (*Marine Corps Times* 2003). This new situation calls for recruiters to educate the people who advise young people, as well as young people themselves, about the values and benefits of joining the military.[21]

The decrease in numbers of military parents suggests that a smaller share of recruits will come from military families. Still, children from such families will no doubt have a higher propensity to enlist, as it is common for young adults whose childhoods were shaped by their parents' occupations to pursue the same occupations themselves. This is true, for instance, of people who grow up in a family business, particularly a business that provides the family home, such as a family farm. People who grow up on or near military bases, attend schools for military children, and socialize largely with other military families may be more likely to choose a military career than those who are unfamiliar with military life.[22]

GENERATIONAL CHANGES

Over the decades of the AVF, a fundamental change has taken place among young Americans. Both legally and statistically, age 18 is the age of maturity. However, the intersection of economic and demographic change has delayed the onset of adult activities for young people to well beyond that threshold. In contrast to their parents, relatively few Americans currently aged 18 to 24 have taken on the major adult roles of financial independence, marriage, or parenthood. Instead, this life stage has turned into one with a great many demographic activities (demographic density) undertaken in no particular order (demographic diversity) (Riche 2000). In this context, "density" is a measure of such demographic markers as leaving school; departing the parental home for independent living; moving from one county, state, or region to another; getting married; having children; and gaining full-time employment. "Diversity" in this context refers to the increasingly varied sequence in which young people transition to adult work- and family-roles.

The military is not the only institution interested in understanding the changing behavior and motivations of young adults. Given the important position young adults occupy among the nation's consumers, advertisers and marketers regularly research the values and attitudes of each new generation as they succeed one another. (Currently, the marketer-dubbed "Generation X" is succeeding "Generation Y" in the military's target recruiting ages.) These analyses are useful for developing recruitment messages, and for considering changes to the array of benefits the military offers.

However, since these analyses stress differences, not similarities, it is important to bear in mind that the principal drivers for fundamental decisions by individuals are very similar and rarely change over time, though attitudes and values may change the way people perceive them. It is true that current conditions can alter an individual's priorities, such as choosing schooling over work.[23] Nevertheless, the recent National Academy of Sciences investigation into attitudes and aspirations of American youth concluded, "Youth attitudes toward the importance of various goals in life, preferred job characteristics, and work setting have changed very little over the past 25 years" (Sackett and Mavor 2003).

Thus, attitudinal trend analysis is useful, but it is dangerous to place too much weight on it. For instance, much was made of the baby boom generation's differences from previous generations; meanwhile, large numbers of baby boomers have led lives very similar to their parents'. The important task for the military is to distinguish marginal changes in young adults' values and attitudes from fundamental changes in their behavior. The fact that many baby boomers tried illicit drugs and danced wildly to strange music turned out to be less significant than such fundamental changes as widespread college enrollment and new roles for women.

The baby boom made another significant change in fundamental behavior that is very relevant to force planners: baby boomers reproduced their parents' lives to a great extent, *but they did so at older ages*. In essence, by delaying marriage, parenthood, and permanent attachment to the labor force, that generation created a new life stage—a sort of postadolescence devoted to exploring career and life options—that takes place during the ages that are most salient to the AVF: 18 to 24.

Succeeding generations have solidified this trend. By and large, young adults are taking longer to finish their education and to become attached to the labor force (Riche 2000). They are also delaying marriage and child bearing, compared to Americans in previous generations. And many are delaying leaving their parents' home for independent living. In 2002, fully 50 percent of the civilian population aged 18 to 24 was living with parents or other relatives (U.S. Census Bureau 2003b).[24] Thus, the ages 18 to 24 span an extended period in which young adults are at least partially dependent upon their parents and society. These years have become a postadolescent life stage in which young people prepare for adult life by engaging in a variety of activities, in a variety of places, simultaneously or consecutively, and in no particular order.

Sociologists who are examining this transition focus on the age-group 16 to 19, when high school graduation should normally take place. In 2000, 3.4 percent of this age-group were high school graduates who were neither in school, in the military, nor at work; nor were 5.5 percent who had not earned diplomas. Thus, roughly 9 percent of these youth could be viewed as "spinning their wheels" before getting traction in an adult activity—almost as many as the 10 percent who were employed. (Nearly 80 percent were enrolled in school, many combining school with work [Riche and Gaquin 2003].)

Given this postponement of what has been considered "normal" adult life, military service offers many attractive transitions to further education and eventual civilian work life. This is all the more so because the military provides a variety of educational benefits to attract recruits—tuition assistance, Montgomery GI bill benefits, and college enlistment bonuses are the most important. Currently, as an incentive to enlist, some recruits are offered loan repayments for college-related federal loans.[25] To attract potential recruits with some college education, the Army has a pilot program called "College First" that allows high-quality recruits to enlist in the Army's delayed entry program for up to two years while in college. Participants receive either a monthly stipend or loan repayment and enter the Army at the advanced rank of E-4 (after at least 30 college credits have been earned).

All services offer tuition assistance for college courses taken while on active duty, and service members can obtain college credits for some military training courses. As a result, in a direct parallel with the trend among young civilian adults to combine work and schooling, service members can combine postsecondary education with active duty. Moreover, all enlisted recruits have the opportunity of participating in the GI bill program. Although these benefits are usually utilized after leaving the military, members can use these benefits while on active duty.

Thus, although the rise in the educational aspirations of young Americans could shrink the pool of future recruits, it could just as well expand that pool if military service helps recruits make career choices, acquire appropriate training, and earn benefits that ease the costs of college once they return to civilian life. Cost-cutting pressures on institutions of higher education increase the value of such benefits, as tuition costs continue to rise and financial aid for poor students continues to contract. Getting a "second chance" to learn and earn after high school could also be relevant to those young people who find they are not fully prepared for college, or who leave college for personal or financial reasons.

OTHER LIFE COURSE CHANGES

The early years of the AVF coincided with a tendency toward early retirement among Americans. In that context, a full military career fulfilled the work life expectations of Americans, particularly men. Whether military or civilian, at that time Americans' mental model of a "career" generally entailed serving continuously with a single employer or industry, learning a variety of skills on the job, rising through the ranks to higher and higher pay levels, and retiring at a fixed age with a full pension.

Now, however, the trend toward early retirement has stopped, and increasing proportions of older Americans are still in the work force. In 2002, half the civilian population aged 62 to 64 was in the labor force, along with a quarter of those aged 65 to 69. (About 80 percent of people aged 25 to 54, the prime working ages, are in the work force [U.S. Bureau of Labor Statistics 2003].) Effectively, there is no standard retirement age anymore. Wiatrowski (2001) notes that "in 100 years, the Nation has gone from a society that needed few retirement benefits, through a period of closely structured retirement plans and ages, to a more flexible period characterized by varying plans and ages." The age at which people can receive full Social Security benefits is rising, while an increasing variety of retirement plans no longer tie a specific number of years with an employer to a specific retirement age.

On balance, Americans have become accustomed to the idea of changing both employers and skill sets throughout their work lives. They are also beginning to accept that a longer life expectancy brings with it an expectation for a longer work life, with possible interruptions for learning new skills, concentrating on family, or simply experiencing life. These developments are based in part on a business climate that rewards responsiveness to change, and in part on changes in employees. Longer life expectancy is an obvious demographic influence. Less obvious is the effect of parallel, though not necessarily identical, work lives for men and women, and thus husbands and wives.

Since 1975, job separation rates have been relatively stable, but the separations have become more likely to be voluntary than involuntary, especially among more-educated workers. They have also become more voluntary across all age-groups, unlike the historical pattern in which job shopping largely took place among young people (Stewart 2002). To be sure, the unusually strong economy of the 1990s made it relatively easy to risk unemployment by changing employers, but so did the increase in the proportion of couples for whom the wife's earnings accounted for a considerable share of the household's income. In 1975, men earned more than 60 percent of income in 77 percent of married couples; by 2000, only 58 percent of married couples fell into this category. Over the intervening quarter century, women had become the primary earner in 12 percent of couples (up from 6 percent in 1975), while the proportion of equal-earner couples rose from 17 to 29 percent (Stewart 2002).

In this new world of worker mobility, multiple careers, midlife retooling, and flexible working ages, a military career no longer parallels a civilian career, but rather complements it. For all but the very senior officers, it precedes entry into the civilian work force. It provides many individuals with an enhanced educational background. And it positions the over 20,000 individuals per year who retire after a full military career to take full advantage of civilian career possibilities.

With a guaranteed annuity equal to about half of their basic military pay, military retirees have the resources to acquire more education and credentials if they like. At an average age of 43, they have enough work-life-expectancy remaining to make undertaking a new career worthwhile (U.S. Department of Defense 2003a). Their annuity may also give them the ability to choose a relatively low-paying career, like teaching, that attracts them, or a light schedule that will allow them time to enjoy other pursuits. This ability may explain, at least in part, why the wages of recent military retirees have been lagging behind those of their civilian counterparts throughout their civilian careers. Adding military pensions to retiree wages eliminates the gap between retiree and civilian earnings (U.S. Department of Defense 2002a). Hence, military human resource planners need to monitor developments in civilian work lives, in order to situate military careers, compensation, and benefits in the most effective context. Like the other demographic developments described in this paper, this one calls for more precise targeting for recruiting and compensation planning.

IMMIGRATION

Trends in immigration and citizenship also interact with trends in military service. Although the proportion of international migrants is not increasing, the large increases in global population over the past half century have increased the numbers of migrants commensurately, and the United States continues to be a prime destination. Nearly 12 percent of the U.S. resident population was foreign-born in 2002, and over half of them (7 percent of total residents) were not citizens (U.S. Census Bureau 2003b).

Citizenship is not required for U.S. military enlistment, but recruits must have at least a green card. The active duty military includes about 35,000 noncitizens, and the military recruits about 8,000 noncitizens yearly (Defense Manpower Data Center 2003, direct communication). Representing over 200 different countries, almost half come from Mexico, the Philippines, or Jamaica. Military service provides a unique opportunity for noncitizens to both serve the country and accelerate the citizenship process. Given that immigration is likely to remain an important factor in U.S. population growth, recruiting planners will want to pay careful attention to immigrant youth.

At least partly in response to the terrorist attacks on September 11, 2001, the President signed Executive Order 329 in July 2002, allowing noncitizen military members to apply for citizenship as soon as they enter the military. Previously, military personnel needed three years of qualifying service (versus five years for civilian personnel) before they could apply. The military is also assisting service members with this process, as well as providing follow-up to shorten the period between application and the granting of citizenship. Thus, a successful route to citizenship is a benefit the military offers to the increasing numbers of immigrants in the recruiting pool.

REPRESENTATION ISSUES

Part of the rationale for developing the all-volunteer force was demographic. First, there was considerable public concern that minorities, particularly African Americans, represented a disproportionate share of fatalities during the Vietnam War.[26] Second, although the Gates Commission, which recommended establishing the AVF, did not mention women in its report, there was a growing recognition that including women in the active duty force would significantly increase the potential pool of educationally qualified recruits (Gates 1970). By all accounts, today's AVF is a success story of inclusion along both racial and gender dimensions, from entry-level to top leadership positions.

Thirty years on, military researchers have found that the top enlisted and officer ranks are more inclusive of minorities and women than the accession cohorts they came from (Quester and Gilroy 2002). Indeed, raw comparisons of demographic composition miss what may be the most meaningful measure of diversity: diverse leadership. Notably, "The military is the only large organization in which large units (comprised mostly of men) are led by women, and large units (comprised largely of whites) are led by minorities" (Quester and Gilroy 2002, 111). Still, the public's expectation that the military should, to the extent possible, mirror the composition of the population it defends is likely to continue to challenge military recruiters.

The most notable demographic difference between the military and the public is the youthful nature of the AVF, and this difference drives other differences such as the racial and ethnic composition of the force. The gap between the age composition of the military and the civilian work force is wide and will widen even further in the coming years, given that the growth in the American population is most rapid among people age 45 and older.

Figure 11 shows the age composition of the military as well as the U.S. labor force. The striking contrast underscores the unique nature of the military as an employer. Many other industries have a primarily youthful labor force (the advertising, entertainment, and information industries come to mind), but in these industries the public is unlikely to be concerned about the relative lack of representation of older age-groups, as they can turn to alternative suppliers if they wish. However, unlike other industries, the military needs to maintain the trust and understanding of the population as a whole. Thus, military leadership will need to monitor the potential effects of the increasing age gap between the forces and the public.

FIGURE 11. AGE DISTRIBUTION OF THE ACTIVE DUTY FORCE AND CIVILIAN WORK FORCE, 2002

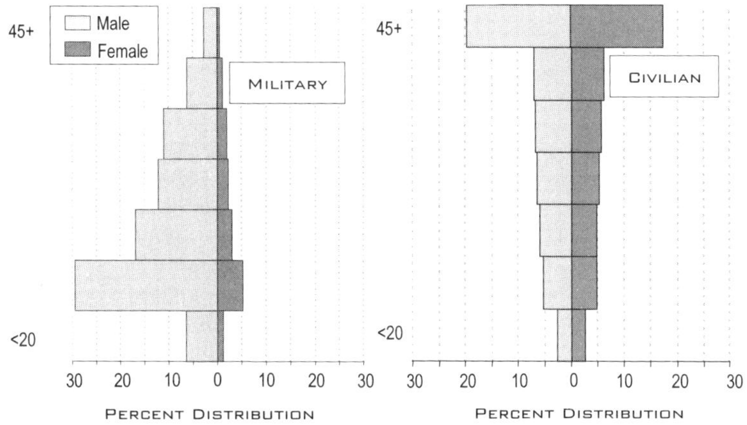

Source: U.S. Department of Defense 2003b; U.S. Bureau of Labor Statistics 2003.

Meanwhile, public representatives will no doubt continue to monitor the racial and ethnic makeup of the AVF versus the civilian population (figure 12). The disparity between the age composition of the military and the civilian labor force makes achieving representation elusive, if only because the minority population is considerably younger than the white population (table 4).

FIGURE 12. COMPARISON OF DIVERSITY BETWEEN
THE ACTIVE DUTY FORCE AND THE CIVILIAN WORK FORCE, 2002

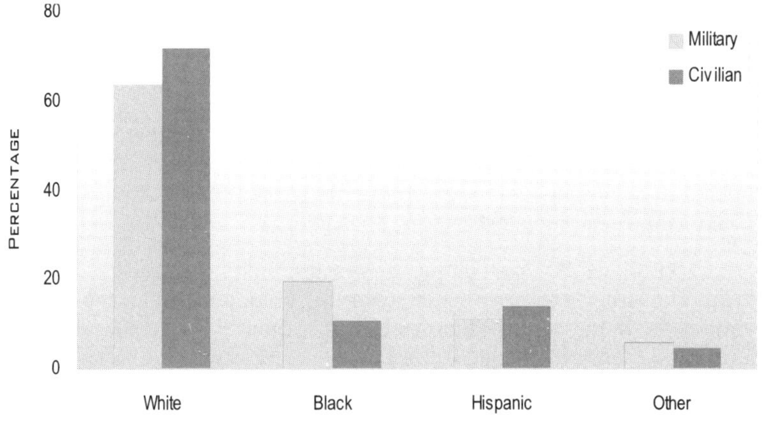

Source: U.S. Department of Defense 2003b; U.S. Census Bureau 2003a.

Since the civilian work force extends across all age-groups, it is not surprising that non-Hispanic whites make up a much larger share of that population than they do of the military. This difference is significantly smaller when considering the prime age population for military accessions (figure 13). Indeed, annual monitoring of the racial and ethnic composition of the enlisted force shows that by and large, the racial and ethnic composition of new accessions largely mirrors the civilian population aged 18 to 24, with Hispanics being somewhat underrepresented and African Americans somewhat overrepresented (U.S. Department of Defense 2003a).

Looking directly at projections of the racial and Hispanic origin of the population aged 15 to 19, the underrepresentation of Hispanics in the military because of lagging educational attainment may become an even greater challenge in the years ahead. It is hard to see how the military can compensate for basic differences in the alternative choices available to young adults in different population groups, particularly those based on education. The civilian sector bears the onus for rectifying or ameliorating these differences, although the military must continue to be responsive to them. For instance, given the importance the military attaches to high school graduation, military leaders could consider more actively supporting the Department of Education's initiatives to encourage high school completion.

Meanwhile, women have contributed significantly to the success of the AVF, both in terms of numbers and accession quality (figure 14). Over the AVF's history, women's representation in the enlisted force has increased from 2 to 15

SUSTAINING THE FORCE: RECRUITING AND RETENTION

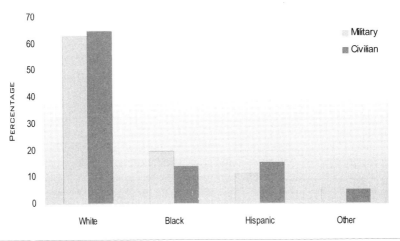

Source: U.S. Department of Defense 2003b; U.S. Census Bureau 2003a.

FIGURE 14. WOMEN IN THE ENLISTED FORCE, 1970–2002

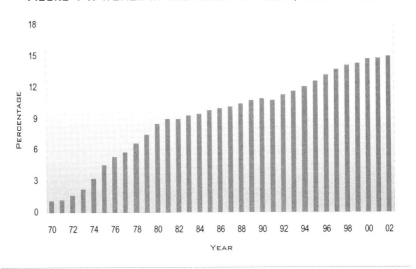

Source: U.S. Department of Defense 2003b.

percent—the highest in the world (Quester and Gilroy 2002, 115). In addition, the AVF has led the civilian sector in remedying "gender tracking," widely considered a primary cause of women's lower work status and earnings relative to men. When the AVF began, almost 90 percent of enlisted women were in administrative or health specialties. Now almost half of enlisted women are in occupations that are considered "nontraditional" for women.

It may be time for the military to acknowledge that it cannot be completely representative in terms of race and Hispanic origin as well as gender. The fact that the military is a unique internal labor market characterized by a hierarchical structure with little lateral entry may increase its relative attractiveness to women and minorities who have historically faced discrimination in the civilian labor market. The advancement process is both well defined and based on merit, and the promotion process looks at everyone (Quester and Gilroy 2002). This makes "over" representation likely for population groups that perceive that they are not treated equally in the civilian labor market. Beyond simple discrimination, individuals with family or other personal connections can be advantaged in civilian employment, while women, in particular, are disadvantaged when they are juggling family responsibilities (U.S. General Accounting Office 2003).

OTHER SALIENT CONTRASTS

Another important difference between the AVF and the civilian labor force is the disproportionate share of military personnel involved in raising children. This difference is occurring because the shifting age pattern of the population is increasing the percentage of the civilian labor force that is beyond the major child-rearing ages. At present, the average American, male or female, spends just over a third of the time between the ages of 20 and 70 raising children (King 1999). Since the prime parenting ages coincide roughly with the armed force's age profile, the military may well be the nation's largest employer called to address issues related to balancing work and family. Its success in doing so will likely bear on its success in retention. Indeed, just as the AVF has put the military in the forefront of equal opportunity employment, its retention needs may put it in the forefront of successful management of work-family issues.

In this context, it is important to recognize that military counts of dependents encompass a broad range of dependency needs. For example, a single parent with a child likely has a more demanding work-family situation than a service member whose dependent is a nonworking spouse. A recent report acknowledges that "the enlisted force has moved from a predominantly single male establishment to one with a greater emphasis on family," but the report analyzes marital status rather than the numbers of dependents who require caregiving (U.S. Department of Defense 2003a).

Though the military population is significantly more "married" than the civilian population across all age-groups, there are differences for men and women at different ages (table 7). Under age 30, both men and women service members are more likely than civilians to be married. This difference is so striking that it suggests that some form of bias is present: perhaps people who are likely to marry earlier than average select the military, or perhaps the military offers incentives for people to marry early (or disincentives to remain single).

TABLE 7. MARITAL STATUS BY AGE AND SEX, 2002
(PERCENT MARRIED, SPOUSE PRESENT OR ABSENT)

	MALE		FEMALE	
AGE	MILITARY	CIVILIAN	MILITARY	CIVILIAN
18 to 19	5.6%	1.8%	9.7%	5.2%
20 to 24	26.5	13.2	32.5	22.9
25 to 29	59.8	40.5	51.6	50.4
30 to 34	78.3	57.6	60.4	63.7
35 to 39	85.6	66.2	62.0	67.3
40 to 44	88.0	68.7	61.8	68.6
45+	90.0	71.5[a]	58.5	66.9[a]

Sources: U.S. Census Bureau 2003a; U.S. Department of Defense 2003a.
a. 45 to 54.

There may be a simple explanation for this pattern. The average age at first marriage has been rising in the civilian population in large part because many young adults cohabit instead of or before marrying.[27] In other words, age-based trends in union formation have not changed significantly, but the nature of the union has shifted for young adults from marriage to cohabitation, particularly when no children are involved. Thus, the nature of the military and its living arrangements no doubt prevents service members from adopting the civilian trend of delayed marriage. After age 30, the marriage rate among female service members lags slightly behind that of civilian women, but male service members are overwhelmingly married, and considerably more so than civilian men.

However, the need for caregiving, more than marriage, produces work-family conflicts, and in a predominantly young work force, children are the family members most in need of care. Others have noted that enlisted service members have children somewhat earlier than civilians do. (See, for example, Morrison et al. 1989.) Different data concepts make it difficult to neatly contrast the parenting demands on the AVF versus the civilian work force.[28] However, nearly half of married military couples (with either one spouse or both in the military) aged 20 to 24 had children in 2002, compared to a fifth of married civilian couples of the same age (U.S. Department of Defense 2003a).

In 2002, the 1.2 million enlisted service members had almost 1 million children. Thirteen percent of the 607,000 single enlisted members were parents. At the grade of E-4, the grade where most enlisted members complete their first term of service, 29 percent had dependent children. At the grade of E-5, 54 percent had dependent children (U.S. Department of Defense 2003a). To the extent that retaining service members is important, family and parenting issues no doubt come into play. Thus, a thorough investigation of the work-family status of the active duty force, with a focus on caregiving responsibilities, may offer useful directions for retention strategies.

CONCLUSION

Unlike other industrialized countries, the United States is not confronted with a declining youth population. Indeed, the population aged 15 to 19 is projected to grow slowly over the next quarter century. At the same time, it is projected to become more racially and ethnically diverse. Meanwhile, changes in educational patterns and employment plans offer the military an opportunity to attract young adults who seek both life experiences and access to further education as they transit from youth to maturity and from education to work. These changes also call for more attention to "stay in school" efforts if the military is to continue its emphasis on regular high school graduation as the relevant credential. And they call for careful monitoring of alternative work life patterns and opportunities, in order to maximize retention goals.

From a demographic perspective, it is hard to see how the all-volunteer force can meet the public's expectations of a force that is representative of the population as a whole. The military has been successful in overcoming the national history of racial and sex discrimination, but because it offers a unique bundle of employment characteristics, it has become particularly attractive to certain population groups. It also has a unique set of demands for its personnel. Meanwhile, the relatively youthful nature of the force makes it less and less representative of the age and household composition of the U.S. population, as growth in the population is largely occurring among people over age 45.

APPENDIX

IMMIGRATION ASSUMPTIONS

In the absence of official population projections updated for the 2000 census results (scheduled for release by the U.S. Census Bureau sometime in 2004), projections by age and racial and ethnic origin were prepared by Martha Farnsworth Riche and Thomas G. Exter for this paper as well as one for the Department of Housing and Urban Development. The projections are based on the 2000 census counts, using a standard cohort-component model and incorporating most of the Census Bureau's assumptions for its middle-series projections, issued in 1999. However, Riche and Exter modified the bureau's immigration assumptions in projecting race and ethnic origins, and made group-specific projections for Hispanics and Asians. As figure 15 shows, this procedure raises the projections for these groups above the Census Bureau's 1999 middle series level, though not to the level of its high series.

FIGURE 15. IMMIGRATION ASSUMPTIONS

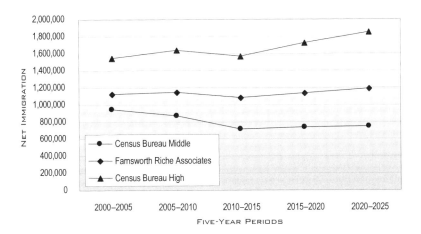

NOTES

1. The military cannot access recruits until age 18 (17 with parental permission). Recruiting efforts are aimed at teenagers who are nearing that age, primarily 15–17.

2. The G-7 economic grouping refers to Canada, France, Germany, Italy, Japan, the United Kingdom, and the United States.

3. In his useful survey of the population situation in Europe, Demeny (2003) remarks: "Having children is a risky adventure that imposes responsibilities but also offers unique rewards."

4. The declines projected for eastern European countries are particularly susceptible to modification, once they complete their economic transition. During the current disruption, large numbers of citizens are emigrating in search of work, and migrants are disproportionately people in their 20s. Thus, the projections assume loss not only of current emigrants, but also of their future children.

5. According to the International Labour Office, rates of youth unemployment are already alarmingly high in many countries: "Around the world, youth unemployment rose by 8 million between 1995 and 1999 . . . aggravated by underemployment where people are working much less than their capacities would permit or that they might want" (International Labour Office 2002, 3).

6. Recall, for instance, the difficulties faced by the United States in the 1970s when, simultaneously, the large baby boom cohort reached the working ages and women of all ages entered the paid labor force.

7. Brazil is a developing country that has sharply slowed the growth of its youth population. According to population experts, military leaders concerned about accession quality (poor eyesight and other effects of poor nutrition and health) induced the government to support family planning programs (Gelbard 2003).

8. The current representation profile (U.S. Department of Defense 2003a) incorporates the findings of the recent National Academy of Sciences panel on the youth population and military recruitment. That report (summarized in Chapter 9 of the profile) uses projections based on pre-2000 census population projections and estimates from the Census Bureau. Pending updated projections from the Bureau, this paper incorporates projections of race and ethnic composition using assumptions developed by Farnsworth Riche and Thomas Exter for this paper (as shown in the appendix) and applied to the Census Bureau's interim 2000-based projections of the population by age and sex, as presented in its International Data Base (U.S. Census Bureau 2003a).

9. "Persons of Hispanic origin . . . were those that indicated that their origin was Mexican, Puerto Rican, Cuban, Central or South American, or some other Hispanic origin." www.census.gov/population/www/socdemo/hispanic/hispdef.html.

10. There is virtually no lateral entry, except for people in some specialties, such as doctors, dentists, lawyers, chaplains, and musicians.

11. Even if the learning is negative, i.e., guiding the recruit away from rather than toward an occupation, it is personally useful.

12. Educational attainment data combine people who completed high school with a GED certificate with people who earned a regular high school diploma.

13. Until 1973, data for whites included Hispanics, who, when forced to choose a racial origin, tend to say they are white; since 1974, data have been available for both whites and white non-Hispanics.

14. Perhaps the most important milestone revealed by the 2000 census was the aging out of the prime working ages (to 65 and older) of the last generation to contain large numbers of people who did not complete high school.

15. These projections assume a continuation of current patterns. (It should also be remembered that high school attainment numbers and projections include GEDs.) If fundamental changes should take place, such as expanded use of graduation standards and/or diminished use of social promotion, these levels may not be attained (Day and Bauman 2000).

16. The projected improvement is mainly driven by large expected increases in high school completion by foreign-born Hispanics, which the authors find "less plausible" than other predictions from their model (Day and Bauman 2000).

17. Tyler (2003) reports that about seven hundred thousand to eight hundred thousand people who have dropped out of high school attempt the GED exams each year. The GED credentialing program is supported by federal funds. His article provides a useful survey of recent research on GEDs.

18. As long as the state does not have a higher minimum than the federal minimum of 16 years, a teenager may take the GED examinations at 16 (Chaplin 1999).

19. U.S. Department of Defense (2002a) features an extensive analysis of the role of educational benefits for both recruitment and retention in chapter 2.

20. For instance, southwestern states like Texas have large numbers of young Hispanics; if the new graduation standards are encouraging students who are struggling to leave high school before graduation, as some assert, these likely recruits may be lost to the military.

21. In June 2003 the Pentagon announced a new advertising campaign to "reconnect Americans to the military." Unlike traditional recruiting commercials, the new spots bypass young people and take aim at more mature Americans who have some notion of what it takes to succeed in the world. Magazine and television ads feature veterans who discuss how military values such as commitment and teamwork helped them to forge successful lives (*Marine Corps Times* 2003).

22. Businesses know that the bulk of their customers tend to be repeat customers; i.e., it is more effective to market to people who have already bought than to cultivate a brand new customer.

23. For instance, enrollment in graduate schools of business increases when unemployment rates increase.

24. This percentage may be mildly inflated by college students home for spring break during the survey week.

25. In a recent development, designed to compensate for an unprecedented concentration of employees who have reached the ages when they can retire, civilian agencies of the federal government are also permitted to offer this benefit.

26. According to researchers cited in Quester and Gilroy (2002), this concern was not factually based.

27. The National Survey of Families and Households, sponsored by the Department of Health and Human Services and conducted by the University of Wisconsin, has spawned a large body of research into this and other changing household and family patterns among the civilian population.

28. One problem in making these comparisons is that civilian data on families are based on coresidency, while military data are based on allowances for dependents. These differences obviously reflect the different goals of public policies that address families in each universe.

REFERENCES

Chaplin, Duncan. 1999. *GEDs for teenagers: Are there unintended consequences?* Washington, D.C.: Urban Institute.

Chaplin, Duncan. 2002. Tassels on the cheap: The GED and the falling graduation rate. *Education Next* Fall: 24–29. Washington, D.C.: Urban Institute.

Day, Jennifer C., and Kurt J. Bauman. 2000. *See* U.S. Census Bureau. 2000b.

Demeny, Paul. 2003. Population policy dilemmas in Europe at the dawn of the twenty-first century. *Population and Development Review* 29(1): 1–28.

Gates, Thomas S. 1970. *Report of the President's Commission on an All-Volunteer Armed Force.* Washington, D.C.: U.S. Government Printing Office.

Gelbard, Alene. 2003. Personal communication.

Gibson, Campbell, and Kay Jung. 2002. *See* U.S. Census Bureau. 2002b.

International Labour Office. 2002. *Youth and work: Global trends.* Geneva.

King, Rosalind Berkowitz. 1999. Time spent in parenthood status among adults in the United States. *Demography* 36(3): 377–85.

Marine Corps Times. 2003. *The military: They also serve who encourage youth.* July 14.

Morrison, Peter A., Georges Vernez, David W. Grissmer, and Kevin F. McCarthy. 1989. *Families in the Army: Looking ahead.* Santa Monica, Calif.: RAND Corporation.

Population Reference Bureau. 2003. *2003 world population data sheet of the Population Reference Bureau.* Washington, D.C.

Quester, Aline O., and Curtis L. Gilroy. 2002. Women and minorities in America's volunteer military. *Contemporary Economic Policy* 20(2): 111–21.

Riche, Martha Farnsworth. 2000. America's diversity and growth: Signposts for the 21st century. *Population Bulletin* 55(2). Washington, D.C.: Population Reference Bureau.

Riche, Martha Farnsworth, and Deirdre A. Gaquin. 2003. *The who, what, and where of America: Understanding the census results.* Lanham, Md.: Bernan Press.

Sackett, Paul, and Anne Mavor. 2003. *Attitudes, aptitudes, and aspirations of American youth: Implications for military recruitment.* Washington, D.C.: National Academies Press.

Stewart, Jay. 2002. Recent trends in job stability and job security: Evidence from the March CPS. Working paper 356. March. Washington, D.C.: U.S. Bureau of Labor Statistics.

Toosi, Mitra. 2002. A century of change: the U.S. labor force, 1950–2050. *Monthly Labor Review* May. U.S. Bureau of Labor Statistics.

Tyler, John H. 2003. Economic benefits of the GED: Lessons from recent research. *Review of Educational Research* 73(2): 369–403.

United Nations, 2003. *World population prospects, the 2002 revision.*

U.S. Bureau of Labor Statistics. 2003. *Household annual averages, table 3: Employment status of the civilian noninstitutional population by age, sex, and race.* http://stats.bls.gov/ [August 19, 2003].

U.S. Census Bureau. 1975. *Characteristics of American youth: 1974.* Current Population Reports: Special Studies. Series P-23, no. 51. April. Suitland, Md.

———. 2000a. *Educational attainment in the United States: March 2000 (updated).* P20-536, table A-2. http://www.census.gov [July 28, 2003].

———. 2000b. Have we reached the top? Educational attainment projections of the U.S. population, by Jennifer C. Day and Kurt J. Bauman. Working Paper Series no. 43. May. Washington, D.C.: Population Division.

———. 2001. *Overview of race and Hispanic origin,* Census Brief, March 2001.

———. 2002a. *International data base,* www.census.gov/idb/ [Oct. 12, 2002].

———. 2002b. *Historical census statistics on population totals by race, 1970 to 1990, and by Hispanic origin, 1970 to 1990, for the United States, regions, divisions, and states,* by Campbell Gibson and Kay Jung. Working Paper Series no. 56. September. Washington, D.C.: Population Division.

———. 2003a. *International data base.* http://www.census.gov/ipc/www/ idbnew.html [July 15, 2003].

———. 2003b. *Current population survey, March 2002,* Internet release, June.

———. 2003c. *Educational attainment in the U.S.: March 2000* (update). http:// www.census.gov/ [July 28, 2003].

U.S. Department of Defense. 2002a. *Report of the Ninth Quadrennial Review of Military Compensation: Volume I.* Washington, D.C.: Office of the Under Secretary of Defense (Personnel and Readiness).

———. 2002b. *Active military demographic profile: Assigned strength, gender, race-ethnic, marital, education and age profile of the active duty force.* September. Arlington, Va.: Defense Manpower Data Center.

———. 2003a. *Population representation in the military services, fiscal year 2001.* Final report. March.

———. 2003b. *Special tabulation.* Arlington, Va.: Defense Manpower Data Center.

U.S. General Accounting Office. 2003. *Women's earnings: Work patterns partially explain difference between men's and women's earnings.* GAO-04-35. October.

Warner, John T., and Beth J. Asch. 2001. The record and prospects of the all-volunteer military in the United States. *Journal of Economic Perspectives* 15(2): 169–92.

Wiatrowski, William J. 2001. Changing retirement age: Ups and downs. *Monthly Labor Review* April. U.S. Bureau of Labor Statistics.

COMMENTARY

DENNIS D. CAVIN

It's a great day to be a soldier. Manning the force, and thus meeting today's young men and women who choose to put on the uniform, is probably the most rewarding job I have had since I joined the military. I had a good mentor. I had the opportunity to work as the aide for Max Thurman when he was the commanding general of the U.S. Army Recruiting Command. Little did I know that 20 years later I would come back to lead that organization.

I was present on the day the first note of "Be All You Can Be" was played on Fifth Avenue in 1981. Twenty years later, I was present when the first words of the Army's new recruiting slogan "An Army of One" were unveiled on January 11, 2001. My experiences with recruiting have come full circle and have influenced my views on the all-volunteer force.

One of the most important things to recognize is that the all-volunteer force is really an *all-recruited* volunteer force. A tremendous amount of effort and resources are required to maintain this volunteer force. This year marks 30 years of success of this recruited volunteer force—an experiment that most people said would not succeed. Yet, the achievements of this force in recent months—in Afghanistan and in Iraq—are a testament to those who envisioned an all-volunteer force and believed it was possible.

The future of the all-volunteer force is now. The challenges that we who are responsible for the force will face over the next 2, 5, 10, and 15 years are upon us today; how we prepare for those challenges will have a tremendous impact on the future. Two words apply to my perspective on the future: ready and relevant. How must we man the force—of soldiers, sailors, airmen, Marines, and

★ ⎯⎯⎯⎯⎯⎯⎯⎯⎯⎯⎯⎯⎯⎯⎯⎯⎯⎯⎯⎯⎯⎯⎯⎯⎯⎯⎯⎯⎯⎯⎯⎯⎯⎯⎯⎯⎯

coastguardsmen—so that it is ready to fight *and* relevant to the needs of the nation? This is the challenge.

In this discussion, I will focus on four aspects of the recruiting environment over which the services have influence. In each of these areas, many questions must be addressed to ensure success in the future. The four areas are personnel quality, the youth market, advertising, and the recruiting establishment.

QUALITY

Maintaining a high-quality force is essential. The paper by Paul Hogan, Curtis Simon, and John Warner (chapter 5, this volume) summarizes the findings from many studies that show the positive effects of personnel quality on military readiness. High-quality personnel have proven their value time and time again, and they will continue to do so. Much is understood about the two important indicators of quality used today: the high school diploma and scores in the upper half of the Armed Forces Qualification Test. (Recruits with such scores are classified as being in aptitude categories I–IIIA.) Whether these metrics will remain relevant in the future is in question.

What defines a high school graduate today, and what will define one in the future? As Martha Farnsworth Riche and Aline Quester document (chapter 7, this volume), significant changes are occurring in civilian educational attainment. For example, more youth are obtaining the General Educational Development (GED) certificate, more youth are being schooled at home, and fewer are attaining the traditional high school diploma. These trends raise some concern, since preliminary evidence shows that youth who hold alternative high school credentials behave differently in the military than do traditional high school graduates, with the former leaving the military at a significantly higher rate.

A second question is whether the traditional aptitude categories I–IIIA are still appropriate as a standard, particularly as the Department of Defense (DOD) renormalizes the Armed Services Vocational Aptitude Battery (ASVAB) this year, a question explored thoughtfully by David Armor and Paul Sackett (chapter 6, this volume). Will these two metrics continue to be meaningful as the department looks to the future? I believe they will; but the department may also need a clearer, and perhaps broader, definition of quality in the future.

Along with a more expansive definition of quality, improvements are needed in prescreening to better identify high-risk individuals who are interested in joining the military—that is, those individuals who are least likely to fulfill their service obligation or perform well on the job. Today the services use the ASVAB to measure aptitude, and it has been a great tool. But a new battery of tests are needed to measure other important characteristics. Pilot tests developed by the Army and the Navy to measure motivation and adaptability to military life have not proven completely successful, but show promise. The services also use medical screening; but a large number of youth are inappropriately disqualified from service because of inadequate screening mechanisms for a number of specific medical conditions, such as asthma.

We who are manning the armed forces need to do a better job of separating out those among high-risk populations who will, in fact, succeed in the military. Much research has been undertaken to show the relationship between aptitude and on-the-job performance and between high school diploma attainment and first-term attrition. However, DOD needs to invest in more research to develop prescreening metrics for other recruit characteristics, such as medical and psychological well-being.

The services also need to invest in higher levels of preconditioning for their young recruits. If an individual volunteers to serve in the military, the services are obligated to ensure that he or she is on a path to success. How can these new recruits be better prepared, mentally and physically, prior to arriving for training? These issues relate to the overall quality of the force and are among those that need further study as policy makers prepare for the future of our volunteer military.

In the conscripted force, terms of enlistment were short; therefore, the services did not have to spend a lot of time training the draft-era force. The services minimized their investment in individual members of the force because those individuals departed at a high rate. Yet training budgets were high because personnel turnover was high. Today, military personnel are of higher quality and are staying in the military longer. The services are now investing in what I call lifelong learning. Should they continue on this course? I certainly think so, because the return on that investment is high.

UNDERSTANDING THE MARKET

As the paper by Hogan, Simon, and Warner argues, success in recruiting and retention requires a good understanding of the marketplace. Should the services attempt to recruit a force that reflects the socioeconomic makeup of the nation at large? Is that the right goal for the future force? As Riche and Quester demonstrated with their analysis, the makeup of today's youth population is very different from that of the past. Thus understanding the market is a dynamic process and requires more than just understanding youth demographics and the youth population.

There are many aspects of the market that the military cannot control, including unemployment, general economic conditions, and competition. Furthermore, it cannot directly control the propensity of youth to enlist in the military, although it attempts to influence propensity through advertising programs. Yet although these factors are not under the military's control, it must understand them and respond to changes in market trends. For example, the military's view of its competition has changed in recent years. We who man the force used to believe that colleges, universities, and industry were, to some degree, the competition. Today, the degree of competitiveness with these institutions has diminished, because the services are working with them through a number of partnership programs.

The Bureau of Labor Statistics reports that about 65 percent of the high school graduation class in 2002 enrolled in colleges and universities in the fall (U.S. Department of Labor 2002). Yet about 42 percent of students entering four-year institutions and 69 percent of students entering two-year institutions do not complete their degrees within six years of entering college (Berkner, He, and Cataldi 2002). The Army has begun to partner with colleges and universities to access that market. Furthermore, when university administrators realize how many students are attending postsecondary educational institutions with benefits earned through military service—such as the Montgomery GI Bill basic benefit, the Army and Navy College Funds, and other tuition assistance programs—they have more appreciation for the value of allowing recruiters on campus.

Competition with industry has also changed. Many businesses agree that hiring someone with military experience is less difficult than finding a person of the same quality elsewhere. Hiring an individual with prior military service means hiring someone with discipline, with values, and who understands teamwork. The Army is partnering with industry through a program called the Partnership for Youth Success, which offers service members positions in industry after completing their service obligations. This program is only one example of promising partnerships. In the future, the military should look for more opportunities for partnering and changing the way it has traditionally manned the force.

ADVERTISING: RECONNECTING WITH AMERICA

The notion of "reconnecting with America" has many facets. The first is to understand prospective recruits. The Army has learned a lot about 17 to 24-year-olds. Understanding what entices youth to join the military—whether patriotism, or skills, or education—is extremely important. It is equally important to know what matters to those who have influence on the youth population—their parents, teachers, coaches, and counselors.

The profile of the "typical recruit" is changing. Among the group of young men and women recruited in 2003, almost 25 percent had completed at least one semester of college (U.S. Department of Defense 2003b). Hogan, Simon, and Warner state that the secular decline in propensity to join the military is partly linked to rising college attendance, but I take exception to this point. While their perspective might be true early on, a relatively large fraction of college attendees drop out or "stop out" (leave college for a period of time), and look to the military as a viable short-term or career option. This fact is not known by the average American, many of whom view military service in general, and service in the Army in particular, as a last choice.

The military was not the last choice for an E-4, Specialist Ming Ho, whom I met recently when he was in his second week of training at Fort Leonard Wood. This young man has an electrical engineering degree from California State Polytechnic University and had worked for Sun Microsystems designing computer chips. He is 29 years old. When I asked him why he joined the Army, he said that when he was 70 years old he wanted to look back on his life and know he had made a difference. He may sound like a rare individual, but he is not; many recruits are similar to him. The Army must leverage that kind of initiative throughout the American population.

The Army has also learned that targeting its recruiting message is extremely important. A national marketing message may or may not be relevant to potential recruits depending on whether they are Hispanic, African American, Caucasian, or of another ethnic group. The same message may also be received differently in different parts of the country. What works in San Antonio may not work in Miami or Chicago, for example. To effectively recruit, the Army must make sure its message is understood by everyone across America despite ethnic and cultural differences. Doing so requires more than translating the message into a variety of languages: that approach was tried, and it does not work. Getting the Army's message across to a diverse youth population is critical; it is an area in which continual improvement is needed.

We in the Army also have to better understand how to measure the return on our investments in marketing research and advertising. We will be continually challenged from both within and outside the department as to the effectiveness of advertising. We will need to be able to demonstrate the relationship between advertising expenditures and propensity to enlist or actual number of enlistments. The Army needs to build more sophisticated models to understand this relationship.

THE RECRUITING ESTABLISHMENT

The Army recently integrated its recruiting, officer accession, officer training, and initial enlisted entry training elements under a single command that I now lead: the U.S. Army Accessions Command. This command brings together the training base and recruiting and accession processes. The greatest payoff from this restructuring has been a more holistic perspective on first-term soldier attrition—a major problem for the military in general, and the Army in particular. Attrition in the Army's 1999 cohort, during its three-year enlistment term, was about 33 percent (U.S. Department of Defense 2002). The Army's goal at one point was to reduce attrition in the training base to 12 percent. Once we began to look at attrition more broadly, however, we realized that holding training attrition (artificially) low can increase attrition later in the enlistment term. We would do better to hold first-term attrition to its pre-1990s level of, say 28–29 percent, and try to move that attrition as close as possible to the start of the pipeline, before significant training resources have been invested. To reach this goal requires the right kind of tools, both in accessing the force and conditioning recruits for success.

Adequately sizing the recruiting establishment and providing the recruiting forces with appropriate tools is essential to effective recruiting. It is also a very expensive element of manning the force. Both the Army and Navy have recently reduced the size of their recruiting force. If recruiting goals do not change significantly, by 2005 the Army's recruiting force will be 20 percent smaller than it was in 2003. It is critical, however, not to cut these resources too far—to understand the minimum level required to sustain the force. If recruiting skills are lost, it takes a tremendous amount of time to recoup those lost skills—to train the right kind of person with the right kind of commitment, who can make 200 phone calls, get 199 negative responses, and not be discouraged. But the Army also needs to examine the enlistment process in its entirety and look for opportunities to speed up the process and to reduce costs, without diminishing effectiveness.

Another concept for future consideration is recruiting stations without walls. Running 2,162 Army recruiting stations across America is expensive. The Army must take better advantage of mobile recruiting efforts and Internet capabilities that are currently very successful. Today's youth are visual people. They gather information from visual media more so than any other source. As a result, the Internet and television will be important ways to reach future recruits. The Army runs an Internet chat room five days a week using 38 recruiters. The conversion rate from these leads is about 12 percent, compared with a conversion rate of about 4 percent using more traditional recruiting means (U.S. Department of Defense 2003a).

Innovation in recruiting is essential. Today's youth are often frightened to walk into a recruiting station. They are convinced that they will not be able to leave without signing a contract. That perspective is largely due to the gap in understanding between the military and the American people that Hogan, Simon, and Warner talked about—a result of the diminishing number of veterans in communities today. We who are responsible for manning the force need to leverage innovative recruiting approaches even more in the future and understand how they can help us grow and sustain our force.

An all-volunteer force—an *all-recruited* volunteer force—is never going to be inexpensive. It has to compete in the marketplace and it has to be fairly compensated. The professionalism of the noncommissioned officers at the service training bases and recruiting stations is exceptional. These individuals perform important and demanding work and should be recognized and rewarded. But more important is the result of their work: the quality force we have today, some 30 years after the all-volunteer force began—a force that is the best this nation has ever had and one that continues to meet the challenges placed before it.

It's a great day to be a soldier.

REFERENCES

Berkner, Lutz, Shirley He, and Emily Forrest Cataldi. 2002. *See* U.S. Department of Education 2002.

U.S. Department of Defense. 2002. Unpublished recruiting data. Fort Knox, Ky.: U.S. Army Recruiting Command.

———. 2003a. Unpublished recruiting data. Fort Knox, Ky.: U.S. Army Recruiting Command.

———. 2003b. Unpublished recruiting data. Fort Monroe, Va.: U.S. Army Accessions Command.

U.S. Department of Education. 2002. *Descriptive summary of 1995-96 beginning post secondary students: Six years later,* by Lutz Berkner, Shirley He, and Emily Forrest Cataldi. December. Washington, D.C.: National Center for Education Statistics.

U.S. Department of Labor. 2002. *College enrollment and work activity of 2002 high school graduates.* Press release. June 25. Washington, D.C.: Bureau of Labor Statistics.

★ ★ ★ ★ ★

GERRY HOEWING

The military should be proud of both the success of the volunteer force concept and of the volunteers themselves. One does not have to look any further than the daily newspaper to see how fantastic and how committed these young men and women are. I do not believe the nation could have accomplished what it did in Afghanistan or in Iraq without the type of talent and motivation that exists in our servicemen and servicewomen.

It is also important to recognize that these service members are people who want to serve. They want to be in uniform, wearing, as our Chief of Naval Operations likes to call it, the "cloth of the nation." These are people with more education, with more experience, and, quite frankly, of higher quality than we have ever seen in the military before. Our force's outstanding readiness is directly attributable to that fact.

Indeed, the Office of the Deputy Under Secretary of Defense for Military Personnel Policy recently published a report on manpower quality in the all-volunteer force. It was partially prompted by speculation from outside the Department of Defense that the military included a disproportionate number of individuals from disadvantaged educational backgrounds. The report, issued in January 2003, contradicted this perception, stating, "Today's military is . . . smarter than the general population: over 90 percent of new recruits have a high school diploma while only 75 percent of American youth do; 67 percent score in the upper half of the enlistment (math/verbal aptitude) test. These attributes translate to lower attrition, faster training, and higher performance" (U.S. Department of Defense 2003).

Naturally, this finding came as no surprise to those of us in the Navy who witness firsthand the accomplishments of our sailors in training and in the fleet, as they operate complex pieces of machinery and master increasingly sophisticated war-fighting technology. The high caliber of recruits has enabled the Navy not only to meet, but also to exceed, mandated quality standards in its accessions. Fully 94 percent of Navy accessions in fiscal year 2003 were high school diploma graduates, and 66 percent of them scored in the top half of the Armed Forces Qualification Test (AFQT). These results reflect an increase from the fiscal year 2002 levels of 92 and 65 percent, respectively. David Armor and Paul Sackett discuss the link between manpower quality and performance (chapter 6, this volume). I believe that the performance of sailors in the Navy today demonstrates the value of high-quality recruits. I want to begin this discussion where Armor and Sackett did, by addressing the relationship between the AFQT and quality, in terms of training and job performance.

AFQT AND TRAINING PERFORMANCE

The relationship between AFQT scores and training performance is the primary rationale for the aptitude portion of the Navy's selection standards. It provides the basis for our service's validation research and guides its classification system. While figure 1 in the Armor and Sackett paper reports a high correlation between AFQT and training performance, a few important caveats are associated with that relationship.

First, a critical intervening variable between cognitive ability and performance is matching the right person to the right job. Performance is optimized when an individual is moderately challenged in a job, and it will be suboptimal when a person is either understimulated or overwhelmed by a job's demands. Not every job is the same, and not every sailor is equally challenged.

People are best assigned to jobs that correspond to their ability level. The Navy has developed a new classification technology to match ability and job demands using expected-performance algorithms. These algorithms will be augmented with another new program for assessing applicant job preferences and matching those preferences with Navy jobs. Research indicates that using job preferences, together with sailor aptitude, during job assignment increases job satisfaction, which reduces attrition and increases performance (Ali, Blanco, and Buclatin 1998; Schmitz and Nord 1991).

Second, the relationship between AFQT scores and performance, as represented in Armor and Sackett's figure, is based on performance in an aggregation of jobs. Yet this relationship is not necessarily true for every job individually. Cognitive ability, as measured by the AFQT, is a good predictor of general job performance. On the other hand, technical aptitude—as measured by other parts of the Armed Serviced Vocational Aptitude Battery (ASVAB)—can be a better predictor of training success for specific jobs and is an important component of the Navy's classification composites. The new data being used to renormalize the ASVAB reveal a slight decline in technical aptitudes in the youth population (Segall forthcoming). Research will be needed to better understand the implications of this trend as weapon-systems technology becomes increasingly sophisticated.

AFQT AND JOB PERFORMANCE

Of course, the ultimate criterion for determining recruiting effectiveness is on-the-job performance. The Joint Services Job Performance Measurement Project was a crucial study for linking manpower quality and on-the-job performance, because it achieved the difficult task of capturing performance in a realistic setting rather than the contrived setting of a schoolroom (Green and Mavor 1994).

Armor and Sackett are quick to point out that the hands-on job performance assessment approach espoused in the study highlights "the 'can do,' rather than the 'will do,' aspects of performance. The assumption is that incumbents will give their best effort when being observed during the HOPT [hands-on performance testing]." Armor and Sackett assert, "That an incumbent can perform a task correctly when observed is no guarantee that the same level of performance will be exhibited on a day-to-day basis without similar close observation." Another important finding of the joint study is that job performance mirrors training performance as it relates to personnel quality. The lesson for the military services is that given good manpower quality, optimal job assignment, and effective training, good job performance will result.

What is quality and performance if they are not linked to readiness? Readiness is the military's bottom line, if you will—the ultimate measure of its effectiveness as an organization. It is conceptually distinct from performance, though related: "performance" describes how well our people do their jobs, while "readiness" describes how well that performance contributes to combat capability. Manpower quality is an important factor in determining personnel readiness because of its relationship to training success and attrition. Obviously, these factors directly contribute to war-fighting capabilities and preparedness, which are at the heart of what the Department of Defense does as an institution. In effect, then, manpower quality is the prerequisite of personnel readiness. It is the foundation of effective personnel classification, training success, retention, and on-the-job performance.

TRENDS IN QUALITY

Given the evidence regarding the relationship between manpower quality and performance, it is clear that the services depend on quality in the youth population to reach their accession goals and to meet their mission requirements. The prospects of maintaining quality levels in the future appear promising. As Armor and Sackett make clear, "On the potential supply side, the projected trends in the number of youth, high school graduation rates, and aptitudes suggest there are sufficient numbers of high-quality youth in the population at large, and those numbers should remain adequate for at least the next 10 years."

I am heartened by these findings but not surprised. I believe that the potential for future recruit quality is not only a product of better education and aptitude, but also a reflection of the growing importance of the idea of service to country. Service has tremendous meaning right now, and the Department of Defense is able to leverage that circumstance through many of its processes.

A caveat related to this discussion is that some studies — including one in particular conducted by the Herman Group — suggest that the nation could face a shortage of skilled labor on the magnitude of 10 million or more people in the next 10 years (Herman, Olivo, and Gioia 2003, 49). So in spite of the fact that the numbers are good, the quality is good, and propensity to enlist remains good, I believe some real challenges await us in the future when it comes to getting the right skill mix and the right quality of recruit into the service.

NAVY MANPOWER INITIATIVES

In the Navy we are hard at work on many initiatives to address the challenges described above. First and foremost, we are emphasizing diversity. We are taking, for the first time ever, a strategic approach. The Navy is endeavoring to recruit and retain the absolute best that the United States has to offer, including people of all races and ethnic backgrounds. We know from the demographics that we are going to have to continue to improve in these efforts, particularly in the officer ranks, in order to capitalize on the diversity that is America.

Performance is another focus area. I have discussed performance as it relates to training and to the quality that is available in the civilian youth population. The Navy ties virtually everything it does — in advancement programs, force-shaping programs, and even new compensation programs — to performance. It can afford to do this, thanks in no small part to the high retention levels it is enjoying right now. The Navy has a tremendous opportunity to be selective about whom it recruits and whom it retains. Therefore, it has a great opportunity to secure not only a high-quality force, but a high quality of service in that force.

In the future, the Navy leadership believes that both goals—a high-quality force and a high quality of service—will be met by a new system we call Sea Warrior. Sea Warrior is a new human capital management system currently under development that recognizes the importance of the human resource in combat capability. Underpinning Sea Warrior are three very exciting programs aimed at providing the Navy with the right sailors, in the right job, at the right time, and with the right skills. These programs are as follows: Improving the Navy's Workforce; Revolution in Training; and the Career Management System (figure 1).

FIGURE 1. SEA WARRIOR: ENABLING INITIATIVES

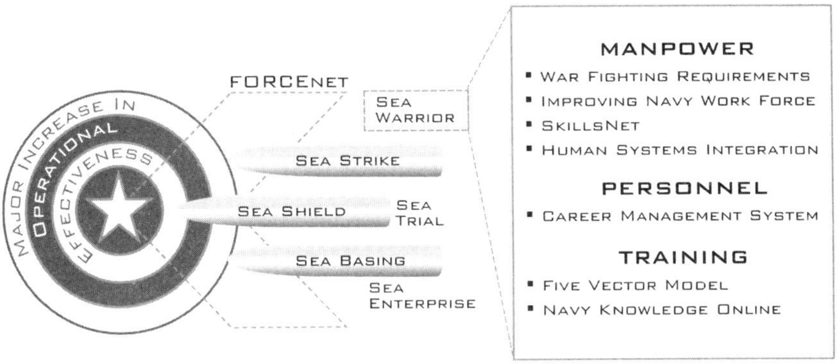

Under Improving the Navy's Workforce, our service is identifying, for virtually every job in the Navy—officer, enlisted, and soon civilian—the tasks that we expect the incumbent of that job to perform. Once we know what tasks are to be accomplished, we can then determine what knowledge, skills, abilities, and tools the incumbent needs to possess in order to be successful. Under the Revolution in Training, we are identifying the individual knowledge, skills, and abilities possessed by every sailor in the Navy. Between these two efforts, embodied in the Career Management System, detailed databases and computerized intelligent agents will be used to make the most appropriate matches between sailors and jobs.

Through Sea Warrior, the Navy will be able to identify sailors' precise capabilities and match them to well-articulated job requirements in a way that far exceeds the simplistic criteria used today. What Sea Warrior will give the Navy is the power that comes from allowing individual choice. Sailors will be involved in the career decision process from the beginning. They will be involved in their own career path development, to include career path choices that are optimal for their specific situations and families.

There will be other benefits to Sea Warrior as well. It will help to optimize sailor performance because Navy platforms and systems will be designed around the war fighter from the outset. It will translate the mission-essential tasks assigned to striking groups into a more precise and easily manageable language. It will implement different types of incentives and flexible rotation dates and move the Navy toward a job-based compensation system. In short, Sea Warrior is a man-power, personnel, and training management system that employs cutting-edge systems and technology to shape the force and achieve the right skill mix. It imposes business efficiency in the production and delivery of optimally trained sailors—both active and reserve—to an optimally manned fleet. The result will be a dramatic increase in operational effectiveness.

Sea Warrior is also connected to something about which the Chief of Naval Operations is so proud: "covenant leadership." Put simply, covenant leadership exists when leaders are empowered to personally invest themselves and stay involved in the growth and development of their people. Personnel develop-ment bolsters the Navy's ability to meet the combat capabilities required in the future. Sea Warrior's focus is on developing individuals' capabilities beginning the moment they walk into a recruiting office through their assignments as mas-ter chiefs or flag officers, using a career continuum of training and education that gives them the tools they need to operate in an increasingly demanding and dynamic environment.

HIGH SCHOOL EXIT EXAMS

Let me close with comments on two other topics covered by Armor and Sackett. The first relates to high school exit exams. The authors present the new devel-opment in high school graduation credentials as a challenge for the Department of Defense, "because it affects the meaning of high school graduation." On the contrary, I see it as an opportunity to refine accessions policy. Regardless of the characterization of a student's high school completion by one state versus another, the student's quality is still the same. Potential recruits are still the same people, but now one more level of definition is available for use in select-ing among them. Instead of just using high school diploma status as the selec-tion criteria, the services will have the opportunity to consider the additional category of certificates of completion. The expanded definition of educational status may reflect different levels of personal initiative, discipline, and commit-ment that translate into important attrition-related outcomes. The challenge will be in establishing standards for evaluating these expanded definitions. I concur with the recommendation for further research into attrition patterns for the dif-ferent educational alternatives.

RENORMALIZING THE ASVAB

The other topic I would like to address is the current effort to renormalize the ASVAB, which I believe is necessary. The ASVAB is the psychometric tool used to measure recruit aptitude for technical training. Renormalizing the tool will align the services' scale of recruit quality to more accurately represent the cur-rent youth population. This step is critical for maintaining accuracy in recruit-ing metrics, since the current norms are based on the 1980 youth population.

The Navy sees this effort as a "good news" story, as the need for renormaliza-tion reflects the fact that the American youth population is getting smarter. Renormalizing the ASVAB is good testing practice. It merely constitutes a recalibration, and, like any other tool, the ASVAB needs to be recalibrated periodically. Our success in exceeding current quality standards should ensure that when the ASVAB is renormalized, the Navy will continue to meet the standards set in the department's planning guidance.

Armor and Sackett are correct that renormalizing the ASVAB will alter qualification rates, but we can control this impact through policy modifications. Policy makers and force planners should remember, as the armed forces make the transition to the new scale, that the organization's greatest imperative is maintaining performance; quality standards exist for that purpose. Any changes in qualification rates that occur as a result of renormalizing will not reflect actual changes in quality, but only in the scale by which it is measured.

CONCLUSION

Professors Armor and Sackett did an outstanding job wrapping their minds around some very exciting and very challenging issues affecting the future quality of the all-volunteer force. Key to their arguments is the distinction they make between what individuals "can do," that is, their maximal performance, and what they "will do," which is typical performance. Maximal performance is determined not only by one's abilities, but also by motivation, and motivation is the critical element of the all-volunteer force.

Without motivation, individuals are unlikely to reach their performance potential, and the relationship between quality and performance is ultimately degraded. The importance of motivation is perhaps the greatest argument for maintaining the way the military does business: the all-volunteer force produces motivated, quality volunteers. When properly classified, well-trained, and provided with ample resources, these volunteers perform to the very best of their ability. It is my belief that the all-volunteer force is delivering exactly what this nation needs, and that it is here to stay. The nation is enormously proud of its accomplishments.

REFERENCES

Ali, Aghar Iqbal, Tom Blanco, and Ben Buclatin. 1998. Theory and methodology goal network programs: A specialized algorithm and an application. *European Journal of Operations Research* 106: 191–97.

Green, Bert F., and Anne S. Mavor, eds. 1994. *Modeling cost and performance for military enlistment.* Washington, D.C.: National Academies Press.

Herman, Roger E., Tom Olivo, and Joyce Gioia. 2003. *Impending crisis.* Winchester, Va.: Oakhill Press.

Schmitz, Edward J., and Roy D. Nord. 1991. The Army's enlisted personnel allocation system. In *The economic benefits of predicting job performance*, 49–72. Edited by J. Zeidner and C. D. Johnson. New York: Praeger.

Segall, Daniel O. Forthcoming. *Development and evaluation of the 1997 ASVAB score scale.* Report no. V3.7.06. Arlington, Va.: Defense Manpower Data Center.

U.S. Department of Defense. 2003. *Conscription threatens hard-won achievements and military readiness.* Washington, D.C.: Office of the Under Secretary of Defense (Personnel and Readiness).

$\star \star \star \star \star$

GARRY L. PARKS

I consider it a great privilege to contribute to this celebration of 30 years of the all-volunteer force, and I welcome the opportunity to comment on the interesting chapter by Dr. Martha Farnsworth Riche and Dr. Aline Quester (chapter 7, this volume), which examines the impact of socioeconomic changes on the all-volunteer force—past, present, and future. With regard to the past, part 1 of this volume describes, in a fascinating level of detail, the background of the all-volunteer force and how it arrived at where it is today.

The papers in part 2 examine various challenges in recruiting and retention. Considering these challenges brings to mind a comment made by Christopher Jehn that I find worth repeating, as it reflects my own experiences. Jehn made the observation that "I have seen smart, I have seen dumb, and smart is way better." Thirty years ago, I was a company commander at Marine Corps Recruit Depot Parris Island. The year was 1973. It was evident to me then, and it is even clearer to me today: smart is way better. Thanks to the all-volunteer force, today our nation's military is far, far better than it was 30 years ago.

The most striking success of the all-volunteer force has been evident in the performance of America's military in Desert Shield, Desert Storm, and most recently in operations in Afghanistan and Iraq. The force's success on the battlefield, the small number of casualties, and the professionalism and competence of our service members, are the result, in part, of improved training and better-motivated servicemen and servicewomen who create fewer disciplinary problems than existed in the days of conscription.

Longer first-term enlistment contracts have magnified the productivity effects of improvements to training and have given taxpayers a higher return on training dollars. Military effectiveness has increased because the services are focused on attracting the best that our nation has to offer. The armed forces are now more selective. The services need fewer recruits than they did during the draft and can therefore focus recruiting efforts on high-quality youth. Improvements in retention mean that our force is more mature and more experienced—another factor that has increased effectiveness.

In addition to celebrating the past 30 years, this volume also looks forward. I had an opportunity a few years ago to address an audience composed mostly of Marines, and I offered some comments about the quality of our all-volunteer force. I said, "We have the best Marine Corps today that I have seen since I have been on active duty and, I would submit, since there has been a U.S. Marine Corps." Perhaps not surprisingly, a retired gunnery sergeant in the back of the audience said, "But, sir, the corps was pretty darn good when I was in."

This Marine's pride was evident, and his thinking logical and appropriate. Nevertheless, my view, on balance, is that the success of the all-volunteer force, as it has evolved over the past 30 years has been phenomenal. That said, when we celebrate the 60th anniversary of the all-volunteer force in 2033, our focus should be on the quality of America's military at that time. Hopefully, we will all look back and be able to note the improvements that we have made since 2003 and how much better the all-volunteer force has become in those 30 years.

RECRUITING SUCCESSES AND CHALLENGES

The Gallup Poll reports that in 1975 the American people gave the military services a 58 percent confidence and approval rating. By 2002 that same rating had risen to 79 percent (The Gallup Organization 2003). The tragedy our nation experienced on September 11, 2001, has given us a profoundly deep sense of nationalism. We all see it. We all feel it. Military recruiters are seeing it as well. They are encountering more cooperation from communities across our nation, particularly from secondary schools. Although some of this cooperation is an outgrowth of congressional mandate, much of it is because the services and their recruiters are simply being creative in reaching out to the appropriate institutions and organizations. Concurrently, these institutions are recognizing the military's value in a way that they perhaps did not fully appreciate in the recent past. Similarly, the American people see more clearly what service members are contributing to this nation's freedom. Unfortunately, that success does not always translate into a great surge of enlistment interest, and when it does, it may not result in a great number of fully qualified applicants.

Marine recruiters have enjoyed great success with the Hispanic community, the fastest growing segment of the U.S. population. Relative to recruits of other backgrounds, Hispanics have much lower training attrition over the entire first term of service (Hattiangadi, Lee, and Quester 2004, 61–71). This statistic is very encouraging and presents an opportunity that must be more fully taken advantage of by the service recruiting commands. An obvious question before military recruiters is how to maximize success with Hispanic recruitment. I think that each military service is looking at this challenge and trying to be creative; yet they need to continue to explore new avenues. Efforts to date have resulted in a "good news" story, both for Hispanic recruits and for the military services. Force planners can look at this population as a positive indicator of what lies ahead for the all-volunteer force as our country's demographics continue to change.

The positive impact that women have had on our military and on the success of the all-volunteer force is another "good news" story. The number of servicewomen in our nation's military has expanded markedly in the past several decades, and they play a much more pronounced role than they did 30 years ago. On balance, the changes that were made to allow women to play a greater role in the military were proper changes. We as a nation are better for having advanced the contributions of women in America's military.

Let me turn to the topic of diversity in the force — of balancing diversity represented in society writ large with the desired diversity of the all-volunteer force. As Riche and Quester state in their paper, the most notable demographic difference between the military and the civilian work force is the youthful nature of the all-volunteer force, not differences in racial or ethnic composition. They also note that ethnic identifications are beginning to blur (youth often check more than one ethnic category when asked to identify their background), which changes the dynamic of the diversity comparison. A military that mirrors America is an admirable goal, yet it is a goal that is difficult to achieve.

Moreover, it will not necessarily ensure a ready force. Today's military requires a population that is smarter than a pure cross section of America. It also requires a more physically fit population than is found in the general public. The services need to concentrate on ensuring that they have the right quantity of the right quality enlistees to sustain the all-volunteer force, not simply a random sample from the larger society.

There are other types of recruiting challenges that the military faces — driven not by ethnicity or gender, but by shortages in critical skills. One of the challenges the services have faced during the last few years, for example, is the need for more linguists, driven primarily by the global war on terrorism. At issue is how the services can overcome their recruiting shortfall in this important area. I will share a story from a couple of years ago about an individual managing recruiting in the San Francisco area. He came to me and said, "I need a Chinese linguist so I can recruit more Chinese-Americans." Knowing the end state he sought, I approached the military occupational field sponsor and said, "We need a Chinese linguist." The field sponsor said he could not spare one because Chinese linguists were in such short supply throughout the service.

What is the point of this recollection? Simply stated, if the department had made available just one Chinese linguist, it could have recruited perhaps another 25 or more Chinese speakers by the end of that year. Sometimes things are looked at with blinders on, and we in the recruiting business must work to counter those tendencies. I bring this up because today the Department of Defense still does not have enough linguists, currently exemplified by the shortage of Arabic speakers.

Connecting with the eligible population has always been a challenge from the recruiting standpoint. The armed forces meet that challenge by advertising what they are about. Understanding who constitutes the enlistment-age population and what motivates them are the keys to successful recruiting. Today's young people surf the Internet, yet remain anonymous in their quest for service information. Their approach is similar to that taken by we older Americans when we are going to buy a car: we often use the Internet to assist us in learning the price of an automobile and its options before we talk to the salesman, or even before we enter the dealership. That is what these young people are doing today: using the Internet to obtain information before they speak to a recruiter.

THE RECRUITER

Although we are celebrating the success of the all-volunteer force, I would underscore that this force is a delicate ecosystem. We must be very careful if we make significant changes because, much like changes to the balance resident in nature, they can have unintended consequences in later years. The one change that, in my opinion, should not be entertained is "who the recruiters are." In order to project an appropriate image, the Marine Corps assigns some of its very best people to recruiting duty; that is how we approach it in my service. We put top-notch officers and noncommissioned officers on the streets of America and task them with the mission of recruiting and sustaining our force. A young person considering military service today, or at least exploring that option, is not thinking about the job that is 10 years hence, and is certainly not thinking about retirement. Instead, the potential recruit is looking at an individual, the

156 ★
SUSTAINING THE FORCE: RECRUITING AND RETENTION

recruiter, and asking, "Do I want to be like him or her?" If we continue to place the proper role models in the heartland of our country—and those role models are the best noncommissioned officers in each of our services—then youth will answer this question affirmatively, and we will succeed in attracting the best young men and women that our nation has to offer.

In terms of the composition of the recruiter force, I would approach with caution the idea of civilian recruiters. Perhaps civilians could be incorporated into the overall recruiting process to replace some active duty service members, but a civilian should not be the first face-to-face contact for a potential recruit. Recruits need to see, meet with, and be nurtured by a uniformed military member when they are discussing enlistment opportunities for the first time.

Similarly, I do not advocate centralized or "joint service" recruiting. Each service has a unique ethos and culture, and the respective recruiters project that image. A person who is attracted to one service is not necessarily attracted to another. By continuing to make each service responsible for recruiting its future members, the department attracts those interested in exploring the different service cultures. A joint recruiting system or one that relies on civilian recruiters could jeopardize current recruiting success.

TRENDS IN YOUTH EDUCATION

The success of the all-volunteer force has in part been due to the requirement for tier 1 recruits, primarily those who hold a traditional high school diploma. I have two concerns about the findings on educational attainment reported by Riche and Quester. First, while federal projections for high school graduation rates may appear good, these graduation measures include tier 2 recruits (that is, recruits who hold General Educational Development [GED] certificates). The projections additionally suggest that the proportion of young people with regular high school diplomas may be falling and that the proportion with GEDs is increasing.

The military places youth with GEDs in tier 2 because it has not had good experiences with recruits with GED backgrounds. Over the last decade, for example, Marine Corps first-term attrition rates were 31 percent for traditional high school graduates and 53 percent for those with GEDs (Hattiangadi, Lee, and Quester 2004, 14). Suggestions that the Defense Department pay more attention to "stay in school" efforts should be strongly considered since those who graduate with a traditional high school diploma have a much higher probability of completing their first enlistment term. The department needs to ensure that recruiters will not have greater difficulty finding youth who meet enlistment standards in the future.

Additionally, our nation has become a more mobile society, which has spawned several nontraditional educational forums. One of these is home schooling. The Department of Defense has extended the definition of tier 1 to include recruits with a home-schooling background on a trial basis. Should we incorporate this change permanently? This question is a piece of the larger challenge of defining what it means to be a high school graduate. Several criteria have to be met before the military will be able to equate completion of alternative programs to a regular high school diploma. Some educational programs, including home schooling, may be better than a traditional program of instruction at keeping students interested enough in school to graduate; yet, at the same time, others may not be. How should the services achieve balance between the variety of educational programs available and what they need to maintain their quality standards?

THE INFLUENCE OF VETERANS

The declining number of veterans in the population could certainly have a negative effect on the military's ability to recruit in the future. Today, veterans make up only about 13 percent of the U.S. population, and of that number, 27 percent are 65 or older (U.S. Department of Veterans Affairs 2000). Furthermore, I am sad to say, we are losing many of these great veterans every day. In the 18 to 64-year-old population group, less than 10 percent of Americans are veterans. Despite these statistics, however, my experience has been that most families are not antimilitary, though many are ill informed. One reason is that the dwindling veteran population is not there to sit on the back porch and relate to youngsters the value of a positive military experience. Further, veterans, perhaps better than anyone, can explain the value of the freedoms that we enjoy in this country and what it is like to live in a foreign land without those freedoms. Unfortunately, the vulnerability of our country, and thus those freedoms, was brought home to Americans tenfold on September 11, 2001.

These comments about veterans also relate to advertising. Army General John Vessey has remarked on the need to ensure that young men and women understand that they join the military to fight (chapter 16, this volume). Veterans can help the armed forces' advertising effort in this regard. But I think the military services also need to reinforce an understanding of why the nation is bringing people into its service and how the nation may have to employ them. The services must let the public know why taxpayer dollars are obligated to maintain an all-volunteer force. Servicemen and servicewomen are recruited, trained, and equipped to guarantee the nation's freedom, and to fight and win the nation's wars when necessary.

I believe that the Department of Defense needs to do everything it possibly can to ensure that the citizens of our country understand that military service is the ultimate expression of public service. That is to say, the department must articulate through multiple means the dedication that is required by our military service members and the sacrifices each of them makes on our nation's behalf. Those who make these sacrifices are precious assets, and all Americans need to understand this. We as a nation need to continue to show our appreciation through our thoughts and actions.

EXPECTATIONS

I will conclude by commenting on an issue concerning quality of life—what I categorically refer to as "expectations." American society and the young people that the armed services recruit today have far greater material expectations than generations past. They have been raised in, and are surrounded by, an environment that provides many material things for them. These are the young people who make up the recruit population today and who will make up the military ranks tomorrow. Therefore, the department needs to be attuned to youths' expectations in a number of different areas—a wide selection of leisure time activities, access to the Internet, and a variety of outlets for consumer goods, for example. Yet quality of life goes well beyond meeting the material expectations of today's youth. The Department of Defense cannot realistically afford everything that these youngsters may expect. However, consideration of what young people actually need and attentiveness to their expectations will help enhance success on the battlefield.

In closing, Lieutenant General Cavin noted in his commentary (part 2, this volume) that America's military is an all-recruited volunteer force. I cannot emphasize enough the importance of that observation. Wonderful young men and women across America serve as military recruiters. They work extremely long hours to perform a demanding, dynamic, and vitally important role in manning the all-volunteer force. This volume celebrates the success of our all-recruited force. If we in the military services continue to view recruitment as a *mission* at which we simply cannot fail, then we will also celebrate the success of the all-volunteer force tomorrow.

The department's proactive recruiting outreach should highlight the opportunities that are available for the children of our nation through military service. The military offers to the youth of our country what American mothers and fathers want for their children: incentive to stay in school and graduate with at least a high school diploma, advanced educational opportunities, physical fitness, a strong work ethic, activity in communities and schools, and a drug-free environment. The services must broadcast this message more effectively. They must project it in a way that makes young people want to join the military and makes their parents confident about their choice.

It has been my pleasure, over the last 30 years, to serve with what I think are the finest people that our country has to offer. I applaud the all-volunteer force.

REFERENCES

The Gallup Organization. 2003. *Military, police top Gallup's annual confidence in institutions poll.* Gallup News Service. June 19. http://www.gallup.com.

Hattiangadi, Anita U., Gary Lee, and Aline Quester. 2004. *Recruiting Hispanics: The Marine Corps experience.* D000907.A2. Alexandria, Va.: Center for Naval Analyses.

U.S. Department of Veterans Affairs. 2000. Data tabulations from Census 2000. http://www.va.gov/vetdata/Census2000/c2kbr-22.pdf.

KENNETH T. VENUTO

The U.S. Coast Guard is one of five branches of the U.S. armed forces and falls under the jurisdiction of the U.S. Department of Homeland Security. During the period between 1967 and 2002, the Coast Guard was part of the U.S. Department of Transportation. The Coast Guard is the country's oldest continuous seagoing service, with responsibilities that include maritime security and safety, search and rescue, maritime law enforcement, aid to navigation, ice breaking, environmental protection, port security, and military readiness. The Coast Guard's fiscal year 2003 recruiting requirement of 5,375 active duty and reserve personnel represented less than 2 percent of the annual recruiting requirements of the armed services (U.S. Department of Homeland Security 2003), and with its mission profile has a very different recruiting challenge. It is also worth noting that the Coast Guard has always been an "all-volunteer force" and has far more than 30 years of experience in that environment.

The Coast Guard is organized such that the assistant commandant for human resources is responsible for recruiting, personnel management, and training for all segments of the work force—active duty, reserve, and civilian—and for military health care. In order to accomplish its missions, the Coast Guard's 39,000 active duty men and women, 8,000 reservists, 7,000 civilians, and 35,000 auxiliary volunteers serve in a variety of job fields ranging from shipboard operators to aviators, communication specialists to small-boat operators, personnel specialists to contracting officers, and lawyers to electronic technicians.

The Coast Guard recruited 4,488 young men and women in fiscal year 2003 to sustain its active duty force level of 39,000. Recruiting continued to be successful, as 92 percent of new recruits hold traditional high school diplomas and 69 percent scored in the upper half of the Armed Forces Qualification Test (U.S. Department of Homeland Security 2003)—results above the quality benchmarks of 90 and 65 percent, respectively, established by the Department of Defense.

The Coast Guard, during an average day, will

- provide continuous maritime security in the nation's ports and waterways
- conduct 109 search-and-rescue cases
- save 10 lives
- assist 192 people in distress
- protect $2,791,841 in property
- launch 396 small-boat missions
- launch 164 aircraft missions, logging 324 hours
- board 144 vessels
- seize 169 pounds of marijuana and 306 pounds of cocaine worth $9,589,000
- interdict and rescue 14 illegal immigrants
- board 100 large vessels for port safety checks
- respond to 20 oil or hazardous chemical spills totaling 2,800 gallons
- service 135 aids to navigation (U.S. Department of Homeland Security 2004)

QUALITY, RECRUITING, AND RETENTION

The chapter by Hogan, Simon, and Warner (chapter 5, this volume) summarizes the issues and pressures we in the armed forces need to be concerned about as we look beyond this 30th year of experience with the all-volunteer force. My conclusion is that the retention of high-performing, highly committed servicemen and servicewomen should be our preeminent goal. However, retaining people increases the complexity of the personnel management systems—so there is no free lunch on the horizon.

I think Hogan, Simon, and Warner say it well in a key conclusion in their paper: "Allow voluntary choice where possible, and care for personnel where it is not." Indeed, our experience in the Coast Guard is that one size does not fit all, and we strive to enable our people to make their own rational, informed career decisions wherever possible.

Armor and Sackett (chapter 6, this volume) alert us to an equally powerful axiom: quality is not cheap. The preceding chapters have described the complexities involved in sustaining a high-quality force. Given these complexities, we in the field of personnel management need to be particularly careful about how we define and measure the multiple dimensions of what we call quality.

In the Coast Guard, our reference variable is *readiness*. In our multi-mission service, we define readiness in terms of the capability we have just before we use it. Our use of the term readiness is quite expansive and includes the systems we use to manage the business as well as the systems we use to conduct operations. Mission performance consumes readiness, which must then be replenished. By measuring in this way, we can calibrate prevention, response, and mitigation activities. Our experience suggests that any definition of force quality must be linked to, and eventually predictive of, readiness.

Riche and Quester (chapter 7, this volume) point to the challenges the services will continue to face because of social and economic changes in the nation in general, and specifically as the services interact with society at large. The market for talent will change continually and will provide the armed forces with new challenges every day, just when we thought we could declare the all-volunteer force a victory.

LESSONS FROM THE COAST GUARD

To supplement the valuable lessons and challenges described in the previous chapters, I offer a few observations that come from the Coast Guard's long experience recruiting and retaining an all-volunteer force.

THE ROLE OF LEADERSHIP IN FORCE QUALITY

Recruiting talented individuals with the right aptitude is the Coast Guard's starting point in achieving force quality. Selecting the best recruits and retaining the best of the best are both part of the quality equation. But in this equation, there is also a significant role for leadership. Units composed of tremendously capable people can suffer wild swings in readiness or performance based on the quality of the leadership they are provided. Unit cohesion, coherence and consistency of action, trust in colleagues, trust in leadership, and trust in the organization are all influenced by leadership. Many researchers conclude that these factors are the great differentiators between the effectiveness of the U.S. armed forces and those of other nations.

Perhaps as we study in more depth the link between quality and performance, we will discover that there are multiple dimensions of quality — such as "potential and kinetic" or "latent and active" — that will help us understand the role of leadership in developing quality in situ. Currently quality is viewed mostly as an innate characteristic of a work force.

CAUTION DEMANDED AS THE JOURNEY CONTINUES

When I think about change — and change is important — I have to reflect on a remark made by Lieutenant General Parks. We of the all-volunteer force live in a delicate ecosystem. Changes to foundational structures, such as compensation and other force-shaping tools, must be undertaken with caution and with a full understanding of the complexities of those structures. There will be unintended consequences to any change we make, many of which will not be predictable. It will challenge all of us to predict and mitigate any adverse effects that occur and to watch vigilantly for signals of unintended consequences we could not predict. There are no perfect solutions. In some respects, I wonder if, despite our best efforts, we merely transform problems. The seeds of tomorrow's challenges may lie in the solutions we impose today.

INSTITUTIONAL VERSUS OCCUPATIONAL FORCES

Just like our colleagues in the other services, the leaders of the Coast Guard are engaged in a thoughtful discussion about the nature of our forces. We sometimes wonder if we have strayed too far toward Charlie Moskos's description of an occupational, as opposed to an institutional, model (chapter 3, this volume). Is the officer corps becoming so overspecialized that there will inevitably be an insufficient number of officers with the breadth of experience necessary to provide a base of institutional knowledge and service leadership? Finding individuals with sufficiently broad experience to lead is increasingly challenging. We create outstanding managers with the necessary skills to operate the Coast Guard as a business, but that is not enough. We must also develop outstanding leaders who create and communicate a vision for the organization, who communicate organizational values, and who inspire commitment and dedication from our service members. Achieving the right balance between creating a technically specialized work force and fostering leadership development will be a significant and growing challenge. I predict we will be discussing this challenge in greater detail on the 40th anniversary of the all-volunteer force.

LINKING QUALITY TO MISSION ACCOMPLISHMENT: RESULTS

As I mentioned above, assessing force quality is crucial to managing human capital. A clear understanding of the linkage between quality and results — however those results are measured — is an absolute necessity if the services are to maintain their credibility and ensure mission success.

A quality force and quality leaders are crucial to mission performance. The armed services must acknowledge that the compensation, personnel support, and human resource management systems they employ can affect their readiness to perform their missions as much as the traditional facets of readiness. Our collective experience in managing the all-volunteer force has been successful, but the years ahead will continue to present great challenges. We in the armed forces must remain vigilant and attentive to work force needs that will keep recruitment and retention of the best people high, and keep our forces ready and able to perform for America.

REFERENCES

U.S. Department of Homeland Security. 2003. Recruiting statistics. Washington, D.C.: United States Coast Guard, Office of the Assistant Commandant for Human Resources.

———. 2004. U.S. Coast Guard mission statistics. http://www.uscg.mil/overview/ [May 2004].

PART III

RESERVE COMPONENT CONTRIBUTIONS TO THE ALL-VOLUNTEER FORCE

INTRODUCTION

WILLIAM A. NAVAS JR.

Looking back on some of our nation's most traumatic historical events, it appears that such events have frequently led to bold changes in policy — changes required for the nation to survive that event and move forward. For example, the attack on Pearl Harbor arguably helped to trigger the passage of the National Security Act of 1947. Defense policy makers had already been considering the idea of unifying the armed forces. But only with the attack, the failure to predict it, and the resulting perception of a lack of coordination between the Army and Navy in the Hawaiian Islands was there sufficient momentum to push for unification.

Similarly, as was discussed in part 1 of this volume, the debate in America surrounding the Vietnam War and growing distrust of the draft helped to trigger the establishment of the all-volunteer force. Vietnam set the stage for the debate over "who should serve" and how the armed forces should be manned. It created sufficient momentum for a presidential candidate to embrace the notion of ending the draft and ultimately for Congress and the public to support the policy as well.

The September 11, 2001, tragedy, leading to the global war on terrorism, was perhaps another such triggering mechanism — this time, forcing the Department of Defense to evaluate the effectiveness of the total force concept and how best to utilize the reserve component of that total force. Today the nation has an all-volunteer force — a total force of active and reserve components — that has served the nation very well. But when we as policy makers celebrate that success, it is largely in the context of the cold war — a *bipolar, industrial-age* context. The Department of Defense and the military services need to transform this force to be effective and efficient in a new environment — a *global, information-age* environment. That transformation is today's challenge.

★

In my view, change is at best inconvenient and few people find change pleasant. It is tough to achieve, but often essential to success. Part 3 of this volume addresses the total force and, in particular, the contributions made by the reserve component—contributions that have changed dramatically in magnitude and in kind since the transformative events of September 11. These changes now necessitate adjustments in how the Department of Defense and the military services manage the reserve component.

The papers in this section address a broad spectrum of issues regarding the reserves, including who they are, how much they contribute, who employs them, and how employers are managing in a new era of the total force. They address the challenges that the department faces, and will face in the future, in recruiting and retaining a reserve component that is no longer a "force in reserve," but instead an integral part of the total force; the need to manage the force judiciously, respecting the reservists' part-time status; the need to rebalance the mix of active and reserve forces so that those reservists in high-demand specialties are not repeatedly called to duty; and the need to adequately fund the reserve components so that they are properly trained and equipped with the most modern systems.

Reservists, their families, and their employers understand the importance of the reserve components in fighting the war on terrorism. Reservists are ready and willing to serve. However, we in the department cannot expect them to indefinitely sustain the level of effort that they are now being asked to put forth. The papers in this section highlight a number of issues that should be among the department's priority concerns in managing its reserve components. They offer insight into solutions and direction for the future. To borrow a quotation from Shakespeare's *Julius Caesar*, we are at one of those places in history where "we must take the current when it serves, or lose our ventures" (4.3.223–24).

★ ★ ★ ★ ★ ★ ★ ★ ★ ★ ★

CHAPTER 8

THE ALL-VOLUNTEER FORCE:
AN EMPLOYER'S PERSPECTIVE

ROBERT K. STEEL

INTRODUCTION

Historically, the role of the nation's guard and reserve was to augment the active force in times of national emergency. The guard and reserve constituted a force held in reserve for the next big war. But with the collapse of the Soviet Union, that role began to change. The Department of Defense (DOD) developed a new strategy that called for increased reliance on the guard and reserve to perform day-to-day missions. Then came the events of September 11, 2001, which, in terms of reserve usage, combined the demands of the reserve's traditional role and those of the new increased-use strategy; reservists are now being called into military service in numbers that approach World War II levels and that were exceeded in modern history only by the one million reservists called up for the Korean War.

This increase in the use of the reserves has created a challenge for civilian employers. During the conscript era and in the early years of the all-volunteer force (AVF), the impact of young men and women's military service on employers was minimal. However, employers have increasingly been affected by military service in what I would like to term the "modern all-volunteer force era," which I will describe below.

Today, employers are losing more reservist employees to military service and for longer periods of time. Once that service is complete, the employer must by law reemploy the returning veteran and, for some purposes, treat the employee as if he or she had been continuously employed by the company during the period of military service. No company or employer is immune to the possibility of losing a reservist employee during a military call-up, as members of the reserve components reside in nearly 5,000 cities across the United States—from New York City to small townships in rural America.

★

In light of these employer challenges, an important concern for the Department of Defense is the attitude of the business community toward the military and toward the all-volunteer force. How the business community treats its reservist employees can have a direct impact on recruiting and retention in the reserve components. Quite simply, we in business and in the Department of Defense share employees. Many of the men and women who serve in the National Guard or reserves also work in the private sector. So there are two fundamental questions worthy of consideration. How successful have we been in sharing our employees? And can we do better? To address these questions, this paper examines the following issues:

- The changing use of the reserves.

- Who employs reservists?

- How have employers responded when they lose a reservist employee to military duty?

- What motivates employers in their treatment of reservists?

- The economic impact of mobilization on employers.

- Areas for further exploration.

THE CHANGING USE OF RESERVISTS: FROM THE CONSCRIPT ERA TO THE MODERN ALL-VOLUNTEER FORCE

During the conscript era, most of our nation's soldiers entered military service directly out of high school or college before embarking on a civilian career. As military veterans left the service, businesses welcomed them. Employers knew they were hiring mature, disciplined young people who were ready to work and make a significant contribution to a company — as they had already made a significant contribution to society through their service in the military. Even those service members who remained in military service for an additional tour or two generally did not "reenter" the civilian job market upon leaving the armed forces but, like the one-term draftee, entered the civilian job market for the first time.

When draftees chose membership in the guard or reserves as their service commitment, or chose to continue their military career on a part-time basis in the guard or reserve, employers were easily able to accommodate their military obligation. Their absence from the workplace typically occurred during a consecutive two-week period during the year, often in the summer months. Periodic training occurred on weekends and thus generally did not affect the employer. Reservists' absence from work was only noticed when they were mobilized.

In the early years of the all-volunteer force, the impact of military service on employers remained basically unchanged from the conscript era. Men and women still entered the military directly after completing school. And for those who entered the guard and reserve, the reserve training regimen remained the same. From the employer's perspective, the construct of military service remained essentially unchanged from World War II up to the Persian Gulf War of 1991. The call to military service only touched employers when the reserves were mobilized — and they were not mobilized very often (table 1). In fact, after the Korean War and prior to 1991, relatively few reservists were mobilized.

TABLE 1. RESERVE MOBILIZATION FROM WORLD WAR II
THROUGH THE VIETNAM WAR

CONFLICT	DATE	NUMBER OF GUARD AND RESERVE MOBILIZED
Vietnam (& the Pueblo Crisis)	1960s	37,000
Berlin Crisis	1961 and 1962	148,000
Cuban Missile Crisis	October 1962	14,000 Air Force reservists
Korean War	1950s	Nearly 1,000,000
World War II	1941–1945	About 400,000 as the military expanded

Source: Office of the Assistant Secretary of Defense for Reserve Affairs.

Employers began to see a change, however, with the convergence of three events that began in late 1990. First, with the end of the cold war, the Department of Defense began to reduce the size of the active duty force. The Defense Department was seeking to create a smaller, leaner force; like businesses across the country, it was looking for ways to maximize the productivity of its entire work force. The second event, and probably the most significant for employers with respect to their reservist employees, was the mobilization of reserves for the 1990–1991 Persian Gulf War. This mobilization clearly signaled the military's commitment to use the guard and reserve under the "total force" doctrine. For employers, this commitment meant that they would have to more frequently face the challenge of accommodating the absences of their reservist employees because of military duty.

The third event was the adoption by the Defense Department of a new strategy that called for increased reliance on the guard and reserve in performing day-to-day missions. To support the new strategy, reservists began to be called away from the civilian workplace even more often and for longer periods of time (figure 1). Prior to 1989, the number of "duty-days" — that is days in which a reservist performs active or inactive duty — that the reserve components contributed to total force missions was minimal. Although the use of reserve component members began to slowly climb in 1990, the first sharp increase occurred with the mobilization of the reserve components for the Persian Gulf War. Following the Persian Gulf War, employment of the guard and reserve grew to a steady state of 12–13 million duty-days per year between 1996 and 2001 — a period which witnessed several smaller presidential call-ups of reserve component members. The terrorist attacks of September 11, 2001, which triggered a partial mobilization of the ready reserve, generated another spike in reserve utilization.

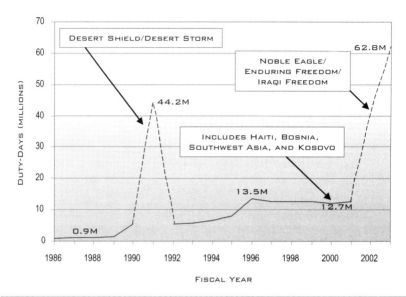

FIGURE 1. RESERVE CONTRIBUTIONS TO TOTAL FORCE MISSIONS

Source: U.S. Department of Defense 2003c.
Note: Data show direct support only, not indirect support such as recruiting, United States Property and Federal Officers (managers of federal property provided to state governors for use by the state National Guards), and most active guard and reserve support. Data include U.S. Coast Guard.

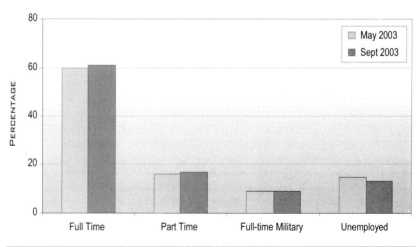

FIGURE 2. RESERVISTS IN THE LABOR FORCE

Source: U.S. Department of Defense 2003a and 2003b.
Note: Margin of error is ± 2 percent.

This series of events marks the beginning of what I refer to as the modern era of the all-volunteer force—an era in which the very nature of reserve service changed, resulting in a much greater impact on employers.

WHO ARE THE EMPLOYERS?

Before examining how employers have responded to reserve usage in this new era, let us first look at who actually employs guard and reserve members. DOD is in the process of gathering data on the civilian employers of guardsmen and reservists. Since those data are not yet available, the best source of information on civilian employers is from periodic surveys conducted by the Defense Department, with the most detailed information collected in 2000.[1]

Figure 2 depicts the employment status of reservists in the labor force, including both those who are employed and those who are unemployed. The survey results show that about 60 percent of reservists who are in the labor force work full time in nonmilitary jobs, while another 16 percent work part time. Nine percent of the reservists are in the military full time, either as full-time employees of reserve or guard units or as augmentees to the active duty force. Finally, 15 percent are unemployed and looking for work.

For reservists who have jobs, figure 3 shows the sector in which they are employed. Fifty-nine percent of reservists with jobs work in the private sector, 32 percent work in the public sector, and 11 percent work for themselves or for a family business. The distribution of reservists by sector of employment differs significantly from that of civilians. Of civilian males aged 18–59, 74 percent are employed in the private sector, a rate 15 percentage points higher than for reservists. Only 14 percent of civilian males are employed by the public sector, compared to 32 percent of reservists. Furthermore, 13 percent of reservists are federal employees, while only 4 percent of civilian males are. Clearly, reservists are much more likely to be employed in the public sector and by the federal government. Interestingly, the fraction of reservists who are self-employed or work in a family business (11 percent) is similar to the fraction of civilians so employed (12 percent).[2]

Figure 3 also shows the breakdown of reservists who are employed in the private sector by firm size. About half of reservists employed in the private sector are in large firms (those with 500 or more employees). Another 20 percent work in firms having 100 to 499 employees, while the rest (29 percent) work for firms with fewer than 100 employees. Among all civilian males who work in the private sector, 43 percent work for firms with 500 or more employees, 16 percent work for intermediate-size firms, and 41 percent work for small firms (having fewer than 100 employees). These figures indicate that reservists employed by the private sector are more likely to work for large firms than are civilians (51 percent versus 43 percent) and less likely to be employed by small firms (29 percent versus 41 percent).

These comparisons paint a clear picture: reservists are more likely to be found in jobs that make reserve service easier (such as federal employment) or for which the costs to employers of hiring reservists are smaller (large firms). Large entities—the federal government, state and local governments, and large private firms—have more flexibility to cover periodic deployments of reservists and are arguably more able to absorb the costs imposed on them by such deployments. Consequently, reservists may be more attracted to larger entities by their better ability to provide benefits (such as health care) that reservists will find attractive and to continue to provide those benefits during deployments.

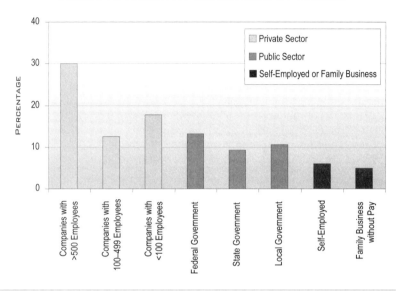

FIGURE 3. RESERVIST EMPLOYMENT BY SECTOR

Source: U.S. Department of Defense 2002.
Note: Percentages exceed 100 perecent due to the possibility of members working multiple jobs. Margin of error is ± 1.1 percent.

HOW HAVE EMPLOYERS RESPONDED?

Historically, the business community has understood the sacrifices guard and reserve members make to defend the freedom our country enjoys. Employers have worked with their reservist employees to help them balance a civilian career and a part-time military career. Even with the Defense Department's increased-use strategy, companies have been willing to accommodate the military requirements of their reservist employees. This accommodation has placed a greater strain on some companies as they struggle to cut overhead and increase productivity in order to remain competitive.

The events of September 11, 2001, however, have placed even greater demands on the reserve components and have had a significant impact on the ability of employers to accommodate reservist employees. We in America will never forget the horrific images that flashed across the television screen that day. The call-up of the guard and reserve to respond to those attacks was considered necessary and appropriate, and businesses responded by supporting their employees who were called to military duty.

My personal experience with reserve employment has been in my job as vice chairman of The Goldman Sachs Group. As a company headquartered in New York City—just blocks away from the World Trade Center—the tragedy of September 11 is especially meaningful to Goldman Sachs. As good corporate citizens and as a company of patriotic Americans, Goldman Sachs—without hesitation—will meet the highest standard asked by the government to support our military. Corporations like Goldman Sachs want to demonstrate, by word and by deed, that they will meet whatever the federal government sets as the gold standard of personnel policy for companies with reservist employees.

Satisfying such standards is, for Goldman Sachs, simply a matter of knowing what has been established as the gold standard and then meeting it. It is an easy decision for Goldman Sachs to make. Of the 20,000 Goldman Sachs employees, only a handful serve in the guard or reserve. We are a very flat organization, which enables us to easily move people around to cover the absence of employees who are called up. But even if we employed hundreds of reservists, the decision would be the same: meet the gold standard. Most large corporations want to and can afford to do the same, as indicated by their current policies, discussed later in this chapter. Large, medium, and even small companies will meet the gold standard if they can.

The National Committee for Employer Support of the Guard and Reserve (NCESGR)[3] has communicated with many employers and found that many have policies to

- pay both the employer's portion and, in many cases, the employee's normal share of the health insurance premium during mobilization, permitting the families of mobilized reservists to remain in the company's health plan and continue to use the health care provider with whom they have an established relationship

- pay their mobilized employees any difference between their civilian and military salary, and in some cases, continue to pay their employees their entire salary, at least for some portion of the employee's mobilization

- maintain contact with their mobilized employees and their families to the extent possible during the mobilization and provide other company benefits

In fact, data from the May 2003 Status of Forces survey reveal the level of support provided by employers (figure 4). The most significant benefits that companies continue to provide are company pay and employer-sponsored health care for the family. Employers are not required to continue to pay their reservist employees when they are absent to perform military duty. Yet, as the figure shows, over one quarter of companies do continue to pay their employees, at least for some period of time, depending on the employer's policies.

While employers are required to allow continued health care coverage under the company plan, they may require the reservist employee to pay the entire premium plus a 2 percent administration fee if the period of service is for more than 30 days. But over one third of the employers pay the entire premium for their reservist employees who elect to remain in the employer-sponsored health care plan, and an additional one quarter continue to pay the employer share of the health plan premium (figure 5).

However, this level of support is difficult for some companies to offer. There are companies that already struggle financially. There are companies that have a large number of employees who serve in the guard and reserve relative to the size of the company. There are also small businesses, individuals who are self-employed, and small-business owners who are in the guard or reserve. These companies are at the greatest financial risk. Even the loss of a single employee can have a disastrous effect on a small business.

Because of the financial risk to a reservist who is a small-business owner or who is self-employed, one might question whether such an individual should in fact be in the guard or reserve. But this decision is one that each individual must make after carefully evaluating the risks and determining how the business would be managed in case of a call-up. A cardinal rule of behavioral economics states that people tend to undervalue negative outcomes and overvalue positive outcomes. Said another way, a small-business owner may underestimate the possibility of being mobilized and overestimate his or her capacity to sustain the business during an absence due to mobilization. Therefore small-business owners and the self-employed may continue to serve in the guard or reserve despite the fact that even a short absence from their business could result in a substantial decline in business or even possible loss of the business.

A more delicate problem is faced by the owners of small businesses who employ reservists, particularly if the reservist is critical to the operation of the business. The law protects the employment and reemployment rights of employees regardless of the size of the business. Additionally, the employer may not discriminate in hiring based on an individual's military obligation. On the other hand, the small-business owner may have a difficult time sustaining the business during an extended absence of a reservist employee. While fewer reservists are likely to be employed by small businesses, as reflected in the discussion of figure 3, this problem is still potentially significant for small-business owners who do employ individuals who serve in the guard or reserve. Thus, this set of circumstances is something the federal government needs to closely examine.

WHAT MOTIVATES EMPLOYERS TO SUPPORT THEIR RESERVIST EMPLOYEES?

Probably the top reason that employers support their reservist employees is patriotism. Employers appreciate the freedoms we in America enjoy. But more importantly, they recognize that everyone who lives in a free society must con-

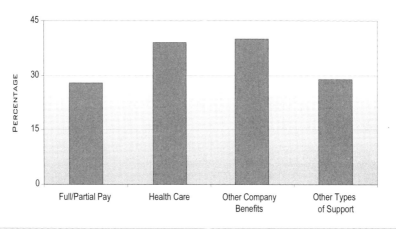

FIGURE 4. COMPANY BENEFITS PROVIDED BY EMPLOYERS

Source: U.S. Department of Defense 2003a.
Note: Margin of error is ± 3 percent.

FIGURE 5. SOURCE OF PAYMENT FOR EMPLOYER-SPONSORED
HEALTH CARE INSURANCE DURING ACTIVATION

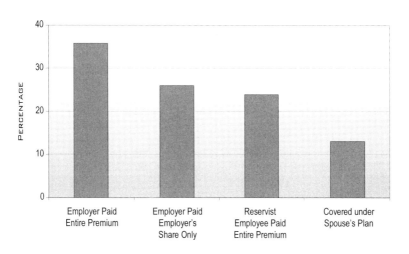

Source: U.S. Department of Defense 2003a.
Note: Margin of error is ± 4 percent.

tribute in some fashion to maintain that freedom. Employers understand and appreciate the challenges their reservist employees face as citizen-soldiers, particularly when they are sent into harm's way. These citizen-soldiers are not nameless faces; they are the company's workers, supervisors, and executives.

Equally important, these citizen-soldiers bring military training, discipline, and leadership skills to their civilian jobs. Supporting their reservist employees is in no small part businesses' way of supporting their very way of life. In return, they benefit from more motivated employees who appreciate the support their employers provide.

Legal Responsibilities

Of course, some employers are strictly motivated by the law, which protects the job rights of citizen-soldiers. The Uniformed Services Employment and Reemployment Rights Act, or USERRA, was enacted in 1994 and codified in chapter 43 of title 38 of the United States Code. USERRA requires that an employee who is absent from his or her place of employment be promptly reemployed upon return from military service. In addition to this basic protection, there are a number of other important protections and benefits provided by USERRA to a reserve member upon returning to civilian employment:

- *Status.* The employee must be placed in the same position or a comparable position, as if he or she had never been absent from the workplace—the "escalator principle."

- *Seniority.* The employee must be given any rights or benefits that accrued as if the employee had been continuously employed.

- *Other benefits.* Any non–seniority-based benefits must be provided if these benefits are offered to other employees who are on furlough or on a nonmilitary leave of absence.

- *Training or other accommodations.* The employer must provide any training necessary to recertify the employee for an appropriate position or to qualify on new equipment.

- *Health care.* The employee must be given the option to continue under an employer-sponsored health care plan for up to 18 months, and to be promptly reinstated in the plan upon return to work with no waiting period or exclusion for preexisting conditions (other than a condition that resulted from military service).

- *Pension plan.* The employee has the right to make up any employee contributions to the pension plan during his or her military absence, and the employer must make any matching contributions. Also, the period of military service counts toward any vesting period or service requirements under the pension plan.

- *Protection against discharge, discrimination, or reprisal.* The employee is protected for a period of time (dependent on the length of service) against discharge, other than for cause. Also, there are protections against discrimination and reprisal based on military service.

The employee has responsibilities also. The employee must provide notice to the employer of upcoming military service. The Defense Department has strongly recommended that reservists provide this notice in writing and give notice at least 30 days in advance if at all possible. Upon release from active duty, the employee must also return to work or provide notice of the intent to return to work within the period specified by law, which is based on the length of the military duty. Finally, an employee who is absent from the workplace for more than 30 days because of military duty must provide the employer with documentation of such service if requested by the employer.

The rights and benefits provided under USERRA are not indefinite. There is a five-year limit; that is, the employee can be absent from the workplace to perform military duty for a cumulative period of five years. However, certain duty is not counted toward the five-year limit; service that is exempt from this accounting includes training duty and involuntary calls to active duty.

It is also worth pointing out that although USERRA was enacted in 1994, the reemployment rights of military members have been protected since 1940. The predecessor to USERRA was a law commonly known as the Veterans Reemployment Rights. USERRA updated and codified what had become a confusing patchwork of statutory amendments to the Veterans Reemployment Rights and numerous court rulings. USERRA modernized the law to provide clear and consistent rules.

As previously indicated, some companies will exceed the basic requirements of the law, while others are only able to provide the support required by the law. The level of support a company is able to provide is based in large measure on its economic position in the marketplace. The business community has faced many challenges in recent years, given a lagging economy and stiff competition in the global marketplace. Some industries and some companies have been pushed to the limit. In the same way that the military reduced its work force in the 1990s, businesses are becoming leaner and demanding more of their employees in order to remain viable and productive. Sharing human resources is not free, from an employer's point of view, and some companies face significant challenges when their employees perform extended periods of military duty.

EMPLOYMENT-RELATED PROBLEMS

Despite these challenges, businesses want to support their employees who are willing to serve our country. In fact, employers have been more supportive of activated reservist employees than the employees themselves expected. The May 2003 Status of Forces survey asked reservists about the degree to which they expect to encounter certain employment-related problems if called to active duty. The same series of questions was asked of reservists who were actually called up. In virtually every case, the expectation of problems was greater than the actual problems experienced. Figure 6 compares expectations (the column

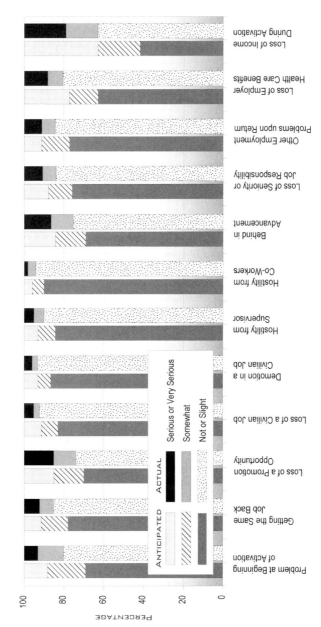

FIGURE 6. ANTICIPATED VERSUS ACTUAL
EMPLOYER-RELATED PROBLEMS

Loss of Income
During Activation

Loss of Employer
Health Care Benefits

Other Employment
Problems upon Return

Loss of Seniority or
Job Responsibility

Behind in
Advancement

Hostility from
Co-Workers

Hostility from
Supervisor

Demotion in a
Civilian Job

Loss of a Civilian Job

Loss of a Promotion
Opportunity

Getting the Same
Job Back

Problem at Beginning
of Activation

Serious or Very Serious

Somewhat

Not or Slight

ACTUAL

ANTICIPATED

100   80   60   40   20   0

PERCENTAGE

Source: U.S. Department of Defense 2003a.
Note: Margin of error is ± 3 percent.

on the left) to the actual experience (the column on the right) in relation to 12 potential problem areas.

Obviously, situations arise in which a particular provision of the law, as it applies to a particular employee, is disputed. When such a dispute occurs, an individual can file a complaint with the Department of Labor, which is the federal agency charged with investigating and adjudicating USERRA complaints. The graph in figure 7 depicts the number of cases opened by the Department of Labor in which a reservist has filed a formal complaint alleging an employer violation under USERRA or its predecessor statutes. The figure illustrates several interesting points. The first is the spike that occurred in 1991, which coincides with the mobilization of over 265,000 reservists for the Persian Gulf War. The second is the increase in the number of cases that occurred after USERRA was enacted in 1994.

FIGURE 7. EMPLOYMENT/REEMPLOYMENT CASES
INVOLVING GUARD OR RESERVE MEMBERS

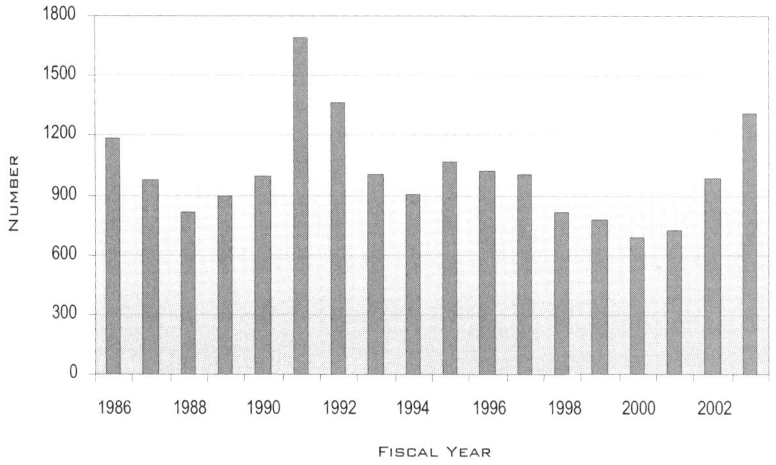

FISCAL YEAR

Source: U.S. Department of Labor 2003.

But the most interesting statistic is the number of cases opened during each of the last two years. While the number of cases has increased—as one would expect with the mobilization of over 300,000 reservists for the global war on terrorism—fewer cases have been opened as compared to the smaller mobilization that occurred in 1991. Although there tends to be a natural lag between reemployment after a deployment and when a reservist might file a complaint, most reservists mobilized over the past two years served on active duty for about one year. So even with this lag, the data still provide an indication that employers are supportive of their reservist employees when compared to the large number of reservists who have been mobilized.

To elaborate further, figure 8 shows the types of problems reservists experienced upon returning to work. These data are results from a survey of reservists rather than actual case files maintained by the Department of Labor. However,

THE ALL-VOLUNTEER FORCE: AN EMPLOYER'S PERSPECTIVE

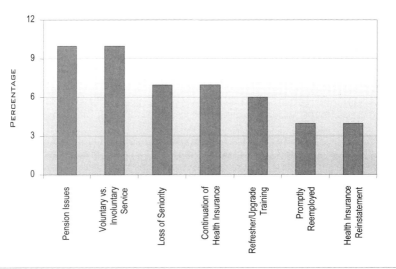

FIGURE 8. ACTUAL EMPLOYMENT PROBLEMS
EXPERIENCED BY ACTIVATED RESERVISTS

Source: U.S. Department of Defense 2003b.
Note: Margin of error is ± 2.

FIGURE 9. SUPPORT FOR RESERVE SERVICE

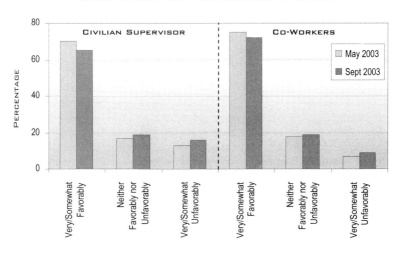

Source: U.S. Department of Defense 2003a and 2003b.
Note: Margin of error is ± 2 percent.

there should be a strong correlation, since the Department of Labor cases are based on complaints filed by employees.

While employer support for their reservist employees must start at the top, leadership-level support may not always permeate throughout the company. The most immediate and direct impact on the company when an employee is absent to perform military duty is experienced by supervisors who must ensure the work continues without interruption and co-workers who may be asked to take on additional responsibilities. Responses to several survey questions provide some insight into the level of support given reservists by supervisors and co-workers (figure 9). As the figure shows, when reservists were asked how supervisors and co-workers viewed their participation in the National Guard or reserve, reservists responded that they thought 65–70 percent of supervisors and 72–75 percent of co-workers had a favorable or somewhat favorable attitude.

The reasons reservists give for not volunteering for additional duty further demonstrate the relatively favorable attitudes of their supervisors and co-workers, and also reflect the loyalty reservists have to their civilian employers. The second-most-reported reason for not volunteering for additional duty is that it would result in time away from work. One might also consider work commitments as being a factor in the top reason given—not enough time. Note also that a lack of employer support and hostility from supervisors and co-workers rank very low on the list of reasons given. These particular indicators are highlighted in figure 10.

FIGURE 10. REASONS FOR NOT VOLUNTEERING FOR ADDITIONAL DUTY

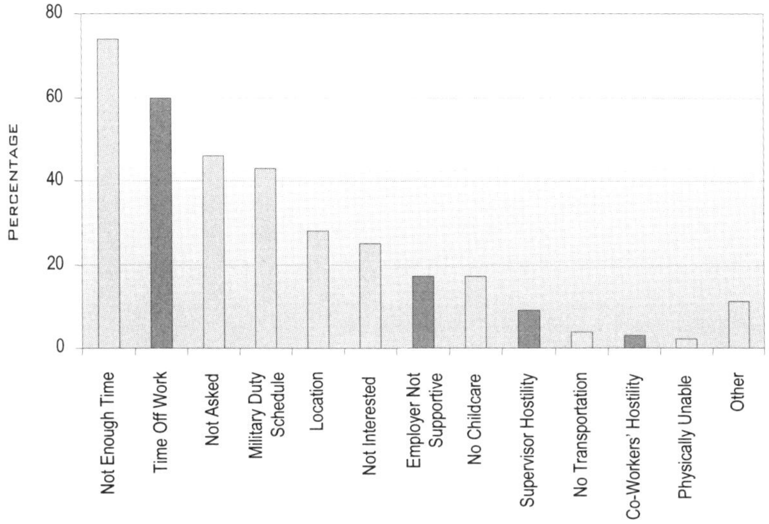

Source: U.S. Department of Defense 2003b.
Note: Margin of error is ± 3 percent.

THE ALL-VOLUNTEER FORCE: AN EMPLOYER'S PERSPECTIVE

One of a reservist employee's most important responsibilities, and one that can help the employer the most, is to provide as much advance notice of pending military service as possible. Employers need as much time as possible to adjust to the pending absence of an employee. The loss of an employee on short notice, particularly when the period of absence will be for an extended time, can cause significant disruption in the workplace. Unfortunately, the track record on this issue is not particularly good. As shown in figure 11, many employers (60 percent) receive a week or less of notice, and only 15 percent are given 30 days or more advance notice. This area is clearly one in which improvement on the part of DOD is needed.

FIGURE 11. ADVANCE NOTICE GIVEN TO EMPLOYERS

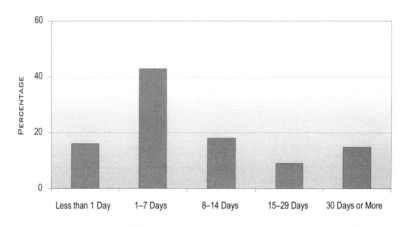

Source: U.S. Department of Defense 2003a.
Note: Margin of error is ± 4 percent.

Related to advance notice is the time a reservist employee needs to prepare for activation. Sixty-two percent of reservists report a need for time off from work to prepare for activation—with the largest number of requests being for four or more days (figure 12). Despite the additional problems posed by this additional time away from work, reservist employees report that their employers appear supportive of this need (figure 13).

WHAT IS THE ECONOMIC IMPACT ON EMPLOYERS?

Employing guard and reserve members imposes several burdens on employers. First is the effect on their work force. When a reservist employee is absent from the workplace, the employer must determine how to accomplish the work normally done by that employee. When the period of military duty is short, the burden to accomplish the work may simply fall back on the reservist employee—to be accomplished either before or after the absence for military duty. But if the military service is for an extended period of time, the employer may have to redistribute the work, assign another employee to do the work, hire temporary

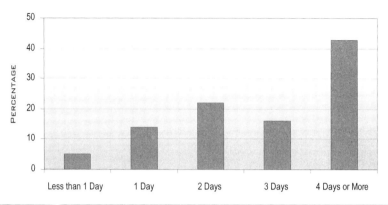

FIGURE 12. TIME TAKEN OFF FROM WORK
TO PREPARE FOR ACTIVATION

Source: U.S. Department of Defense 2003a.
Note: Margin of error is ± 4 percent.

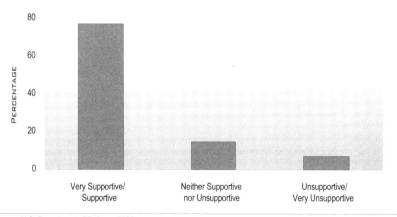

FIGURE 13. EMPLOYER SUPPORT FOR
TIME TO PREPARE FOR ACTIVATION

Source: U.S. Department of Defense 2003a.
Note: Margin of error is ± 4 percent.

help, or take other personnel actions. The reservist employee's reemployment rights can be a factor in what an employer is able to do.

The employer may also be faced with morale issues from other employees who are assigned additional work when a reservist employee is absent to perform military duty. This situation may occur more frequently when reservist employees volunteer for military assignments. Even though a reservist volunteers for duty, the military may use an involuntary authority (such as partial mobilization) to help dampen any negative attitudes that an employer, supervisor, or co-worker may have.

When the reservist employee is absent to perform military duty for fewer than 31 days, the employer must continue to pay the employer's share of any employer-sponsored health insurance premiums, if the employee elects to retain his or her company health insurance during the period of military duty. The law provides some relief for employers if the period of service is for 31 days or greater. The employer may pass along the entire premium cost (plus 2 percent of the total premium to cover administrative costs) to employees who elect to continue in their employer-sponsored health care plan. As stated earlier, the employee has the right to retain this benefit for up to 18 months.

Survey results reveal that of the 71 percent of activated reservists who are covered under an employer-sponsored health care plan, 54 percent elected to retain their coverage under that plan. For reservists who were covered by an employer-sponsored health care plan, 62 percent of employers continued to pay their share of the premium for the company health care plan, or to pay the entire premium for their activated reservists (figure 5).

Another cost to employers relates to pension plans. The employer is required to treat military service as service with the employer for purposes of a company pension plan, to include making any required contributions to the plan on behalf of the employee, and matching any make-up contributions by the employee to the extent that the employer normally makes matching contributions. This requirement has been characterized by at least one company's human resource manager as an unfunded mandate by the federal government (Gotz 2003, 3). When combined, these costs can place financial pressure on an employer — particularly on small-business owners with few employees and who may be operating with a very small profit margin.

THE SMALL-BUSINESS ISSUE

The issue of how to sustain a business in the absence of a reservist employee might easily prove to be the greatest challenge facing small-business owners, since they are more apt to rely heavily on a small cadre of employees. The extended absence of any one employee could significantly impact the operation of the business and the morale of other employees. Small businesses are also less likely to be able to fill critical positions quickly or easily, particularly when they are required to reinstate a reservist employee upon his or her return from military service.

Some assistance is available to small-business owners affected by the absence of a reservist employee and to self-employed reservists. The Small Business Administration offers financial relief through its Military Reservist Economic Injury Disaster Loan Program. The program is designed to provide funds to an eligible small business to meet ordinary and necessary operating expenses that it is unable to meet because an essential employee was "called up" to active duty as a military reservist. An eligible business can receive a 30-year loan of up to $1.5 million at a maximum interest rate of 4 percent.

EMPLOYERS WITH RELATIVELY LARGE COMPLEMENTS OF RESERVISTS

Not only can small businesses be hit hard when reservist employees are absent to perform military duty, but an industry or a company that employs a large number of reservists can feel the impact as well. One of the best examples is the airline industry. There is a natural relationship between the military, which is a fertile training ground for pilots, and the airlines, which are eager to hire experienced pilots. Moreover, the scheduling system used by the airlines provides reservist pilots an ideal opportunity to perform military duty in the guard or reserve on a frequent basis.

The airlines have routinely been able to accommodate dual-career pilots under the traditional reserve training regimen. But the increased use of the guard and reserve in response to the global war on terrorism has placed a strain on some airlines. During an airline symposium hosted in March 2002 by the NCESGR, which brought together military leaders and airline representatives to discuss how they could work together to optimize their shared pilot assets, one airline representative noted that for every four pilots employed by his airline who are in the guard or reserve, the company must hire one additional pilot just to cover normal flight operations.

Moreover, the terrorist attacks of September 11 had a devastating effect on an already struggling airline industry. The combination of a sluggish economy, already fierce competition, and the sudden "fear of flying" that resulted from terrorists using commercial airliners as lethal weapons, has had an impact on airline revenues, causing some airlines to furlough employees. During the 2002 airline symposium, only one airline indicated that it was able to provide more than the minimum benefits required by law to reservist pilots called up for military duty.

AREAS FOR FURTHER EXPLORATION

What does all of this information tell us? First and foremost, anecdotal information and survey results from reservists indicate that employers appear to be supporting their mobilized reservists today. It also appears that employers were able to navigate through the conscript era and the early all-volunteer force era with few problems. But the modern AVF era—with its more frequent and longer absences for reservist employees—has created a new set of challenges for businesses. And it may be difficult for many businesses to sustain the current level of employee support over the long term without some change in the relationship between the Department of Defense and the business community.

Today the Defense Department lacks comprehensive information on the employers of reservists. There are also few data available on employer problems vis-à-vis their employees who serve in the guard or reserve. The Defense Department must direct efforts to develop an empirical body of evidence on employers and the effects that reserve service is having on them. DOD must be able to assess the types and magnitude of problems and the financial burden placed on employers. It can no longer rely on anecdotal information in developing personnel policies that directly or indirectly affect employers, if it wants to sustain the level of employer support that reservists have historically enjoyed. This effort is critical if DOD plans to use its reserve components to the same extent in the future as it has over the past 10 years—and particularly if the Defense Department plans to use them at the rate now being experienced in the global war on terrorism.

Still uncertain is the long-term effect of the Defense Department's current strategy to rely more heavily on the guard and reserve. The Defense Department is taking some steps to bring more predictability to the employment of the reserves. The Secretary of Defense has directed the services to rebalance their force structure in order to limit involuntary mobilization of guard and reserve members. He has directed that guidelines be established to limit the mobilization of guard and reserve members—possibly to no more than one year in every six. He has also directed the services to position the force so that the reserves would not have to be mobilized in the first 15 days of a crisis. These steps are important to employers because they provide a measure of predictability, which employers have indicated is one of the most significant steps the Defense Department can take to assist them.

A Blueprint for Future Action

Glenn Gotz (2003, S-1–S-3) identifies several steps for future action. These steps, described below, provide the Defense Department with a road map to success. DOD has already taken preliminary steps to implement several of the actions.

> *Establish a mandatory-reporting employer database.* DoD should require reservists to identify their employers. A well-populated employer database—identifying reservists' employers and linked to Reserve personnel files—is essential for developing early warning indicators of employer support problems. . . .

> *Obtain timely information for early warning of problems.* DoD should develop a short, frequently administered employer survey . . . [to gather data that will help] to uncover changes, warn of new problems, and identify reasons for changes in employer attitudes and behavior. . . .

> *Provide more timely information to employers.* DoD should notify employers about call-ups and activation for training as early as possible. With this information employers might be able to improve workload planning and lower costs, and reservist-employees might encounter less resentment from their immediate supervisors and coworkers. . . .

Decrease uncertainty about call-up frequency and duration. DoD should consider actions that would decrease employers' uncertainty about call-up duration and frequency. Setting definite deployment lengths and keeping to them appears to have value for employers. It might also help employers if call-ups and annual training were structured to avoid peak business periods. . . .

Conduct experiments and demonstrations. DoD should test or demonstrate the effectiveness of costly or potentially risky initiatives before implementing them nationwide. . . . And DoD should run experiments to assess the costs and effectiveness of various strategies for offsetting employer costs attributable to Reserve call-ups.

The Quadrennial Defense Review stated that DOD can no longer solely rely on "lagging" indicators such as retention and recruiting rates to assess the impact of military operations on employers if the Defense Department intends to continue to use reservists to the extent they have during the last 10 years. By the time these indicators highlight a problem, it is too late. DOD needs to develop early-warning indicators of reserve recruiting and retention problems, and should have an action plan for offsetting significant employer support problems if they are shown to exist or if early-warning indicators predict them.

Before the Defense Department can determine what steps it should take to maintain and enhance the support of employers, it must first have empirical information. The Defense Department has already taken the first critical step in this direction, by establishing an employer database. It is now in the process of making reservist reporting of employer information mandatory. Once the database is established, DOD will be able to gather information from affected employers and identify actions that would yield the greatest return in enhancing employer support.

A FINAL WORD

Employer support will continue to be a critical element of the all-volunteer force—particularly as it relates to those members who serve in the guard or reserve. The steps identified by Gotz (2003) are prudent if the Defense Department is to sustain the support employers have demonstrated thus far in the modern all-volunteer force era. But much remains to be done before the Defense Department is able to undertake a comprehensive program that will sustain the level of support necessary for continued use of guard and reserve members at current rates or even at the rate of 12–13 million duty-days per year that was typical of the late 1990s.

Employers will continue to do their part, but the federal government must also step up with a more systematic, focused approach to working with those employers who employ guard and reserve members. Policies and practices that facilitate military service, both from an employer perspective and from that of the reservist employee, need to be developed.

The easy first step for large companies is to simply let them know what the gold standard of support is. The much more complex problem is how to ameliorate the potentially significant impact that the mobilization of even a single employee may have on the small-business owner. Even with the assistance that is available from the Small Business Administration, much more needs to be done in this area.

NOTES

1. The Defense Manpower Data Center (DMDC) conducts periodic surveys of active duty and reserve members for the Department of Defense. Prior to 2003, surveys of reserve component members were administered approximately once every five or six years. Beginning in 2003, DMDC has conducted quarterly "Status of Forces" surveys. Results presented in this paper are taken from reservist responses to the reserve component surveys in U.S. Department of Defense 2002, 2003a, and 2003b.

2. The statistics comparing employment of military reservists with that of males in the civilian population (in this paragraph and in the one that follows) are tabulated from U.S. Department of Labor 1998, 1999, and 2000.

3. The National Committee for Employer Support of the Guard and Reserve was established in 1972 as an agency within the Department of Defense. Its mission is to promote cooperation and understanding between reserve component members and their civilian employers and to assist in the resolution of conflicts arising from an employee's military commitment. NCESGR operates through a network of more than 4,500 volunteers, with 55 committees, one located in each state, the District of Columbia, Guam, Puerto Rico, the Virgin Islands, and Europe.

REFERENCES

Gotz, Glenn A. 2003. *Strengthening employer support of the guard and reserve.* D-2755. Alexandria, Va.: Institute for Defense Analyses.

U.S. Department of Defense. 2002. *2000 Survey of reserve component personnel.* August. No. 2002-009. Arlington, Va.: Defense Manpower Data Center.

———. 2003a. *Status of forces survey of reserve component members, May 2003.* Arlington, Va.: Defense Manpower Data Center.

———. 2003b. *Status of forces survey of reserve component members, September 2003.* Arlington, Va.: Defense Manpower Data Center.

———. 2003c. *Employment of reserve component forces & effects of usage (A profile of the reserve components, 1986–2003).* Washington, D.C.: Office of the Assistant Secretary of Defense for Reserve Affairs.

U.S. Department of Labor. 1998. *Current population survey.* March. Washington, D.C.: Bureau of Labor Statistics.

———. 1999. *Current population survey.* March. Washington, D.C.: Bureau of Labor Statistics.

———. 2000. *Current population survey.* March. Washington, D.C.: Bureau of Labor Statistics.

———. 2003. *USERRA Information Management System (UIMS) database.* Washington, D.C.: Veterans' Employment and Training Service.

✱ ✱ ✱ ✱ ✱ ✱ ✱ ✱ ✱ ✱ ✱

CHAPTER 9

FROM THE HOME FRONT TO THE FRONT LINES: U.S. RESERVE FORCES ANSWER THE CALL TO DUTY

Edward L. Schrock

THE ROLE OF THE RESERVE AND NATIONAL GUARD IN THE TOTAL FORCE

The first Air Force casualty during Operation Iraqi Freedom was a member of the selected reserves: Major Gregory L. Stone of the 124th wing of the Idaho Air National Guard.

Today, the reserve component of the U.S. armed forces is no longer simply the "force of last resort." The reserves are a critical element of the total force of the 21st century, characterized by balanced capabilities and flexible strength. Composed of 1.2 million servicemen and servicewomen, the reserve component accounts for almost half of the U.S. military's total force. It is an increasingly important element of the U.S. armed forces.

The contribution of the reserve component has increased dramatically over the past decade, from 1.4 million duty-days in 1989 to almost 13 million duty-days in 2001. However, as of 2003, the number of duty-days worked during the year had risen to over 60 million days. Since September 11, 2001, and as of August of 2003, about 300,000 of the 1.2 million reserve and National Guard members have been called to active duty (U.S. General Accounting Office 2003). These men and women have fought on the front lines in Iraq; worked to track and apprehend members of the Taliban and Al Qaeda in Afghanistan, Asia, and Africa; and participated in Balkan peace-keeping operations. They have also taken on a number of domestic security missions, including airport security and security at the Salt Lake City Olympics. The reserve component is key to the successful implementation of the Department of Defense strategy that calls for evolution toward a balanced, integrated, and seamless total force.

The reserve force must play a leading role in the shift from a threat-based approach to a capabilities-based approach to national defense mandated by the

★

2001 Quadrennial Defense Review (U.S. Department of Defense 2001). Reservists are so valuable because they offer a unique mix of core competencies and skills, enhanced by civilian experience, to support a broad portfolio of military capabilities and a continuum of service marked by flexible strength. In many cases, the reserve force is the major (or sometimes only) source of personnel with critical skills, such as military police and civil affairs teams.

When the world changed on the morning of September 11, 2001, it became apparent very quickly to civilian and uniformed leaders at the highest levels in our nation's military that the United States faced a long and draining struggle against terrorism. We realized that our intelligence capabilities and focus must evolve. We shifted our focus in planning for military operations from predictable cold war rotations and station keeping to maintenance of a sharp force, ready to surge large numbers of war fighters to quickly overwhelm an asymmetrical threat. Thankfully, years of prudent investment in special operations capabilities, communications systems, and joint-interoperability served the Department of Defense well. It also became apparent that policy makers would have to reevaluate the assumptions under which the military maintained its reserve forces.

In support of current operations in Iraq and Afghanistan, and to meet already existing global commitments, by August of 2003 over 280,000 reservists and National Guardsmen had been activated, as mentioned previously. Although every effort has been made to limit their overseas tours to one year or less, many reservists called to serve in Iraq had already completed one or more prior periods of active duty service. This trend has produced a fundamental change in the effect that military service has had on the personal and professional commitments of reservists, and the nature of the job for which they signed up.

The bottom line is that the reserve force has become a full partner with the active duty force, with significant numbers of reservists being activated in support of almost every conflict in which the United States is engaged worldwide. The reserve component is a critical part of today's total force and is central to the success of current and future U.S. military operations.

EFFORTS TO CORRECT DISPARITIES BETWEEN THE ACTIVE AND RESERVE COMPONENTS

All men and women in uniform who actively serve our nation and strengthen our total force deserve equitable compensation and benefits for the service they provide, regardless of whether their duty is classified as "active" or "reserve." Congress and the Department of Defense must continue working to ensure that our reserve components have the training, equipment, and supplies that make them seamlessly interoperable with their active duty counterparts.

Unfortunately, disparities in the types of equipment issued to units in Iraq have often existed between the reserve and the active components. Too often, with regard to the most advanced types of body armor, or the most capable antimissile systems available for troop transport helicopters, the "haves" are the active duty units and the "have-nots" are the reserve units. The undeniable fact in this latest conflict is that these units are exposed to equally significant threats from insurgent and guerrilla forces each and every day. We as a nation have not only failed by sending them into harm's way without the best personal protective equipment available, we have also dealt a stiff blow to their morale.

In order for the Department of Defense to realize the force-multiplying and transformational benefits sought by the mandates of the 2001 Quadrennial Defense Review, the department must equip, train, and deploy the reserve component in the same manner as the active component. If we Americans expect our reservists to be called to active duty, to make the associated sacrifices and give of themselves, even their lives, then we must provide them no less than their active duty counterparts. This provisioning will require additional money and a commitment on the part of the active components to allow funds allocated for their respective reserve components to be used to procure the equipment and supplies and provide the training required for seamless integration. Such action is the only way to ensure that our reserve components have the equipment, training, and supplies to quickly and seamlessly integrate with active duty forces and facilitate the surge capability that the war on terrorism demands.

Recognizing the multiple disparities between treatment of the active and reserve components, Congress moved as quickly as possible in 2003 to correct these differences. Congress directed the U.S. General Accounting Office to review (1) income protection for reservists called to active duty, (2) family support programs available to reservists, and (3) reservist and National Guard access to health care. Congress also sought to erase differences in the compensation and benefits provided to reserve members and their families and those provided to active duty forces.

Acting on testimony from the U.S. General Accounting Office and other organizations, and on insights gained from monitoring the activation of reserve and National Guard personnel in support of Operation Iraqi Freedom, the Congress sought to correct as many disparities as possible. The 2004 National Defense Authorization Act recognizes the heightened responsibility of reserve component members and further proposes to equalize their compensation, benefits, and capability with those of the active duty force to the maximum extent possible. The 2004 National Defense Authorization Act provides additional support in the following ways:

- *Training and readiness.* The act allocates $730.5 million to enhance reserve and guard facilities and improve force training and readiness; this allocation includes $360.9 million beyond the amount requested by the administration.

- *Financial compensation.* The act improves the financial compensation offered to reservists who provide critical support to military operations. In particular, the act authorizes special pay, bonuses, and student loan repayments for reserve members who serve in high-priority units during time of war as well as members who face hostile fire and imminent danger. The act also authorizes reimbursement of lodging expenses for mobilized reservists and recalled retirees.

- *Access to TRICARE coverage for reservists and their families.* The act provides immediate medical and dental screening for selected reservists who are assigned to a unit that has been alerted or notified of mobilization. It permits family TRICARE enrollment on a cost-share basis for reservists who are unemployed or whose employers do not offer medical insurance. It grants access to TRICARE up to 90 days prior to the start of active duty and extends from 120 days to 180 days the eligibility for transitional medical care after the reservist separates from active duty.

- *Access to commissaries.* The statute authorizes the secretary of defense to modify the current policy in order to grant reservists the same access to commissaries as is enjoyed by active duty members and their families.

- *Access to Department of Defense dependent schools.* The act extends to dependents of all mobilized reservists the opportunity to enroll, on a space-available, tuition-free basis, in Department of Defense dependent schools.

- *Correction of disparities in equipment.* The act provides for an additional $5.2 million to procure Up-Armored High Mobility Multipurpose Wheeled Vehicles for the Army National Guard and to increase protection from antitank mines, antipersonnel mines, and armor-piercing munitions in peace-keeping operations.

- *Increase in end strength for the reserve and National Guard.* The act provides for a 1,779-person increase in end strength, to include activation of 12 more weapons of mass destruction–civil support teams.

The chairman of the House Armed Services Committee, Congressman Duncan Hunter, remarked on Congress' efforts to do better by our reserve and National Guard soldiers: "Extremely high deployment rates for members of the National Guard and Reserves have taken a toll on these personnel and their families. [This bill] recognizes their sacrifice and works to support their needs" (U.S. Congress 2003).

THE REAL CHALLENGE AHEAD:
"SEAMLESS" INTEGRATION OF FORCE COMPONENTS

In this most recent conflict in Iraq, the nation asked its reservists to answer the call of their country on what was basically a moment's notice. Many men and women were asked to leave their jobs, businesses, families, and obligations behind with as little as 72-hours notice. They answered the call and performed magnificently. Congress has worked with the Department of Defense to identify and provide funding to address as many inequities in their compensation and treatment as possible. However, we policy makers must not sit back and wait for the next conflict to prod us into action. We must not count on our reserve and National Guard to continually set their lives aside with little notice and deploy for indeterminate missions and shifting periods of time. We know that we cannot maintain a ready and viable active component in this manner, so we should not expect to maintain the reserve component this way.

To a certain extent, the nation's experience in its last major conflict, the 1991 Persian Gulf War, prevented policy makers from fully realizing the extent of the demand that would be placed on reservists during the sustained war on terrorism. Approximately 220,000 reservists and National Guardsmen were activated in the six months building up to Operation Desert Storm (U.S. General Accounting Office 2003). Almost all of them were able to return home within a year or less of their date of activation. The short duration of the Persian Gulf War, and the fact that forces deployed in that conflict were not exposed to prolonged, guerrilla, and insurgent attacks failed to highlight some of the inadequacies in equipment, training, and compensation levels that have become evident during the current conflict in Iraq.

The 220,000 reservists called up for the Persian Gulf War were called up with just 10 separate mobilization orders. This number contrasts sharply with the 264 mobilization orders signed to date to activate the 280,000 reserve members called to serve in the operation in Iraq. Policy makers must continue to ask whether we have achieved the ability to integrate reserve and National Guard troops with their active component counterparts in the "seamless" manner required to fully realize the benefits and capabilities of the total force concept. The answer to that question is complex, but I would submit that at this point the answer is no, we have not.

The change in the world after September 11 also changed the challenge of integrating the reserve and active duty components. In preparation for the first Persian Gulf War, military commanders activated and deployed reserve forces according to existing operational plans. These plans called for the activation of entire reserve units in support of broad mission statements. The international political environment was much more stable. Coalition partners during the first Gulf War were committed to supply a certain measurable amount of assistance. Access to bases was more certain. National Guard and reserve forces had not been called up in previous years to fly combat air patrols over domestic cities or to provide security at airports all over the country. Much more uncertainty existed in the months leading up to the current conflict in Iraq.

As existing operational plans proved inadequate at identifying requirements for the Iraqi conflict, the Department of Defense began using a modified mobilization process, activating reservists in much smaller units, and sometimes individually. Coordination was much more difficult, and much slower. As can be expected, radical change without time to plan highlighted the shortcomings and inflexibility of existing mechanisms. Readiness-reporting systems could not provide enough detail on the equipment and training readiness of the smaller subunits that were being called up. Some units were kept on alert for more than a year without ever being mobilized. In some cases, the services could not track who had been deployed and for how long.

The manner in which reservists were deployed in the early stages of this conflict leaves much to be desired. A recently completed study states that in response to the modified mobilization process, Air Force officials drafted a revised mobilization instruction to reflect changes in the "roles and responsibilities of personnel and the flow of information that had occurred under the modified mobilization process" (U.S. General Accounting Office 2003). However, the instruction was never finalized and never signed. Regardless, some Air Force mobilization officials followed the draft provisions while others stuck with the original instruction. In some cases this led to Air Force components being mobilized without their parent headquarters' knowledge.

The Department of Defense must continue to work to understand the new environment in which the total force must operate and ensure that the system in place has the flexibility to deploy servicemen and servicewomen in as orderly and predictable a fashion as possible.

Another important facet of the reserve component's readiness to seamlessly integrate with the active component is the state of its equipment and training. The current conflict in Iraq focused a bright spotlight on some glaring deficiencies in the equipment available to the reserve component. Stories of frantic parents attempting to buy substitute body armor plates for their children who are either reserve or active component soldiers still equipped with Vietnam-era flak jackets are truly shocking in a nation that spends close to $400 billion each year on its armed forces. While the 2004 Authorization Act included some funding to improve reserve component equipment, far more remains to be done.

A recent DOD report projects a $16.5 billion equipment shortage among the reserve component.

> Many of the Reserve Components received a large portion of their equipment by cascading equipment models from the Active Component to the Reserve Component. As the Active Component received newer and more modern equipment, the older, less efficient, and less capable equipment it replaced was transferred to the Reserve Component. This transfer, although improving equipment on-hand readiness, creates a host of maintenance and compatibility issues related to equipment age and modernization. The Reserve Components often face the dilemma of receiving the Active Component's most aged equipment and not having adequate resources to repair and maintain it in proper warfighting condition. In some instances, commercial production lines to manufacture repair parts have been shut down and repair parts were simply not available (U.S. Department of Defense 2003, 1–5).

These shortages are particularly severe in aircraft modernizations.

The fact that the U.S. reserve force is not equipped to the same level as the active duty force reflects a budget decision that may have seemed prudent in a pre–September 11, 2001, world in which large-scale reserve deployments were expected to have long lead-up times when equipment and training shortages could be addressed. However, as the events of the last year have shown, the armed forces no longer have the luxury of long advance warning times.

After September 11, 2001, active component military commanders came to Congress and explained that the current environment compelled them to invest heavily in readiness versus procurement. Congress applauded their foresight and prudence; their wise investment was evident in their performance and readiness to surge and overwhelm an adversary in Iraq. The nation must applaud the reserve component for stepping onto that same tortured landscape with confidence and resolve, knowing that they did not have the most advanced protective systems with which their active duty counterparts were equipped.

If the nation is to remain committed to a total force concept, it can no longer tolerate such great disparities between the active and the reserve components as those that presently exist. The Department of Defense and the Congress must continue to work with active and reserve component military commanders to ensure that the units they command are properly equipped and trained to fight together on short notice.

There is no question in my mind that the United States has the finest military in the world. The fact that it is an entirely volunteer force reflects the great patriotism and sense of duty of successive generations of Americans. The nation has repeatedly called on its military to do the impossible, and it has never failed us. Often, when intractable, complex, and messy disasters and conflicts threaten American lives or interests at home or abroad, and the resources of civilian or international agencies are not up to the task of resolving them, our military commanders are asked to find a way—and they always do.

War is a shocking, terrible experience that forever changes the lives of servicemen and servicewomen who endure it. The nation's leaders must always think long and hard about asking our young men and women to go into harm's way for their country. Military commanders will tell you that our military force has the highest morale when it is actively engaged overseas, doing the job for which it was trained, and helping protect American lives and interests at home and abroad. U.S. soldiers sign up for a reason. They believe in that for which our country stands. They are willing to fight to protect those ideas and to fight to allow others to enjoy the same liberty and freedom that we protect so zealously. They willingly put themselves into harm's way because they understand that the American people are behind them. They trust their commanders to make the correct decisions to accomplish their mission and protect the lives of those in their charge. They also expect to be properly equipped, trained, and compensated for the job we ask them to do. We must not fail in doing so.

There is no way the United States could have been successful in the Persian Gulf War, in Operation Noble Eagle, in Operation Enduring Freedom, or in Operation Iraqi Freedom without the reserve forces. The reserve component is an increasingly critical element of the total force that secures our homeland and powers our efforts abroad. Every member of the reserves swears an oath to support and defend the constitution of the United States of America. They vow to obey the orders of those appointed over them. This is the same oath that each and every active duty member makes. All, if called to action, are willing to sacrifice their lives, time with their families, and their futures to protect our nation, our freedoms, and our way of life. Because of their commitment and sacrifice, the United States Congress and Department of Defense have a responsibility and obligation to support, train, and equip the men and women of our reserves just as they do the members of the active force.

REFERENCES

U.S. Congress. 2003. House Armed Services Committee. Press release on completion of 2004 Defense Authorization Bill. Washington, D.C.: House Armed Services Committee Press Office.

U.S. Department of Defense. 2001. *Quadrennial defense review.* Washington, D.C. Office of the Secretary of Defense.

———. 2003. *National Guard and reserve equipment report for fiscal year 2004.* Washington, D.C.: Office of the Assistant Secretary of Defense for Reserve Affairs (Materiel and Facilities).

U.S. General Accounting Office. 2003. *Military personnel: DOD actions needed to improve the efficiency of mobilizations for reserve forces.* GAO-03-921. August. Washington, D.C.: U.S. Government Printing Office.

RESERVE COMPONENT CONTRIBUTIONS TO THE AVF

★ ★ ★ ★ ★ ★ ★ ★ ★ ★ ★

CHAPTER 10

MANNING THE FORCE WHILE AT WAR: A CRITICAL CHALLENGE

James R. Helmly

Manning the force, from my perspective, *is the most critical issue* facing both the active and reserve components. I remember several years ago being invited to Capitol Hill for a breakfast for leaders of the reserve components. The chief or the deputy chief of each of the reserve components was in attendance. Unexpectedly, we were asked a question by the congressmen present. "Would each of you please take the podium and tell us what you believe to be your top three critical issues?" I was then a brigadier general and thus was last to respond.

Each of the chiefs in turn remarked that they needed funding for various weapons and systems—airplanes, radar systems, naval vessels, trucks, tanks— for construction projects, or for training. When it was my turn, I said, "In my judgment, I believe the three most critical issues that we face in the Army Reserve, and that in fact we all face, whether active or reserve component, are manning the force, manning the force, and manning the force." That statement still expresses my judgment today.

CHANGED REALITIES

Although the world has changed, we in the Department of Defense continue to create expectations for our most critical element—our people—based on the realities of a world that no longer exists. I know of no better example of this fact than a photo of an Army truck that I saw on the Internet several months ago. With the power of modern technology, I was able to zoom in on the photograph in order to see all of its details. In the front window, the truck had a small, hand-lettered sign that read, "One weekend a month, my butt."

Various people in the Pentagon became alarmed when it was discovered that the photograph was of an Army Reserve truck. They asked if I was concerned. I had two observations: that I am not and that I am. My first observation was

★

simply that the soldiers were having their day and sharing some humor, which should be allowed and was no cause for concern. On the other hand, I was concerned because the photograph illustrated that the expectations we in the reserve components have set for our force are no longer realistic. We have set the expectation that Army Reserve soldiers serve for one weekend per month and two weeks in the summer, and are rarely called up to participate in operations. This expectation certainly does not describe the experiences of our reserve soldiers today.

THE ARMY CULTURE

The Army's culture is based on the notion of mobilizing the force. The Army garrisons the force and then mobilizes it for a large war of a discrete nature. The war begins on a specific day, it involves masses of people and machines that fight against an opponent's mass of people and machines, and it ends on a given day. These expectations were well matched by the Desert Shield and Desert Storm experience. That war began in early August 1990. The first reserve unit was mobilized on August 9. At the height of the war, in January 1991, the Army Reserve had 84,000 soldiers mobilized. By the following October, every Army Reserve soldier had been demobilized, and most of the active component soldiers had also returned home to yellow ribbons and parades. The war was over. The task for the Army was completed.

That paradigm, however, is not serving the Army Reserve well in this new war — the global war on terrorism — and the friction of operating in a new world under an old paradigm is beginning to show. The Army Reserve has been in a continuous state of mobilization since December 1995. Since that time, the Army has done little to change the way it is manning the force, supporting the force, or training the force — all of the things that affect the recruiting and retention of its people. It is not surprising that reserve members still believe, "One weekend a month, two weeks in the summer, and I will not be mobilized except to fight a 'big war' of a discrete nature, and then for a relatively short duration."

A BRIEF HISTORY

Before discussing policies and practices, I would like to offer a brief history of the Army Reserve. The Army Reserve was organized in 1908. The history of our nation's reserve components is rich, tracing back to 1636 when the militia was formed. The modern-day version of the militia is the state National Guards — both Air and Army — that serve proudly alongside the federal reserve components.[1]

The Army Reserve was the first organized federal reserve component, created largely to perform as an auxiliary to the regular Army. The regular Army, at that time, found that it needed certain capabilities only during times of war — such as medical support on the battlefield. But the Army could not afford to retain such skills in the regular Army, within the strength levels or budget resources authorized by Congress. As a result, the Army petitioned Congress to establish, and then created, an organized medical reserve corps, as an auxiliary to the regular Army.

Today, the Army Reserve again serves primarily as a provider of auxiliary capability, referred to as combat support and combat service support capability, rather than as a force in reserve—that is, a supplementary force with a balance of combat arms and support capabilities such as is found in the Army National Guard. Yet the Army Reserve continues to organize, man, train, sustain, and mobilize the force as a force in reserve. Little change has been made in the way the Army does business to accommodate how the reserve forces are actually being used.

A RETURN TO THE DRAFT?

I agree with Stephen Herbits, who wrote earlier in this volume about the need to appropriately manage the many "knobs and dials" that have an impact on the all-volunteer force—those knobs and dials being the various policies, practices, and procedures that govern how the services man the force (chapter 1, this volume). If the Department of Defense does not fine-tune its manpower and personnel policies, we in the military leadership will unfairly force our nation to return to the debate over conscription versus a volunteer force.

I believe this statement to be true because of an experience we had in the Army soon after September 11, 2001. The Army held a high-level planning session to address the longer-range implications of the global war on terrorism. A number of senior officers from the retired community participated in these discussions. One of these retired generals remarked that the Army was no longer going to be able to effectively man the force—that it would be necessary to return to the draft. I believe this pronouncement was a knee-jerk reaction, which I challenge.

Conscription does not result in the kind of force that is needed in the Army today—that supports the way the Army must fight and provides the kind of skills required. A draft functions as an inefficient, ineffective mobilization. It generates a large quantity of raw, untrained manpower, which must be trained and infused into organized units to provide a capability. It does not mobilize already-trained personnel who can be organized and structured into agile, flexible units.

During the conscription era, the Army trained draftees to skill level 10, which prepares service members for a job at the rank of private. But skill-level-10 manpower does not fly rotary-wing aircraft at 10,000 feet and higher; it does not refuel over a 1,000-mile flight to insert highly trained special forces soldiers into remote areas; it does not intercept messages and decode Farsi into English; and it does not map out campaign plans against terrorist cells. In short, the Army needs highly skilled manpower. A draft cannot provide that level of skill. The all-volunteer force does.

I believe the knee-jerk reactions consisting of calls for a return to the draft are fueled by concern over whether the services will be able to continue to call on individuals in the reserve components in the quantity and with the frequency needed. The question is asked, "Will the nation sustain a mobilization?" If the answer to this question is no, then the resulting view is often that the Army needs to grow in size and to resort to a draft to man the force. This approach reflects industrial-age thinking. It has no place in today's information-age war against terrorism: a war of indeterminate length and punctuated by intense, volatile, and violent campaigns of shorter duration—a characterization suggested by our experiences in Afghanistan and Iraq. So the challenge is to figure out how to use the volunteer force we have, to fight the war that we face, without breaking down the very fabric of the force—its people.

TRANSFORMING POLICIES AND PRACTICES

In the early years of the all-volunteer force, the Army focused on manning the active component. This focus was appropriate, as the active component is indeed the "point of the spear." But the reserve components were manned as an accidental by-product of active component recruiting. There was not an intentional and deliberate policy to man the reserve component in a way that was appropriate for the tasks that they would perform. There is no place for such a casual approach today. The Army needs to move past industrial-age impediments to manning the force in order to succeed in an information-age war.

STRUCTURE

First, let me address the issue of structure: the number, size, and composition of units in the force. When I assumed leadership of the Army Reserve, I conducted an assessment of the organization to identify the challenges and strains it was experiencing. I found that our force structure called for 226,000 Army Reserve soldiers, but that our authorized strength was only 205,000. This anomaly is not unique to the Army Reserve; it is also evident in the active component of the Army and in the Army National Guard. The imbalance between structure and strength reflects an industrial-age model that assumes a linear mobilization process dependent on a mass infusion of manpower. Instead, the Army Reserve needs to structure its manpower requirements to be equal to or slightly below the authorized strength of 205,000. In doing so, we will be able to fully man our units with trained personnel.

Further, the Army Reserve is not structured as a mirror image of the regular Army. The regular Army and the Army National Guard are both balanced forces with a mix of combat, combat support, and combat service support units. In contrast, the Army Reserve is structured almost entirely to provide combat service support. Twenty percent of this structure consists of service members in the medical discipline; ten percent are in civil affairs. In over 50 of the Army's 196 occupation specialties, over half the capability is in the reserve. Some of those specialties require training in excess of 30 weeks before a soldier is qualified in the discipline. Yet there are no policies to provide specialized training to inactive-duty reserve soldiers in those specialties.

HIGHLY SKILLED SPECIALTIES

The length of the Army's service obligation can be at odds with requirements for many highly skilled specialties. In general, the Army Reserve has an eight-year mandatory service obligation. In a number of highly skilled occupational specialties, the attrition rate is over 50 percent during a soldier's initial enlistment of six to eight years. Recruits are interested in training for these specialties, but not in the lengthy service obligation. So they participate in the training and the one-weekend-per-month requirement, but then rapidly leave the selected reserve for the individual ready reserve. Today, there is no penalty for making this move. Yet a large part of the problem is that the Army recruits individuals for these highly skilled specialties in the same way that it recruits infantry soldiers—relying on the same marketing, advertising, and subsequent training. Using an industrial-age approach to recruiting will not work in the future.

The medical specialty provides a particularly good example of why more than one approach to recruiting and retention is needed. The U.S. Army's medical care capabilities are resident in the reserve. For over seven years, the Army Reserve has failed to recruit physicians in sufficient numbers. I have developed an increasingly close relationship with Lieutenant General James B. Peake, Surgeon General of the Army. General Peake is extremely knowledgeable about the Army's dependence on its reserve medical units and physicians to provide critical medical care around the world. Yet until 1995, little had been done to craft an approach to recruiting and retaining physicians in a way that is appropriate for this discipline. As a result, I chartered a process action team to recommend a focused approach to recruiting and retaining medical care personnel—one that is not tied to structure but instead to inventory availability. Today, the Army has a 90-day rotation policy in place for physicians, which allows them to serve in the reserve without disrupting their private practices. Manpower requirements for physicians will no longer be based on unit structure, but will instead be based on the number needed to provide the Army Reserve with a three-year capability to sustain 90-day rotations.

CIVILIAN-BASED SKILLS

A number of the tasks performed by the Army Reserve require skills that are primarily civilian based, such as skills related to civil affairs. Some of these skills are in high demand today. One approach that has been suggested to reduce the stress on these career fields is to increase the capability in the active component. I challenge that approach. I believe we should increase the capability in the Army Reserve to a level where we no longer have to mobilize the same reserve soldiers continuously. The Army Reserve is working to develop a structure that would involve mobilizing individual reserve soldiers for a single 9-to-12-month period within a five-year window.

COMPENSATION

To develop and sustain a more focused method of recruiting and retention requires resources. Today, the law requires the Army to provide each reserve soldier no fewer than 48 inactive-duty training periods and 14 days of annual training. An inactive-duty training period is defined as lasting a minimum of four hours, for which a reserve soldier receives a day of pay but no allowances. Over a two-day weekend, a reserve soldier works four training periods and receives four days' pay. I am in favor of the concept of compensating reserve soldiers with a day of pay for a day of work. But if this approach is adopted, the reserve soldier also needs to receive a portion of the allowances and special pays that would be available to an active duty soldier.

In many specialties — such as aviation and linguistics — reservists must meet the same qualification standards as active duty soldiers, but they receive a smaller amount of proficiency pay. The reserve aviator must fly the same number of hours per month to be fully qualified, yet the reservist receives a smaller amount of proficiency pay. (For example, if the reservist flew the required hours in two days during weekend training, he or she would receive $^2/_{30}$ of a month's flight pay.) This same situation applies to medical specialists, parachutists, and intelligence specialists — members of career fields in which the Army faces shortages and is very dependent on the reserve force. This industrial-age entitlement process must be changed.

TRAINING

Training must be improved. The readiness and availability of reservists will improve as we in the Army fully man the force and implement a new approach to training. Reserve training needs to begin prior to mobilization. The Army Reserve has created an "individuals account" to better track people who are temporarily unable to perform their mission with their unit — that is, individuals between assignment to units, in initial entry training, in hospitals, and in school. As this approach is implemented, the reserves will be more ready and more available to fulfill their mission.

EMPLOYERS AND FAMILIES

Even if the Army is successful in reducing the frequency of deployments and providing greater predictability to its reserve soldiers, it must be sensitive to the fact that the primary income for a reserve member comes from his or her civilian employment. Furthermore, the training and skills that Army Reserve soldiers bring from the civilian sector are one of the strengths of the reserve components. So it is important that the Army Reserve work in closer cooperation with members' civilian employers.

Similarly, the Army needs to work more closely with the families of its members. While great progress has been made in many aspects of family support, there is much to be done to improve communication. This need was evident recently when the Army announced its intention to lengthen mobilization tours to support ongoing operations in Iraq. The Army did not approach this announcement with care. We used "Pentagonese" — the language military leaders use to communicate about military operations. Families do not understand this language; they understand English. Families need background information and a more careful explanation of what is required of them. This recent experience was a big lesson for the Army.

CULTURE

Culture must change. The change in military culture that is required to fit the realities of the global war on terrorism is very much like the change in culture that was required when the department moved from a conscripted force to an all-volunteer force. The Army needs to change the reserve culture that is based on "one weekend a month, two weeks in the summer." Instead, reservists need to believe that they are soldiers who use civilian-based skills in the performance of their military duty. They need to understand that they will be used — that they will be mobilized for periods of time, but in a way that will allow them to simultaneously maintain their civilian career. This means that the Army needs to ensure that members receive adequate notice in advance of deployments and that deployments are more predictable in length. This is the challenge we in the Army Reserve face.

CONCLUSION

I am proud of the quality of our force in the Army Reserve. Our new Army Reserve recruits meet the same high enlistment standards, in terms of education and aptitude, as do their active duty counterparts. The Army Reserve has traditionally exceeded the Department of Defense benchmarks of at least 90 percent of recruits having a high school diploma and 60 percent scoring in categories I–IIIA on the Armed Forces Qualification Test. About half of its members have prior service experience and about half do not; thus much of this quality is coming from the civilian community directly into the Army Reserve. The Army also has more female soldiers in its reserve than are in any other component of the armed services — owing largely to the fact that most of the Army Reserve structure is open to women.

I would like to close by returning to Steve Herbits's analogy of the knobs and dials — the policy tools available to manage the force. Whether we fail or succeed in the global war on terrorism will be directly linked to how we sustain the all-volunteer force. I believe it is too soon to evaluate the overall impact of ongoing operations in Afghanistan and Iraq on the all-volunteer force in general and the Army Reserve in particular. Regardless, there are areas where we can learn from this experience and where improvements can be made. For example, when the Army mobilized the reserves to support Operation Iraqi Freedom, our service members were too often faced with unexpectedly short notice of mobilization — sometimes five days or fewer from alert to mobilization. Due to the nature of the war, a large number of soldiers were quickly mobilized, but then many of those soldiers found themselves waiting for several months at mobilization stations. Some were demobilized; thousands were then remobilized. In the future, the Army must do better, because the way we use the force is directly related to our ability to recruit and retain the force. Once again, it is about how we manage the knobs and the dials.

NOTES

1. The federal reserve components are the Army Reserve, Air Force Reserve, Marine Corps Reserve, Naval Reserve, and Coast Guard Reserve.

★ ★ ★ ★ ★ ★ ★ ★ ★ ★ ★

CHAPTER 11

THE RESERVES AND GUARD: STANDING IN THE CIVIL-MILITARY GAP BEFORE AND AFTER 9/11

Peter D. Feaver
David P. Filer
Paul Gronke

INTRODUCTION

Since the founding of the American republic, observers have entertained contradictory worries about how to harmonize the civilian and military worlds. One line of concern has been that a dysfunctional gap could emerge between the military, especially a standing army or later an all-volunteer force (AVF), and the civilian society it has pledged to protect. Another line of concern has been that civil society—reflecting the biases of liberalism and individualism and the hurly-burly of democratic politics—could undermine military capacity by starving it of needed resources or forcing it to fit a civilian mold.

As with many other political concerns, the framers of the Constitution dealt with these concerns through a series of innovative compromises. Responsibility for and power over the military would be shared among civilian institutions; the armed forces themselves would be composed of a small professionalized component and, in an emergency, a larger group of citizen-soldiers, the body of the citizenry embodied in militia or volunteers—men with more than half of a foot firmly planted in the civilian world but armed and ready to defend the state against attacks from abroad (or usurpations of power from within).

The temporary expedient of various forms of conscription during major wars, and then the continuation of selective conscription during the cold war, modified the compromise in various ways but did not erase the underlying tension, which reemerged with greater urgency upon the establishment of a volunteer force in 1973. Although the nation's experience with conscription was short and decidedly mixed, some observers warned that embracing a fully professionalized military could produce a dangerous gap between the military and American society.

★

The worry was multifold. Fewer and fewer civilians would have military experience and thus perhaps fewer and fewer would possess the knowledge and wisdom to wield civilian control. A self-selected and isolated, but large and capable, military caste might develop a sense of superiority and come to reject the basic democratic values that it had pledged to defend. A citizenry disengaged from the responsibility of military service might lose basic civic values. A professional military might devolve into a mercenary force seeking foreign adventures; and so on.[1] "Gap critics" were balanced by those who postulated that the AVF would lead to a growing (and sometimes problematic) convergence between military and civilian institutions. Forced to compete with the private sector for labor, the military would increasingly lose its distinctive nature and become "just another job," catering to the vagaries and sensibilities of "employees," and, when necessary, compromising military effectiveness to meet recruiting and retention goals.[2] Finally, many simply dismissed the concerns of both varieties of critics.

The shift to the AVF coincided with the increase in importance of the institutional descendants of the old militia, by this time embodied in the reserves and National Guard and newly prominent in the total force concept. The impetus behind the total force was the need to preserve combat power even while shrinking the number of active duty troops. The total force brought with it, however, a side effect that at least some senior military leaders considered beneficial and deliberate: it tied the hands of future presidents and forced them to mobilize substantial public support before committing U.S. military troops in foreign conflicts. The idea was to put enough crucial combat and high-demand units in the reserves and guard that the U.S. military could only be deployed for short periods of time or for minor operations without a politically costly mobilization of citizen-soldiers. Thus, once again the Republic embraced an innovative compromise to address an age-old civil-military tension.

Thirty years into the AVF experience, it is clear that the worst fears of the critics have not materialized. Along many dimensions, the AVF has maintained a healthy connection with American society. At the same time, the worsening civil-military problems in the 1990s demonstrated that some of the concerns proved prophetic. In particular, the vigorous debate about a possible gap between the beliefs and values of America's military members and those of its general citizenry refocused attention on the costs and benefits of the AVF and, by extension, the possible role to be played by the reserve components of the total force.

In this light it is worth asking whether the reserves and National Guard have functioned as a citizen-soldier bridge between the American people on the one hand and a professional standing army on the other. This paper provides a partial answer to this question, or rather a series of partial answers, deduced by comparing various beliefs of reservists with those of civilians and active duty service members. We attempt to ascertain whether there is indeed a gap between the beliefs of military members and other citizens, and where the beliefs of reservists fall along this spectrum. We assume that if reservists hold beliefs resembling those of the American citizenry but differing from the active force, then reservists might serve to introduce those beliefs to the military. On the other hand, if reservists hold beliefs resembling those of active duty military members but differing from other civilians, then reservists might serve to introduce such beliefs to the civilian world.

Within the limits of our data, we find that today the reserves and National Guard are able to function as a citizen-soldier bridge, but one that runs primarily in one direction. In most respects, the guard and reserve bring military values into society, providing a vital source of contact between the civilian population and the armed forces. There is little evidence to suggest that the guard and reserve communicate civilian values to the military. Much to the contrary, the views and values of guard and reserve members are found to be "more military" in some respects than their active duty counterparts—a concept that we will explain later in our analyses.

We begin this paper with a brief summary of the prominent debate over the so-called civil-military gap, paying particular attention to the relevant findings of the project launched by the Triangle Institute for Security Studies (TISS). We next report the results of analyses that compare survey responses, drawn from the TISS data, of different groups of military members and civilians on a variety of issues related to civil-military relations. Since our data were collected before the September 11, 2001, attacks, we also address, in a necessarily more speculative manner, the possible ramifications of the new era for our findings. We close with a brief discussion of follow-on research questions raised by our analyses.

THE 1990S GAP FLAP

Civil-military relations became a hot topic in the 1990s, and numerous high-profile issues reflected a turbulent civil-military undercurrent. Among the issues with a civil-military component that initially emerged during the tenure of the elder George Bush were the debate over whether African Americans were disproportionately at risk in Desert Storm combat; the Tailhook controversy and the broader question of opening combat opportunities to women; the roles and missions debate and the question of undue Joint Staff influence in designing the post–cold war drawdown of forces; and vigorous allegations that senior military leaders were blocking possible U.S. military involvement in the former Yugoslavia. Yet it was the election of President Clinton—the first president of the Vietnam generation and a man personally associated with considerable civil-military controversy—that took civil-military problems to a new level and led some observers to worry about a "crisis" in American civil-military relations.

Of course, there was no "crisis" by comparative standards. There was no real question of a coup and, despite all the problems that were experienced during this period, it was still possible to boast, as President Clinton often did, that the U.S. military was the best equipped, best trained, most capable fighting force in history. After reviewing a litany of civil-military problems in the United States, one expert from a NATO ally observed to the authors, "In our country, we can only aspire to reach the depths of civil-military gap problems to which you are claiming the United States has sunk."

At the same time, there was no question that civil-military relations were stormy by U.S. historical standards. Numerous anecdotes pointed to the possibility of a more systemic problem. President Clinton encountered a bureaucratic revolt when he attempted to end the military's ban on openly homosexual men and women serving in uniform. The Joint Chiefs of Staff protested and encouraged protests from the retired military community. Congress acted to block the President, and Clinton was forced to make a humiliating retreat, settling for a "don't ask, don't tell" policy that clearly violated his campaign promises. The controversy stirred up so much ill will that an Air Force general gave a speech at an officers' banquet in which he referred to the President as that "draft-dodging, pot-smoking, skirt-chasing" commander in chief (Lancaster 1993). The antipathy seemed to be reciprocated: one low-level Clinton staffer at the White House allegedly told Lieutenant General Barry McCaffrey, "I don't talk to the military" (no author 1993), and the paucity of veterans in senior Clinton administration posts was taken by some to be a reflection of President Clinton's own antimilitary feelings. After all, as repeated by his critics, the President at one time wrote in a letter explaining his position on the draft that his generation "loathed the military" (Mathis 1992).

The age-old debate over a civil-military gap thus emerged as especially prominent: did these problems stem from a gap between the military and American society that was harmful and widening, or were these problems the product of a misguided attempt by ignorant civilians to remake the military in the civilians' image and thereby narrow what was in fact a functional gap. There were ample anecdotes to support either view.

Supporting the idea of a widening gap was Thomas Ricks (1997), a prominent defense correspondent who tracked a group of Marine recruits through basic training.[3] Ricks reported on how alienated the individuals were towards civilian society once they had successfully become Marines. The transformation from "slacker" to warrior apparently filled them with a strong sense of superiority with respect to their former civilian counterparts. Ricks saw parallels in the accounts by military analysts about military involvement in the culture war and connected these to other dots: the prominence of conservative evangelical religiosity among the military and the partisan exploitation of military symbols by Republicans in the 1992 and 1996 elections.

Supporting the idea of a deleterious narrowing of the gap were all of the accusations of unproductive and rampant "political correctness" in the ranks (Webb 1997, 1998; Hillen 1999; Kitfield 2000). The Clinton administration pushed for the expansion of combat opportunities for women, and numerous critics worried that military effectiveness was compromised. The gays-in-the-military imbroglio, of course, was framed precisely in this fashion: was it unacceptable or was it a military exigency for the military to discriminate against homosexual Americans in a fashion that would not be permitted in civilian society? Similar concerns were raised about holding the military to ever rising standards, whether with regard to the protection of the environment or the convergence of the military and civilian legal systems.

The debate was lively, but it was largely conducted at the level of dueling anecdotes. Accordingly, the Triangle Institute for Security Studies set out, at the urging and with the support of the Smith Richardson Foundation, to conduct a more systematic and comprehensive examination of the "gap" issue. In its study, TISS examined three questions: What is the nature of any gap or gaps? What factors shape these gaps? And what does any of this matter for civil-military cooperation and military effectiveness — that is, for national security?[4] To address these questions, the TISS team administered a survey designed to measure attitudes and beliefs about a range of domestic, defense, and foreign policy concerns — producing a one-of-a-kind data set on civilian and military opinions about civil-military relations. The survey was administered to elite (up-and-coming) military officers in all branches of service, including a small sample of officers from the reserve and guard; civilian elites in career stages comparable to the military officers; as well as to veterans and nonveterans in the general public.[5]

Viewed as a whole, the TISS study offers several major findings. First, there is not one civil-military gap but many civil-military gaps, or at least many dimensions to an overall gap. Second, along some of its dimensions, the gap appears to be widening, while along others it appears to be narrowing. Third, some of the gaps are functional and should be preserved; other gaps seem potentially dysfunctional and are candidates for remedial measures.

In broad terms, the military responses to most survey questions tended to fall somewhere in between those of the general public and those of the civilian elites, especially on domestic and foreign policy issues where responses tracked along a traditional left-right continuum. Civilian elites offered the most liberal responses; the military and the general public offered more conservative ones, with the latter often the most conservative of all. In some cases, though, the military was clearly an outlier. On some issues, such as support for higher defense spending, the outlying results are neither surprising nor particularly significant. On others, the results may be unsurprising but are potentially more significant. For instance, the small numbers of officers reporting "independent" or "no party" affiliation and the corresponding large numbers reporting "Republican," combined to create an eight to one Republican to Democrat split. When compared with historical data since the beginning of the AVF, this marked a dramatic decline in the number of "independents" and a corresponding rise in "Republicans;" such a shift could move the military away from its historical position of political neutrality to one of a more partisan cast.

The TISS project confirmed the long-standing finding that the public professes a high degree of confidence in the military. This encouraging poll result appears to mask, however, underlying friction and potential fault lines that could make that support more brittle than otherwise imagined. For instance, public confidence in the military is propped up by the significant presence of veterans in the civilian population, a feature that is on the decline as the World War II and Korean War generations pass on. There is, in other words, a growing "experience gap," or lack of military experience in the civilian population — most pronounced among the political elite yet also evident in the general public — and this gap will certainly widen over time.

For example, through the better part of the 20th century, there was a veterans premium among elected representatives—that is, more veterans in Congress than in the comparable demographic cohort in the general public. Over the last quarter century, however, that premium evaporated, and in 1994 there were even fewer veterans in Congress than in a comparable slice of the civilian population.

Moreover, along with expressions of support, the public also holds opinions that point to a more cynical view of the military. Civilians expect the military to act as a self-interested, strategic bureaucracy. For their part, military officers express strong support for the principle of civilian control but also harbor views that are at odds with the norms of civilian control. Incidentally, survey responses confirmed that civilians, both mass and elite, are even more confused than the military about the basic tenets of democratic civil-military relations theory.

There appear to be numerous factors at work in shaping the convergences and divergences of civilian and military opinion. The shift from a conscripted force to an all-volunteer force is an obvious and potentially critical factor, but it is not the only one. Changes in the structure of American parties, the erosion of the pro-defense wing of the Democratic Party, the end of the cold war, and, undoubtedly, the "Clinton factor" all play a role. Moreover, as we discuss below, changes since the TISS survey, most notably the response to the September 11 attacks, have probably also had an effect.

The experience gap appears to matter, at least insofar as the use of force is concerned. In a pattern that extends for most of American history, when veterans are amply represented in Congress and the executive branch, the United States is less likely to initiate the use of force; when the percentage of veterans is low, the United States is more likely to initiate the use of force. Moreover, military officers and civilian elites buy into a myth about the public being afflicted with a "body-bag syndrome." But the public is not casualty-phobic; it is defeat-phobic. Properly mobilized public support can be assured even for missions that risk significant American military casualties.

In summary, there is no gap-induced crisis in civil-military relations; certainly the TISS study uncovered no problem so severe as to require urgent and drastic action. At the same time, some of the trends discovered could grow into problems, and some of those problems are potentially important enough to merit the attention of senior leadership. In other words, there is enough of a gap to wonder whether today's guard and reserve members—citizen-soldiers with a foot planted firmly in a civilian occupation but at the same time wearing a uniform of the armed forces—can provide a human bridge between civilian society and military institutions, and potentially serve to close the gap.

STANDING IN THE GAP:
THE ROLE OF MILITARY RESERVES

Stephen M. Duncan (1997, 243) stresses the importance of the military reservist in American society: "I believe that the absence of mandatory military service for all Americans, the tenets of effective democracy, and a concern for proper balance in our civil-military relations will continue to require citizen volunteers who can assume the warrior in the interest of country, and return to their figurative ploughs when danger passes."[6] Duncan implies that the military reservist is someone who can share the good news of military service with those who otherwise would fail to have such knowledge and can carry ideals consistent with democratic society into an authoritative, hierarchical military. He claims that this function is critical for "the proper balance in our civil-military relations."

William Blackstone, in commenting on the American citizen-soldier, wrote: "[A man] put not off the citizen when he enters the camp; but it is because he is a citizen, and would wish to continue so, that he makes himself for a while a soldier" (Duncan 1997, xi). American military reservists are interesting because they are *soldiers* and at the same time they are *civilians*. They are, so to speak, a mixed breed. The necessary question to ask then is: When they "enter the camp" do they bring the citizen with them? Likewise, when they return home, do they bring the soldier? In other words, are military reservists attitudinally closest to their civilian counterparts, and do they thus bring with them civilian attitudes and beliefs when they perform their military service? Or do they have a belief system more similar to that of their comrades in arms and bring military values and beliefs with them when they return to civilian society? Or might they think like the military on some issues and like civilians on others, possibly transferring military belief systems to civilians and civilian belief systems to the military?

Studies concerning military reserves focus on several different aspects of the citizen-soldier in both military and civilian realms. Binkin and Kaufmann (1989), Brehm (1992), and Heller (1994) look to find the mix of reserve forces and active duty military forces that will maximize the fighting effectiveness of the military at a minimum cost. Hart (1998) and Jacobs (1994) provide a rich history of reserve forces that includes the American saga of the citizen-soldier. This past, grounded in the militia clauses of the Constitution and the founders' distaste for large standing militaries, has normative implications for the future of the American military force. Cragin (1999), Duncan (1997), and Kirby et al. (1997) consider the effects on citizen-soldiers of their recent increased uses for wartime as well as contingency missions.

The American citizen-soldier, long a symbol of an American's right and desire to protect his or her nation, today serves on par with his active duty counterpart in all branches of the military. Although there is still and always has been debate over the effectiveness and readiness of military reserves (see Binkin and Kaufmann 1989 and Duncan 1997), mobilization of the active duty force for war or any armed conflict would be impossible without military reserve support (Duncan 1997). Indeed, since the end of the cold war, the President has called on the reserves several times (Cragin 1999), and military reservists have served even more often on a voluntary basis. Military reserves, including the National Guard, make up roughly one half of the nation's military fighting strength (U.S. Department of Defense 2004). As reserve forces are deployed with active duty forces, at home and abroad, for many types of contingencies and missions, the lines between active and reserve forces are increasingly blurred.

Louis Zurcher (1986) suggests that military reserves are suited for a "bridging" role between the active duty military and civilian institutions. He proposes that military reserves can be "networkers" or "constructive brokers" by "balancing diverse ideologies through the processes of civilianizing and militarizing." "Networking," according to Zurcher, "is the activity of individuals to coordinate, polarize, or somehow enlist the cooperation of components of the multiorganizational field toward an accomplishment desired by the net workers or by those whom they represent." The accomplishment here, of course, is the improvement of national defense, and reservists, as effective networkers, can and should work toward mobilizing the resources of the military and civilian sectors to that end. Networking does not mean that they necessarily have to procure defense-related money or equipment (although Zurcher is quick to point out that they have the capability in some cases to do so), but that reserves should network people and ideas across whatever boundaries exist between civilian and military sectors.

Zurcher focuses more on the reservist having the potential to "civilianize" the military, although he says that they can also "militarize" civilian society, and that both of these efforts are important to civil-military relations. Given what he calls a "functionally marginal position," or membership in both worlds, reservists can and should represent and merge the orientations of the different groups with which they are affiliated. It is this function that he labels constructive brokering.

Our paper examines the attitudinal profile of military reserve officers and tests the hypothesis that military reserves, as part civilian and part soldier, "leaven" not only the attitudes, beliefs, and values of the military, but also leaven the attitudes, beliefs, and values of civilian society.[7] Where Zurcher primarily focuses on reserves as possible "civilianizers" of the military force, we explore the possibility that military reservists might effectively bring military attitudes and values to civilian society as well. Therefore, the military reserves may act as a bridge to both sides, not a bridge built by only one side to reach the other, and may theoretically reduce the culture gap between civilian society and the military. Where Zurcher's study relies heavily on theory without much empirical evidence, we use unique data that allow us to determine the attitudinal profile of military reserve officers, in relation to the attitudes of their civilian and military counterparts, on a variety of different issues.

THE NATURE OF MILITARY RESERVISTS

Not much has been written about the attitudinal characteristics of military reservists. Within the all-volunteer force, one may surmise that military reservists serve by choice—which sets them apart from their counterparts in civilian society who do not serve and may make them attitudinally closer to their military counterparts, who also elected to serve. Even those senior officers who initially came into service under conscription (both active duty military and military reservists) remain in the force by choice. Duncan (1997, x) says, "Most senior American reservists, officer and enlisted, have experienced active service in uniform. Many have several years of active service. Many have combat experience. All are volunteers. This necessarily sets them apart from the vast majority of their fellow citizens who have never served."

In addition, Duncan points out that to understand the military reservist, one must understand the "warrior culture," of which military reserves, by the very fact of their service in uniform, are a part. "Service in uniform," he says, "in the last half of the last decade of this century attracts a special breed of American citizen and influences its adherents in unique ways." Finally, Duncan asserts, military service in general "casts a spell on people who engage in it" (Duncan 1997, xii). His implication is that the "spell" of service, whether active or reserve, causes the beliefs of the military to diverge from those of civilian society. Therefore, we might expect members of the active duty military and military reserves to be attitudinally similar because they share at least the experience of service.

Conversely, military reservists might be closer attitudinally to their counterparts in civilian society because, despite their intermittent military service, they are civilians. Therefore, they conceivably could bring a value system more consistent with civilian society to the military. Samuel Huntington (1957, 17) claims that military reservists have values and beliefs that are aligned with those of civilian society. He asserts that the reservist "only temporarily assumes professional [military] responsibility," because his primary roles in society are elsewhere. Consequently, military reservists have greatly different values, motivations, and behavior than do professional career military officers. Simply stated, they think more like civilians. Zurcher (1986, 225) agrees that the ideological perspectives of reservists are different from those of military careerists. He points to studies of naval reservists that show they are likely to be politically diverse; critical as well as supportive of the military on certain issues; conservative, but "not remarkably so," given that they are primarily civilian in their views; and "much more satisfied with democratic than with authoritarian leadership." Zurcher points out that the reserves infuse the military with a civilian perspective, and, though not "ideologically homogenous," are "different enough" from military careerists to provide an exchange of perspectives and open up a dialogue.

The very institution that originally trained college students to be military reserve officers, the Reserve Officer Training Corps (ROTC), was based on an assumption that educating and training civilians who have a classically liberal background and education would produce officers that would leaven the military with civilian values. Michael Neiburg (2000, 2–3) claims that the creation and evolution of ROTC has been grounded in the intensely held American belief, shared by educators, politicians, and college students alike, in the importance of populating the military with "nonprofessional" officers produced outside the traditional military academies. Officers educated in civilian institutions would have a wider and more well-rounded set of experiences. Analogous to some claims about the guard and reserves, ROTC officers would bring to the military a value system more consistent with that of the larger American society.

How Leavening Might Work

The military reservist provides a potential solution for marginalizing the culture-values gap between civilians and the military by bringing military ideals and values to civilian society. Using logic derived from Huntington's mention of the military's role in the National Defense Act of 1920 (which provided soldiers as instructors at government-sponsored youth summer training camps in an effort to influence society's support for a strong national defense), one can envision a like role for military reserves in "leavening" civilian society.[8] The military reservist who serves with the active force returns to home and hearth, to his place of business or government service job, and to his church, and relates things military to those around him. Civilians glean from the reservist an understanding of military values and gain a measure of support for the military as an institution. As a prescription for the use of military reserves, Duncan (1997, 237) argues that "reservists should be visible in Heartland America." The presence of military reserve units in each state (to include Army and Air National Guard units) enhances public support for the nation's armed forces generally, as well as for each particular service represented.

Conversely, military reservists could be the vehicle that carries "meaningful integration with civilian values" to their active duty military counterparts. In other words, military reservists could leaven the military by bringing civilian values with them when they serve with the active duty force. The military has a difficult time accepting civilian values because "the forms of military social life and the social origins of the military profession make the cosmopolitan outlook difficult" (Duncan 1997, 211). Honor, rigidity, and traditionalism discourage military elites from changing their views. Military reservists, serving with the active duty force, might not be so inhibited by military values. They could have the "cosmopolitanism" and detachment that Janowitz (1971) says is required of military managers. Through contact with reservists, cosmopolitanism could "rub off," so to speak, on the active duty service members. In this way, "civilian values" could be integrated into the active duty military.

Zurcher provides other examples of how leavening might work. What we refer to as leavening, Zurcher calls "networking." Reservists, by simply demonstrating a willingness to "occupy" both civilian and military statuses, can influence others' views of the civilian or military sectors. When a reservist consciously undertakes this task, he or she becomes an asset to *both* sectors. Zurcher says that reserves can reverse the process of structural divergence in ideologies between civilians and the military if the process is unproductive, or speed it up if it is productive. Similarly, reservists who call themselves "professionals" in their civilian occupations may consciously encourage the maintenance of professionalism in the military as well. And those who hold "occupations" in civilian life might actively support "emerging occupationalism" in the military — that is, approaching military service as "just another job" that is evaluated primarily on the material rewards (pay and benefits) it offers (Zurcher 1986, 229).

DESCRIBING THE CIVIL-MILITARY GAP

Data from the TISS survey are used in this paper to study the attitudes of military reservists as a way of describing the nature of the civil-military gap in some detail. As mentioned previously, the TISS questionnaire was administered to both military personnel and civilians. More specifically, the results described here reflect the responses of three primary groups of survey respondents: "up-and-coming" active duty officers (military elites), comparable officers from the reserve and guard, and civilian elites.[9] Data reflecting the views of the general public (referred to as the "mass" subgroup) — both veterans and nonveterans — are used for comparison for some of the issues evaluated. In this paper, we examine seven issue areas: military change and effectiveness, domestic economic and social issues, moral and social traditionalism, confidence in the military, the military's functional and social imperatives, views of military and civilian culture, and military inclusion of homosexual Americans and better opportunities for women serving in the military.

For each issue, we ascertain whether military reservists are attitudinally aligned with civilians, the active duty military, or neither.[10] Thus, these analyses help us determine whether reservists leaven civilian society or the military, and are thereby *citizens-first reserves* (those that are attitudinally closest to civilians), *soldiers-first reserves* (those that are attitudinally closest to the military), or *hyper-military reserves* (those that are attitudinally "more military" than their active duty counterparts).[11] Of course it is entirely possible that military reservists can be soldiers-first or hyper-military reserves on certain issues and citizens-first reserves on others. If military reservists are soldiers-first reserves or hyper-military reserves on some issues and citizens-first reserves on others, we can claim that military reservists leaven in both directions.

MILITARY CHANGE AND EFFECTIVENESS

Military reserves appear to be "citizens-first" on only one issue: they agree that the military needs to change some behaviors to" keep up" with civilian society. One battery of questions in the TISS survey asked respondents to comment on issues that may prevent the military from being effective during times of war.

Taking the battery as a whole, civilian and military subgroups (including guard and reserve) are in general agreement over what causes a military to be ineffective during wartime.[12] These items include Americans' lack of trust in the uniformed leaders of the military; a system for promotions and advancement in the military that does not work well; sexual harassment in the military; the military having no confidence in its political leaders; and inaccurate reporting about the military and military affairs by the news media. There seems to be similar consensus over what *does not* hurt military effectiveness. For example, "the tensions created when women entered the workplace," elicited responses of "isn't happening," or has "no effect" for just over a majority of respondents in all subgroups queried.

When we probe deeper, however, a slightly different pattern emerges. We broke the issues introduced for comment into two clusters. The first cluster consists of conditions or policies that allegedly exist in the military today, which if the military does nothing to change, may lead to ineffectiveness during times of war. Some examples of conditions that could be seen this way are sexual harrassment in the military and military adherence to old-fashioned views of morality (figure 1). The second cluster consisted of items where respondents were asked whether the military, due to civilian influence, could be seen as having changed too much, and where acceptance of these changes by the military could lead to ineffectiveness during time of war. Some examples of these issues proposed in the battery of questions are the military becoming less male-dominated or the military banning language and behavior that might otherwise be thought to encourage comradery among soldiers.

FIGURE 1. ATTITUDES ON ISSUES RELATED
TO MILITARY EFFECTIVENESS

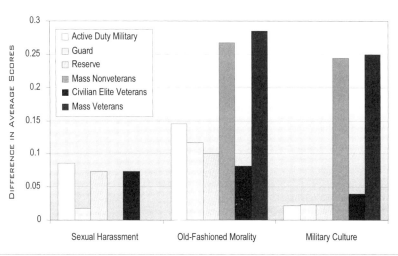

Note: Average scores for each group are relative to the civilian elite nonveterans baseline. Positive values mean that a group is more likely to disagree that this issue is a problem for military effectiveness (as compared to the views of civilian elite nonveterans).

Analyzing just the first issue cluster, we find that the guard and reservists diverge from their active duty counterparts. Guard members and reservists appear to be somewhat more willing to believe that a military that fails to change certain perceived behaviors is harmful to military effectiveness during war time (figure 2). With regard to this first issue cluster, the attitude of both military reserves more closely aligns with that of civilian elites (citizens-first).

Analyzing just the second issue cluster, active duty officers and guard officers appear to have no concern (or possibly do not believe) that society has changed the military to the detriment of effectiveness. It appears, however, that reserve officers (as distinct from guard and active duty officers) do believe that a "changed" military, or ramifications of changes brought about by civilian influence (such as gender-mixed basic training) do indeed hurt military effectiveness. In sum, the guard officer thinks like the active duty military officer here (soldiers-first), whereas active reserves portray an attitude more conservative than their active duty counterparts (hyper-military) with regard to a military influenced by civilian change and the implications for military effectiveness therein (figure 2).

FIGURE 2. ACCEPTANCE OF MILITARY CHANGE

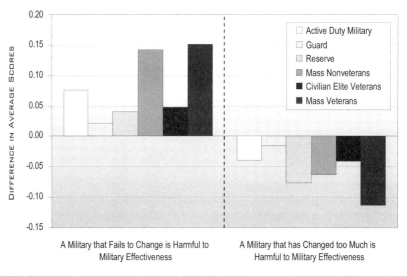

Note: Average scores for each group are relative to the civilian elite nonveterans baseline. Positive values mean a group is more likely to disagree; negative values indicate a group is more likely to agree.

If senior policy makers are concerned that the military may drag its feet on matters of social change, then the guard, and to a lesser extent the reserves, may very well help counter that situation, if one accepts the premise that reservists may transmit societal values to their military counterparts when the two serve together.

DOMESTIC ECONOMIC AND SOCIAL ISSUES

On domestic economic and social issues, military reserves are attitudinally closest to their active duty military counterparts. A question on the TISS survey asked respondents to comment on their positions with respect to various domestic social and economic issues. Domestic social issues included, for example, school busing, abortion, prayer in public schools, and the death penalty. Domestic economic issues included, for example, uses for the then-anticipated budget surplus, environmental regulations, and tuition tax credits.

By comparing the responses of our different subgroups with respect to economic and social issues, we concluded that military reserves think like their active duty counterparts. While all groups are more conservative (that is, opposing school busing and abortion but supporting prayer in public schools and the death penalty) than the civilian elite nonveterans, the guard and reserves are as conservative on social issues and more conservative on economic issues than their military and civilian-veteran counterparts (figure 3).

FIGURE 3. ATTITUDES TOWARD SOCIAL AND ECONOMIC ISSUES

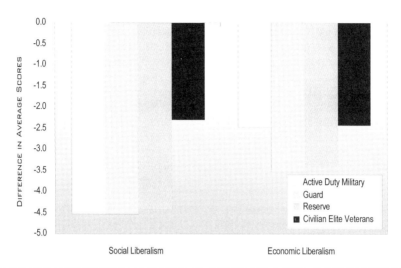

Note: Average scores for each group are relative to the civilian elite nonveterans baseline. Negative values indicate more conservative views as compared to the baseline.

When controlling for other factors that shape individual attitudes toward domestic issues—such as gender, age, race, level of education, political views, region, religion, and contact with those in the military—we found a difference in attitudes between the military subgroups (active duty, guard, and reserve) on the one hand and the civilian elites on the other. We also found that members of the Army or Air National Guard or any type of military reserve organization have similar attitudes regarding domestic social issues as do members of the active duty force. Therefore, *military reserves are soldiers-first with respect to certain domestic social issues.*

Military reserves appear to be more conservative than the active duty military with respect to domestic economic issues. We also found a discernible difference between both subgroups of military reserves and the active duty military with respect to domestic economic issues. When we accounted for all other factors that might shape individual opinion toward domestic economic issues, we discovered that military reservists appear *more* conservative (that is, more opposed to higher taxes and higher government spending) than the active duty military on these issues. Therefore, on domestic economic issues we classify them as hyper-military reserves.

The findings suggest that military reserves have the potential to pull the military in a conservative direction fiscally. The findings could also have implications for policy making in government, given that most legislators that have served in the military have done so in either the reserves or the National Guard.

MORAL AND SOCIAL TRADITIONALISM

Military reserves are soldiers-first with respect to certain moral and social traditional values. The TISS survey compared military and civilian attitudes on selected traditional moral and social issues. For example, respondents were asked whether "the decline in traditional values has contributed to a breakdown in society" and whether "civilian society would be better off if it adopted more of the military's values and customs." Reserve officer attitudes appear to track closely with the attitudes of their active duty military counterparts on both of these issues (figure 4).

FIGURE 4. ATTITUDES TOWARD MORAL AND SOCIAL VALUES

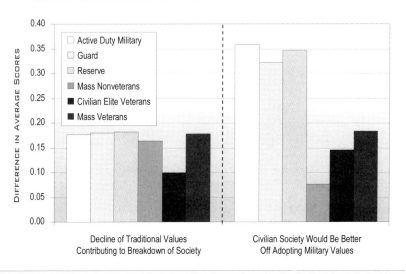

Note: Average scores for each group are relative to the civilian elite nonveterans baseline. Positive values indicate higher levels of agreement compared to civilian elite nonveterans.

Our analyses show that on the issue of a breakdown in traditional values contributing to the breakdown of civilian society, the military reserve subgroups agree most with the active duty military. Because they think most like the active duty military, military reserves have the capacity to leaven civilian society to military values. Interestingly, both civilian veterans and mass civilian nonveterans *also* agree that the decline in traditional values is leading to a breakdown of society.

The military appears to exhibit a stricter and more conservative attitude than do civilian elites with respect to moral and social traditionalism, an attitude which Janowitz might have predicted. Certainly the reserves are no help if the solution to bridging any values gap is for the reserves to leaven the military. Interestingly, the civilian mass appear more conservative than civilian elites with respect to at least these moral issues. It may be that the military (reserves included) is suited to bridge the gap between the civilian mass and civilian elite.

CONFIDENCE IN THE MILITARY

Military reserves have more confidence in the military than do civilian elites or even their active duty counterparts. Respondents to the TISS survey were asked to rate their confidence in the ability of our military to perform well in wartime and, for example, whether they expected that 10 years from now America will still have the best military in the world. On this issue, military reserves appear to have a very high level of confidence in comparison to all subgroups (figure 5), acting here as hyper-military reserves, thus theoretically leavening not only civilian society, but the active duty military as well, with respect to confidence in the nation's armed forces.

FIGURE 5. CONFIDENCE IN THE MILITARY

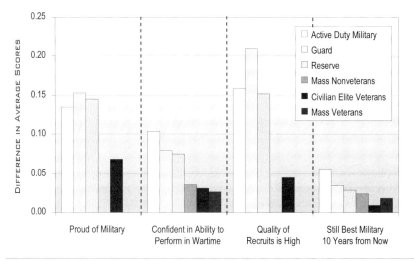

Note: Average scores for each group are relative to the civilian elite nonveterans baseline. Higher scores indicate a higher level of confidence.

Another question on the TISS survey asked respondents to agree to differing levels with the statement, "I would be disappointed if a child of mine joined the military." Guard and reserve members have a more favorable attitude towards a child joining the military than do active duty members themselves (figure 6). We believe this result is an indication that guard and reserve membership may serve as a bridge between the military and civilian worlds. This finding is also good news for recruiters, as children of reservists may be primed for service and a viable source of future accessions.

THE MILITARY'S FUNCTIONAL AND SOCIETAL IMPERATIVES

Peterson-Ulrich (2002, 246–47) writes of the military's sometimes conflicting roles, which she refers to as the military's functional imperative and the military's societal imperative. The functional imperative is to provide for the national defense. Its societal imperative is to preserve and protect democratic values within the institution itself. Said another way, the societal imperative is for the

STANDING IN THE CIVIL-MILITARY GAP

FIGURE 6. DEGREE OF DISAPPOINTMENT
IF A CHILD JOINED THE MILITARY

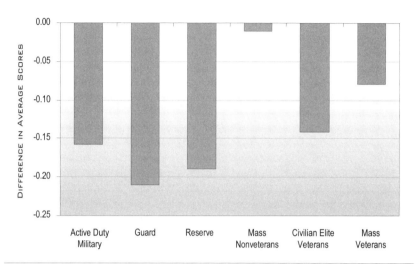

Note: Average scores for each group are relative to the civilian elite nonveterans baseline. A larger negative score indicates disagreement with the statement "I would be disappointed if a child of mine joined the military."

military to resemble as closely as possible the society it has sworn to protect. Peterson-Ulrich points out that the two imperatives cause inherent tensions between senior leaders in the military and those in civilian society. Often, the military's societal imperative is looked upon by the military as an attempt by civilians to implement social engineering (such as the attempt by the Clinton administration to allow homosexual men and women to serve openly) at the expense of the functional imperative (military effectiveness).

One question in the TISS survey asked respondents to comment on issues relevant to these two imperatives. We broke the issues considered in this question into two clusters. The first cluster we labeled "functional imperatives" — things that are perceived as necessary for the military to function, necessary for its mission of providing national defense. Some examples of the functional imperative items are a culture built on strength, toughness, physical courage, and a willingness to make sacrifices; uniforms and medals; and ceremonies and parades that are necessary to build morale, loyalty, and comradery. We labeled the second issue cluster "societal imperatives." This cluster consisted of items that are perceived as necessary for the military to fulfill its role of preserving and protecting democratic values. An example of these items is the military's more impressive record of eliminating racial discrimination than that achieved by American society in general.

There seems to be great consensus across all subgroups of respondents, civilian and military alike, about the importance of the military's "functional" imperative. All subgroups of respondents agree at rates of greater than 90 percent with statements that claim the importance of particular features linked to this functional imperative (table 1)—statements such as, "An effective military depends on a very structured organization with a clear chain of command." Consensus on issues forming the societal imperative cluster, however, is not as evident—that is, responses to statements such as, "Even though women can serve in the military, the military should remain basically masculine, dominated by male values and characteristics."

TABLE 1. MILITARY'S FUNCTIONAL AND SOCIETAL IMPERATIVES

STATEMENTS PEOPLE HAVE MADE ABOUT THE AMERICAN MILITARY	PERCENTAGE WHO "AGREE STRONGLY" OR "AGREE SOMEWHAT"				
	ACTIVE DUTY MILITARY	GUARD	RESERVE	CIVILIAN ELITE NON-VETERANS	CIVILIAN MASS NON-VETERANS
Functional imperatives					
An effective military depends on a very structured organization with a clear chain of command.*	98	98	98	97	–
Military symbols –like uniforms and medals –and military traditions –like ceremonies and parades –are necessary to build morale, loyalty, and comradery in the military.	97	100	99	91	94
Even in a high -tech era, people in the military have to have characteristics like strength, toughness, physical courage, and the willingness to make sacrifices.	99	100	99	94	95
Societal imperatives					
Even though women can serve in the military, the military should remain basically masculine, dominated by male values and characteristics.	47	37	47	34	50
The U.S. military has done a much better job of eliminating racial discrimination within the military than American society in general.	96	90	95	66	–
On most military bases there are company stores, child care centers, and recreational facilities right on the base. It is very important to keep these things on military bases in order to keep a sense of identity in the military community.	79	84	84	67	–

Note: All differences are significant at the .01 level unless otherwise noted.
* p<.05.

Reserves are closer to the active duty military (soldiers-first), and the guard is closer to civilian elites (citizens-first), with respect to attitudes about the military's societal imperatives. We find no significant difference between the views of reserve officers and active duty officers with respect to societal imperatives, which makes them soldiers-first with respect to this category of issues. Guard officers appear to take a middle position, similar to that of elite veterans, between active duty officers and civilian elite nonveterans. For instance, whereas the military overwhelmingly agrees that the military has done better than civilian society in eliminating racism, civilian elite nonveterans are more skeptical and guard respondents are somewhere in between. However, the guard is *slightly* closer to civilian elite nonveterans on societal imperative issues than it is to the active duty military on most of these questions, and therefore the guard acts like citizens-first military reserves. This finding suggests that to the extent that National Guardsmen serve with the active duty military, they may leaven military attitudes about the importance of the societal imperative role.

Military reserves may have the effect of "intensifying" the active duty military's attitudes about the functional imperative. The top-level results, reported in table 1, show little difference between the active duty military, guard, and reserves. However, when we performed statistical analysis (not reported here) that controlled for age, gender, and other factors, the differences between groups were larger than the differences in the results reported in table 1. The guard thinks most like its active duty counterparts, and reservists feel more intensely than active duty members that functional imperatives are important. In a manner of speaking, the reserve views are "more military" than those of the active duty military. The guard acts as soldiers-first reserves, and the reserves act as hyper-military reserves.

VIEWS OF MILITARY AND CIVILIAN CULTURE

Military reserves leaven in both directions with respect to positive views of civilian culture. The TISS survey asked respondents to make judgments about civilian and military culture. Respondents were given a list of both positive and negative adjectives (such as honest, hard-working, creative, self-indulgent, or lazy) and were asked to mark all that apply to civilian culture and all that apply to military culture.

There is some agreement between the military subgroups and civilian subgroups as to the nature of both civilian and military cultures (figure 7). Analyses reveal that all groups except mass veterans see the military in a positive light (that is, they disagree with negative adjectives applying to the military), and most groups stereotype civilian society negatively (although both groups of civilian veterans view civilian culture in a more positive light).

Serving as a military reservist seems to enhance positive views of civilian society. On the one hand, military reservists hold a positive stereotype of military culture (they reject negative portrayals of the military) that is in line with how the active duty military sees military culture. Therefore they are soldiers-first reserves with regard to their views on military culture. On the other hand, reservists are more likely than active duty military (and guard members) to attribute positive traits to civilian culture. They are citizens-first reserves with respect to civilian culture. Hence, on the issue of views of civilian and military cultures, military reserves leaven civilian society, and because the military sees civilian society in a more negative light than civilian elite nonveterans, the reserves reduce the military's negative outlook on civilian society.

FIGURE 7. ATTITUDES TOWARD MILITARY AND CIVILIAN CULTURE

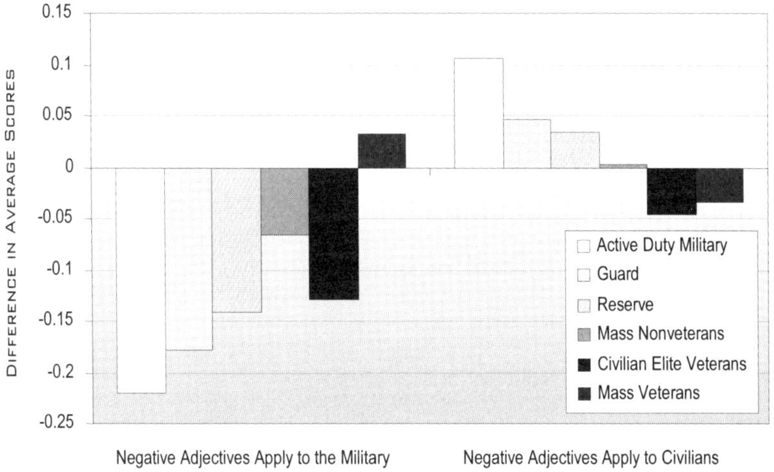

Note: Average scores for each group are relative to the civilian elite nonveterans baseline. Negative values mean a group is more likely to disagree with negative adjectives applying to the military or civilians. Positive values mean a group is more likely to agree with negative adjectives.

HOMOSEXUAL SERVICE MEMBERS AND BETTER OPPORTUNITIES FOR WOMEN SERVING IN THE MILITARY

With respect to issues of homosexuality and better opportunities for women in the military, military reserves are soldiers-first. On these two sensitive issues, we examined four questions posed by the TISS survey.

First, we analyzed two questions that we felt captured the issue of better opportunities for women serving in the military: "Do you think women should be allowed to serve in all combat jobs?" and "If, under present standards, your commander was female, how would you feel?" There was a substantial split in opinion between the military and veteran subgroups on one side, and the civilian nonveteran subgroups on the other side, with regard to further integrating women into combat positions. Over 60 percent of all three military subgroups answered "no" to this question, whereas only 35 and 42 percent of civilian elites and civilian mass, respectively, answered "no." Interestingly, between 67 and 72 percent of the three military subgroups *would* feel comfortable with a female commander.

To capture respondents' feelings about homosexual men and women serving openly in the military, we also examined the responses to two questions: first, "Do you think gay men and lesbians should be allowed to serve openly in the military?" and second, "If, under present standards, your commander was gay, how would you feel?"

With respect to homosexual Americans serving openly in the military, there was a wide split between the views of military respondents and those of civilian respondents. Well over 70 percent of all three military subgroups responded "no" to the question of whether gays and lesbians should be allowed to serve openly. Conversely, only 30 percent of civilian elite nonveterans and 34 percent of civilian mass nonveterans responded "no." The elite and mass veterans were relatively more opposed to gays serving openly than were their nonveteran counterparts, with 51 and 45 percent of elite veterans and mass veterans answering "no," respectively. When asked, "If . . . your commander was gay . . . ?" the split remained basically unchanged.

These findings reveal a difference of opinion between societal elites and military elites on the questions of open service for homosexual Americans and increased opportunities for women. That the reservists track with their active duty counterparts means that reservists will not be influential in changing the minds of active duty members with respect to these two sensitive issues. On issues of gender- and sexual orientation–based integration into the military, the guard and reserves act as soldiers-first reserves.

SUMMARY

In conclusion, we see that both reserves and National Guardsmen are attitudinally aligned with their active duty military counterparts on most of the issues we analyzed (table 2). As a result, they are theoretically best suited to leaven civilian society with military attitudes and values. Our results suggest that successful "leavening" in the other direction will be limited.

MILITARY RESERVE ISSUES POST–9/11

The American political landscape has changed significantly in the wake of September 11, 2001. We in America have recently witnessed the most significant reorganization of government since the National Security Act of 1947. With a new Department of Homeland Security, questions arise as to the proper role of the military in a domestic setting. We have seen armed soldiers in the streets of New York City, Patriot missile batteries defending the skies of Washington, D.C., and F-15s creating an umbrella over other major cities.

The nation is, for the second time in two years, at war. The capacity of the military is arguably as stretched as it has ever been. Given the current operations tempo, we ask some pointed questions about the post–September 11 world and the meaning of the total force concept today.

September 11 probably narrowed some gaps between civilian society and the military in that it made security concerns seem personal, immediate, and thus somehow more real to civilians. And, to a remarkable extent, the military reserves have been demonstrably relevant in addressing those security concerns.

TABLE 2. SUMMARY OF FINDINGS ON ATTITUDES
OF MILITARY RESERVES

ISSUE	GUARD	RESERVES
Civilian realm		
Domestic social issues	Soldiers-first	Soldiers-first
Domestic economic issues	Hyper-military	Hyper-military
The decline of traditional values is contributing to the breakdown of our society	Soldiers-first	Soldiers-first
Civilian society would be better off if it adopted more of the military's values and customs	Soldiers-first	Soldiers-first
Military realm		
The military has changed too much —Effectiveness	Soldiers-first	Hyper-military
The military has not chang ed enough—Effectiveness	Citizens-first	Citizens-first
The military's societal imperative	Citizens-first	Soldiers-first
The military's functional imperative	Soldiers-first	Hyper-military
Connection between military, civilian		
Positive views of civilian culture	Citizens-first	Citizens-first
Positive views of military culture	Soldiers-first	Soldiers-first
Further integration of women into the military	Soldiers-first	Soldiers-first
Homosexuals serve openly in the military	Soldiers-first	Soldiers-first

Since September 11, 2001, military reserves have participated in a variety of activities that have brought them increased visibility. They have provided airport security throughout the nation, guarded military installations, stood watch over the nation's critical infrastructure (its bridges, water supplies, and nuclear power plants, for example), constituted weapons of mass destruction teams, and trained civilian first responders in a variety of critical tasks. And most recently, the military reserves have deployed to Afghanistan and Iraq to fight with their active duty counterparts. As of November 12, 2003, 154,183 reserve and National Guardsmen from across the services were deployed.

In today's climate, it is harder to describe reservists as "weekend warriors" or dismiss them as second-rate soldiers. This changed attitude potentially magnifies the positive effect that contact with reserves in everyday life will have on civilian society and the civilian-military gap. That is, these gaps may continue to decrease.

It is possible, of course, that the greater exposure of reserves cuts the other way. Perhaps "familiarity breeds contempt," or possibly the public will grow tired of the militarization of the public sphere. Certainly, the revived concern over the Posse Comitatus Act shows that some of the nation's long-standing tradition of distrust of a standing army in our midst is still present.[13] Nevertheless, given the strong public consensus undergirding the war on terror, it is likely that the public today has a greater appreciation for the role of the military in its day-to-day life than was the case several years ago. In this regard, it is striking that even antiwar protests have made a point of linking opposition to the war in Iraq with support for the troops.

September 11 has paradoxically narrowed the gap in risks that used to separate civilians, reservists, and the active forces. More American civilians died in the opening salvo of the war on terror than have American soldiers in the fighting of the war. Given the prominence of reservists on the casualty lists, the active-reserve line of risk has been blurred as well. If this trend becomes a characteristic of the new era, it could reshape civil-military relations in unforeseen ways. At the very least, it suggests that the old bargain—the military risks its life so that civilians do not have to—is being renegotiated.

The effect of 9/11 on recruitment is harder to discern. The patriotic revival has not translated into a groundswell of volunteers; the effects of the economic downturn seem more important in propping up recruitment than simply patriotism per se. Indeed, increased deployments and operational tempo may have the opposite effect, intensifying recruiting and retention challenges, especially as the economy recovers.

A major wild card is the attitudes of civilian employers of reservists. To date, they have been remarkably supportive, and if civil-military gaps truly have narrowed, perhaps this support will persist. On the other hand, civilian employers are being asked to shoulder loads that would have been unthinkable several years ago. The public will eventually need its police, its fire fighters, and its teachers back.

THE BOTTOM LINE

So why should it matter that the views of reservists are closer to those of their active duty counterparts than to those of civilians on most issues we examined? The bottom line is that if one is worried about the views of civilians drifting from those of the military, reservists can help. But if the primary concern is a military with values drifting from those of civilians, military reserves are probably not much help.

One potential role of the citizen-soldier—to bring civilian social and civic values into the military—is probably not being performed and should not be overemphasized in mission rhetoric. Military reserves may, however, bring into the military other civilian attributes such as business techniques or technical expertise. Similarly, where the active force is not doing a good job of influencing civilian society with its point of view—such as in teaching basic civil-military relations—the active reserves and National Guard are likely to be just as hampered.

Readers should remember the caveat that these analyses are from active reserve and National Guard samples that have limitations in terms of how well they represent the reserve components. A more comprehensive study should include a wider range of reserves and National Guard officers, enlisted soldiers, and post-Clinton and post–September 11 data.

However, there are some useful points that policy makers might take away from this study. First, civilian contact with the military may help civil-military relations. Our analyses show that time and time again, contact with someone in the military was a significant variable. People with high levels of contact with someone in the military also view the military very favorably. Of course, we cannot be certain of a strong causal relationship running from contact with someone in the military to favorable views. Perhaps the causal arrow moves in the opposite direction, with favorable views leading to more contact, or even that both are the result of some third unknown factor. Our results, however, offer prima facie support for programs designed to increase civil-military interactions as a way of "getting the military message" out to otherwise hard-to-reach audiences.

Second, the reserves and National Guard can "represent" the military in settings and locales where the active force cannot. This mission for the citizen-soldier should be adequately resourced and rewarded. Programs and policies that enhance this representation function have value not easily captured in monetary or operational measures. Simplistic bean-counting efficiency measures of regionally isolated reserve and National Guard units are likely understating their true value. Reservists and National Guardsmen may be particularly well suited for interactions with "hard-to-reach" civilian groups such as elites, especially academic elites.

Third, military reservists may play a crucial role in shaping the military perspectives of the political elite. The military perspectives of the political elite, in part determined by the percentage who are veterans (reserves or active duty), shape the actual use of force. Gelpi and Feaver (2002) show there is a growing experience gap in the political elite.

Furthermore, in this rising post-Vietnam generation, a large fraction of military veterans gained their military experience in the active reserves and National Guard. In the 108th Session of the House of Representatives, 70 percent are non-veterans, whereas only 22 percent had ever served on active duty and 14 percent served either in the active reserves or the National Guard (including those reservists who also served on active duty). In the Senate, 62 percent have never served, while 30 percent are active duty veterans, and 16 percent have served in the reserves or with the National Guard (again including some who also served on active duty). Of the 15 House members who joined the military after Vietnam, 9 were in the active reserve or the National Guard (60 percent). The single senator who joined the military after Vietnam (Senator Sessions) was in the Army Reserve.

As the percentage of the political elite with military experience continues to decrease, the reserves and guard will increasingly provide the military perspective within that group. The implications for the use of force—which will be based on the decisions of a political elite whose experience is largely and increasingly in reserve service—cannot be understated, especially with the nation currently at war.

CONCLUSION

The reserves and guard make an indispensable contribution to American military power. They can also play a vital role in American civil-military relations. By standing in the gap between people with no military experience and the active duty force, reservists are able to facilitate communication between those spheres. Our research suggests that the attitude profiles of the reserves and guard make them best equipped to represent military values in civilian settings, rather than civilian values in military settings.

The findings raise interesting follow-on questions. Do reservists see this communication as a role for themselves? In what ways do they carry out this role, either intentionally or unintentionally? How effective are they? The TISS project was not designed to answer these ancillary questions, but future research projects could. Future research could also determine whether the events of September 11 and their aftermath have brought civilian and military viewpoints closer together or whether demographic and other trends continue to widen the gaps. Whatever the results, we expect future efforts to confirm that the reserves and guard are more than just factors in combat mobilization. Instead, they shape, as the Republic's framers expected, American civil-military relations in meaningful ways.

APPENDIX

DATA AND METHODOLOGICAL ISSUES

The TISS study was multimethod, multidisciplinary, and multipersonnel. Political scientists, historians, sociologists, policy analysts, and public opinion experts—some with no military or government experience, others with a wide range of such exposure—participated in the study. The scholars worked as a team, but each reached independent conclusions. Moreover, the findings of one part, for example, the analysis of survey results, are best interpreted in the light of the findings of another part, for example, the analyses made by military historians. Thus, the summary and conclusions offered in this chapter reflect the views of the authors and do not necessarily reflect the views of other TISS researchers.

DATA

The TISS study produced a one-of-a-kind data set on civilian and military opinion about civil-military relations. From late fall 1998 through late spring 1999, the TISS team administered a survey consisting of 250 questions. It was designed to measure attitudes and beliefs about foreign and defense policy issues, domestic concerns, culture, values, religion, and military relations with civilian society. In addition, the questionnaire asked respondents to provide information about their demographic backgrounds. Respondents included 1,143 elite members of the military in all branches of the service and at various stages in their careers: precommissioning; at the staff-college level (roughly a decade into their career); at the war-college level (roughly 17 years into their career); and upon promotion to flag and general officer rank (after roughly 25 years of service). A similar, though smaller, sample of officers from the reserve and guard was also included.[14]

The same survey was also administered to 935 civilian elites at comparable stages in their careers: a sample of undergraduates at an elite university as well as civilian leaders drawn from various sources including *Who's Who in America*, lists of academic experts, and other groups such as State Department and foreign-service officers, foreign policy experts, and media and labor leaders. Finally, a shorter version of the survey was prepared for a representative national telephone survey of 1,001 selected members of the general public, to obtain what might be considered "mass" opinion on the issues.

The TISS data have limitations, however. The sampling design focused on elite officers; the enlisted ranks were not surveyed and, within the officer corps, an effort was made to identify future leaders rather than capture a representative sample of the officer corps as a whole. In addition, because some organizations declined to participate, the sample is somewhat skewed across the services. (More Navy and Army officers, fewer Air Force officers, and the same percentage of Marines are represented in the group of respondents in comparison to the officer corps as a whole.) Also, the data represent a snapshot of opinion, rather than a time series over several years. Finally, and perhaps more problematic, the survey coincided with the height of the Clinton impeachment scandal. Thus, the TISS data are best thought of as blazing the trail for future collection and research rather than providing the final word on the subject. Nevertheless, to our knowledge, there is no other resource available for comparing civilian and military (active and reserve) attitudes across so many different issues and dimensions.

METHODOLOGY

Using the TISS data, we compare the attitudes of seven subgroups of respondents. We categorize these subgroups by kind of military experience and by type of civilian group. "Active duty military" are officers in any of the services currently serving in the active duty force. "Reserve" respondents are officers currently serving in the reserves of one of the military services. "National Guard" respondents are officers in the Army National Guard or the Air National Guard. In discussing our findings, we refer to both reserve and National Guard officers as "reserve officers" or "military reserves" unless we have a reason to distinguish them. "Civilian elite nonveterans" come from the elite sample and have never served in the military. "Civilian elite veterans" are from the elite sample and have previously served in the military in some capacity. "Civilian (general public) mass nonveterans" are respondents from the mass sample and have never served in the military; "civilian mass veterans" are respondents who have previous military experience.[15]

We examine issues from three settings: the civilian domain, the military domain, and where the two areas are connected. All three lie within the "realm of ideas and values" (as opposed to more "policy-based" areas, such as the use and scope of military force or foreign policy preferences), where the "gap" between civilian and military leaders is thought to be "wider and more pervasive" than it is in other spheres (Holsti 2001, 29).

The areas we analyze include domestic issues (social and economic); beliefs on the status of morals in civilian society (i.e., is the decline of traditional values leading to the breakdown of American society?); views of civilian and military cultures; ideas about what does or does not harm military effectiveness (focusing on value-based ideas); and views on military traditionalism. Additionally, we analyze two sensitive policy issues: further integration of women into combat roles and allowing homosexual men and women to serve "openly" in the military. These two issues were contentious at the time of our survey, and continue to be so today. They exemplify the core of the culture gap debate.

We use two types of statistics to analyze the data. The first are descriptive statistics that cross-tabulate the survey responses of the subgroups for items of interest and assess the likelihood that any differences we observe are due to chance. Second, we use multivariate analyses to look deeper into the findings of our descriptive statistics. We control for a number of effects including age, gender, race, region, education, religion, and political views. We also control for the amount of contact a respondent has had with those who are currently serving or have served in the military. For ease of presentation, we report only summary results; readers interested in more detail should contact the authors.

Our measure of the gap is operationalized as the absolute difference between an individual's score on a set of measures and the average military score (for the military gap) or the average civilian score (for the civilian gap) on those measures. For example, a large value on the civilian gap score indicates that an individual gave a response that was largely different from the average civilian elite response. We also subject these differences to multivariate analysis, allowing us to explain why a respondent may be more similar or different from the average civilian elite or military respondent.

NOTES

1. See Hayes 1973 and Kohn 1974. Other concerns like this were discussed and rejected by the *Report of the President's Commission on an All-Volunteer Force* (Gates 1970).

2. See Janowitz 1973, Segal et al. 1974, Sarkesian 1975, and Moskos 1977.

3. See also Weigley 1993, Kohn 1994, and McIsaac and Verdugo 1995.

4. The published TISS findings are only briefly summarized in this paper. Preliminary answers to these questions were given in a series of publications, with three meriting special attention: Feaver and Kohn 2000 and 2001b and Feaver and Gelpi 2004. The reader is invited to review these works for a fuller discussion of the results.

5. Data and methodological issues are described in more detail in the appendix. See also Newcity 1999.

6. Other sources that imply that reserves play an important role in civil-military relations include Cohen 1997; and Feaver, Kohn, and Cohn 2001.

7. We use the term "leaven" in this paper when the inclusion of one group (for example, the reserve) as part of a larger group (civilian society) changes the estimated average opinion of the larger group, because the first group has systematically different opinions. So, for example, when we say military reserves *leaven* the military, we mean that the reserve opinions are systematically closer to civilian opinions, and thus the reserves may be available as potential agents of persuasion.

8. The National Defense Act of 1920 authorized a detail of regular officers as instructors in youth summer training camps. The goal was to build a nationwide organization so that every community in the country would have representatives of at least one of the Army components in its midst, whose views would be felt among their neighbors until all people came to appreciate the prudence of supporting a strong national defense (Huntington 1957, 283–84).

9. The sample of active duty military personnel responding to the TISS survey comprised an elite group of officers—those who have attended the war colleges, command and staff colleges, the capstone course, or the National Defense University, for example. The enlisted ranks were not included in the survey. There was no effort made to capture a representative sample of the active duty force. These facts represent a limitation in the TISS data set. The civilian elites are at comparable stages in their careers (as compared to the active duty military group) and include a sample of undergraduates at an elite university as well as civilian leaders drawn from various sources. Thus, civilian elites are used as a baseline for comparison with the elite military sample.

10. In figures 1 through 7, the average score for each subgroup is expressed as a deviation from the average score of the civilian elite nonveterans subgroup for the issue in question.

11. Military reservists might also leaven civilian society with values that are not traditionally military, or that are not in the best interests of either the military or civilian society; that is, they might reproduce error in civilian society that will make society and the military worse off. For an extreme example, see Dunlap 1992–1993, 2–20.

12. Well over 60 percent of all subgroups felt particular items "somewhat hurt" or "greatly hurt" military effectiveness in times of war.

13. The Posse Comitatus Act (of 1878) prohibits the use of military personnel for civilian law enforcement purposes, except where explicitly authorized by the Constitution or by act of Congress.

14. The "elite military" sample includes respondents from: Naval War College (N=334), Army War College (N=72), Command and Staff College (N=93), National Defense University (N=156), Capstone Course (N=68), Army War College Reserves (N=210), Army National Guard (N=62), National War College Reserves (N=57), and National Defense University Reserves (N=91) (Holsti 2001, 4).

15. Not all issue items on the survey were asked of the mass civilian subgroup. Therefore, it is impossible to conduct analysis comparing military elites and civilian mass nonveterans for certain items.

REFERENCES

Binkin, Martin, and William W. Kaufmann. 1989. *U.S. Army guard and reserve: Rhetoric, realities, risks*. Washington, D.C.: Brookings Institution Press.

Brehm, Philip A. 1992. *Restructuring the Army: The road to a total force*. Carlisle Barracks, Carlisle, Pa.: Strategic Studies Institute.

Cohen, Eliot A. 1997. Civil-military relations (Are U.S. forces overstretched?) *Orbis* 41(2): 177–86.

Cragin, Charles L. 1999. The demise of the weekend warrior, *Defense Link News*. http://www.defenselink.mil/news/Jul1999/n07091999_9907092.html [May 13, 2004].

Davis, Richard A. 1989. *Role of the reserves in the total force policy*. Testimony before the Subcommittee on Readiness, House Committee on Armed Services, Washington, D.C. February 23.

Duncan, Stephen M. 1997. *Citizen warriors: America's National Guard and reserve forces and the politics of national security*. Novato, Calif.: Presidio Press.

Dunlap, Charles. 1992–1993. The origins of the American military coup of 2012. *Parameters* 22(4): 2–20.

Feaver, Peter D., and Christopher Gelpi. 2004. *Choosing your battles: American civil-military relations and the use of force*. Princeton, N.J.: Princeton University Press.

Feaver, Peter D., and Richard H. Kohn. 2000. The gap: Soldiers, civilians, and their mutual misunderstanding. *The National Interest* 61 (Fall 2000): 29–37.

———. 2001a. Media and education in the U.S. civil-military gap. *Armed Forces and Society* 27(2) (special edition): 173–317.

———. eds. 2001b. *Soldiers and civilians: The civil-military gap and American national security*. Cambridge, Mass.: MIT Press.

Feaver, Peter D., Richard H. Kohn, and Lindsay P. Cohn. 2001. Introduction to *Soldiers and civilians: The civil-military gap and American national security*, Edited by Peter D. Feaver and Richard H. Kohn. Cambridge, Mass.: MIT Press.

Gates, Thomas S. 1970. *Report of the President's Commission on an All-Volunteer Armed Force*. Washington, D.C.: U.S. Government Printing Office.

Gelpi, Christopher, and Peter D. Feaver. 2002. Speak softly and carry a big stick? Veterans in the political elite and the American use of force. *American Political Science Review* 96(4): 779–94.

Gronke, Paul, and Peter D. Feaver. 2001. Uncertain confidence: Civilian and military attitudes about civil-military relations. In *Soldiers and civilians: The civil-military gap and American national security*. Edited by Peter D. Feaver and Richard H. Kohn. Cambridge, Mass.: MIT Press.

Hart, Gary. 1998. *The minuteman: Restoring the army of the people*. New York: Free Press.

Hayes, M. Vincent, ed. 1973. Is the military taking over? *New Priorities: A Magazine for Activists* 1(4).

Heller, Charles E. 1994. *Total force: Federal reserves and state National Guards*. Carlisle Barracks, Carlisle, Pa.: Strategic Studies Institute, 43–57.

Hillen, John. 1999. Must U.S. military culture reform? *Orbis* 43(1).

Holsti, Ole R. 2001. Of chasms and convergences: Attitudes and beliefs of civilians and military elites at the start of a new millennium. In *Soldiers and civilians: The civil-military gap and American national security*. Edited by Peter D. Feaver and Richard H. Kohn. Cambridge, Mass.: MIT Press.

Huntington, Samuel. 1957. *The soldier and the state: The theory and politics of civil-military relations*. Cambridge, Mass.: Harvard University Press.

Jacobs, Jeffrey A. 1994. *The future of the citizen-soldier force*. Lexington, Ky.: University Press of Kentucky.

Janowitz, Morris. 1971. *The professional soldier: A social and political portrait*. New York: Free Press.

———. 1973. The social demography of the all-volunteer force. *Annals of the American Academy of Political Science* 406 (March): 86–93.

Kirby, Sheila N., David Grissmer, Stephanie Williamson, and Scott Naftel. 1997. *Costs and benefits of reserve participation: New evidence from the 1992 Reserve Components Survey*. Santa Monica, Calif.: RAND Corporation.

Kitfield, James. 2000. The pen and the sword. *Government Executive* 32(4): 18–28.

Kohn, Richard H. 1974. The all-volunteer army: Too high a price? *Proceedings of the U.S. Naval Institute* 100(3): 35–42.

———. 1994. Out of control: The crisis in civil-military relations. *The National Interest* 35: 3–17.

Lancaster, John. 1993. Accused of ridiculing Clinton, general faces Air Force probe. *Washington Post*. June 8, 1993: A1.

Mathis, Nancy. 1992. Clinton launches damage control. *Houston Chronicle*. February 13, 1992: A1.

McIsaac, James, and Naomi Verdugo. 1995. Civil-military relations: A domestic perspective. In *U.S. civil-military relations*. Edited by Donald Snider and Miranda Carlton-Carew. Washington, D.C.: Center for Strategic and International Studies.

Moskos, Charles. 1977. From institution to occupation: Trends in military organization. *Armed Forces and Society* 4(1): 41–50.

National Opinion Research Center. 1996. *General social survey*. Chicago: National Opinion Research Center.

Neiburg, Michael. 2000. *Making citizen soldiers: ROTC and the ideology of American military service*. Cambridge, Mass.: Harvard University Press.

Newcity, Janet. 1999. *Description of the 1998–1999 TISS surveys on the military in the post cold war era*. Paper prepared for the TISS Project on the Gap Between the Military and Civilian Society, October 27–29, Cantigney Estate, Wheaton, Illinois.

No author, 1993. Clinton's quick steps to better relations; after summit jog, general snubbed at White House has warm words for president. *Washington Post*. April 6, 1993: A7.

Peterson-Ulrich, Marybeth. 2002. Infusing civil-military relations norms in the officer corps. In *The future of the Army profession*. Edited by Donald Snider and Gayle L. Watkins. Boston: McGraw-Hill.

Ricks, Thomas E. 1997. The widening gap between the U.S. military and U.S. society. *The Atlantic Monthly* July.

Sarkesian, Sam C. 1975. *The professional Army officer in a changing society*. Chicago: Nelson-Hall Publishers.

Segal, David R., John Blair, Frank Newport, and Susan Stephens. 1974. Convergence, isomorphism, and interdependence at the civil-military interface. *Journal of Political and Military Sociology* 2(2): 157–72.

Shultz, Fred L., ed. 2000. Interview: James Webb. *Proceedings of the U.S. Naval Institute* 100(4): 78–81.

U.S. Department of Defense. 2004. *The defense almanac*. http://www.defenselink.mil/pubs/almanac/ [May 14, 2004].

Walter, Scott. 1997. Tradition and the military. *American Enterprise* 8(2): 46–49, 70.

Webb, James. 1997. The war on military culture. *The Weekly Standard* 2(18): 17–22.

Webb, James H. Jr. 1998. *Military leadership in a changing society*. Address given to Naval War College Conference on Ethics. November 16. Providence, R.I.: Naval War College.

Weigley, Russell F. 1993. The American military and the principle of civilian control from McClellan to Powell. *The Journal of Military History* (October): 27–58.

Zurcher, Louis A. 1986. The future of the reservist: A case of constructive brokering. In *Citizen-sailors in a changing society: Policy issues for manning the United States Naval Reserve*. Edited by Louis A. Zurcher, Milton L. Boykin, and Hardy L. Merritt. New York: Greenwood Press.

★ ★ ★ ★ ★ ★ ★ ★ ★ ★ ★

COMMENTARY

REGINALD J. BROWN

The 30th anniversary of the inception of the all-volunteer force commemorates the beginning of what has been a far-reaching transformation of the armed forces of this nation. In a fundamental way, this transformation—the move to an all-volunteer force—also represents a return to America's military heritage. The soldiers of the American Revolution were volunteers to a man. Though great powers of that period relied extensively on conscription and universal service, the American approach was different. Our nation achieved and maintained its first half century of independence based exclusively on volunteerism. Involuntary service was first introduced in the United States for several years during the Civil War, reintroduced for two years in World War I, and instituted again from 1940 to 1973. Viewed from that perspective, the transition to the all-volunteer force was less a radical experiment than a return to the principles upon which this nation was founded. Indeed, the United States has had a con-scripted or involuntary force for only 35 years of its 225-year life as a nation.

The parallel between the armed forces today and those of the Revolutionary period is important to note. The forces of the American Revolution were a mix of local militia and a smaller group of trained regulars known as Continentals. Membership in both groups was voluntary. U.S. forces today are structured in a similar fashion, with large numbers of reserve personnel acting in concert with a smaller number of full-time active component troops. As was true for their Revolutionary War forebears, reservists and active component soldiers today serve on a voluntary basis. Needless to say, there are dramatic differences between the soldiers of these two eras, but the nature of their volunteerism is very much the same.

★

Though often maligned by the professionals of the Revolutionary War, militia forces played a vital role in retaining control of colonial territory not physically occupied by the British during that conflict. British control of the colonies throughout that struggle rarely extended beyond the range of British guns. Militia control of the majority of the colonies helped ensure that the days of British rule were numbered.

The importance of today's guard and reserve soldiers to the overall military strategy of the United States is similar to that of the colonial militias in the Revolutionary period. As Representative Edward Schrock noted, "The reserve component is key to the successful implementation of the Department of Defense strategy that calls for evolution toward a balanced, integrated, and seamless total force" (chapter 9, this volume).

Today's reservists and National Guard soldiers perform dramatically different roles than did their predecessors. While the roles and missions of the colonial militiamen and their comrades in the Continental Line units differed greatly from one another, there is virtually no difference between the missions assigned to the two components today. Indeed, the National Military Strategy of the United States makes little if any distinction between active and reserve component organizations, focusing instead on capabilities and their relationship to the international environment. Modern day reservists and colonial militia members retain a shared philosophy and lineage of volunteerism, but play different roles in the makeup of the total force.

How successful is the current approach to the use of our reserve component forces? By any objective measure, use of reserve component soldiers in meeting the needs of the nation's military strategic aims has been remarkably successful. This was true well before the events of September 11, 2001. The efforts of the reserve components since that tragic day have simply revalidated what has been long known. Our reserve component forces have become more than a contributor to the nation's security; they have become absolutely essential.

Essential is a strong word, but I believe that it is apropos in this case. As Representative Schrock noted, reserve component participation in meeting real-world mission requirements has grown steadily since the 1980s, from 1.4 million duty-days in 1989 to nearly 13 million duty-days annually in the years prior to September 11. Since that event, reserve component participation in a host of new missions has dramatically exceeded even that level. Congressman Schrock also notes that, as of August 2003, approximately 300,000 reserve component soldiers have been mobilized since September 11, 2001, a number that will certainly grow in the months and years ahead. To place this number in the proper context, one need only realize that the active component force numbers less than 500,000 personnel. The fact that reserve component forces represent nearly 40 percent of the forces employed since September 11 demonstrates how critical the reserve component contribution is in the global war on terrorism.

While 300,000 is certainly a large number, it does not tell the entire story. Like any military force, the reserve component can never be perfectly structured to meet the needs of any given contingency. This limitation means that some elements of the reserve component will find themselves employed more frequently and more extensively than others. Reserve component military police and military intelligence units have been hard pressed to meet the emerging requirements of the post–September 11 security environment. Specialized organizations like civil affairs units and psychological operations units, which reside almost completely in the reserve components, have been even harder hit. Congressman Schrock is absolutely correct in noting that the reserves provide unique capabilities to the total force, particularly in such areas as civil affairs and military police. Finally, the ongoing demands of Operation Iraqi Freedom mean that virtually every combat brigade in the Army National Guard will mobilize in the coming months and years.

In the case of the post–September 11 effort, the limitations of a preexisting force structure in a new and different security environment also mean employing soldiers and units in functional roles that would have been unthinkable just a few years ago. One need only speak with an artilleryman performing military police duties to understand the significance of this particular manifestation of the global war on terror. These mission shifts are not limited to the reserve components, as numerous active component units have also been retrained and reequipped for unanticipated requirements.

Congressman Schrock goes on to argue that disparities in the equipment, training, and supplies provided for the reserve versus active forces must continue to be addressed by Congress and the Department of Defense. The equipment and well-being of reservists must be provided for to the same extent as are those of the active component.

With the global war on terrorism occupying center stage, it is easy to forget that the U.S. military has other ongoing commitments as well. These other missions — in Bosnia, Kosovo, the Sinai, and elsewhere — are, to an increasing degree, being accomplished by reserve component forces. The men and women of the guard and reserve will find themselves serving in almost every corner of the world for the foreseeable future.

Military operations are never risk free, and this latest effort is no different. A major risk this time, however, has little to do with defeat in military action. A danger the services face today lies in the potential for overuse of our reserve component soldiers. Many of these personnel are now facing a second year away from home, away from their jobs and their families. Two years away from friends and family is a long time for any soldier. For members of the reserve component, who must reintegrate themselves into the civilian work force upon their return, the prospect of a two-year absence is truly daunting.

The challenge for the services does not end there. Not only must these soldiers cope with reentering civilian life, but large numbers of them must also be convinced to remain in the reserve components in the future. Recruitment of new soldiers cannot by itself meet the needs of the future reserve component force. Seasoned, experienced leaders and soldiers will also be essential. In fiscal year 2003, 53 percent of accessions to the reserve component were new enlistees (individuals with no prior service), while 47 percent had prior military service (U.S. Department of Defense 2003).

If there is a positive aspect to the situation faced by members of the reserve components, it is that these issues are being addressed aggressively at all levels of the Department of Defense. One aspect of this attention, as noted by Congressman Schrock, is an ongoing effort to eliminate disparities in compensation received by members of the active and reserve components. It goes without saying that soldiers going into harm's way should be compensated equally regardless of whether they are active or reserve.

Compensation is only one of many efforts designed to limit the impact of current and future operations on reserve component personnel. The services are working constantly to ensure that reserve component families receive the support they need to cope with the absence of their reservist family member. Just as importantly, organizations like the National Committee for Employer Support of the Guard and Reserve are working to ensure that reservists can look forward to employment upon release from active duty. Legislative efforts in recent years have addressed many of these issues, but much more remains to be done.

One approach to addressing the challenges faced by the services in both recruiting and retention might be a greater reliance on programs like the Army's Partnership for Youth Success (PAYS). In this program the Army helps soldiers obtain jobs (to be performed by reservists when they sign up, and active duty troops when they leave the Army) with designated partnering employers. This match between recruit and employer is made before the soldier ever enters the Army. Through PAYS, soldiers sign up for specific jobs, learning skills that are needed by participating companies. The Army invests in these individuals, trains them in needed skills, enjoys the benefits of their training while they serve, and returns them to their community as more valuable citizens. The companies that hire these soldiers benefit from receiving well-trained, proven employees.

Another benefit of this program is that the Army is not in competition with business for scarce experienced employees. Rather, the Army's PAYS program effectively adds to the pool of skilled workers. PAYS is a win-win-win-win proposition for the soldier, the Army, the employer, and the country. A key benefit of this program is its potential to enhance employer support for the guard and reserve. The Army currently has partnerships with 68 companies and is negotiating with more. The companies participating in PAYS and providing jobs across the country include Hospital Corporation of America, Goodyear, Sears Auto Center, Southwest Airlines, and The Pepsi Bottling Group.

The men and women of the Army Reserve and the Army National Guard will continue to play a pivotal role in the global war on terrorism and in meeting the security needs of the nation as a whole. That much is clear; but that acknowledgment does not mean that the defense establishment takes their participation for granted. A large proportion of my time, and of those throughout the Army and Department of Defense leadership, is consumed with ensuring that we mobilize no more reserve component personnel than are absolutely necessary to accomplish the mission. We have gone to great lengths to ensure that members of highly stressed career fields like the military police and civil affairs do not find themselves mobilized indefinitely. Our efforts have paid off: only volunteers have been mobilized for more than 24 months in support of current operations, and an absolute minimum number of units have been mobilized for a second year. Needless to say, we will continue to make every effort to minimize the impact of current and future operations on the members of the reserve components.

CONCLUSION

While stress on the reserve components will continue to present a challenge to the Army leadership, I believe that the future is bright. Talented, motivated men and women continue to join the reserve component in large numbers. As we commemorate the anniversary of the all-volunteer force, guard and reserve personnel are reenlisted even as they are deployed overseas. The willingness to serve our nation in a time of crisis is a hallmark of the reserve components, and their actions in the wake of September 11 have been no different.

In focusing on the reserve component of the all-volunteer force on this 30th anniversary, I believe that we get a good look at what America and the American military are all about. Reserve component soldiers volunteer not once, but over and over again as they deploy around the world. These men and women lie at the heart of the all-volunteer force, and I am quite certain that they will never let our nation down.

REFERENCES

U.S. Department of Defense. 2003. Reserve component accessions data. Washington D.C.: Office of the Assistant Secretary of Defense for Reserve Affairs.

★ ★ ★ ★ ★

THOMAS F. HALL

With almost 34 years of total active service, and over 20 of those years spent in the all-volunteer force, I have survived many transformations. Anyone associated with the Department of Defense has seen change come and go with each new world crisis. In simplified terms, transformation in the 1960s involved the expansion of forces for the Vietnam War; in the 1970s, it was the contraction of the force following the Vietnam War; in the 1980s it was high defense spending to win the cold war; in the 1990s, transformation was reducing defense spending following the victory in the cold war.

Today, the department is undergoing transformation to achieve a more responsive, lethal, and agile military force that is capable of responding to a wide range of enemy capabilities. This transformation must respond to the global war on terrorism — the first war of the new millennium — triggered by the attacks of September 11, 2001, on New York City and Washington, D.C.

Over the past decade, the reserve components have been used extensively to support military operations. Reserve members have supported all contingency operations, both as volunteers and through involuntary call-ups. They have supported counterdrug operations, responses to domestic emergencies, and major military exercises, as well as provided other direct support to the combatant commands and the military services.

As the Department of Defense moves forward with the prosecution of the global war on terrorism, certain issues need to be addressed—issues that are central to effectively using the reserve components as part of the total force. Actions that need to be taken include improving the mobilization process; establishing predictability of service for reserve component members; addressing the repeated mobilization of units that are in high demand; supporting service rotational policies; and examining service force structure and end strength.

In the sections below, I will address a number of the key issues affecting the reserve components today: their value and contributions to the total force, the impact of high operational tempo on recruiting and retention, stress on the force and how rebalancing efforts might help to ease that stress, and the challenges for training and family support in the future.

THE RESERVE COMPONENTS: A VALUABLE ASSET

Reservists add punch and potency to America's war-fighting capability. They are people with varied talents whose problem-solving skills are force multipliers that cannot be quantified. In addition to their military skills, their civilian-acquired skills can benefit military forces, as these skills sometimes represent expertise not readily available or maintained in the active forces. For example, in Afghanistan, a National Guard military police sergeant who is a building contractor in civilian life was able to use his construction knowledge to help his unit build holding cells for terrorist prisoners well before military engineers could be at the site.

Both President George W. Bush and Secretary of Defense Donald Rumsfeld have recognized that the National Guard and reserve play an essential role in fighting the global war on terrorism. As of the fall of 2003, approximately 300,000 reserve component members bear testimony to that truth, having served in some capacity since September 11, 2001. Nearly 90,000 have served or are serving in a second year of mobilization. As I will discuss in more detail in a following section, the level of contribution by the reserve components has been high; but the reserve components have experienced reductions in size and structure. Over the past seven years, funded reserve strength decreased by just over 50,000 personnel, to about 883,000 members—a reduction of just over 5 percent. The selected reserve now constitutes 38 percent of a total force of over 2.3 million members. In addition, there are some 284,000 individual ready reservists who may be called to active duty in times of national emergency. Total funding resources for the reserve component have increased to about $29 billion, or 7.9 percent of the total Department of Defense budget (figure 1). Congressman Schrock has told us that efforts to correct disparities between the active and reserve components may involve additional outlays in the years ahead; this spending will be necessary to ensure that the reserves are properly equipped, trained, and compensated (chapter 9, this volume).

RESERVE COMPONENT CONTRIBUTIONS TO THE TOTAL FORCE

Over the past two years, the Department of Defense has initiated the largest mobilization of the National Guard and reserve effected since the Korean War. By any pre–21st-century measure, the pace of America's global military missions today would be classified as hectic. In the past 13 years, U.S. forces have been dispatched to no fewer than seven separate and quite dissimilar engagements, primarily in Afghanistan and Iraq (table 1). (The largest were Operations Noble Eagle, Enduring Freedom, and Iraqi Freedom.) In fact, over the past 13 years, in only 1 year—1993—were no reserve component members involuntarily called to active duty. The pace of operations has only increased since then, as U.S. military forces, including members of the National Guard and reserve, have been involved around the globe in missions of varying size, intensity, and duration.

FIGURE 1. RESERVE COMPONENT FUNDING
(AS A PERCENTAGE OF THE TOTAL DEFENSE DEPARTMENT BUDGET)

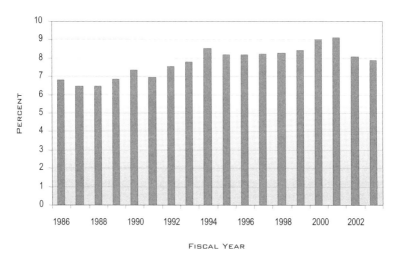

FISCAL YEAR

Source: Office of the Assistant Secretary of Defense for Reserve Affairs.

Reserve component members have supplemented and bolstered the full-time active component in ever increasing numbers, as figure 1 in Robert Steel's paper shows (chapter 8, this volume). In 1993, reserve component members contributed over 5.7 million duty-days of operational support. Total duty-days grew to 13.5 million in 1996 and then fell to an average of about 12.5 million duty-days each year thereafter until the events of September 11, 2001. The total reserve component support to the active component grew to over 41 million duty-days in fiscal year 2002 and to over 60 million in 2003.

In 2001, the reserve component response to the September 11 attacks on America can only be described as phenomenal. Within minutes, Air National Guard aircraft responded to the reported aircraft hijackings. By the end of the day, literally thousands of reserve component personnel were being deployed to assist with rescue efforts and to protect vital national assets. Many members responded without awaiting orders, simply reporting for duty to their armory or reserve center.

TABLE 1. RESERVE COMPONENT SUPPORT TO CONTINGENCY
OPERATIONS, 1990 TO PRESENT

	DATES	INVOLUNTARY	VOLUNTARY	TOTAL
Desert Shield/ Desert Storm	August 1990– August 1991	239,187	26,139	265,326
Somalia	December 1992– May 1993	0	343	343
Haiti	September 1994– May 1996	6,250	2,088	8,338
Bosnia	December 1995– present	32,404	25,322	57,726
Southwest Asia	February 1998– present	6,108	32,911	39,019
Kosovo	April 1999– present	11,426	5,900	17,326
Noble Eagle/ Enduring Freedom/ Iraqi Freedom	September 2001– present	348,284	34,093	382,377

Source: Office of the Assistant Secretary of Defense for Reserve Affairs.
Note: Data include U.S. Coast Guard.

From the outset of Operation Enduring Freedom and Operation Noble Eagle in 2001 through Operation Iraqi Freedom in 2003, nearly 350,000 reserve component members have been mobilized. They span the breadth of military specialties and have come from every section of our nation. In support of each of these operations, members of the reserve components responded quickly and with military skill and efficiency. The integration of the full-time active component and part-time reserve component forces met the expected readiness standards. In fact, integration of the active and reserve forces in all aspects of the all-volunteer force has been successful. By all indicators, throughout the many contingency operations in the last 13 years, there were no insurmountable problems in going to war using the guard and reserve.

IMPACT ON RECRUITING AND RETENTION

With this operational tempo as a backdrop, it is noteworthy that recruiting and retention for the selected reserve have remained stable and on target each year. Since fiscal year 1997, the reserve components have cumulatively achieved better than 99 percent of their authorized end strength for the seventh consecutive year and over 100 percent for the past four years (figure 2). At the same time, the composite attrition rate for all seven components remains at a very low level (figure 3).

While support of real-world missions appears to have a positive impact on most reserve component manpower and personnel indicators, the high operational tempo may have the opposite effect in certain areas. A macro view of end strength achievement can mask serious concerns in certain high-demand reserve units and specialties that are experiencing above-normal levels of attrition. Thus it is necessary to examine other force metrics to determine whether the high operational tempo of recent years is having an adverse impact on the reserve components.

STRESS ON THE FORCE

Since September 11, 2001, nearly 37 percent of the total selected reserve has been called up to support military operations. This level of operational tempo has forced the Department of Defense to ask an important question. Are we putting too much stress on the reserve components? To determine the level of stress that today's operational tempo is placing on the reserve forces, the department is evaluating several factors: the frequency of use, the percent of inventory used, and the duration of call-ups.

FREQUENCY OF USE

Frequency of use refers to how often reserve component members are called up — for separate contingencies or multiple deployments within a given contingency. During periods of high demand on the reserves, it is a challenge for the military services to manage repeated mobilizations of individual reservists, particularly for members of career fields that are in high demand. However, in looking at the frequency of call-ups going back to the Gulf War in 1990–1991, and including those associated with the Haiti, Bosnia, Kosovo, and Southwest Asia contingencies, as well as the current operations, the number of reserve members called up for more than one contingency make up a relatively small percentage (less than 10 percent) of those on active duty today and an even smaller percentage of the total selected reserve population (less than 4 percent).

The data in table 2, which represent call-ups over the last seven years, show that only a relatively small number (11,802) of those members on active duty today have been called up for previous operations. But the number of members being recalled more than once for the current operations, though not large (only 15,982, or 1.8 percent of the selected reserve, as of December 2003), is more of a concern and is increasing as the department continues to call up reserve members. The number of multiple call-ups is currently at an acceptable level, but it must be closely monitored — especially for those reservists in high-demand career fields.

PERCENTAGE OF INVENTORY USED

The percentage of inventory used is the amount of the reserve force that is used in a given time as compared to what is available. Up to 30 percent of 159 enlisted career fields and 20 percent of 56 officer career fields in the reserve components

FIGURE 2. END STRENGTH ACHIEVEMENT IN THE RESERVE COMPONENTS, 1987–2003

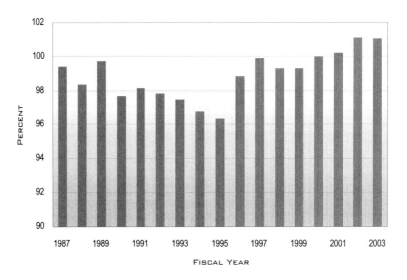

Source: Office of the Assistant Secretary of Defense for Reserve Affairs.
Note: Data include U.S. Coast Guard.

FIGURE 3. ATTRITION IN THE RESERVE COMPONENTS, 1987–2003

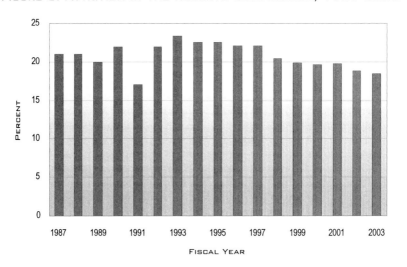

Source: Office of the Assistant Secretary of Defense for Reserve Affairs.
Note: The attrition rate equals total personnel losses divided by average strength. Data include U.S. Coast Guard.

TABLE 2. MULTIPLE CALL-UPS FOR RESERVE COMPONENT
(AS OF DECEMBER 2003)

MULTIPLE CALL-UPS SINCE 1996[a]

NUMBER	OPERATION	NUMBER OF RESERVISTS	PERCENT OF SELECTED RESERVE
2 Call-ups	ONE/OEF/OIF + 1 PRC	10,263	1.2
3 Call-ups	ONE/OEF/OIF + 2 PRCs	1,424	0.2
4 Call-ups	ONE/OEF/OIF + 3 PRCs	115	0.0
Total		11,802	1.3

"DOUBLE TAPS" SINCE SEPTEMBER 11, 2001[b]

RESERVE COMPONENT	NUMBER OF RESERVISTS	PERCENT OF SELECTED RESERVE
Army National Guard	4,465	—
U.S. Army Reserve	1,850	—
U.S. Naval Reserve	437	—
U.S. Marine Corps Reserve	872	—
Air National Guard	4,295	—
U.S. Air Force Reserve	3,269	—
U.S. Coast Guard Reserve	794	—
Total	15,982	1.8

Source: Office of the Assistant Secretary of Defense for Reserve Affairs.

a. Multiple call-ups, in this portion of the table, refer to those selected reserve members serving in Operation Noble Eagle (ONE), Operation Enduring Freedom (OEF), or Operation Iraqi Freedom (OIF) who also served in a previous presidential reserve call-up (PRC), such as Bosnia or Kosovo.

b. Double taps are the number of selected reserve members having served more than one tour in current operations (ONE/OEF/OIF).

have been heavily used in the past two years. Career fields exhibiting a high usage rate — 35–40 percent or higher over the past two years — could be considered stressed fields (figure 4). Examples of stressed career fields include law enforcement, civil affairs, installation security, intelligence, special forces, air crews, and transportation.

DURATION OF CALL-UPS

Duration is the amount of time for which reserve component members are called up — the duration of the mobilization tour. Historically, the maximum tour of duty for reservists in contingency operations has been nine months (270 days). By comparison, in current operations, the majority of call-ups have been for 300 days or longer (table 3). The data clearly show that the duration of tour lengths has increased to support the requirements of the global war on terrorism.

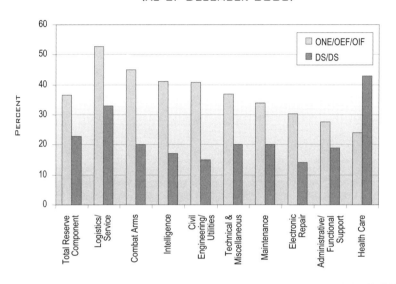

FIGURE 4. PERCENTAGE OF RESERVE COMPONENT MEMBERS
MOBILIZED FOR MAJOR CONTINGENCIES BY CAREER FIELD
(AS OF DECEMBER 2003)

Source: Office of the Assistant Secretary of Defense for Reserve Affairs.
Note: The percentages for ONE/OEF/OIF reflect the total number of mobilized reserve component members (319,193) divided by the selected reserve strength (875,607) as of December 2003. The percentage for Desert Shield/Desert Storm (DS/DS) reflect the total number of reserve component members (267,330) divided by the selected reserve strength (1,166,427) as of September 1991.

TABLE 3. DURATION OF CALL-UPS FOR
RESERVE COMPONENT MEMBERS

CONTINGENCY	AVERAGE NUMBER OF DAYS
Desert Shield/Desert Storm	156
Regional Contingencies (Kosovo, Somalia, Southwest Asia, Bosnia, Haiti)	~200
Noble Eagle/Enduring Freedom/ Iraqi Freedom	319

Source: Office of the Assistant Secretary of Defense for Reserve Affairs.

Overall, these indicators suggest increasing stress on the reserve components, particularly on those individuals and units in high-demand specialties.

Reducing stress is a top priority for the department; it is finding the right solution that is the challenge. There have been calls for an increase in end strength, which is certainly one option. Secretary Rumsfeld has repeatedly said that he would support an increase in end strength if he were convinced it was necessary. But this option should not be exercised until the military services first review the adequacy of their overall military capabilities and determine whether changes can be made in the mix of active and reserve forces to meet current and projected operational requirements while relieving stress on the force. In other words, the services first need to determine if they are effectively using the forces they currently have — the subject of the next section.

REBALANCING THE FORCE

Change, inevitable as it is, seems to spark concerns. Although the experiences of the Department of Defense in the past few years have clearly highlighted a number of areas where changes must be made, implementation is frequently fraught with challenge. An issue that has generated particular interest is that of rebalancing the force.

WHAT IS REBALANCING?

Simply put, rebalancing is asking if the military services have the right type and mix of forces for the missions the Department of Defense must undertake. If the type and mix of forces is not correct, the services need to consider what changes could be made in order to better utilize the scarce resources they have to meet the department's mission.

As the department considers rebalancing, it must first look at specific career specialties that are highly stressed — specialties such as civil affairs, aircrews, special forces, operational and counterintelligence, military police, installation security, and law enforcement. Statistics on the usage rates in some of these specialties are indicative of stress. For example, 54 percent of civil affairs officers in the reserves (and 72 percent of the total force inventory) have been called up. Further, 76 percent of reserve enlisted installation security specialists (and 30 percent of the total force inventory) have been called up. To better optimize force capability, it would be prudent to better distribute the skill mix in the total force to relieve some of the stress placed on members of these and other high-demand career fields.

OPTIONS FOR REBALANCING

Rebalancing initiatives should focus on three areas: enhancing early responsiveness of the force, relieving pressures on service members in stressed career fields, and employing innovative management practices. Specific rebalancing initiatives include

- Reviewing possibilities for converting military positions to civilian jobs. Secretary Rumsfeld has asked if outsourcing nonmilitary jobs can create more billets for essential military positions. When possible, the services can and should recover military billets by contracting functions to nonuniformed personnel. Indications are that over 10,000 military personnel could be put back into the operational force in the near term, if the positions they currently occupy were filled by civilians.

- Identifying useful manpower realignments in the active and reserve component capabilities mix. Specific options include transferring some active duty billets from one career field to another; creating more reserve component billets in the stressed career field, thereby establishing a deeper rotational base in the reserve component pool; migrating active component missions to the reserve component; migrating reserve component missions to the active component; or a combination of these options. In addition to realignment, another option is creating either blended units (composed of active and reserve forces) or specialized reserve units that are prevolunteered for very rapid employment.

- Employing management approaches such as the continuum of service, reach-back operations, rotational overseas presence, and improvements in the mobilization process to enhance access to individual skills and capabilities.

The military services moved some 10,000 positions within and between the active and reserve components in fiscal year 2003. Another 20,000 positions are scheduled for rebalancing in each of the next two years, fiscal year 2004 and fiscal year 2005, for a total of 50,000 rebalanced positions in three years, with the potential of reducing the need for reserve mobilizations and relieving stress on reserve capabilities in high demand.

None of these rebalancing concepts have emerged in a vacuum. The department and the services have been examining these concepts since before the events of September 11. My office, the Office of the Assistant Secretary of Defense for Reserve Affairs, has been open and collaborative in working with service staffs. We have kept the Congress informed as these ideas have developed, and we have included the reserve military associations in our discussions. We all share the imperative of winning the global war on terrorism.

The department is serious about making transformational changes in the *near term*. Secretary Rumsfeld has asked the military services to examine rebalancing with the intent of making real changes this year and next, not five or six years from now.

OTHER NEAR-TERM CHALLENGES

There are other areas where improvements can be made in managing the reserve component. Two important areas are training and family and employer support.

TRAINING

In order to achieve the agility in the force that the global war on terrorism demands, the military services need to change their reserve training philosophy from *mobilize-train-deploy*, to *train-mobilize-deploy*. The services need to be more creative in developing programs to train reservists before they are mobilized for an operation. There is no longer time to prepare for the fight against a well-defined enemy during a long build-up schedule. Today's military forces have to meet stateless enemies on accelerated conflict timelines.

One way to introduce flexibility into premobilization training is to ask if the one-weekend-drill-per-month paradigm — the 38-day annual training requirement — is sufficiently responsive to today's operational demands. Other options might include a more concentrated training cycle, such as two two-week training periods or a one-month training block. There might be cases where individuals could drill virtually, using computer technology and connectivity from remote locations. The intention of this concept is not to do away with weekend drills or to cut overall annual reserve pay and compensation. The goal is to introduce more flexibility into the current training structure in a way that might better prepare the force to rapidly respond to mission requirements.

FAMILY AND EMPLOYER SUPPORT

Another important area of concern is family and employer support. Judicious and prudent use of the reserve components is extremely important. The department understands the potential long-term effects of lengthy, multiple deployments. It is acutely aware that its ability to maintain strength and fulfill troop commitments in the global war on terrorism depends largely on the readiness and support of service members' families and employers. Toward this end, enhancements have been made in family and employer support programs. Robert Steel has emphasized the importance of employer support, but described the difficulties faced by small businesses in particular (chapter 8, this volume). He also describes the implications of the Uniformed Services Employment and Reemployment Rights Act, the law that protects the job rights of citizen-soldiers.

The services monitor employer and family-related issues and concerns for early indications of potential problems. Because reservists are being called upon more than they have in the past, the impact on their families and employers is changing. Although the services are currently achieving their strength objectives, as discussed earlier, it is important to remain vigilant about future enlistment and reenlistment behavior and trends.

In speaking with reservists around the country and around the world, and with their employers, there seems to be a consensus that being mobilized once is expected, and twice might be okay, but that the third time really becomes a point of concern. Reserve component members and their families and employers want predictability of service; they want to know when they will deploy and when they will return. Steps to improve predictability of service will go a long way toward maintaining family and employer support.

THE ACID TEST OF THE RESERVE COMPONENTS

In the end, the acid test for the nation's reserve component members is this: are we providing the right reservists, with the right equipment and training, in the right number, at just the right time, to help the total force fight and win our nation's conflicts? The goal for the department is to have not one more reservist on active duty than needed and to have not one reservist fewer than required to accomplish the mission. That goal is driven in part by cost factors and in part by the necessity for equitable treatment of reservists, their families, and their employers.

These transformational concepts are worth every ounce of energy that the department can muster. We owe no less to the fathers and mothers of America who have given us a sacred trust: the lives, the fortunes, and the futures of their children and of our nation.

★ ★ ★ ★ ★ ★ ★ ★ ★ ★ ★ ★

PART IV

Transformation in Military Manpower and Personnel Policy

★ ★ ★ ★ ★ ★ ★ ★ ★ ★ ★

INTRODUCTION

Ken Krieg

Previous parts of this volume have addressed the all-volunteer force from a number of perspectives — from a historical perspective, from a forward-looking one, and from one that focuses on the reserve component. The all-volunteer force has taken the art of war to levels heretofore unknown. It has succeeded in the many challenges it has faced and has done so in spite of difficult circumstances. Looking back over the past three decades, however, we also see that this force was built on a set of strategic conditions that no longer reflect the planning environment of the 21st century. As a result, many of the tools and policies used to manage this force emphasize stability rather than innovation.

The transformation of the armed forces that is ongoing today reflects the need for the Department of Defense to adapt to a changed and changing security environment. Much of the public debate and discussion about transformation focuses on "big-ticket" investments in flashy platforms — on high-end weapon systems with tremendous capabilities. But we in the Department of Defense understand that transformation is also about policies and practices, including, I am glad to say, military manpower and personnel policies.

A quick review of transformation literature reveals that the most important elements of transformation are not the hardware but in fact the "soft" issues — the way people and organizations think and work together, their culture and values, what they are about, and why they are engaged in their particular endeavors. Technology facilitates change; it does not guarantee it. Only people working with technologies and systems can make change a reality.

The papers in part 4 of this volume address many questions concerning the future of military manpower and personnel policy. What characteristics are needed in our military forces in the future? Do current policies undermine the development of these characteristics — characteristics such as innovation and

★

risk taking? What innovations in policies and practices are essential if the department is to build the cadre of soldiers needed to fight and win the wars of the future? Is the force well organized to get the most out of its active and reserve components? Is there room for a new philosophy of force management that more closely integrates the department's full- and part-time workers; that enhances its ability to surge; and that could expand its overall capability without a large increase in overall troop strength?

In many respects, the answers to these questions, offered by the authors of the papers in this section, serve as important agenda items for a transformation in manpower and personnel policy. They also have application to the civilian work force in the Department of Defense — a segment of the department whose transformation is not the focus of this volume, but one that is important to remember. Although such policy transformation takes time and will require much debate and discussion, the process must begin now. Indeed, the department has taken a number of steps in the right direction. Yet more steps certainly must be taken in order to ensure that the all-volunteer force remains the great national asset that it is today.

★ ★ ★ ★ ★ ★ ★ ★ ★ ★ ★

CHAPTER 12

LOOKING TO THE FUTURE: WHAT DOES TRANSFORMATION MEAN FOR MILITARY MANPOWER AND PERSONNEL POLICY?

Beth J. Asch
James R. Hosek[1]

INTRODUCTION

Each decade of the all-volunteer force (AVF) has brought with it new challenges in meeting military manpower supply requirements—challenges that have been successfully met by the Department of Defense (DOD) and Congress. During the first decade, in the 1970s, the challenge was to transition from a conscripted to a volunteer force. Meeting that challenge involved an unprecedented increase in military pay. In the 1980s, the volunteer force was sustained with both another large increase in military pay—made necessary because military pay had been allowed to fall relative to civilian pay during the late 1970s—and an expansion of recruiting and retention resources such as bonuses and educational benefits. This period was also notable in that the recruiting effort became more sophisticated in describing local markets, motivating recruiters, and developing effective advertising programs, and thereby accessing high-quality personnel at acceptable costs. The third decade, the 1990s, witnessed the end of the cold war, the increase in operations other than war, and an unusually robust civilian economy that again challenged DOD's ability to recruit and retain high-quality personnel. This challenge was successfully met with another substantial increase in military pay that helped restore it to pre-boom levels relative to civilian pay; a restructuring of pay that gave larger increases to personnel who earned promotions faster; and an increase in recruiting and retention resources.

The AVF is now at the beginning of its fourth decade. While the future is unknown, DOD is transforming itself to ensure that it is prepared to meet future threats. Such transformation requires a reassessment of the military's current manpower and personnel policies and therefore the factors that will affect the continued success of the AVF over the next decade and beyond.[2]

★

This paper provides input relevant to that reassessment. We begin with a description of how the ongoing transformation of the military has been defined, drawn from statements and testimony of DOD leadership and documents such as the 2001 Quadrennial Defense Review (QDR). We then discuss the likely implications of transformation for military manpower requirements. Given the likely changes in military manpower goals, we then ask whether the existing military personnel management and compensation systems support these transformation-related goals. Finally, we discuss the types of personnel management and compensation policy changes that might be required.

WHAT IS MEANT BY TRANSFORMATION?

The purpose of the military's transformation effort is to ensure that it has the capabilities it needs to defend the United States against a spectrum of unknown and uncertain threats. Transformation is not a one-dimensional concept or a pre-determined recipe for change. Instead it is commitment to innovative approaches to war fighting and the support of war fighters.[3]

The 2001 Quadrennial Defense Review report outlined a new defense strategy that relies on transformation for its success. That strategy shifts the focus of military planning from defense against predetermined threats and preparation for two major, simultaneous wars to the identification of potential but uncertain threats and the development of capabilities to deter and defend against them. The QDR identified six major goals. They are to

- protect the U.S. homeland and bases overseas and defeat weapons of mass destruction and their means of delivery

- project and sustain power in distant environments

- deny sanctuary to the nation's enemies by developing capabilities for persistent surveillance, tracking, and rapid engagement

- protect U.S. information networks from attack

- use information technology to link different U.S. forces

- maintain unhindered access to space and protect space capabilities from enemy attack

Achieving these goals will require intellectual, cultural, and technological changes within not only the armed forces but also DOD as a whole. Defense Secretary Donald Rumsfeld has stated that transformation calls for a revolution in culture in terms of "the way we think, the way we train, the way we exercise, and the way we fight." Transformation must "encourage a culture of creativity and intelligent risk taking" and "promote a more entrepreneurial approach to developing military capabilities." As described by Chairman of the Joint Chiefs of Staff, Richard Myers, intellectual change means that people must have "the mental agility to match their capabilities to new and unprecedented missions," and cultural change means that they must develop an "attitude that values educated risk taking and cooperation that spans organizations." Moreover, transformation requires change in doctrine, organization, training, and logistics, bolstered by change in technology.

Although the definition of transformation is not tied to particular initiatives, several specific reforms have been defined as vital for future war fighting. These reforms relate to jointness in military planning and operations, improved personnel management and compensation, and improved acquisition and use of technology.

At its extreme, jointness means the full integration of the different service divisions, where capabilities are "born joint." According to General James P. McCarthy (U.S. Air Force, Retired), this integration would be achieved through joint training, the development of "tailorable" joint-force modules, and the creation of a joint command-and-control capability to plan missions and conduct operations. Jointness would be far more prevalent than it has been in the past, and would penetrate further into each service. This concept of jointness seems consistent with each service retaining the responsibility and authority to create and sustain specific defense capabilities; but the services would engage jointly in planning the capabilities needed, allocating the capabilities across the services, deciding on battle plans, and tailoring the modules to be deployed.

A second area of reform is the management and organization of personnel to allow for greater speed and flexibility in deployment, to allow for more decentralized forces that enable subordinate commanders to exploit windows of opportunity, and to allow for greater intelligent risk taking and innovation.

A third reform required by transformation is to improve the use and acquisition of technology within the fighting forces. Although technology is already a priority, transformation will require that the force is fully connected and networked to ensure that a common picture of the battlefield is shared. Further, the military must continue to take advantage of rapidly changing technologies. Although defense officials argue that changing technology is only one part of transformation, it is clear that dramatic changes in technology are central to the rationale behind and the progress of transformation.

Transformation is also expected to be an ongoing process, rather than a one-time change. Transformation is viewed more as a framework for generating and embracing fundamental change than a process with an end point. Thus, it seems likely that the meaning of transformation itself, and the specific reforms that are pursued, will continue to evolve as the capabilities and challenges facing the armed forces unfold.

WHAT ARE THE IMPLICATIONS OF TRANSFORMATION FOR MILITARY MANPOWER REQUIREMENTS?

Transformation will clearly require fundamental change throughout the military, including requirements for military manpower. In this section we argue that transformation will not just change military planning and the resulting numerical manpower requirements for manning various kinds of units, but will change how things are done. Specifically, there will be a greater need for flexibility in personnel management as well as a change in military culture that both promotes and results from the greater flexibility.

A SHIFT FROM THREAT-BASED TO CAPABILITIES-BASED PLANNING

The following is a simplified characterization of the process that was used for determining manpower requirements in the pretransformation era. The threats associated with two major theater wars would be identified in broad terms: strategists would identify the possible adversaries, their military capabilities, the potential types of battle (in the air, at sea, or on land), and the possible geographic locations of battle. From these projections, the strategy and battle plans would be devised. These would detail the roles and missions of each force and the allocation of force "building blocks" to the theaters. (Examples of "building blocks" are air wings, ships, submarines, Marine expeditionary forces, and Army divisions.) From these decisions would flow the logistics and manpower requirements.

Planning would thus be based on a specific set of threats, and the services would configure the design of their missions, equipment, training, and unit organization to meet those threats. The implicit assumption was that a conservative estimation of the nature of the possible threats would ensure that the planning and resources needed to meet them would also be sufficient to handle smaller operations. Given unit organization (that is, the number of personnel in each unit by rank and skill) and an estimate of the numbers and types of units needed, manpower requirements followed.

This simplified description of the planning process leaves out the many variants of major theater war, regional conflict, and ancillary missions that were addressed through planning exercises, field exercises, and investments in the development of doctrine and training. These activities, and the experience that accrued as successive generations of planners and leaders faced a changing national security environment, helped provide assurance that the force had the capability — and the manpower — to meet foreseeable threats on several fronts.

However, the 2001 Quadrennial Defense Review shifted the focus for military planning from a specified set of threats — and an assumption that if these threats could be met, then so also could other threats be met — to a focus on the development of capabilities as the key to meeting diverse and uncertain threats. Under capabilities-based planning, planners must decide upon a threat distribution, meaning the types of threats possible and the likelihood of their occurrence, singly or simultaneously. For each type of threat, planners devise robust approaches — that is, operational plans that can surmount unforeseen circumstances as they arise. Also, planners consider whether it is possible to anticipate types of threats and take action to deter or influence ("shape") them. Capabilities-based planning recognizes that because threats are unknowable beforehand, it is advantageous to be able to select particular capabilities from within each service and combine them to effect a joint response.

The distinct emphasis on jointness in capabilities-based planning may mark a new phase of interservice cooperation, although joint planning has occurred for decades and was directly addressed as a priority by the Goldwater-Nichols Reorganization Act of 1986. Advances in sensors, communication, situational awareness, precision-guided munitions, and command-and-control technology now enable ground, air, and sea forces to establish closer working rapport than ever before. This improved rapport has enlarged the range of maneuver, increased the size of the supportable front, and permitted rapid and accurate strikes and counterstrikes, all of which contribute to a greater overall technical capability and, arguably, to a growing sense of trust in joint planning and joint operations. Furthermore, technical change and cultural change (increased trust) appear to allow the concept of jointness to be implemented at lower and more decentralized levels of military operations. This phenomenon enables the services to be more mutually reliant rather than self-reliant, and it increases the likelihood that tailored forces, which combine units or parts of units from each service, can be created and placed under joint command without incurring the resistance and resentment of unit commanders.

Capabilities-based planning is not structured to produce a single estimate of manpower requirements determined by a prespecified set of threats. Instead, one can think of a relationship between manpower and the probability of meeting the threats in the threat distribution. For example, at a given level of manpower the predicted probability of success might be 100 percent for 60 percent of the possible threats, 90 percent for 30 percent of them, and 80 percent for 10 percent of them. Adding capability, that is, adding certain types of units and the manpower to staff them, increases the predicted probability of success across the identified range of threats. Capabilities-based planning therefore provides information about the level of preparedness with respect to that range and may enable planners to obtain a more precise idea of the trade-offs involved when choosing among different types of units for inclusion in the force. By not focusing primarily on two major theater wars, capabilities-based planning provides an effective way to assess how to support the strategic goals outlined in the 2001 QDR, which are, once again, defeating weapons of mass destruction and their means of delivery; projecting and sustaining power in distant environments; developing capabilities for persistent surveillance, tracking, and rapid engagement; protecting information networks and space capabilities from attack; and using information technology to network U.S. forces. In the end, this assessment helps support decisions about weapons investment, roles and missions, organization, and force size.

Planning may consider units to be preconfigured with respect to their organization, equipment, and personnel, or may call for the reorganization of existing unit types or the creation of new unit types. (Recently created new unit types include Army light divisions, Stryker brigades, and Patriot missile units.) Once the number and kind of units required has been designated, manpower requirements have also largely been designated.

As articulated by Secretary Rumsfeld, transformation will require changes throughout the defense community. Nobody knows exactly what the changes will be, but they will affect needed capabilities, doctrine, organization, and technology, and hence manpower requirements. In the context of compensation and personnel policy, transformation will require innovative and flexible ways of using personnel. Furthermore, personnel are likely to have different kinds of careers than they do now. Various studies and commissions have defined what is meant by more flexible use of personnel within the context of the current compensation and personnel management systems. Proposed features include

- More variation in the length of the military career across skill and occupational areas, implying careers that extend beyond 30 years and, more controversially, careers that exceed 10 years but end before 20 years. Such variation in career lengths would result in differences in the experience mix of different occupational areas.

- Greater emphasis on conserving active duty positions for combat-essential activities, along with a shift of noncombat-essential support to civilian contractors or DOD civilians, thereby increasing the number of available active duty combat and combat support personnel. The Office of the Secretary of Defense and the services have begun to explore the opportunities for such shifts.

- Continued reliance on the selected reserves in overseas deployments and in the manning of domestic positions vacated by deployed active duty personnel, but enhanced by development of the continuum-of-service concept, whereby qualified reservists may be called to serve, or volunteer to serve, for a variable number of days in an active assignment.

- Longer time in an assignment for officers and noncommissioned officers (NCOs), allowing individuals more time to learn a job and allowing the services to capture the returns provided by more job experience.[4] Longer assignments are feasible if longer career lengths are possible, or if average assignment length remains the same but some assignments are shortened while others are lengthened.

- Fewer moves, that is, fewer permanent changes of station, enabling longer time in an assignment and reducing disruption in the lives of military families.

- More variation in time-in-grade and hence in-grade progression (that is, more variation in the timing and probability of promotion), enabling members to stay in a grade longer rather than being moved up to a more supervisory grade or forced out by up-or-out constraints. (This concept is sometimes described as an "up-or-stay" approach.)

- Development of multiple career tracks for officers and NCOs to take advantage of gains from specialization and facilitate a better match between career track and individual skills and preferences. (The Army has developed such tracks for officers.) The tracks could allow varying time in grade. For example, those on a leadership track might experience faster grade progression and achieve a higher grade at the end of their career. Those on a more technical track might enter at a higher grade (reflecting more civilian education) but progress more slowly up the grades.[5]

This proliferation of ideas and initiatives for greater flexibility in personnel management should contribute both to greater military capability and increased member satisfaction.

The greater need for flexibility and the call for more innovation and intelligent risk taking will require a changed military culture. The transformed culture will place a premium on adaptability to emergent situations, interoperability and jointness, rapid responsiveness, agility to capitalize on opportunities in the field, and a small logistics footprint.

Culture refers to how things are done and defines the tacit rules that influence actions in a wide variety of situations. Culture is rooted in a set of values, beliefs, rituals, symbols, and assumptions, and it provides a common language and common knowledge about the norms of behavior.[6] Because it shapes behavior, culture is a strategic human resource tool that can affect performance and capability. Importantly, culture can act as a partial substitute for explicit rules of behavior under a range of uncertain circumstances.

To support the goals of transformation, the values and beliefs that define military culture need to emphasize innovation and entrepreneurship within the bounds of the military's chain-of-command environment, and need to recognize the importance of flexibility in managing personnel. Furthermore, jointness and interoperability must be important norms of behavior, and innovative use of personnel and technology must be defined and rewarded. Leaders will play a particularly important role in communicating these values and rewarding behavior that conforms to them. Strong leadership and an effective means of disseminating information about the importance of new values are critical for creating and maintaining a culture that values innovation and entrepreneurship. Later in this chapter, we discuss incentives that can help support innovation and cultural change.

Given the far-reaching changes implied by transformation, a key question is whether the existing military compensation and personnel systems can accommodate these changes or whether, in fact, these systems must change too. The current personnel management and compensation systems have shown an impressive capacity to respond to evolutionary change in the past, leading to success in attracting and retaining the quantity and quality of personnel required. As illustrated over the past three decades of the AVF, the personnel and compensation systems have helped ensure that talented individuals are encouraged to enter and stay in the military in sufficient numbers; that personnel have the incentive to perform well, to pursue activities that develop and reveal their capabilities, and to seek positions where those capabilities are put to their best use; and that arduous duties in hazardous conditions and in places far from home are recognized.

But despite this success, policy makers and analysts have little objective information on whether personnel and compensation policies have generated a defense work force that is well-equipped or likely to embrace the creativity, risk taking, and flexibility called for by transformation. Also lacking is an objective basis for determining whether past policies produced the right amount of flexibility and risk taking. Such a measure would be valuable for assessing the gains from increases in creativity, risk taking, and flexibility under transformation. Furthermore, as discussed in the next section, despite its many successes, the current military compensation and personnel systems seem to hamper rather than promote the flexible use of personnel and produce remarkably similar personnel outcomes, in contrast to the call for more variation in the kinds of military careers offered. The lack of personnel management flexibility produced by the current system has been a common theme in recent studies of the system, including the *Report of the Defense Science Board Task Force on Human Resources Strategy* (U.S. Department of Defense 2000).

ARE THE CURRENT PERSONNEL MANAGEMENT AND COMPENSATION SYSTEMS ADEQUATE?

Is there any reason to believe that the current systems will not provide the flexibility needed to support transformation? Does the current military culture incorporate values and norms that conform to the goals of transformation? In this section we argue that the current military culture seems to place particular emphasis on conformity rather than on flexibility and risk taking. This emphasis is evident in the high degree of equity in the pay outcomes and in the career lengths and experience mixes across occupational areas produced by the military's compensation and personnel systems. Still it is important to recognize that these systems also have attractive features, which we will discuss as well, including a successful track record during the AVF years.

The culture of the U.S. military reflects the military's historical antecedents, including the nature of war fighting in the past, the geography of warfare, the varied purposes of war fighting (waging war for the defense of the nation-state, domestic operations, peace keeping), and the environments in which war fighting has occurred. As these antecedents tend to be service-specific, the most powerful cultural elements are the service branch subcultures, and not the DOD culture as a whole. Various analysts argue that the Goldwater-Nichols Act has done little to change the preeminence of service cultures or to form a truly joint culture.[7]

The service branch subcultures reflect their assigned domain of war on land, at sea, or in the air. As discussed by Builder (1989), important to defining culture across the service branches are the identity of the war fighter, the size of the service's capability, and the relative importance of technology versus personnel skill in each service. Specifically, the Air Force sees air power and the role of the pilot as the decisive element in war. Capability is measured in terms of numbers of wings of bombers or fighters, and technology is a defining characteristic, with specific platforms, or even airframe models, being intimately connected with the notion of the pilot's identity. The Navy also relies on technology, but personnel are more likely to associate themselves with the Navy as an institution, or with a specific community (air, ship, or submarine) than with a specific ship or platform. Capability is viewed in terms of command of the high seas and is measured in terms of the stock of ships. The Army culture values basic skills in soldiering and war fighting over technology or equipment, with capability often measured in terms of end strength, not equipment. The Marine Corps is often thought to have one of the most distinct cultures, with identity being most closely tied to being a Marine, rather than being part of a specific unit. These subcultures affect the services' strategic approaches to war and how they conceptualize and prepare for war.

From a personnel standpoint, the military culture has several defining elements, as discussed by Snider (1999). "Discipline" is a critical element that helps minimize the confusion on the battlefield and that, together with "ritualization," provides rules on how and when military personnel can violate the usual social prohibitions against killing and violence. A related element is "professionalism," which defines codes of conduct. "Cohesion" and "esprit de corps" address the issue of unit morale and the willingness of unit members to execute the unit's mission. From the standpoint of the compensation system, a key element of the culture is equitable and fair treatment with respect to pay and career opportunities. This feature reflects the common burden of service, regardless of service branch and career field. Furthermore, equitable treatment with respect to pay, as well as fairly applied personnel policies, reflects the value of cohesion as a cultural element and recognizes the divisiveness of unfairly applied compensation and personnel policies. These cultural elements have given rise to compensation and personnel policies that are well defined, openly applied, and subject to considerable oversight by the DOD and Congress.

While these policies have been quite successful along many dimensions, there are elements that are likely to hinder transformation. An important example is the military's promotion process, which assesses performance in terms of well-defined criteria. While the system is an invaluable tool for providing performance incentives, it also arguably gives incentives to members to perform in a predictable manner that conforms to well-defined cultural norms. When there is relatively little variance in performance among promotion-eligible members, and therefore relatively little variance in individual promotion opportunities, each member has an incentive to "play it safe." Even small mistakes or undesired outcomes arising from informed risk taking can have serious consequences in terms of promotion timing. Frequent rotations exacerbate the climate of "zero tolerance for mistakes," because the best way to demonstrate high performance when one's duty tour is short is to follow the path of one's predecessor and conform to expectations. The lack of lateral entry and the hierarchical chain-of-command-environment can also magnify the tendency to conform: responsiveness to leadership is a cultural norm, yet those who become leaders in the chain of command achieved those positions precisely because their performance conformed to expectations. Because the promotion system is the key incentive mechanism for high performance in the military, these pressures embedded in it — pressures for predictable and uniform job behavior — are likely to hinder efforts to foster greater innovation, intelligent risk taking, and entrepreneurship. In short, the current military culture, as reflected in the compensation and personnel systems, places a higher value on predictability and conformity than on flexibility and risk taking.

FLEXIBILITY OF THE CURRENT COMPENSATION AND PERSONNEL SYSTEMS

As we will show, the military compensation system leads to highly similar pay by year of service across the branches of service and across occupational areas within a service. While this outcome results in a high degree of equity in compensation, and indeed equity of opportunity in compensation might be a useful policy in its own right, it is questionable whether an organization engaged in many different activities and employing many different technologies should find it efficient to have essentially the same labor experience mix in each activity. It is more likely that efficient management is achieved when different skills have different career lengths. For example, infantry and combat-related occupations may require mostly younger personnel in top physical condition for shorter careers, whereas some support occupations such as mechanics may require skilled technicians for longer careers. Career lengths reflect retention patterns that in turn are a response to the military's compensation system.

Within the compensation system there are numerous special and incentive (S&I) pays that can be varied across personnel and over time, and we find that most of the variation in military cash compensation across personnel at a given year of service is attributable to variation in these special and incentive pays. S&I pays provide a targeted, efficient way of increasing the level of compensation in response to more arduous or hazardous military duties, higher market wages, or changes in those wages over the business cycle. But with available information, we (and arguably, policy makers) cannot tell whether special pays are being used to maintain similarity in experience mix and promotion opportunity, or to provide the best-suited experience mix for producing output. As we show below, the compensation system leads to highly similar retention profiles across occupational areas.

Cash compensation for military personnel can be divided into regular military compensation (RMC),[8] S&I pays, bonuses, and miscellaneous allowances and cost-of-living allowances (COLAs).[9] Average cash compensation in 1999 was around $32,000 for enlisted personnel and $65,000 for officers (tables 1 and 2), and regular military compensation accounted for over 90 percent of these totals. S&I pays, such as proficiency pay, career sea pay, parachute duty pay, and hostile fire pay, averaged $300 to $1,300 for enlisted personnel and about $1,000 to

$3,000 for officers. These averages are taken over all personnel and most personnel do not receive any given S&I pay. Many S&I pays are not large. For instance, the average amount of proficiency pay for airmen who received it was $2,285, and only 3 percent received it. The same story was true of bonuses, miscellaneous allowances, and COLAs. For example, the average aviation officer continuation bonus in the Navy was $12,163, and only 7 percent of Navy officers received it. The average overseas COLA for soldiers was $1,849, and only 25 percent of soldiers received it.

TABLE 1. AVERAGE ENLISTED PAY, 1999

CATEGORY OF CASH COMPENSATION	ARMY	AIR FORCE	MARINE CORPS	NAVY
Regular military compensation	$30,509	$31,398	$28,241	$30,655
Special and incentive pays	482	301	317	1,345
Bonuses	372	381	11	777
Miscellaneous allowances and COLAs	832	1,015	785	967
Total	32,195	33,095	29,355	33,743

Source: Asch, Hosek, and Martin 2002.

TABLE 2. AVERAGE OFFICER PAY, 1999

CATEGORY OF CASH COMPENSATION	ARMY	AIR FORCE	MARINE CORPS	NAVY
Regular military compensation	$61,689	$61,599	$58,707	$59,761
Special and incentive pays	927	2,810	1,889	3,134
Bonuses	673	1,695	756	2,172
Miscellaneous allowances and COLAs	837	779	810	872
Total	64,125	66,883	62,161	65,940

Source: Asch, Hosek, and Martin 2002.

Figures 1 and 2 show how average cash compensation varies over the military career for enlisted personnel and officers, respectively. Average cash compensation in 1999 for enlisted personnel ranged from just over $20,000 at entry to over $40,000 at the 20th year, representative of an increase of a bit more than $1,000 per year (figure 1). Average cash compensation increased abruptly at year 20, as lower-ranking members exited and began drawing military retirement benefits; the remaining members had a higher average rank and received higher pay. Between years 20 and 30, pay grew by about $1,500 per year, topping out in the low $60,000 range. For officers, pay ranged from just below $40,000 at entry into commissioned service to about $115,000 at year 30, representing a steady increase of about $2,500 per year (figure 2). There was no discontinuous jump at

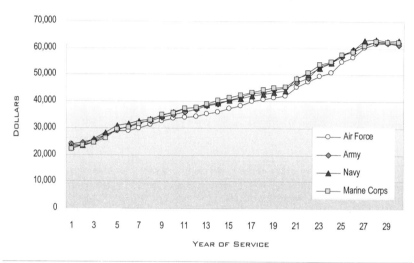

FIGURE 1. AVERAGE TOTAL ENLISTED PAY
BY SERVICE AND YEAR OF SERVICE, 1999

Source: Asch, Hosek, and Martin 2002.

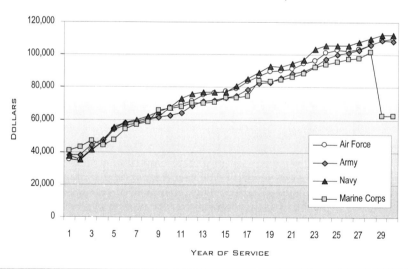

FIGURE 2. AVERAGE TOTAL OFFICER PAY
BY SERVICE AND YEAR OF SERVICE, 1999

Source: Asch, Hosek, and Martin 2002.
Note: Marine Corps averge pay drops off beyond year of service 26 due to a data anomaly.

year 20, because officer promotions occur within particular year-of-service intervals, and officers not promoted to the rank of major at 10–12 years of service are eliminated by the up-or-out constraint. The officer promotion system leads to less variation in rank than exists among enlisted personnel.

Although the services share a common pay table, and longevity increases are automatic, the promotion system incorporates strong incentives for performance and can create pay differences among personnel in different occupations. Promotion speeds for enlisted personnel vary across the services: service members in the Marine Corps are promoted to E-5 most quickly, and those in the Air Force are promoted most slowly, a statistic that largely accounts for the Air Force having lower average pay than the other services after the sixth year of service.[10]

Variation in enlisted pay comes primarily from S&I pays and bonuses and, secondarily, from differences in promotion speed. Pay variation in the Air Force in 1999, shown in figures 3 and 4, is illustrative of that for the other services. At each year of service, the standard deviation of compensation was computed for increasingly inclusive measures of compensation, starting with regular military compensation, adding S&I pays, then adding bonuses, and finally adding miscellaneous allowances and COLAs.

For airmen, the standard deviation of cash pay was about $4,000. That is, the pay earned by most airmen was the amount shown in figure 1 plus or minus $4,000. Much of the pay variation in the first 10 years of service derived from enlistment and reenlistment bonuses. After that, the variation increasingly came from regular military compensation. Given that personnel are on a common basic pay table and would receive the same pay at a given year of service if they were all of the same rank, the variation in regular military compensation occurred because of differences in rank—some members were promoted more quickly, some more slowly. Also, the amount of the housing allowance depends on whether a member has dependents, and while most junior members did not have dependents, most career members did.[11] The range of variation in enlisted pay can also be compared with that in the private sector. Looking across all enlisted personnel, the difference in pay between those at the 10th percentile of the pay range and those at the 90th percentile at the 10th year of service was $10,000 in 1999. In the private sector, the range of variation in pay between those at the 30th and 90th percentiles of the income spectrum was $23,000 for men with some college education.[12]

Among Air Force officers, pay variability rose substantially beginning in the midcareer, at around 10 years of service. Much of this variability was due to the addition of bonuses. The major bonus categories were aviation officer continuation pay, medical officer retention bonus, incentive specialty pay for medical officers, nuclear officer accession bonus, nuclear officer retention bonus, and nuclear career annual incentive bonus. Although only a small percentage of officers received these bonuses, their large dollar amounts significantly increased pay variation. For Navy and Army officers, pay variability that begins in the midcareer continues into the later career, between 20 and 30 years of service.

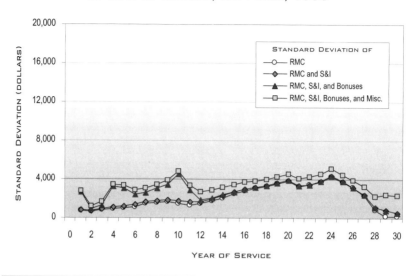

FIGURE 3. STANDARD DEVIATION OF ENLISTED PAY
BY YEAR OF SERVICE, AIR FORCE, 1999

Source: Asch, Hosek, and Martin 2002.

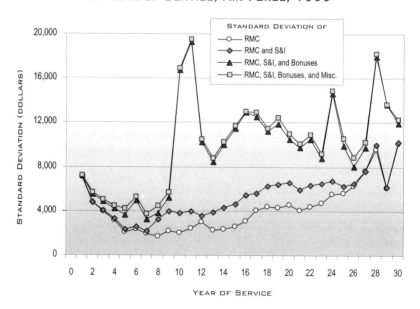

FIGURE 4. STANDARD DEVIATION OF OFFICER PAY
BY YEAR OF SERVICE, AIR FORCE, 1999

Source: Asch, Hosek, and Martin 2002.

As the main sources of pay variation in the military, S&I pays and bonuses represent the services' primary tool for influencing the retention decisions of service members, and in the aggregate, for shaping the experience mixes of personnel in different occupational areas. A question of interest is whether the services have used S&I pays and bonuses to flexibly manage personnel and achieve variable career lengths with different experience mixes across occupational areas. An examination of the years-of-service or experience mix of personnel across occupational areas within a service suggests that the service branches have generally relied on special and incentive pays and bonuses to generate similar, not varied, careers across occupational specialties. That is, the variation in these pays has resulted in conformity in the experience mix of the career force, particularly after the first five years of service.

Tables 3 and 4 show the enlisted and officer years of service distribution by one-digit DOD occupational code for fiscal year 1999. The greater "front-end" variation in the fraction of personnel with between 1 and 5 years of service probably reflects differences among career fields in first-term attrition rates and adjustments in recruiting targets driven by unexpectedly high or low retention in higher years of service. Only a small percentage of enlisted personnel, often less than 5 percent, have 21–30 years of service. The patterns for officers, shown in table 4, are similar in many ways, the chief exception being that typically 10–15 percent of officers have 21–30 years of service, while only 20–30 percent have 1–5 years of service, which is much lower than the nearly 50 percent for which this is true in the enlisted force.

Although the experience mix is similar across occupations within a service, there are some differences in that mix across the services. These differences arise from the services' roles and missions and the inherent attractiveness of the training, career tracks, living environments, and opportunities for deployment in each service. The Army and the Navy share many similarities in their experience mix, but the Navy appears to have a more diverse experience mix, perhaps reflecting differences between its seagoing and nonseagoing communities. The Marine Corps has the most junior force. It chooses to use mostly first-term members to constitute its fighting force, and strictly limits continuation into the career force. The Air Force has the most similar experience mix across occupational areas, reflecting its policy of equal advancement opportunity regardless of specialty. It also has the most senior force overall, that is, the highest percentage of personnel with over 10 years of service. The value of career opportunities within the Air Force is the most likely explanation for the seemingly contradictory fact that the Air Force has the lowest average pay but the highest average level of experience.

Our comparisons are at the broadest occupational category, that is, the one-digit level. Within each category, careers typically begin in narrowly defined occupations and feed into supervisory and leadership positions in these occupational areas. Retraining into a different occupational area occurs to some extent, particularly at the time of first-term reenlistment, but this is a relatively infrequent occurrence.

TABLE 3. ENLISTED YEAR-OF-SERVICE DISTRIBUTION BY ONE-DIGIT DOD OCCUPATIONAL CODE, FISCAL YEAR 1999

One-Digit Occupational Area	YOS 1-5	YOS 6-10	YOS 11-20	YOS 21-30
Army				
Infantry, gun crews, and seamanship specialists	57.3%	16.9%	22.6%	3.2%
Electronic equipment repairers	59.3	18.4	20.3	2.0
Communications and intelligence specialists	56.1	17.8	23.5	2.6
Health care specialists	49.3	25.0	23.1	2.6
Other technical and allied specialists	48.0	20.2	28.0	3.7
Functional support and administration	44.6	21.9	27.7	5.8
Electrical and mechanical equipment repairers	55.8	20.8	21.1	2.4
Craftsmen	61.2	19.2	17.7	2.0
Service and supply handlers	56.5	20.5	21.1	1.9
Navy				
Infantry, gun crews, and seamanship specialists	55.3	13.3	28.1	3.3
Electronic equipment repairers	39.2	20.1	37.0	3.6
Communications and intelligence specialists	44.6	20.8	31.5	3.2
Health care specialists	40.3	27.7	28.8	3.2
Other technical and allied specialists	22.8	19.8	50.2	7.1
Functional support and administration	24.8	22.1	47.0	6.1
Electrical and mechanical equipment repairers	46.6	18.7	31.2	3.5
Craftsmen	32.7	22.1	42.4	2.8
Service and supply handlers	28.2	24.5	43.6	3.7
Marine Corps				
Infantry, gun crews, and seamanship specialists	77.1	10.6	10.9	1.4
Electronic equipment repairers	59.9	18.6	17.7	3.7
Communications and intelligence specialists	59.1	17.7	19.6	3.6
Health care specialists	38.3	21.2	36.0	4.5
Other technical and allied specialists	57.9	18.6	19.9	3.5
Functional support and administration	54.7	15.8	22.2	7.3
Electrical and mechanical equipment repairers	63.5	17.0	16.5	3.0
Craftsmen	68.7	14.7	14.8	1.8
Service and supply handlers	70.2	14.2	13.2	2.3
Air Force				
Infantry, gun crews, and seamanship specialists	43.0	17.6	35.0	4.4
Electronic equipment repairers	33.4	18.4	41.9	6.4
Communications and intelligence specialists	35.9	16.8	40.8	6.5
Health care specialists	43.3	24.8	28.6	3.4
Other technical and allied specialists	39.3	16.8	38.2	5.7
Functional support and administration	28.5	19.3	44.3	8.0
Electrical and mechanical equipment repairers	35.5	18.4	39.4	6.7
Craftsmen	36.4	18.6	37.1	7.9
Service and supply handlers	36.0	22.0	35.5	6.5

Source: Asch, Hosek, and Martin 2002.

Table 4. Officer Year-of-Service Distribution by One-Digit DOD Occupational Code, Fiscal Year 1999

One-Digit Occupational Area	YOS 1–5	YOS 6–10	YOS 11–20	YOS 21–30
Army				
Tactical operations officers	31.7%	22.3%	34.1%	11.9%
Intelligence officers	24.4	22.5	43.3	9.8
Engineering and maintenance officers	39.0	20.1	33.1	7.8
Scientists and professional s	23.7	17.9	42.4	16.0
Health care officers	30.4	23.2	35.6	10.8
Administrators	23.1	19.5	41.0	16.5
Supply, procurement, and allied officers	26.6	21.0	41.2	11.2
Navy				
Tactical operations officers	15.8	30.0	39.5	14.7
Intelligence officers	20.5	22.3	43.2	14.0
Engineering and maintenance officers	6.7	7.1	51.1	35.1
Scientists and professionals	17.6	23.5	43.8	15.2
Health care officers	29.0	22.2	36.2	12.6
Administrators	46.7	10.6	31.3	11.4
Supply, procurement, and allied officers	15.2	21.2	45.5	18.1
Marine Corps				
Tactical operations officers	20.6	33.3	36.3	9.7
Intelligence officers	27.1	26.5	34.4	12.0
Engineering and maintenance officers	16.8	20.6	37.9	24.7
Scientists and professionals	31.1	25.5	37.0	6.3
Health care officers	32.7	22.5	36.8	8.1
Administrators	25.9	26.5	33.3	14.4
Supply, procurement, and allied officers	26.7	26.7	33.3	13.3
Air Force				
Tactical operations officers	14.9	26.8	46.1	12.2
Intelligence officers	28.2	23.1	33.1	15.6
Engineering and maintenance officers	26.9	23.1	38.9	11.1
Scientists and professionals	25.0	21.3	39.4	14.3
Health care officers	30.8	22.7	36.2	10.4
Administrators	24.0	21.4	31.1	23.5

Source: Asch, Hosek, and Martin 2002.

The discussion in the previous section focused on the equity of pay outcomes and career lengths among members at the same year of service in different skill areas within a service branch, outcomes that are at odds with what we would expect from an organization that flexibly manages different skill areas. Rather than foster innovation and flexible management, the culture, as reflected in these outcomes, has placed a higher value on conformity. Before discussing issues surrounding transformation of the military compensation and personnel systems, we note some of the attractive features of the current compensation and personnel systems that should not be overlooked when discussing proposed changes to the systems.

The modern military compensation system was developed by the 1948 "Hook Commission" and was enacted into law in 1949. Although various changes have occurred since then, the basic structure — of basic pay tables, various allowances, special and incentive pays, and immediate retirement benefits after 20 years of service — has remained essentially unchanged. The compensation system is highly visible, stable, and equitable. It can accommodate changes in force size, provides rewards for advancement, offers well-targeted supplemental pays, and contains incentives to prolong careers and incentives to exit the force. The published, regularly updated basic pay table, with pay defined in terms of pay grade and years of service, coupled with allowances for housing and subsistence, allows members to easily see how their pay will change through longevity and promotion.

The structure of the basic pay table has been highly stable; changes to the structure are made only after considerable study and deliberation. The stability makes members confident that they can forecast their future earnings, and the absence of radical change precludes invidious comparisons and blatant inequities across different generations of military personnel (that is, those entering service one year ago, five years ago, or fifteen years ago). That the pay table is common across occupations and services underscores the notion of equity — different members in different services are equally valued, given their years of experience and rank — and a shared awareness of equity may well be a unifying concept in wartime and peacetime.

The pay table has held up under increases in force size (as in the cold war buildup), changes in experience mix (associated with Korea and Vietnam), and decreases in force size (at the end of the cold war), and it has done so during both the draft era and the all-volunteer force era. The pay table provides rewards for advancement by structuring pay so that it increases with promotion. The ranks themselves function as explicit rungs on a career ladder. And the opportunity to move up the ranks — and receive higher pay — represents an incentive structure to induce members to exert effort and to reveal their skills and talents.[13]

The supplemental pays have been constructed based on specific rationales.[14] Bonus authorities enable the recruitment of high-quality personnel into hard-to-fill occupations and the retention of trained, experienced personnel with skills where training investments are large (such as for pilots and nuclear-trained officers) and where shortfalls would imperil military capability. Pays related to certain proficiencies (foreign language, parachute, nuclear), specialty-related risks (hazardous material), location disparities (domestic and overseas COLA), persistent separation (sea pay, family separation allowance), hardship (assignments to locations without amenities), and imminent danger are generally accepted as adjustments that are necessary to meet manning requirements and to compensate for unusual circumstances or risks.

The supplemental pays are large in relatively few cases, small in most cases, and typically received by a small fraction of personnel; the clear rationale and narrow targeting prevent them from eroding a sense of equity fostered by the basic pay table. In fact, one can argue that special pays operate to conserve equity, because even though the basic pay table is the same for all personnel, the conditions of work are not the same, and special pays such as sea pay, hazardous duty pay, COLAs, hostile fire pay, and family separation pay help to compensate for these differences. Also, by sustaining retention as appropriate, given manpower requirements, special pays help to maintain similar promotion opportunities across occupations.

Finally, the retirement benefit system, with both vesting and eligibility to retire occurring at 20 years of service, creates a powerful incentive to stay in the military beyond 10 years and to leave after 20 years. The added retention increases the return to training investments and creates a larger pool of experienced members whose knowledge of policy and procedure may help keep activities running smoothly.

In contrast to the compensation system, which focuses on pay, the personnel management system develops, advances, and assigns personnel. Military training helps to build an identity with the organization, unit cohesion, and an understanding of the command-and-control system and the importance of following orders. Advanced training and military professional education contribute to the development of leadership and communication skills and provide a thorough understanding of the roles, missions, equipment, tactics, and decisions required by personnel in positions of authority.

The promotion system clearly defines the rank structure and describes the responsibilities attending each rank. The criteria for promotion are explicit, detailed, and common knowledge among members competing for promotion. In the lower ranks, the use of explicit criteria that depend on objectively measured elements such as written and hands-on tests of skill and knowledge, physical fitness, marksmanship, successful completion of training, awards and decorations, and additional education, help to promote openness and fairness.

The assignment system for enlisted personnel operates centrally and matches available, qualified personnel to position openings (faces to spaces). Although sometimes members are allowed to choose the location of their next assignment as a retention incentive, assignments typically occur independently of individual preferences and therefore offer no opportunity for members to influence assignments. Officer assignments are also made centrally, but recommendations from senior officers are taken into account. Recommendations also influence the assignment of senior NCO positions.

TRANSFORMING MILITARY COMPENSATION AND PERSONNEL POLICY

As we have described, we think the major opportunities to support transformation through changes in the military compensation and personnel management systems lie in increasing the flexibility for managing personnel and providing support for a culture of creativity, entrepreneurial activity, and intelligent risk taking. Another challenge is assuring that the reserve forces will be suitably compensated if they are to be called upon far more frequently than in the cold war era. (This challenge is discussed at length in part 3 of this volume.) In discussing these topics below, we state the case for change, outline approaches for change and concerns about those approaches, and reflect on the factors that may have to align for change to occur.

THE CASE FOR CHANGE

The conformity of the experience mix of personnel across occupational areas, as shown earlier, suggests that the military personnel requirements process is not being driven by what manpower capabilities are needed by the services to accomplish their missions, but instead by what experience mixes are on hand or are delivered by the compensation system. This conformity stands in opposition to ideas such as innovation, intelligent risk taking, and entrepreneurship because it means there is a lack of demand for flexibility. Ideally, the unit structures and personnel mix that support various functions and activities would be determined without consideration of the supply and experience mix of personnel available to those activities but would be determined by the particular needs of those areas.

In effect, the experience mix is determined by the structure of compensation, including promotion policy and the use of special and incentive pays. There are exceptions to this rule—bonuses and special pays can target retention behavior among specific groups of personnel, as can the inherent attractiveness of military careers—but it would be focusing on the trees rather than the forest to ignore the effect of the compensation structure on experience mix. Determining the manpower requirements for a function or activity is in actuality conditioned on the expected flow of personnel by year of service. That is, the compensation and personnel systems operate to provide a supply of personnel, and the manpower system makes allocations subject to supply constraints. In an alternate world, manpower requirements would emerge from an assessment of the effectiveness, and the cost-effectiveness, of different manpower configurations, and the compensation system would be sufficiently flexible to permit the optimal requirements to be obtained.

If it is true that the experience mix present in the services is largely determined by the structure of compensation, then changes in that structure are needed to permit greater flexibility in managing personnel. Such changes would affect retirement benefits, the basic pay table, the use of special and incentive pays, and the personnel assignment system. However, in our view, compensation reform has proven difficult to achieve because there has been little impetus from the demand side of the military for greater flexibility in personnel management.

OBSTACLES TO COMPENSATION REFORM:
THE EXAMPLE OF MILITARY RETIREMENT BENEFITS

For greater flexibility in the management of military personnel to be realized, compensation reform must occur. Yet structural changes in military compensation that fundamentally alter the system rarely occur and the case of military retirement benefits illustrates why this is the case.

Retirement benefits have a strong effect on retention after about the 10th year of service. Both vesting and eligibility to receive retirement benefits occur at year 20. As a thought experiment, consider the consequences if vesting stayed at year 20 but eligibility to receive benefits were set at age 62, as it is for reserve retirement; the incentive to leave service upon reaching 20 years would decline as would the incentive to stay in service to year 20. Clearly, retention behavior is influenced by the retirement benefit structure, and changes in the structure could be devised to allow greater flexibility in shaping careers in different career fields and even at the individual level within a field. Indeed, many of the numerous study groups and commissions that have been convened in the past 55 years to study the military retirement system have come to the conclusion that the retirement system stifles personnel management flexibility.[15]

Asch, Johnson, and Warner (1998) have demonstrated the potential advantages of a retirement reform package in which the age of eligibility to receive benefits were set at 62, the steepness of the basic pay table were increased, a thrift-savings-type program were introduced with early vesting (after five years of service, as occurs through the Employee Retirement Income Security Act), and selective separation payments were introduced. Such a system would sustain or increase retention, strengthen incentives for effort, and cost less than the current system. The selective separation payments would enable the services to tailor each occupation's retention profile. Furthermore, although selective pays like bonuses and separation pays have been targeted toward particular career fields in the past, they could in addition be targeted toward specific individuals. That is, the services could be given the authority to offer such pays to retain particularly well-qualified individuals, or to encourage the exit of individuals who are underperforming but who otherwise would be allowed to complete 20 years of service. The Defense Science Board Task Force on Human Resource Strategy also recommended reforming the retirement system by including thrift-saving-type and separation pay components to enhance flexible management of personnel (U.S. Department of Defense 2000).

There appear to be several reasons why proposals such as these have generated debate but not consensus for action. The call for retirement reform has not been voiced by the services; the gains in military capability from the reform have not been *demonstrated* and quantified; a transition plan has not been specified and the costs of transition have not been estimated; and to some, any revamping of the retirement benefit system raises fears of broken trust, benefit cuts, and an open door to future rounds of disruptive and demoralizing changes. In addition, individual-level special pays raise the question of whether individual-level performance assessments are sufficiently fair, accurate, and efficient to support such actions. These points deserve serious attention and require analysis if such unorthodox change is to be politically feasible, let alone attractive as a mechanism to implement transformation.[16]

The most recent position taken by the services on retirement reform concerned the rollback of REDUX, the acronym for an earlier change in the retirement benefit structure. REDUX mandated a reduction in retirement benefits from 50 percent to 40 percent of basic pay for personnel retiring at their 20th year of service, but allowed benefits to rise to 75 percent of basic pay at year 30, as under the previous system. The change applied to all personnel entering active duty after August 1, 1986. A dozen years later, in the late 1990s, as the reality of this change sank in, the service chiefs heard numerous complaints from the field about the inequity of retirement benefit differences between personnel entering just after, versus just before, August 1, 1986, but otherwise doing the same work and making the same sacrifice.

Ultimately, equity was restored by giving service members under REDUX the choice of the pre-REDUX benefit structure (called High-Three) or receiving a $30,000 bonus at year of service 15 in exchange for a pledge to remain in service for five more years and remain under REDUX. The pressure for this change did not result from quantitative evidence showing that REDUX distorted the efficient allocation of manpower or reduced proficiency in performing mission-essential tasks, but rather from a growing consensus within the services that REDUX eroded morale—therefore negatively affecting military capability—and created a disturbance that would resound in the field, in budget deliberations, and in press coverage over the next decade or more.

The lack of quantitative evidence about the effect of REDUX on military capability seems as if it should have been highly consequential to the policy debate. The REDUX debate perhaps inevitably centered on a core value, equity. REDUX indeed violated equity between cohorts; but additionally, there was no evidence-based case to explain how equity had been traded off for greater military capability or even an improvement in military careers. In effect, REDUX was seen as a cost-saving initiative that reduced pay for part of the force in a seemingly arbitrary way, and it was not accompanied by hard evidence showing that it increased (or did not reduce) military capability. Inequities are tolerated in many other instances, in the form of targeted enlistment incentives, continuation incentives, proficiency pay, and sea pay, probably because these incentives help eliminate inequities in circumstance and support equity in opportunity for promotion. But REDUX affected all personnel reaching or anticipating military retirement, and REDUX was not accompanied by analysis showing that too many personnel stayed to 20 years and too few stayed after 20, that is, that personnel were misallocated.

These points have their counterpart in discussions about increasing the flexibility of managing personnel. Special and incentive pays appear to be an acceptable means of lengthening careers up to a point. However, for careers extending beyond year 10, the pull of retirement benefits becomes stronger, and the services might find too many personnel choosing to stay relative to manning requirements as a result of the retirement system's 20-year vesting rule. Separation pay could help shape retention in years 10 to 20, but absent this adjustment, the higher retention would in due time lead to an increase in retirement costs and in retirement benefit accrual charges. Yet even if pay mechanisms such as separation pay were available to shape the retention profile, there is the question of whether the services would choose to manage personnel and set requirements differently than they do now. This of course is the question about innovation, creativity, and entrepreneurship. It is one thing to have compensation and personnel systems that permit more flexibility, and another thing to demand more flexibility, especially if policies to enhance flexibility are viewed as threatening core values such as equity.

THE DEMAND FOR FLEXIBILITY: AN EXAMPLE

To consider the degree to which the services demand flexibility in their use of personnel, it is helpful to review the current process for determining manpower requirements for a specific activity. While this subject is vast and each service and command has its own approach, the process used by the U.S. Army Training and Doctrine Command (TRADOC) is illustrative. TRADOC develops a command-wide manpower program that takes into account the programmed work load, priorities within that work load, and personnel constraints ("available manpower resources"). The program depends on the technology chosen to accomplish the work (in a sense, the production function), the manpower and equipment required by the technology, the funding required, funding available as set by program budget guidance, and trade-offs involved with accomplishing different portions of the total potential work load.

The process begins with a discussion between the functional manager and the manpower manager to agree upon the types and levels of work to be done, resulting in a "validated work load requirement." The technology choice is then made, and equipment and staffing requirements are determined. "Manpower staffing standards and functional estimating equations" are used, and these models "have a proven relationship between the work required and the work load driver." Priorities and funding are then taken into consideration, and this process leads to a draft manpower program that is reviewed by program directors at the command level, who may make adjustments based on priority changes within their areas. The revised program is then sent to the field, where field commanders can make reallocations across their functional mission areas within the aggregate resource levels assigned in the working plan. Once these changes are incorporated, the program is given a final review by the command. The command plan provides Army headquarters with a unit-level description of manpower requirements and serves as the input to the Army-wide table of distribution and allowances (TDA). The manpower requirements contained in the TDA are the spaces that must be filled by the personnel command. This work load–based system "provides commanders and functional managers with a consistent and objective view of the demand for labor and a process that supports the allocation of available manpower resources against priority missions."

The manpower requirement determination process has proven effective in providing feasible, auditable manpower requirements. The requirements are feasible in that they are sufficient to accomplish the programmed work load, and auditable in that the engineered manpower standards and estimating equations that relate work load to labor demand are open to inspection by those involved with the process. The use of credible, open methods as well as input from functional commanders and field commanders makes the process objective and inclusive. Applying the same methods to each unit avoids disagreements that would result from allowing field commanders to submit manpower requirements based on their own methods. Overall, the manpower requirement determination process is able to function as a resource allocation mechanism in what amounts to a centrally planned economy.

But the process has limitations. Although useful for determining budgets and programming resources, manpower requirements determined by the process are often not fulfilled in practice: authorized, funded positions are usually fewer than the stated requirements. The inconsistency leads to the question of what in fact the requirements represent. Further, although innovations in resource allocations occur, the process does not have strong incentives for innovation because the status quo is defensible in the current period if it worked in the previous period, whereas innovations that create efficiencies run the risk of decreasing an organization's allocation in the future and disrupting its organizational structure (sometimes referred to as eliminating someone's rice bowl).

Innovation requires a special effort to go against the existing manpower standards and estimating equations and thereby upset the basis of the equilibrium among the organizations covered by the requirement determination process. The implementation of innovation—even planning the innovation—may require special budget allocations that can be difficult to obtain, and the innovator may need to develop a consensus among stakeholders to gain support for the innovation. Several years may elapse before the concept, funding, and organizational support are in place. This length of time is often longer than a commander's rotation assignment, and opponents to an innovation may therefore be able to outwait the initiative. Furthermore, innovations often involve a period of learning and adjustment, and innovators face the risks of little immediate payoff and possible failure, either of which could lead to adverse performance appraisals. As discussed in the context of the promotion process, these factors arguably lead to a culture of predictability, conformity, and "yes-people," not one of creativity and innovation. Finally, although we are discussing the manpower requirement process, it is useful to recognize that innovation can occur through changes in that process or, given the process, through changes in targets and rewards for unit performance, which, if successful, can feed back into requirement setting. In other words, we note that requirements are but one area where innovation might occur.

In the private sector, the impetus for innovation among senior managers comes from the profit motive, the behavior of rival firms, the threat of entry of new firms, and the possibility of bankruptcy. In the public sector, efforts to increase efficiency, flexibility, and innovation have employed benchmarking, outsourcing, and reorganization, which can be thought of as counterparts to competition, entry, and bankruptcy. The military does not operate according to a profit motive and does not have a residual claimant such as a manager, owner, or shareholder, who receives all incremental monetary return to greater effort, skill, and ability. But a type of residual claim may be created through other mechanisms, including promotion and nonpecuniary benefits such as recognition and choice in assignments, as discussed next.

APPROACHES FOR CHANGE

To summarize the discussion, tools and policies to achieve more flexible management of personnel exist—as in the case of special and incentive pays—or have been proposed—as in the case of calls to reform the retirement system. While additional tools could be useful, the heart of the problem is not the lack of tools but the lack of incentive or "demand" for flexibility on the part of defense managers. Indeed, the discussion in the previous sections illustrates that existing policies and procedures are used to achieve conformity within each service branch. To achieve greater flexibility in managing personnel and more variable outcomes in terms of career length and assignment length, the demand for flexibility and the incentives to be innovative and work in new ways must increase. Thus, the following discussion focuses less on proposing new tools for flexibility, a topic discussed by numerous studies and commissions over the years, and more on how to use the personnel management and compensation system to produce greater demand for flexibility and innovative behavior.

PERFORMANCE APPRAISAL

The traditional mechanism for the provision of incentive for performance and innovation in the military is the promotion process. Performance is evaluated in terms of predetermined criteria that rely on the metrics mentioned earlier and on supervisor and commanding officer evaluations. Increased incentives for innovation, informed risk taking, and greater use of available flexibilities to achieve more variable results could be improved by expanding the criteria used by commanding officers in their evaluations.

Specifically, performance appraisals could place greater emphasis on innovation, creativity, and entrepreneurship, so that these factors would figure more prominently in promotion decisions. Supervisors and commanding officers now appraise performance, but a "360-degree" appraisal, whereby subordinates as well as supervisors provide input, might offer additional information about receptivity to ideas from below and the effort to put them into action. Performance appraisals would not replace more traditional evaluation methods, such as testing and fitness reports, but would provide supplementary information about dimensions of performance that are verifiable and known to the commanding officer but not easily measured by conventional metrics. Furthermore, traditional metrics might be expanded to include measures of performance related to innovation, when such metrics are available. Expanding the promotion criteria to include transformation-related performance also provides incentives for members who have the ability to be creative and innovative to choose to remain in the military and seek advancement to leadership positions.

When relying on performance appraisals of commanding officers and supervisors, it is important to recognize the potential for "influence behavior." When performance is difficult to measure, or is unmeasured, and promotion decisions depend heavily on the subjective judgment of supervisors, individuals competing for promotion have an incentive to engage in actions to tout their own talents and accomplishments or to diminish those of their rivals.[17] Such influence behavior is costly from the military's perspective because it does not improve performance, just individuals' pay, and, indeed, it can diminish performance if individuals devote time or resources to such activities that would otherwise have been devoted to productive activities. Influence costs can be reduced if subjective evaluations are supplemented with the use of meaningful metrics that are not subject to influence behavior. They can also be reduced if the financial gains associated with promotion are limited. Although limiting the financial gain also reduces the incentive for high performance, such limits may make sense if the costs of influence behavior are substantial relative to the benefits. Or put the other way around, incentives that induce high performance may also be accompanied by influence behavior, the level of which may be tolerable if the benefits of high performance are large.

A challenge in implementing a performance appraisal process that recognizes innovation and greater use of flexibilities will be the difficulty of obtaining meaningful metrics and tying specific actions to desired outcomes. For this reason, documentation of initiatives should supplement the appraisals. Where possible, the documentation could include a description of concept, objective, implementation, and results, such as a quantitative assessment involving not case-study descriptions but before-and-after comparisons of performance relative to that of comparable activities or organizations in the military. Comparisons might be extended to the private sector in certain cases, as has been done in Army logistics, where in the past decade the focus of the logistics philosophy and organization changed from stockpiling spares to high-velocity resupply, computerized tracking of each item, and networked information and ordering systems. Because the majority of noncombat activities occur at multiple sites within a service, share similarities across the services, and have private sector counterparts, the opportunity for quantitative assessment and the expansion of performance metrics seems considerable.

AWARDS

Promotion is but one way to reward desired individual behavior. Awards can be provided in a variety of ways. For example, recruiting commands recognize persistently outstanding recruiters with awards such as rings, certificates, and plaques, and this type of public appreciation could also be used to recognize innovators. More generally, awards can be given for both individual and unit achievement relative to a preset goal, as in recruiting, or based on judgment by a panel of experts, as in awards for excellence such as the Baldridge award. They could also be based on a comparison of units with one another, where the comparison employs metrics related to performance level or performance improvement. When using awards, it is crucially important to know what to reward. Well-chosen objectives and a careful selection process with clearly specified criteria add to the prestige of the award. It is also important to recognize that group-level awards can lead to "free-riding" behavior, whereby individuals within the unit reduce effort and rely on colleagues to extend effort. Incentives for free riding are reduced or offset when group-level awards are supplemented with awards based on individual performance.

Policy statements and actions by the top leadership should reinforce the greater emphasis on innovation, flexibility, and entrepreneurship in performance appraisal and the achievement of rewards. Such emphasis helps ensure that people at all levels take innovation seriously and helps change the culture by disseminating information about changing values and beliefs. A military culture that places greater value on the importance of innovation helps ensure that actions, norms, and decisions reflect this value.

CHOICE OF DUTY AND JOB ASSIGNMENT

An alternative to promotion and recognition as a means of providing incentives for performance that supports transformation is to provide members with more choice with respect to their duty and job assignment. Granting service members a greater voice in selecting their assignments requires a careful weighing of the benefit to the organization and the benefit to the individual. In some cases, the organization may have the flexibility to define a set of acceptable assignments and let the individual choose from within the set; the organization can also define the set of individuals who are allowed to make a choice. Thus the organization can ensure that allowing members some choice will not result in poorer matches between personnel and positions. At the same time, the policy of offering choice should increase the member's ex ante level of satisfaction—that is, with a say in selecting the assignment, the member has a better chance of getting a preferred assignment.

An exciting example of greater individual choice is the Navy assignment incentive program, a pilot program allowing eligible sailors to bid for assignments for shore billets in distant ports. Sea pay will no longer be paid for these billets, and instead the Navy is holding a sealed bid auction on-line. The Navy is willing to pay a maximum of $450 per month in addition to other pays and benefits to staff these billets, but because preferences differ among sailors, some sailors will accept a considerably lower amount (by "bidding" that they will accept $250, say) and yet be satisfied to have been chosen for the assignment. This matching of assignment with individual preferences should result in greater satisfaction and perhaps higher retention than an assignment system that does not factor in individual preferences. If too few qualified bids are made, the Navy reserves the right to make unilateral assignments, that is, to revert to the current method of filling billets. About 4,000 positions will be included in this pilot program when it is in full swing. The program also allows sailors, once chosen for a preferred assignment, to opt to extend their tours, which should reduce the frequency and cost of relocating personnel. Overall, the program should result in mutual benefit to the Navy and the sailor.

The auction-based assignment system, as the Navy has implemented it, does not impede the chain of command. Also, the program is relatively small and has little impact on the usual assignment system; it does not noticeably deplete the supply of personnel available for assignment. However, the program could be scaled up. The benefit to the organization from scaling up would depend on the impact on morale, unit cohesion, proficiency, performance, and retention, as well as on cost. Today, the cost of "matching faces to spaces" is apparently small, because the matching is done by a centralized activity that relies on a computerized model. But to assert that the cost is small is to assume that the accounting cost of the matching system represents the full cost to the organization. Rather, all of the costs and benefits of the system should be judged relative to those of alternative methods. In the past, no real alternative to computerized matching was put forward, and computerized matching was feasible: it got the job done. Yet computerized matching might or might not result in lower benefits and higher cost than a voluntary assignment system once the proper accounting is done.

A voluntary assignment system would look considerably different from the current system. In effect, an internal-market clearing price would be put on each assignment. Theoretically, some personnel would be willing to pay for prized assignments by giving up part of their basic pay. But if such bids were not permitted, then highly valued assignments would be filled by bidders bidding zero dollars, implying their willingness to be chosen for those assignments without any additional pay. If there were an excess supply of volunteers, the service would choose among them. Thus the pool of volunteers would be self-selected, but the choice of volunteers from the pool would be random (or random conditional on minimizing relocation cost). For less-popular assignments, the service would have to pay a positive amount—equal to the minimum bid—for each assignment. There would presumably be an aggregate budget for such payments. This amount might be equal to the expected cost savings, somehow estimated, of the volunteer system relative to the current matching system. Given the budget, the service would have to allocate it across assignments. Depending on preferences, the budget might be high enough to offer the lowest-bid payment to every volunteer. But if not, the service could offer a payment up to a limit for each assignment and, as now, simply fill the remaining billets by direct order. If personnel expected some risk of being ordered to a billet regardless of their preferences, they could be induced to bid less than otherwise (say $150 rather than $250) and thereby increase their chance of assignment to a preferred location and the chance that the given budget would be sufficient for all billets to be filled by volunteers.

Pay for Performance

Pay increase without promotion is another form of incentive to reward creativity, innovation, and entrepreneurship. Pay increase without promotion is also an incentive for members whose grade progression is slower and who spend more time in a given grade, such as those on a technical rather than a leadership career track. The essential question here is how to link the payment to desired behaviors, such as creativity. One approach is to pay members based on an assessment of their performance with respect to creativity, innovation, and entrepreneurship. This is a challenging and even radical proposal because it is a pay-for-performance scheme. Today, the military does not use pay for performance, except in the sense that superior performance results in faster promotion. The military does offer special and incentive pays for proficiency in selected skills, duty in certain locations and circumstances, and retention. These pays designate a group and pay all members in the group either a fixed amount or, in the case of bonuses, an amount depending on term length.

In contrast, pay for performance offers the same incentive structure to all members in a group but pays them according to their performance. Payment can be limited to a single period, as is a lump sum bonus, or paid over time, as is proficiency pay. Performance can be assessed subjectively, objectively, or both, and can consider individual performance, team performance, and organization performance. The assessment can consider both inputs—for example, effort, concept, or planning—and outputs—actual improvement in quantity, quality, timeliness, or cost.

In order to achieve validity, acceptance, and effectiveness as a compensation tool, a pay-for-performance scheme should have relevant, timely, and accurate measures. Where multiple activities and multiple metrics are involved, performance scores should be combined (or weighted) to reflect command priorities. (Recall that priorities are used in determining manpower requirements, so are already formally identified.) Where performance is compared across sites, members and groups ideally should have the same opportunity to perform, and where conditions differ (for example, where differing physical layouts or equipment affect performance) methods should be developed to adjust for the differences. The amount of money at stake needs to be large enough to influence effort, and this amount may be related to how well leadership has established a culture of creativity. Although meeting these conditions is demanding, the overall objective is to embed tangible incentives for transformation in the personnel management system.

There are a number of pitfalls associated with pay-for-performance schemes, and care must be taken to recognize and, if possible, avoid them. The pitfalls have to do with multiple principals, multiple goals, measurement of inputs and results, teams, shirking, risk aversion, and the personal discount rate. The simplest and arguably most positive setting for pay-for-performance schemes is where there is a single, easily measured output, and the amount of output depends on an individual's effort. But the setting in large organizations like the military is typically far more complicated. A unit may report to several principals that have different concerns. Teamwork is the norm, and attempts to identify and reward individual contributions may be arbitrary and divisive.

Many outputs and inputs are not measured in a way that connects inputs to outputs. (Proponents of activity-based analysis chide the stovepiped budgeting system for obliterating this connection.) The value of some outputs, like services, is not easily measured, and adjustments for the quality of outputs are often difficult to make. (This difficulty is well illustrated by problems in adjusting for the quality of consumer goods in the Consumer Price Index.) If incentives are tied to readily measured outputs, the allocation of effort may be distorted toward those outputs and away from other equally important but difficult-to-measure outputs. If incentives are based on team- and organization-level measures, lower overall effort might be expected than under strictly individual incentives because of free-riding behavior, while higher overall effort is possible if there are complementarities in the effort of team members; the result depends on the particular circumstance. Finally, pay-for-performance schemes can be divisive if the system lacks integrity and the awarding of pay is viewed as unfair. In contrast, the current promotion system indirectly links pay with performance and gives the assurance of equity through the use of a common pay table.

If reward for superior performance is delayed, the strength of the incentive will be lower for individuals with high discount rates. Furthermore, pay-for-performance schemes do not necessarily reward individual effort when pay depends on results but results depend not only on individual initiative but factors outside the individual's control. For risk-averse individuals, the greater the risk that pay will decline due to factors outside the individual's control, the weaker the incentive for pay for performance as a component of pay. Moreover, the larger the downside risk the weaker the incentive. Pay-for-performance schemes usually specify a base level of pay and an *increase* in pay as a function of effort or output. But, for example, an officer management system that is believed to have zero tolerance for defects—that is, a huge downside risk—would deter officers from taking a risk to innovate.

These pitfalls of pay for performance suggest that it will not see extensive use in the military or that the amount of money at risk and dependent on performance will be relatively small. While smaller financial rewards imply weaker incentives, even weak incentives can be meaningful. For example, informal evidence about military recruiters suggests that their productivity is responsive to the rewards and public recognition they receive for strong performance, even though the monetary value of the rewards is trivial. Similarly, evidence pertaining to enlistment bonuses shows that the enlistment behavior of young adults is responsive to these bonuses despite the amount being small; the value of bonuses as a compensation tool lies in this responsiveness and in being able to target bonuses toward a particular group, thereby limiting the budget outlay. Thus the use of pay-for-performance methods, even if the incentives are relatively weak, should not be dismissed out of hand, especially for some groups of personnel or for those in particular situations.

CONCLUSION

The gains achievable through transformation depend on technology, culture, and people, and the contribution of people depends on compensation and personnel management policies. Although the current compensation and personnel management policies have many advantages and a proven record of effectiveness in meeting manning requirements, transformation requires a significant change from status quo behavior, and that in turn requires greater flexibility in using people and greater incentives for innovation, creativity, and entrepreneurship.

It would be a mistake to lose sight of the effectiveness of current policies as a foundation for supporting transformation. The policies on the whole have delivered the personnel needed to meet manning requirements, and the planning processes have functioned sufficiently well to modify training and career tracks in response to anticipated changes in requirements. Furthermore, for at least two decades—since the manning crisis in the 1979–1980 time frame—the policies have delivered high-quality personnel. The importance of this achievement cannot be overstated. In the enlisted force, high-quality personnel are more proficient in training, more proficient in duty-related tasks, more likely to complete their first term of service, and more likely to advance to higher grades. In addition, and more subtly, the system has worked well to identify recruits who are particularly well-matched with the military, as evidenced by their performance and reflected by persistently faster promotion than their peers, and these well-matched, high-performing personnel are more likely to reenlist (Hosek and Mattock 2003). The system is therefore pro-selective on quality.

The officer system has also functioned well to train and attract college graduates. Although one could elaborate, it is safe to say that the service academies and Reserve Officer Training Corps programs have been successful in providing high-quality officer accessions in sufficient numbers to meet manning requirements. Well-trained, high-quality enlisted and officer personnel represent a superb reservoir of talent that is necessary to conceive of and carry out the many innovations that constitute transformation. It is therefore important to conserve the strengths of current policies as changes to those policies are contemplated.

The key goals of personnel management and compensation change are, first, greater flexibility in managing personnel; and, additionally, stronger incentives for intelligent risk taking, entrepreneurship (meaning the tendency to launch new initiatives), and greater creativity in all phases of military activity. We have identified a number of personnel and compensation policy changes that can support greater flexibility and stronger incentives, but whether these are pursued will depend on the commitment of top leadership and the demand from within the services at lower levels. Leaders have already stated the need for a change in culture, and there is little doubt their message has been heard. Although change has been occurring, this might have occurred anyway, given the historical record of change in the services. And change has occurred. For example, the Army created light- and medium-weight brigades, the Air Force reorganized into an expeditionary force, the Navy redesigned its assignment system to place greater weight on the career planning and aspirations of the individual sailor, and the Marine Corps, like the other services, modernized its logistics system. Nevertheless, it seems reasonable to suggest that a clear, sustained leadership commitment to cultural change is essential for transformational improvements in flexibility and creativity, especially if changes appear to run counter to other cultural values such as equity.

Incentives at the organizational level and at the individual level are both important.[18] Organizations require incentives to improve status quo methods, procedures, and resource allocations. These incentives may be as straightforward as developing metrics of performance so that it can be monitored and compared across comparable activities at other sites, and so that the effect of innovations can be identified.[19] The old bureaucratic bogeyman of losing resources if cost-effective improvements are made can be weakened if creativity and entrepreneurship become cultural values, esteemed at all levels, and rewarded at the individual level. Innovations that keep personnel in grade longer or that lengthen or shorten careers can be supported by changes in pay and personnel management policy that permit this greater flexibility.

The sharing of information and the rigorous assessment of results are valuable components of change, and hence transformation. Experience in developing metrics, in collecting data on performance, and in storing, retrieving, and analyzing that data should be shared across the services and the analytical community. From this perspective, it is worth considering a broader charter for the Defense Manpower Data Center (DMDC). The birth of the DMDC can be traced to the poor state of personnel data available for analysis at the outset of the Gates Commission and, as events unfolded, to the widespread recognition of the value of personnel data in informing policy. Yet today, the personnel data collected by DMDC are very much the product of the original data templates, and there are virtually no data linking personnel to activity so that metrics of performance can be analyzed with respect to different, and innovative, manpower configurations and incentive structures. Building such a linked database is a large undertaking, but judging from the payoff of the investment in data on personnel and the importance of transformation itself, the effort may well be worthwhile.

Changes in compensation and personnel policy are likely to be accelerated if they are proven to be valuable to military capability. To that end, it would be worthwhile to develop, implement, and evaluate a limited number of demonstration projects in the armed forces to test the validity and effectiveness of new personnel and compensation policies. Such demonstrations could focus on specific activities or specific communities where the lessons learned could be leveraged and applied more broadly. Demonstration projects were authorized for the federal civil service in the late 1970s and included a project at the Naval Weapons Center in China Lake, California, that began in 1980 and that tested a flexible classification system and broad pay-banding system. While such projects in the context of the armed forces would need to be cognizant of unique aspects of uniformed service, the concept of experimentation and documentation would be the same.

Finally, in addition to demonstrating the value of change, future analysis should focus on methods of surmounting the obstacles to transformation of personnel and compensation policy. This paper highlighted the obstacles, and specifically the lack of demand for flexibility and innovation, as exemplified by the conformity of personnel outcomes produced by compensation and personnel policy and the repeated calls for military retirement reform that are usually followed by inaction or by modest change. It also discussed the types of incentives that could be used to increase the demand for flexibility and address the obstacles. Still, more information is needed on the contexts where these obstacles are the greatest and how to navigate the possible tension between existing cultural values and the introduction of new values. Only by demonstrating the value of change and addressing the obstacles to change will meaningful change take place and be sustained in the coming years.

APPENDIX

TRANSFORMATION DEFINED[20]

The term "transformation" has been used by the Department of Defense since the mid-1990s to encompass many different types of change, including radical alterations to defense strategies and more evolutionary modifications to personnel organization and management. In fact, DOD consistently emphasizes that it is undergoing not a single change, but a series of interconnected transformations that will ultimately affect all aspects of the department. However, the multifaceted nature of DOD's transformation makes it difficult to come up with a concrete definition of the term or even to succinctly describe the specific processes involved in "transforming" the armed forces. More than anything else, transformation seems to represent a mandate for generating and embracing fundamental changes to all aspects of DOD, particularly its organization and governing philosophy.

The U.S. Joint Forces Command (USJFCOM) website entitled "What Is Transformation?" offers a description of this term which, although extremely general, provides a good starting point for discussion. The website states, "Transformation is the process of changing form, nature, or function. Within the United States military, transformation requires changing the form or structure of military forces; the nature of our military culture and doctrine supporting those forces; and streamlining our war-fighting functions to more effectively meet the complexities of new threats challenging our nation" (U.S. Joint Forces Command 2003). At various times these processes of change and streamlining have included developing a more deployable and integrated fighting force, redesigning the U.S. base structure, improving training techniques, developing and applying laser technology and robotics, accelerating the missile defense program, improving the competitive acquisition process, and evaluating U.S. alliances with other countries. The challenge, therefore, is to distill from this all-encompassing definition the essence and core of what is meant by the word "transformation."

In an attempt to simplify and direct the process of transformation, DOD has outlined what it has termed the six major areas of transformation. These include: the protection of the U.S. homeland and the defeat of weapons of mass destruction and their means of delivery; the projection and sustainment of power in distant environments; the denial of sanctuary to enemies by developing capabilities for persistent surveillance, tracking, and rapid engagement; the leverage of information to link up joint forces; the protection of information systems from attack; and the maintenance of unhindered access to space and the protection of U.S. space capabilities from enemy attack (Rumsfeld 2002). While these six objectives help to classify the long-term goals of transformation, they still do not shed much light on the more detailed and daily activities required within the process itself.

Top Defense Department personnel justify the abstract nature of these definitions by arguing that transformation is not about technical changes or specific modifications within the armed forces, but rather is predominantly a revolution in the culture and attitude of the military. Secretary Rumsfeld (2002) stated that transformation requires dramatic change in "the way we think, the way we train, the way we exercise, and the way we fight." He went on to comment that transformation had to include not only changes within the armed forces but also within "the Department that serves them, by encouraging a culture of creativity and intelligent risk taking. We must promote a more entrepreneurial approach to developing military capabilities, one that encourages people . . . to be more proactive, to behave somewhat less like bureaucrats and more like venture capitalists." In this sense, transformation is an attempt to change the way DOD works and the way that employees and service members perform and think about their jobs.

Chairman of the Joint Chiefs of Staff, General Richard Myers, expanded on Rumsfeld's explanation of transformation by characterizing the process as having three key parts: intellectual, cultural, and technological (Harper 2003). To explain intellectual change, he refers to the fact that "people must have the mental agility to match their capabilities to new and unprecedented missions." The cultural aspect requires the development of an "attitude that values educated risk taking and cooperation that spans organizations." Finally, there is technological change, which he deemphasized, noting that "changes in doctrine, in our organization, in training [and] in logistics" make transformation possible. These three components contribute to the constitution of a new guiding framework and a refocused mentality for DOD.

Despite the fact that the most prominent Department of Defense officials define transformation almost entirely without reference to particular initiatives, several more specific reforms have been defined as vital to the objective of developing a modern and streamlined military. One such objective is that of "jointness," meaning interoperability and cooperation between the different service divisions. Taken to its furthest extreme, the achievement of a truly "joint" armed force requires joint training and the development of the capacity to carry out joint missions through the establishment of a "standing joint command and control capability" and the development of "tailorable force modules" (McCarthy 2001). Jointness can also refer to greater interagency integration, such as that between DOD and the State Department. At a minimum, jointness will require increased communication between the services and additional flexibility to allow for joint training and missions. It is also important to note that within the concept of transformation, the use of the term jointness stresses a level of interservice and interagency integration that extends above and beyond what has been already achieved or even intended by the term in previous DOD statements.

A second consistently emphasized aspect of transformation is the need for a modification in the management and organization of military personnel. Such changes would streamline the armed forces and DOD and improve the incentives given individuals to perform their jobs effectively. This aspect of transformation includes a change in the organization of the forces to allow for greater speed and flexibility in deployment. It also requires closing unused or unneeded bases and making sure that U.S. troops are stationed in the most effective locations so as to maximize their responsiveness and deterrent force. The 1997 Report of the National Defense Panel noted that transformation had to include "new operational concepts to employ currently planned forces in exploiting asymmetric advantages and reducing the number of required forces" (U.S. Department of Defense 1997, 2). In addition, transformation necessitates that the incentives and compensation programs used by DOD be modified, in order to better encourage personnel to think innovatively and to properly reward them for the changed nature of their work in the 21st century (Hosek 2003).

Such reforms would not only aid in the physical transformation of DOD, but would also contribute to a changed culture in the armed forces; they would transform not only the way U.S. troops fight, but also the way they understand their importance, the way they live, and the way they interact. For some DOD officials, these changes in personnel organization are the most important and influential aspects of transformation. For example, Air Force Lieutenant Colonel Steve Suddarth (2002) comments, "I tend to see the most critical element in the transformation as being how we manage people." This statement suggests that transformation is most essentially an effort to better train, motivate, and employ DOD employees, both civilian and military.

Another integral aspect of transformation is the requirement for improved use and acquisition of technology within the fighting forces. Deputy Secretary Paul Wolfowitz (2002) commented that a large part of transformation involves a revolution in "the manner, speed, and effectiveness with which industrial and commercial tasks can be accomplished" and depends on "the impact of advances in technology in computing, communicating, and networking that taken together constitute an Information Revolution whose effects extend far beyond technology into the organization and even culture of the business and commercial worlds." Furthermore, as the National Defense Panel noted, "The military services will have to tap into rapidly advancing technologies to develop new military systems that can be applied within the framework of new operational concepts" (U.S. Department of Defense 1997, 57).

However, Department of Defense officials, including both Secretary Rumsfeld and Deputy Secretary Wolfowitz, are quick to remind the public that technological development is only one part of transformation and cannot by itself drive a revolution in military affairs. For example, Wolfowitz (2002) stated that "transformation is about more than what we buy or how much we spend on technology. . . . transformation is about changing the military culture into one that encourages 'innovation and intelligent risk taking.'"[21] Despite official DOD reports that downplay the importance of technology within transformation, it seems that, given the radical changes and improvements that have recently occurred in information technology, technology is still central to the rationale behind, and the progress of, transformation.

Along with the many cultural and organizational changes, specific changes to the national security strategy are also included within any definition of transformation. These changes respond to the new international security environment, both that which existed before September 11, 2001, and that which has emerged since. Most dramatically, the Quadrennial Defense Review published in 2001 outlined the shift from the two-major–theater-war force planning towards a new approach which "emphasizes deterrence in four critical theaters, backed by the ability to swiftly defeat two aggressors in the same timeframe, while preserving the option for one major offensive to occupy an aggressor's capital" (Wolfowitz 2002). In addition, transformation is associated with the transition from a "threat-based" strategy to a "capabilities-based" one, which "focuses less on who and where the threats are and concentrates more on what the threats might be—and how to deter and defend against them" (Garamone 2002). Finally, integrated within the definition of transformation is a "new framework for assessing risk," which includes force management risks, operational risks, institutional risks, and those associated with future challenges. This redefined framework enables the military to better anticipate potential threats and to prepare for the future more efficiently and so contributes to the stated objectives of transformation, particularly the defense of the U.S. homeland and the protection of its capabilities.

Lastly, there is the question of how long transformation will take. DOD statements are extremely evasive when it comes to placing transformation within a specific time frame or even estimating how much time the process will require. In general, the transformation project is not defined along a specific timeline and instead is classified as a process which lacks a true "end point." In fact, some DOD officials speak of "institutionalizing transformation," by which they mean that "transformation is not a single event, but a process that needs to go forward in the future so that we are constantly in an evolution of transformation as time goes on" (McCarthy 2001). This statement, when combined with the broad and continually expanding definitions of transformation discussed above, implies that transformation is not simply a temporary objective. Instead, it seems to be a more symbolic concept that embodies a permanent framework intended to initiate, support, and explain innovation and modernization within the armed forces. By classifying certain objectives as "transformational," DOD is able to raise the importance of these policies and to place them within a coherent framework.

This discussion of transformation has explored both the general and more detailed descriptions of this process and has defined its core aspects as being the following: an emphasis on cultural change; the achievement of a new level of jointness; the acquisition and application of new technologies; and a shift in the defense strategy and the assessment of risk. More important than defining specific objectives, this in-depth look at what transformation has come to mean suggests that transformation is above all a tool used to unify and motivate a commitment to enacting change. As a result, it seems reasonable to predict that the meaning of transformation will continue to evolve, and even expand, as the capabilities of, and the challenges facing, the armed forces develop and multiply.

NOTES

1. The authors thank RAND colleagues Jennifer Kavanagh for a review of the concept of military transformation, Bogdan Savych for a review of the management and economics literature on organizational culture, and C. Christine Fair for a review of the literature on military culture. We benefited from comments received at the 30th anniversary conference and from reviews provided by James Dertouzos at RAND and by John White at the Harvard Kennedy School of Government.

2. The Department of Defense typically distinguishes between manpower policies and personnel policies in the following way. Manpower policies deal with the military service's demand or requirement for personnel (often referred to as end strength). For example, decisions concerning the types of weapon and other systems that the department will procure drive demand for manpower—both in terms of the number of operators and the skills needed. Some systems are labor intensive, while others save on manpower (such as the newer classes of Navy ships currently being designed). Policies that govern the geographic distribution of forces at home and abroad and the mix of active and reserve forces are all manpower policies. Personnel policies allow DOD to manage the supply of personnel to meet manpower requirements. The timing and length of training, promotion policies, retirement regulations, education standards, quality standards, and compensation policies are examples of personnel policies.

3. The appendix provides a more detailed discussion of the definition of transformation and contains references for the Rumsfeld, Myers, and McCarthy quotes appearing below.

4. As experience in an assignment increases, the member learns to do a variety of tasks. More time in an assignment may mean becoming specialized, but not narrow in terms of the tasks that can be done.

5. Multiple career paths could be phased in, affecting only a small fraction of personnel at first and allowing them to choose to participate or not. This approach would prevent large disruptions to members who expected and preferred the current system. Depending on the design of a system with multiple career paths, promotion would proceed at the same rate as it does now, but the type of positions would be limited to those within a path.

6. The importance of corporate culture is recognized in the private sector and has been the subject of numerous management studies that focus on the definition of culture, the issue of how to measure it, and its effect on firm performance.

7. See Adolph, Stiles, and Hitt 1995; Chiarelli 1993; Fautua 2000; and Young and Lovelace 1995. However, other authors argue that Goldwater-Nichols has had a large effect on the status of jointness, contending that the awareness of the importance of jointness seems to have increased, as have the Joint Staff institutions created to support that objective (Roman and Tarr 1998).

8. Regular military compensation is the sum of basic pay, the housing allowance, the subsistence allowance, and the federal tax advantage owing to the nontaxability of the allowances.

9. This discussion draws on a study by Asch, Hosek, and Martin (2002) for the Ninth Quadrennial Review of Military Compensation.

10. Promotion rates have been fairly stable over time for each service. See Hosek et al. forthcoming.

11. Enlisted pay variation in the Navy resembled that in the Air Force, while most of the variation in the Army and the Marine Corps came from promotion speed. (In the Army, variation from bonuses is apparent in the first 10 years of service but less prominent than in the Air Force. The Marine Corps makes little use of bonuses and minor use of S&I pays.)

12. We use the 30th percentile of private sector workers because workers at the 10th percentile might not qualify for or be sought by the services. See Asch, Hosek, and Martin 2002 for further pay range comparisons.

13. Direct measures of effort and talent are not available. Promotion requires personnel to acquire necessary skills and knowledge, verified by written or hands-on tests, and also depends on physical fitness, supervisor rating of performance and future potential, awards and decorations, and additional educational attainment. Each of these items requires the exertion of effort. Supervisor rating of performance arguably includes an assessment of talent. Also, evidence shows that members with high scores on the Armed Forces Qualifying Test (AFQT) are promoted more rapidly. See Hosek and Mattock 2003.

14. The pays are described in detail in U.S. Department of Defense 1996.

15. See, for example, the Defense Manpower Commission report 1976 and the report of the President's Commission on Military Compensation 1978. The various commissions offered different solutions to improve management flexibility. For example, the Defense Manpower Commission recommended that the retirement benefit be based on a point system where those in noncombat skills would receive 1 point per year of service, and those in combat skills would receive 1.5 points per year. Thirty points would be required for an immediate annuity while those who had 10 points but less than 30 would only be eligible for an annuity that began payment at age 60.

16. In fact, there was broad consensus that the personnel and compensation systems needed to be reformed well before the concept of transformation emerged. This is consistent with our view of transformation as a rubric for encouraging innovation and reform rather than a newly discovered, specific recipe for change. Of course, possible areas for reform go well beyond the retirement system and include the roles and missions of the active force, the reserve force, civilian personnel, and contractors and the interaction among the services in planning, acquisition, and operations.

17. The issue of influence behavior has been studied in the economics literature. See Milgrom 1988 for discussion of the issue, and see Prendergast 1999 for a review of the evidence in the private sector.

18. In the context of defense, the organizations reside within a hierarchy of organizations having budget and reporting requirements. Therefore, it is meaningful to speak of incentives at the organizational level, just as it is meaningful at the individual level. The concept of transformation appears to be aimed primarily at the organizational level, encouraging organizations and their leaders to become more innovative and entrepreneurial, which in turn may require changes in incentives at the individual level.

19. To be clear, we are not talking about a metric for innovation per se but a metric for unit performance. When compared across innovating and non-innovating units, the metric can reveal the gains, if any, from the innovation.

20. Prepared by Jennifer Kavanagh.

21. Internal quotation marks indicate Rumsfeld's words.

REFERENCES

Adolph, Robert, Charles Stiles, and Franklin Hitt. 1995. Why Goldwater-Nichols didn't go far enough. *Joint Forces Quarterly* (spring): 48–53.

Asch, Beth, James Hosek, and Craig Martin. 2002. *A look at cash compensation for active-duty military personnel.* MR-1492. Santa Monica, Calif.: RAND Corporation.

Asch, Beth, Richard Johnson, and John Warner. 1998. *Reforming the military retirement system.* MR-748-OSD. Santa Monica, Calif.: RAND Corporation.

Builder, Carl. 1989. *The masks of war: American military styles in strategy and analysis.* Baltimore: The Johns Hopkins University Press.

Chiarelli, Peter. 1993. Beyond Goldwater-Nichols. *Joint Forces Quarterly* (autumn): 71–81.

Defense Manpower Commission. 1976. *Defense manpower: The keystone to national security, Report to the president and the Congress.* Washington, D.C.: U.S. Government Printing Office.

Fautua, David. 2000. The paradox of joint culture. *Joint Forces Quarterly* (autumn): 81–86.

Garamone, Jim. 2002. *Flexibility, adaptability at heart of military transformation.* American Forces Press Service. www.dod.mil/news.Jan2002 [January 31, 2002].

Harper, Gene. 2003. *Joint chiefs chairman takes transformation to industry forum.* American Forces Press Service. www.dod.mil/news/Jan2003 [January 17, 2003].

Hosek, James R., and Michael G. Mattock. 2003. *Learning about quality: How the quality of military personnel is revealed over time.* MR-1593-OSD. Santa Monica, Calif.: RAND Corporation.

Hosek, James R., Michael G. Mattock, C. Christine Fair, Jennifer Kavanagh, Jennifer Sharp, and Mark Totten. Forthcoming. *Attracting the best: How the military competes for information technology personnel.* MG-108-OSD. Santa Monica, Calif.: RAND Corporation.

Hosek, Susan. 2003. Taking care of people: The future of army personnel. In *The U.S. Army and the new national security strategy.* Edited by Lynn Davis and Jeremy Shapiro, 217–37. Santa Monica, Calif.: RAND Corporation.

McCarthy, James. 2001. Special DOD Briefing on Defense Transformation. June 12.

Milgrom, Paul. 1988. Employment contracts, influence activity and efficient organization. *Journal of Political Economy* 96(1): 42–60.

Prendergast, Canice. 1999. The provision of incentives in firms. *Journal of Economic Literature* 37(1): 7–63.

President's Commission on Military Compensation. 1978. *Report of the President's Commission on Military Compensation.* Washington, D.C.: U.S. Government Printing Office.

Roman, Peter J., and David Tarr. 1998. The Joint Chiefs of Staff: From service parochialism to jointness. *Political Science Quarterly* 113(1): 91–111.

Rumsfeld, Donald. 2002. *Secretary Rumsfeld speaks on 21st century transformation of U.S. armed forces.* Remarks at National Defense University. January 31. www.dod.mil/speeches/2002/s20020131-secdef.html [July 31, 2003].

Snider, Don. 1999. An uninformed debate on military culture. *Orbis* 43(1): 11–26.

Suddarth, Steve. 2002. *Our transformation focus.* www.airpower.maxwell.af.mil/airchronicles/ct/ci/trans/aftrans.html [July 14, 2003].

U. S. Department of Defense. 1996. *Military compensation background papers: Compensation elements and related cost items, their purpose and legislative backgrounds*, 5th ed. Washington, D.C.: Office of the Secretary of Defense.

——. 1997. *Transforming defense: National security in the 21st century.* Report of the National Defense Panel.

——. 2000. *Report of the Defense Science Board Task Force on Human Resources Strategy.* Washington, D.C.: Office of the Under Secretary of Defense (Acquisition, Technology, and Logistics).

——. 2002. *Report of the Ninth Quadrennial Review of Military Compensation.* Washington, D.C.: Office of the Under Secretary of Defense (Personnel and Readiness).

U.S. Joint Forces Command. 2003. *What is transformation?* www.jfcom.mil/about/transform [July 14, 2003].

Wolfowitz, Paul. 2002. Prepared Statement for the Senate Armed Services Committee Hearing on Military Transformation. Washington, D.C. April 9.

Young, Thomas-Durell, and Douglas C. Lovelace Jr. 1995. *Strategic plans, joint doctrine, and antipodean insights.* Carlisle, Pa.: Strategic Studies Institute.

★ ★ ★ ★ ★ ★ ★ ★ ★ ★ ★

CHAPTER 13

A "CONTINUUM OF SERVICE" FOR THE ALL-VOLUNTEER FORCE

JOHN D. WINKLER
R. WAYNE SPRUELL
THOMAS L. BUSH
GARY L. CRONE

INTRODUCTION

Thirty years after the inception of the all-volunteer force, it is instructive to review the paradigm of military service used by the Department of Defense (DOD), to examine how the nature of military service has changed over the last 30 years, and to ask how the concept of military service may change further in the future. The evolving character of the all-volunteer force, with special attention paid to the role played by the reserve forces, is especially noteworthy.

The contributions made by part-time reserve component members have changed substantially both in degree and in kind in recent years. Reserve component members have supplemented and bolstered the full-time force at increasing levels of utilization. In 1993, the reserves contributed over 5.7 million days of duty; in each of the six years prior to the global war on terrorism, reserve contributions averaged 12 to 13 million duty-days annually, equivalent to the service of 35,000 members on active duty; and with the start of the global war on terrorism, reserve component support to the active component grew to over 41 million duty-days in 2002 and 63 million duty-days in 2003. The reserve components contribute significantly to the full spectrum of operational missions, fighting in our nation's wars, conducting peace-keeping stability operations, and defending the homeland. Particularly relevant to certain capabilities, such as those involving high-technology skills, the reserves bring unique talents to the active component by virtue of their civilian employment, education, and civilian-acquired skills.

As contributions have increased, the nature of reserve participation has also changed—a change which is germane to the all-volunteer force concept now and in the future. No longer can reserve members be viewed as "weekend warriors," performing the minimum number of required training days until mobilized for a high-intensity conflict. As reserve members are now involved in the full range of operational missions, the average number of days of duty performed annually exceeds the minimum 38-day requirement; some individual members' service exceeds that requirement by a significant amount. Inherent to the changing nature of participation is an increased spirit of volunteerism on the part of reservists. Recruiting and retention remain strong, despite increased utilization, and members join the reserves with a greater expectation that they may spend time on active duty.

Yet, to this day, the department's manpower and personnel policies and practices still separate service members into two distinct groups—"full-time" active duty members and traditional "part-time" reservists. This management structure neither reflects the realities of how the total force is being used nor supports optimal employment of the force. For a service member to move from the active to the reserve component requires fairly definitive separation and accession actions. Extensive "work-arounds"—circumventions of the systems dictating how the reserves are employed, resourced, accounted for, and managed—are commonplace, particularly when trying to bring part-time reserve members onto active duty and keep them there for as long as they may desire. Further, the department still depends on mobilization to access reserve component capabilities—a practice that could be viewed as more appropriate for a conscription-based military than for an all-volunteer force.

As the department looks to the future, a more integrated approach to military personnel management is imperative. To acquire and maintain capabilities that will meet a wide-ranging and uncertain set of demands, and to support surges in activity, the military services must have the flexibility to attract and access the most qualified and capable personnel for full-time or intermittent duty, regardless of the composition of the units employed or the personnel category to which individuals belong. The services will need tools that allow them to bring together capabilities existent in active and reserve forces through the creation of new organizations such as "blended" units (units composed of both active and reserve forces) and through greater use of "mixed units," in which reserve component individuals augment active units in operational environments.

A NEW PARADIGM OF MILITARY SERVICE

With these considerations in mind, many in the Department of Defense believe that a transformation in personnel management is needed—a transformation that acknowledges the changes that have occurred in how military service is performed as the basis for establishing a new paradigm for the Department's organization and management of personnel assets. The new paradigm that we envision, which we refer to as the "continuum of service," aims to provide more flexibility in creating needed capabilities and to ensure a more seamless and cost-effective management of military forces. It prescribes both organizational and systemic change in order to more effectively manage individuals throughout their military career, while meeting the full spectrum of military requirements in peacetime and wartime with greater efficiency and economy of resources.

The continuum of service can enhance the spirit of volunteerism by providing more ways in which military service can be performed to support DOD missions. The continuum can provide more opportunities for the part-time force to volunteer for extended service. It can support new affiliation programs through which the military services can attract and access individuals with cutting-edge skills. Finally, it can facilitate transitions between levels of participation. In total, the continuum of service offers a model for addressing the changing characteristics of a work force that is increasingly more educated and more inclined to migrate between jobs in pursuit of enhanced career opportunities. We believe the continuum of service reflects the convergence of two goals: that of an operationally integrated total force and that of a seamless force—one where members can easily move between full- and part-time status.

ENHANCED VOLUNTEERISM AND MORE OPTIONS FOR PARTICIPATION

One element of the continuum of service, relevant to discussion of the all-volunteer force, is the flexibility it offers to capitalize more extensively on the willingness and ability of American citizens to volunteer their services when the nation needs them—an attribute that can serve to alleviate some of the strains inherent in the current system. By making greater use of citizen volunteers and reservists volunteering for extended duty, the department can better support its new defense strategy—the foundation of which is to build capabilities into the force that can meet military requirements that will vary in type, in intensity, and in duration over time. Moreover, short-term volunteers can help meet requirements for specialized skills, such as particular linguistic competencies that may be needed on short notice, as well as those that are frequently in high demand. Greater reliance on reservist and citizen volunteers could further reduce the burdens of involuntary mobilization and repeated activations and deployments among traditional reservists.

The continuum of service helps to create a labor market that will satisfy the varying demands for military capabilities. To provide surge augmentation and support, the continuum seeks to better capitalize on reservists who offer their service on a continuous, part-time basis or for an extended deployment to meet war-fighting requirements. To address a broad range of changing requirements, particularly ones of a technical and specialized nature, the continuum also aims to establish pools of uniquely skilled individuals who participate on a limited or standby basis, but are available as volunteers for short periods or in emergency situations to perform specific tasks. These pools can consist of both reserve members and civilians who may be quickly accessed to serve in or support the military.

These projected characteristics of a new military labor market closely resemble those of the civilian labor market. In the civilian labor market, individuals tend to experience more job transitions than they did in the past; there are more part-time and episodic workers; and there are longer, more frequent interruptions from employment in pursuit of education. The department needs to recognize that these same forces are at work in the military market and begin to capitalize on the opportunities provided by a work force that is increasingly mobile, more educated, and inclined to migrate between pursuits in search of rewarding opportunities.

OPPORTUNITIES FOR EXTENDED SERVICE

The continuum of service envisions that individuals should be able to select among and move between varying lengths of military service and perform military service in new, nontraditional ways. It would allow the force to include

- Full-time members who serve 365 days per year.

- Part-time members who, steadily throughout the course of a year, provide varying levels of service, including the "traditional" 38 days per year but also fewer or more. For example, members might serve for as little as 10 percent of their time, or for as much as 75 percent.

- Part-time members who provide intermittent service in response to specific needs, serving for tours of 60 or 90 days or six or nine months, for example.

- Individuals with specialized skills who do not perform military service on a regular basis, but who are available and volunteer for a period of time if their skills are needed. Their service obligation might be considerably shorter than the traditional six to eight years.

In some segments of the reserve community, participation by reservists already occurs at levels greater than standard part time and less than permanent full time. While observed most frequently in the air reserve components, the practice also occurs among certain individual augmentees and in selected units in other reserve components. In fact, participation levels, measured as the average number of paid duty-days performed by selected reserve members, has exceeded the minimum required for some time. According to statistics maintained by the Office of Assistant Secretary of Defense for Reserve Affairs, reservists performed an average of approximately 45.1 paid duty-days in fiscal year 2000, prior to the onset of the global war on terrorism, compared to the required 38 days; and that figure has since increased. In addition, reserve components have little difficulty finding volunteers for temporary assignments funded as "active duty for special work," which indicates the presence of a labor market responsive to expanded part-time participation opportunities. This market can be capitalized upon more broadly for selected skills.

The creation of a "variable pool of reserves" is one option for managing personnel who may offer their services on a continuous, part-time basis or for extended but intermittent periods of active duty. This tool would represent an expansion of existing methods for employing reserves. The variable pool would consist of a small group of individuals and units, no longer constrained by the traditional 38-day training program for reservists. These personnel would voluntarily commit to continuous or intermittent extended duty through formal agreements to meet war-fighting and other operational requirements. The length of the annual participation requirement would vary by individual or unit and would be stipulated in standing volunteer agreements with a military service.

A variable pool would profitably support the segments of the force where reserve volunteers serve in sizable numbers today. These include Air Force maintenance and air crews, Navy and Marine Corps command staffs, and Army exercise command-and-control elements. It could also support emerging missions such as those related to space, information operations, intelligence, medicine, and certain other high-technology areas. The variable pool could comprise volunteer units and detachments to meet unanticipated operational and support needs, or it could focus on specialized capabilities to include those needed early in an operation, such as cargo handling, transportation, or other "prime-the-pump" capabilities.

The ability to craft formal agreements with individuals and units of a reserve variable pool would provide commanders and the services with greater flexibility to satisfy mission requirements as they evolve. If volunteers can be accessed in selected functional areas, requirements that are not in effect 365 days per year can be met on a timely and as-needed basis. While the traditional 38-day training program might well remain the mainstay of reserve participation, the variable pool would provide the option of a more robust structure for contribution of part-time service. Those reservists in the civilian labor market who frequently change jobs, or who work flexible hours, part time, or in a virtual setting, might find this reserve option more attractive than those that currently exist.

NEW AFFILIATION AND PARTICIPATION PROGRAMS

The establishment of new affiliation and participation programs can be a way to recruit and affiliate individuals who possess state-of-the-art skills that are hard to acquire, develop, and maintain in the regular force.

Some affiliation programs may be aimed at capitalizing more effectively on skills resident in today's reserve forces. Reserve component members bring diverse civilian skills and experience to the military beyond what is available in the regular component. These may include medical, language, information technology, and other technical skills. The reserves also serve as one of the military's most visible links to American society. Reservists and guardsmen are construction workers, teachers, coaches, fire fighters, police officers, nurses, doctors, and lawyers among other things, located in thousands of communities across the nation; and their reserve service ensures a bond between the military and the civilian sector. In addition to exemplifying the importance of combining military service and citizenship, the connection between the reservist and the community may provide a link to skills, resident within that community, that may be needed to support unique, unusual, or specialized military requirements. Expanded options for affiliation and participation can help the department access such skills.

Other programs may be aimed at civilians. One group of particular interest is military retirees. Following the terrorist attacks on the World Trade Center and the Pentagon, many military retirees, both active and reserve, expressed a strong desire to serve in some capacity. Retirees represent a large source of trained and experienced manpower, which is often left untapped. In select situations, retirees may serve most effectively through a return to active duty. In other situations, they could provide useful services to military agencies as civilian volunteers. To take advantage of this valuable source of manpower, the department needs better systems for tracking and utilizing retiree volunteers.

Through more innovative forms of affiliation than currently exist, the reserve components could attract more individuals who might be interested in military service on a part-time basis—appealing to their sense of patriotism and interest in working on challenging national security objectives. By building mutually supportive relationships with corporations, for example, DOD could foster partnerships in key areas such as information technology or other high-technology areas relevant to the military. In addition, partnering with the nation's colleges and universities could allow the services to take advantage of their long history of producing cutting-edge technical innovations and comprehensive social geopolitical insights for the federal government. The following sections offer examples of how such affiliation programs might work.

CIVILIAN-ACQUIRED SKILLS

Reservists offer a valuable reservoir of unique knowledge, skills, and abilities, and may provide the military with knowledge of cutting-edge technology and exposure to new and innovative practices and approaches employed by industry and the private sector in a range of disciplines. A way to capitalize on these competencies is through the self-reporting capabilities being programmed into the Defense Integrated Military Human Resource System, which will aid the department in collecting data on the civilian skills of its reservists. Once the system is in place, the department will be able to craft policies and practices by which the services could better match the specialized skills of reservists with emerging requirements, particularly skills that are not resident, or are resident in small quantity, in the full-time force.

The services can also leverage specialized skills found in the civilian sector by matching these skills directly to military occupations and thereby shortening or eliminating entry-level skills training. This practice is currently employed with doctors, lawyers, and construction workers but could be expanded to a broader set of occupational and skill areas. The Office of the Secretary of Defense has asked the services to examine the Australian Defense Force model of "direct entry"—a program recently endorsed by the DOD's Business Initiatives Council. Under this model, individuals with certifiable civilian skills are mapped against, and used to satisfy, existing manpower requirements. The results in Australia have demonstrated significant savings in training costs.

MANAGEMENT OF THE INDIVIDUAL READY RESERVE

The individual ready reserve (IRR), a subcomponent of the reserves, has largely served as a repository for trained personnel resources exiting the service. It is often thought of as the dead-end street of military participation. As a result, the services have been reluctant to expend resources on this pool of assets. Instead, the IRR could be made an entry point for volunteers with hard-to-acquire or newly emerging skills who want to contribute to the military in traditional or nontraditional ways. We have named this new approach the "controlled specialty" IRR. Here the services could experiment with new and emerging requirements. It is a place where trained individuals could be used to perform active duty for special work. A recent example of such an approach to the IRR is the Army's Arab-American Linguist Program. The Army is now using the IRR to bring native Arabic speakers into the Army and field them to meet a growing requirement for Arabic translators. This program is a model that can be emulated in other specialty areas, including other foreign languages, foreign-area expertise, and information technology.

EXPANDED VOLUNTEER AUXILIARIES

The continuum of service could also accommodate mission augmentation performed by civilian volunteers who are trained to service standards. Volunteer auxiliaries could be expanded to attract individuals from all age-groups who wish to volunteer their talents. Auxiliaries can attract civilian volunteers and expand access to skilled individuals who want to associate and identify with military service, culture, and core values but who do not want to be subject to mobilization or strict military regime (as a member of the uniformed military). Auxiliaries also offer one means of managing and employing those military retiree volunteers who are not required on active duty.

The Coast Guard Auxiliary is a successful example. The Coast Guard considers its auxiliary to be a fourth component, in addition to the regular, reserve, and civilian Coast Guard components. Under the Coast Guard model, civilians regularly deploy on cutters and Coast Guard aircraft as augmentees, just like their active duty and reserve counterparts. The Coast Guard even has a provision through which the Commandant can transfer these auxiliary members into the reserve component. The Civil Air Patrol provides the Air Force with similar operating capabilities. Such models could be extended and adopted more broadly.

COMMUNITY PARTNERSHIPS

By developing partnerships with communities, corporations, and academia, the department can access certain skills and people to meet military requirements that cannot be fully met through traditional contracts. For example, the department is currently implementing the Defense Wireless Service Initiative, which matches experienced wireless engineers with a military need for spectrum managers, who are in short supply in both the active and reserve components. Some of these wireless engineers will become individual augmentees; others may reside in the "controlled specialty" IRR. The keys to developing successful partnerships are twofold: the military's willingness to provide flexible active duty participation options (such as participation from a remote location rather than a military facility) that match an individual's civilian obligations with their military duties; and an active interest on the part of civilian organizations and individuals to partner with the Department of Defense.

FACILITATE TRANSITIONS BETWEEN LEVELS OF PARTICIPATION

One way to attract and retain members to an all-volunteer force, beyond expanding the range of service opportunities that are available, is to facilitate movement between these options. The continuum of service offers such flexibility and, in doing so, expands the traditional definition of a military career. A traditional military career spans the period from accession into the force through military retirement or discharge and is typically thought of as a continuous period of full-time active duty service. The continuum of service offers an opportunity for a career that may include a range of service from full-time active duty to standby or minimum part-time service and all levels of participation in between. While not typically thought of as a part of a "military career," the continuum of service provides greater opportunity for retirees and former members to contribute to defense missions. To effectively implement such an approach, the department must lower the barriers that prevent individuals from changing their level of participation in military service and create incentives that would reward, rather than discourage, appropriate changes over the course of a military career.

The challenge for military personnel managers is to establish policies that facilitate career life cycle management for members regardless of where they reside on the continuum of service, and that provide the tools necessary for managing personnel in response to a dynamic military environment. Among the most important of the changes that need to be made are simplifying the rules for employing volunteer part-time members, streamlining the various forms of service, and removing impediments that hinder changing levels of participation.

One must also ensure that personnel management is sufficiently flexible to accommodate changes in the level of participation. The current system of management and accounting does not support this paradigm. It calls for the reservist to be periodically managed as an active duty asset, then as a reserve asset, and sometimes managed and accounted for under each system for various purposes while serving on active duty. Numerous inconsistencies prevail.

For example, current strength accounting actually masks the true extent of reserve contributions to the full-time force and impedes efficient employment of reservists to accomplish missions in support of combatant and other major commands. Reservists who are activated under section 12302 of title 10 U.S. Code (that governs partial mobilization of reserve personnel) do not count against active duty end strength, but they do count against the number of senior enlisted personnel (E-8 and E-9), field grade officers (O-4 to O-6), and general officers (O-7 to O-10) who are authorized to serve on active duty. (These provisions are frequently termed "controlled-grade accounting.") Additionally, officers and warrant officers who are activated under section 12302 must be transferred to the active duty list (absent the President invoking emergency authorities) and as such, must compete for promotion with career officers or warrant officers. At the conclusion of their activation, these officers will return to their reserve status, and may actually find themselves lower in the chain of command than their reserve peers who were not activated but, in the meantime, were promoted under the reserve promotion system.

Finally, strength accounting and management are contingent upon whether the reservist's active duty is funded from appropriations for members supporting regular force requirements or appropriations supporting reserve force requirements. In other words, the source of funding (active or reserve) can determine the rules for managing personnel. Fundamentally, these practices do not support the continuum of service. The continuum is intended to facilitate, enhance, and reward additional service, rather than to discourage service and disadvantage the reservist who is willing to participate at a higher level.

What can be done? The rules that govern and constrain the effective employment of reserve component personnel must be changed, which in many cases requires legislation. First, Congress and DOD must eliminate the rule that requires reservists who serve on active duty for special work to be included within the active duty end strength if they are on active duty for more than 180 days. Next, consistency between end strength and controlled-grade accounting must be achieved. Management of active and reserve personnel should remain separate so that reservists have a reasonable opportunity to compete for promotion. Finally, the source of funding should not dictate the category in which a person is accounted for or managed.

To accomplish these changes, the department is developing legislation that would provide for a new strength accounting category for "reservists on active duty" — thus eliminating the 180-day rule. Average strength is the metric that could be used to account for the various lengths of service performed by reservists on active duty. Average strength, which measures end strength continuously, allows the services to manage reservists on active duty with greater flexibility and precision. It vitiates the need for arbitrary barriers such as the 180-day-threshold rule, which deters extended participation by reservists, by linking their service to active duty end strength. While average strength is a challenging metric to track, it can provide for more effective personnel management that enhances reserve volunteerism.

There are no controlled-grade limitations associated with this new strength-accounting category. Reservists on active duty would simply continue to be controlled by the strength limits governing the selected reserve. It would be difficult to impose a grade-control structure on this category of reservists on active duty, since reservists are moved to this category to meet ad hoc requirements rather than a standing military structure. For example, a service may find itself in need of an O-4 for 200 days or an E-9 for 55 days. Through this proposed approach, the services can assign reserve members to fill such needs without worrying about an artificial grade structure or limit on the number of days of duty. In doing so, the department would move closer to a model where individual reservists could serve beyond the minimum annual participation requirement, but for less than a full year, making it easier for individuals to serve the needs of the department and the nation.

Additionally, under this proposal reservists who respond to surge requirements would remain within the reserve management structure. There is no need to change the current budget accounting practices when reservists provide extended service. Active duty for special work would still be funded by both active and reserve appropriations. But accounting for reserve personnel on active duty would become the responsibility of a single personnel manager charged with providing the human resource, instead of falling to separate active or reserve personnel managers based solely on the source of money. By using this approach, the department will be able to quickly respond to emerging situations by providing reserve personnel without shifting them between two different personnel management systems.

The services are using reservists on extended active duty within the existing strength accounting and management limits today, but they are doing so by routinely working around the system to avoid accounting for reservists. This "under-the-table" use of reservists is not reported and is only controlled by funding. "Work-arounds" include issuing the same person multiple back-to-back active duty tours of less than 180 days; using two or more reservists to complete a single task—one who starts the task and the next who picks up the task at the 180-day point, so neither count against active duty end strength; or couching a single requirement as several different requirements and then using the same person, under a different set of orders, to work on each phase of the project.

Since the services take measures to avoid strength accounting, the only control on this category is funding. But when the services resort to working around the system, it is often at the expense of the reservist and the reservist's family in terms of continuity of benefits and at the expense of the command in terms of continuity in manpower to complete a project. The new model proposed above benefits both the individual service member and the combatant commander, and places visibility and control where it belongs—in the hands of reserve personnel managers. The model better supports individual reservists serving anywhere from 0 to 365 days a year, and should enable personnel managers to respond more quickly and effectively to the needs of combatant commanders, defense agencies, and other major commands.

FINAL COMMENTS

In essence, the continuum of service establishes a labor market that allows varied forms and levels of military participation, encourages such participation through appropriate incentives, and eliminates barriers to voluntary participation.

Managing within a continuum of service can help to attain and retain skills that are hard to acquire and maintain in the military, to include those in cutting-edge technologies. It will provide opportunities to establish new and innovative affiliation programs and to create partnerships between DOD and industry for individuals willing to support military requirements. By adopting a new availability and service paradigm as the basis for managing active and reserve forces, individuals will be able to change levels of participation with greater ease, and the department will better leverage its investment in training and education to meet operational requirements.

To operate within a continuum-of-service paradigm, the department must work to simplify the rules for employing reserve component members and create conditions that both enhance volunteerism and facilitate a seamless flow of personnel from active duty to reserve and from reserve to active duty over the course of a military career. Barriers to such service must be minimized, thereby eliminating the need for the work-around solutions often in effect today.

The desirability of a continuum of service can be briefly stated in terms of several "demand-side" and "supply-side" advantages affecting active and reserve personnel. On the demand side, the continuum of service

- can be cost effective because it preserves capabilities for surge and augmentation using personnel employed on a less-than-full-time basis

- acknowledges the reality that some capabilities required on a part-time basis face more demand than others

- provides flexibility to enable a wider variety of capabilities to be "banked," or kept in reserve

Similarly, on the supply side, the continuum of service

- acknowledges the fluctuating nature of military requirements by facilitating different levels of reserve participation and enabling surge augmentation in support of operational missions

- capitalizes on labor markets by providing opportunities for individuals who are part-time workers in the civilian labor force, for students, for retirees, and for people moving among jobs or between jobs and school

- provides flexibility by offering opportunities to work a greater or lesser amount or to speed up or slow down one's military career investment, as needs and preferences change

Altogether, the continuum-of-service paradigm can create a military force that is both operationally integrated and administratively seamless and, as such, represents an important step forward for the all-volunteer force.

CHAPTER 14

TOWARD A NEW BALANCE
IN MILITARY CAPABILITIES

ARTHUR K. CEBROWSKI

INTRODUCTION

I begin with what some may believe are outrageous ideas and then explain why their consideration may be overdue.

- The U.S. military force structure—and in particular the active-reserve component relationship—is outdated. Increasingly it is a drag on the military's ability to provide what the nation needs, and it has to be reengineered soon.

- Many argue that the U.S. military is slipping away from American society. Increasingly it is less a reflection of the society from which it comes and more of a self-defined elite. The argument is overblown but calls for action nonetheless.

- The reserve components, and particularly the National Guard, should be less clones of and support for the active forces, and more vanguards of total force transformation and vehicles for changing the active force components.

U.S. military force planning—that is, the way the Pentagon goes about designing future forces—is like the activity guided by the double helix of DNA fame: highly complex interactions are continuously carried out through the guidance of an underlying pattern. In force planning, one of the spirals is the logic that blends past decisions about force size with forecasts of the future political and technological circumstances with which future forces will have to contend. This spiral is manifested in defense programs, budgets, and debates over the fate of weapons systems and manpower levels. The other spiral is what might be called the cultural spiral—the set of assumptions members of the military profession have about their role, character, and purpose. These assumptions are important to the logic stream. They provide the screen through which the military sifts the rapidly expanding force options that technology, globalization, and political change make possible. In an era when fewer of the politicians and citizens who help to decide what the U.S. military will become have any direct experience with the military, how the military sees itself plays an increasingly powerful role in force planning. That role includes narrowing the options and influencing the biases and assumptions of the politicians and citizens who help sort out what the U.S. military will be.

THE CHANGING MILITARY CULTURE

The last draftee entered U.S. military service on June 30, 1973, and the last individual to have been conscripted retired from active duty before the end of the last century. The United States has had an all-volunteer military for a generation and a half, and today, the men and women in uniform are all professionals. They refer to themselves as "warriors." They are certainly the best-equipped, best-paid, and best-trained warriors in the world. By most measures of combat quality, they are the best warriors in the world. They may be the best warriors in history.

Members of the U.S. military have not always called themselves warriors. Before the 1970s, the term "GI" was much more prominent as a generic rubric, and for most of the 20th century, "soldier," "sailor," "airman," or "Marine" worked fine as a descriptor. "Warrior" had never been a particularly laudatory characterization in the American military culture. It was not prevalent in the World War II lexicon, even in the speeches and writings of General George S. Patton Jr. and other luminary leaders. Nor was it used much in the Korean or Vietnam conflicts, possibly because the U.S. military culture then stemmed from another tradition: the decades of the 1940s, 1950s, and 1960s were rooted in the notion of citizen-soldiers, and citizen-soldiers, however proficient they could be as temporary acolytes of Mars, never lionized warriors for very long, nor lost their interest in life and goals outside of the military and war.

The citizen-soldiers got a lot out of the military. And the nation, as has been true throughout its history, got much from its citizen-soldiers. After the Revolutionary War, it was the once–citizen-soldiers who opened the "West" — from the Appalachians to the Mississippi — largely riding the opportunities of the land grants the fledging nation used to pay its revolutionary warriors for their service. After World War II, the GI bill gave the once–citizen-soldiers the educational experience that boosted U.S. productive dynamism through the remainder of the 20th century. For their part, those citizen-soldiers brought to the military the culture of the nation, along with expertise and technological wisdom that helped make the U.S. military so powerful.

But beginning in the early post-Vietnam period, "warrior" emerged as a generic term of choice. Its new prominence reflected the renaissance the U.S. military went through after Vietnam in an institutional effort to restore discipline, morale, and distinction. As the draft ended, "warrior" picked up connotations of dedication and professionalism. It picked up some other connotations too. One was an emphasis on combat specialization. The U.S. military's purpose, the military increasingly said, was to "fight the nation's wars," not to "nation-build," not to further social engineering efforts, not to be a police force, not to "win hearts and minds." American warriors were different from other warriors. They would not be aggressors; they would punish aggression. Their battlefields would not be on U.S. territory; they would fight abroad. They would fight the nation's wars; others would clean up afterward.

FORCE-PLANNING LOGIC FOR THE COLD WAR

Those assumptions and a changing international security environment influenced a force-planning logic chain that helps describe the character of today's military—a logic chain that has evolved over the past three decades.

The chain's first link dealt with the problem of projecting power abroad. In the 1940s this meant establishing military bases throughout the world, and, by the end of World War II, the United States stood astride one of the most extensive, robust military basing systems ever created. Projecting power also meant creating alliances, initially to help prosecute the world war, then to contain Soviet military power. These bases and alliances established the basic character of U.S. military deployments for the next half century.

By the 1960s, U.S. military presence abroad was concentrated in garrisons and particular ports in Europe—mostly in Germany and in the United Kingdom for ground and air forces and throughout the Mediterranean for naval forces—and in Japan and Korea. The strategy for projecting power abroad shifted to maintaining garrisons and stations in strategic locations, and those garrisons, in and around which most of the U.S. forces deployed abroad operated, became an integral part of the physical expression of the containment policy.

There were important exceptions to this pattern. The deployment of half a million military personnel to Southeast Asia during the Vietnam conflict of the 1960s, the buildup of U.S. military strength in the Persian Gulf area in the 1990s, and the U.S. military presence maintained by naval forces and military assistance programs throughout the world all offset the notion that U.S. military forces abroad were concentrated in particular locations and were fairly sedentary and stable. But throughout the last half century, most of the U.S. military (on average, two thirds of the active force) was always located in the United States, and most of the forces deployed abroad were usually (for 42 of the last 50 years) located in the garrisons and overseas bases that had been maintained since the end of World War II in Europe, Japan, and Korea.

The essence of U.S. power projection in that context focused on reinforcing these forward garrisons.

The cold war and strategic nuclear parity forged the next two links in the logic chain: a responsive, event-focused force posture and a punitive force structure. In an era when miscalculation could trigger a civilization-destroying nuclear exchange, the steel thread that ran through decades of planning focused on how to deter that event from occurring. The central strategic problem was how to contain Soviet power and influence without triggering a global holocaust. Crisis *management* was the underlying watchword. Deterrence was the strategy. And U.S. forces were increasingly designed to enhance deterrence by building a convincing capability to defend against Soviet military capabilities in particular scenarios.

The core that ran through this strategy was fundamentally responsive. The United States made it clear that it would always be able to hit back, but for the most part, ceded the initial military moves to potential adversaries. Likewise, the United States took its cues in developing military capabilities from what potential enemies appeared to be trying to develop. That did not mean it would seek to duplicate what they did. But if the Soviets indicated they were going to build heavy tank forces as the core of their ground power, the United States would develop a means of countering that core. Through the decades of the cold war the United States honed its ability to respond. Its forces increasingly took on the capabilities and character that made their response credible. Deployments maintained that credibility. Force planning was unabashedly "threat based," and vast amounts of money were spent defining and specifying the size, character, and operational scheme associated with the Soviet military threat. Contingency planning focused almost exclusively on how the U.S. military would respond to Soviet or Soviet-supported aggression. Increasingly, U.S. force planning centered around the characteristics of its potential enemy.

In the 1980s and early 1990s, the last link in the cold war logic chain was forged: the primacy of access to the battle space. Access had not been an issue through much of the cold war because U.S. garrisons were already in place in Europe and Korea, where both the threat of a military clash with the Soviets, and the stakes if it should occur, were high. But Vietnam had suggested that the likelihood of armed conflict might be higher elsewhere, and by the 1980s the Middle East and Persian Gulf region increasingly appeared to be the next candidate.

The rise of this region in U.S. military planning was sparked by the Arab-Israeli war of 1973, the shock of the oil embargo, and ever growing Soviet naval and airlift capabilities. While the focus of the formal planning framework remained on Central Europe, in 1973 the Department of Defense began a series of assessments of the relative ability of the Soviet Union and United States to move forces into the Persian Gulf region. After the fall of Iran's shah and the Soviet invasion of Afghanistan, the department set up a separate major theater command for Southwest Asia, institutionalizing the region as an area of major U.S. military planning interest. The prominence of the Persian Gulf region in planning grew through the 1980s, and, after the formal demise of the Soviet Union and the first war with Iraq, it became the primary force-planning focus inside the Pentagon.

At that time, there were no large U.S. military garrisons in or near what was referred to as Southwest Asia, and bringing military force to bear there was not going to be easy, especially given sea and land mines and other technologies that could make it very difficult to project naval and ground forces into the region. Accordingly, throughout the last decade of the 20th century the military concern with projecting power increasingly focused on how to overcome concerted "keep-out" efforts by opponents

The forging of this chain of military concern—from force projection and a focus on response to events, through the design of a punitive force structure, to the question of how to get that force into a fight in areas where it was not already garrisoned—took place in the crucible of increasing professionalism. Warriors replaced GIs. Among other things, this professionalization has contributed to a dramatic increase in the efficiency and effectiveness with which the U.S. military can implement the logic chain built over the last three decades. It can project military power better than ever, it can push through an opponent's attempts to keep it out, and, as has been demonstrated over the last decade, it can defeat and destroy enemy armed forces. Today, the United States has the most powerful, effective military in the world. It is so superior that it cannot be seriously challenged militarily for the foreseeable future. It is a profoundly influential instrument of U.S. foreign policy, generally recognized as the standard against which all other martial forces are evaluated, and likely to increase its superiority relative to all other military forces for at least the next five years. As Western movie heroes once explained it, this is "no brag, just fact."

NEW PARADIGMS IN FORCE PLANNING

As wonderful as it is to have such a military, as important as it is to maintain the status it has attained, and as justifiably proud the men and women in the U.S. military are of the institution in which they serve, today's military is insufficient for the tasks it faces today and for the challenges it will face in the future. Military magnificence is not an end in itself. The U.S. military is one of the means—an important one—through which the United States seeks to obtain its international goals. So it should be judged not only in terms of its efficiency and effectiveness relative to other militaries or against its own history. The U.S. military needs to be assessed against how well it helps the United States achieve its international and security policy and shaped to enhance the nation's ability to do so.

The world has changed the utility of the logic chain and the character of today's military. It increasingly emphasizes the need to supplement the magnificence of U.S. military prowess with other capabilities. It is true that the nation needs warriors, for the world is not benign, and as long as other military forces embody great capacity to use violence effectively, the United States will need to be able to defeat them. But it is also true that the United States will have to tap into capabilities beyond destroying armed forces. It must be able to stabilize situations after major armed conflicts have ended and, most important, prevent them from happening. For these purposes, it will need systems enforcers and administrators—experts in sustaining peace and in directing the transition from war to sustained peace.

Particular events continue to drive the use of U.S. military force, as demonstrated by our response to Iraq's invasion of Kuwait in the 1990s and as would occur if the North Koreans attacked the Republic of Korea. But it is also increasingly obvious that the nation needs a capability to supplement its event-focused planning with systematic thought about and planning for a continuum of near-continuous presence and security stabilization, both military and civilian.

The U.S. military will need to continue to improve its ability to access the battle space and to project raw military power, for the nation is shifting its overseas military posture away from garrisons and toward a more flexible presence. Therefore, the armed forces must increasingly focus on their ability to maneuver military force from strategic distances and from the sea—without reliance on fixed, forward positions. Furthermore, "keep-out" military technologies—from mines and barriers to longer-range missiles—are becoming more sophisticated. The U.S. military will need the capabilities not only to overcome and stay ahead of keep-out technologies, but also to increase its ability to bring political victory in addition to military victory to the areas where the United States wishes to gain access.

Defense policy making must continue to be informed by knowledge of the technologies of violence and power. But because of all the other new foci listed above, it must increasingly be informed by moral principle.

These considerations are not driven solely by the current situation in Iraq, however much that situation exemplifies why the supplements are needed. They reflect the underlying dynamics of globalization, modernization, and the emerging information age that increasingly condition human and international affairs. As such they are not just tactical considerations associated with the present. They are strategic considerations that are going to be present for the foreseeable future and probably well beyond.

NEW ROLES FOR THE GUARD AND RESERVES

New force-planning paradigms have implications for the thorny issues of the balance between active and reserve forces and their respective roles and missions. As the current situation in Iraq indicates, one of the consequences of the decisions in the 1970s to shift what are sometimes called "support" functions into the reserves and to make National Guard forces clones of the active forces has been the need to call up reserve components to deal with the aftermath of major armed combat. The department relies on the reserve components—not exclusively, but certainly importantly—for the stabilization process in Iraq, for it is in the reserve components that police, civil affairs, and other skills central to the transition to peace reside. The extended duration of these call-ups often causes considerable stress for the individuals involved, for many of them face extended reductions in salary and growing challenges to their civilian careers.

However, the policy issues here go beyond the problem of inequitable stress on a segment of the American public (and the political implications of that stress). They point to a series of questions about the effectiveness of the current active-reserve force mix of personnel and functions in the U.S. military and, ultimately, to the character of the warrior culture that currently dominates inside the U.S. military.

An example of the concerns over effectiveness is how to address the problem of spreading the forces too thinly, particularly into the new roles demanded by the new era. One can hear about a growing range of solutions to this problem that run from adding force structure to the active and reserve components to reinstituting the draft. These solutions encompass a variety of adjustments to recruiting, reserve call-ups, and training.

Let me add some suggestions.

First, I do not believe the best solution—and by "best" I mean the solution that can be available soonest *and* that has the most beneficial longer-term implications—lies at either end of the range. That is, I tend to dismiss the supposed "quick fix" of adding force structure to the active or reserve components. I do not think it is likely to be very "quick." Post–World War II history shows that adding, manning, training, and equipping a new active Army brigade will take up to two years. And adding more structure to a structural base that needs to, and is going to, change simply promises to slow the transformation of the force when that transformation should be accelerating. Nor do I believe that the other end of the spectrum of potential solutions—reinstituting the draft to generate more military manpower—is politically viable. Besides, it is not manpower, per se, that is needed. It is manpower with particular skills, experience, and perspective.

Second, the best solution involves National Guard and reserve personnel. This is because the skills and talents the department needs are far more prevalent within the reserve components than they are within the active force. I am not talking here about combat skills so much as what I term "system-enforcer and system-administrator skills"—those skills and talents that are particularly needed to stabilize, reconstruct, and democratize, and to otherwise facilitate the transition from armed conflict to a civil society. Thus I am talking mostly about the skills and talents guard and reserve personnel gain more from their civilian careers, training, work, and interests than from their military experience.

The way to tap this reservoir of civil talent is to form a new, hybrid organization within the National Guard. This organization would have a force-protection component, but not necessarily one designed to engage and defeat an organized, combat-equipped opposing military force. It would be an organization from which units could be tailored to facilitate a particular transition to peace at a particular time and location. If that transition happened to require the reconstruction of civil infrastructure, the new unit would have a particularly robust civil-infrastructure-reconstruction component, manned by guard and reserve personnel who, because of their civilian careers, were adept at doing such things. The unit size would depend on the particular stabilization missions, but perhaps a range of brigade-size to division-size provides a notional sense of how large it would be.

The Department of Defense would activate the personnel for this unit for one year rotations. Participation in the unit would be open to those personnel with the requisite skills and experience—from both their civilian careers and military positions—from across the guard and reserve structure and from any service.

Why would guard and reserve personnel be interested in serving on active duty in such a unit? There are at least three reasons. First, the service would meet the nation's needs, and to those service members who share the underlying commitment to the nation we know as patriotism—which by all indications is a common and distinguishing characteristic of those who have chosen to serve in the National Guard and reserve—participation would be a true manifestation of that commitment. Second, participation in the unit would constitute a different kind of military service, one that would be less a diversion from one's civilian career, and more a means of enhancing that career, for the tasks and experience of this service would draw largely from the skills the individuals are honing in pursuit of their civilian careers. Third, because of the importance of this undertaking, the nation ought to adopt special means of compensating those who serve for the full year. Policy makers should look closely at the Israeli approach of filling financial gaps between the military incomes of members of the reserve components activated for service and what they would otherwise be making in their civilian careers.

This last point would, of course, be among the most controversial. It raises the obvious challenge, not that it would be too expensive, but that it would be inequitable. That is, what is it about this kind of active service that distinguishes its importance from that of "traditional" activation? The challenge is a serious one, and should be considered carefully. But I want to point to a few of the underlying implications of what I have sketched out here.

What I have sketched as a new stabilization unit ought to be recognized, if you will, as a vanguard unit for a transformed force. It would represent a significant step away from the half-century assumption that the U.S. reserve components are supposed to be clones of the active force, there to speed the mobilization of the nation to fight industrial-age war on a truly grand, World War II scale.

Instead of iterating this purpose—a purpose which we must not yet abandon entirely—the unit I have outlined would be a means of altering the character of the active force. It could help shape a new total force to better cope with the kinds of problems the nation is more likely to face in the foreseeable future. For example, the unit could become a means of replicating its stabilizing capabilities in the active force. It could accomplish this purpose during the year of its activation by training active duty personnel. The active duty personnel could then serve as the replacements for the activated reserve and guard personnel who transition back to their civilian careers and lives.

In the process, I submit, we could adjust the kind of professionalization of the active force that has been underway since the end of the draft, offsetting the transition toward separateness from the society—a separateness that comes with the services' current "warrior" culture—with a deeper integration.

CONCLUSION

Let me return briefly to the propositions I began with, which suggest a need to change the balance of capabilities in the U.S. military (figure 1). I suggest that this concept for a new hybrid organization is one small way of changing that balance. The Department of Defense needs the reserve components to play a different and more essential role than they do now. It needs them to help it cope

FIGURE 1. CHANGING THE BALANCE

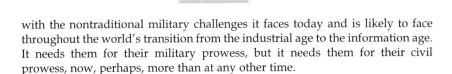

Warriors	System Administrators
Power Projection	Security Exportation
Responsive, Event Focused	Continuous, Transition Focused
Destroy Enemy Forces	Build Civil Society
Access to Battle Space	Access to Political Victory

with the nontraditional military challenges it faces today and is likely to face throughout the world's transition from the industrial age to the information age. It needs them for their military prowess, but it needs them for their civil prowess, now, perhaps, more than at any other time.

COMMENTARY

PATRICIA A. TRACEY

Let me first echo Ken Krieg's comment that our all-volunteer force is a national asset (part 4, this volume). We should celebrate its success. In fact, I would assert that our nation's confidence in achieving the desired outcomes in the global war on terrorism would be very different with a force that was structured around the rules of the Vietnam conscript era.

That said, I have spent much of the last decade of my career jerry-rigging the current manpower and personnel system to make it produce the operators and war fighters that the military services have required. I have found it necessary to skirt the edge of the law and skirt the edge of policy, to "just this once" make something work, because it has to work now. As a result of those experiences, I cannot escape the sense that significant changes are needed in the manpower and personnel policies under which the Department of Defense (DOD) operates.

After reading the paper by Beth Asch and James Hosek (chapter 12, this volume), I realized that I had read the title question differently from the way in which they intended it. The title of the paper asks the question, "What does transformation mean for military manpower and personnel policy?" The authors' answer to that question focuses on how military and personnel policies have to change to enable transformation and transformed capabilities. I read the title as follows: "Are there opportunities for transformation — indeed transformational imperatives — in the area of manpower and personnel policy management and execution?" I believe the answer to this question is yes. And I believe the answer to this second question might provide the sense of urgency that is needed to remove the many barriers to transformation identified by Asch and Hosek.

There are three elements to the manpower and personnel policy equation, but I caution that we do not very well understand how these elements make the all-volunteer force work. The three elements are as follows:

- Pay, compensation, promotion, and personnel policies that allow people to choose to serve. This element tends to receive the most attention.

- A quality of service that enables the men and women who join the military to feel that they can accomplish the missions they are assigned at the level of excellence with which they expect to accomplish them. Ensuring quality of service includes providing the training, the equipment, the spare parts, and the conditions of work that enable people to perform at a high level of excellence.

- Knowledge on the part of service members that their service is valued.

The Department of Defense is at a point where all three of these elements are better balanced than they have ever been. This situation offers us a window of opportunity to consider the changes that are needed to enable the capability of the force to reach the next level. I will address potential changes by commenting on several aspects of the paper that Asch and Hosek prepared, which include a number of assertions with which I take issue.

I will begin with the assertion made by Asch and Hosek, with which I agree, that changes to the department's manpower requirements have, historically, tended to be evolutionary. Most of the services tend to accept that they will make changes by bringing in people at the bottom ranks who have the skills that they need. It takes 20 years to make change that way. I am not sure that approach is compatible with a commitment to transformation.

Legacy systems and transformed systems overlap inside our force. Yet I would argue that our department is not artful about how it manages either the manpower or the personnel transitions that could accelerate the implementation of transformed systems or transformed capabilities. Shouldn't we be developing the manpower and personnel policies that allow us to accelerate those outcomes?

Second, the Asch and Hosek paper talks about the need to value, reward, and provide incentives for flexibility and risk taking. They associate flexibility and risk taking with four characteristics, as assessed below:

- *Adaptability to emerging situations.* If you have watched CNN one night over the course of the last two years, you could not dispute that adaptability to emerging situations characterizes the United States military in the field, both at the individual and the unit level.

- *Interoperability and jointness.* Both have been key characteristics of operations over the last two years, so the force in action is successful in these areas as well.

- *Rapid responsiveness.* In this area the force has both strengths and weaknesses.

- *Agility to capitalize on opportunities in the field.* I say again, if you watched CNN at all in the last two years, you could not avoid seeing that the members of the armed forces were able to capitalize on opportunities in the field.

These characteristics are typically considered in terms of how they apply to individuals and units in the force. The issue that I believe Asch and Hosek are trying to raise, however, is that we in the Department of Defense have been unable to create flexibility and responsiveness in the *system as a whole*. When we need a surge in linguists in a certain skill area, for example, the system is incapable of adapting to that need. When we need a surge in antiterrorism and force protection personnel in order to respond to the increase in physical security demands that have emerged since September 11, 2001, the system has difficulty responding. We are unable to decide what peacetime tasks in our tables of organization are less important under the current real-world circumstances so that we can free up the assets needed to meet emerging demands.

Inside the Navy, we meet this type of emerging requirement by asking the commands, on a fair-share basis, to give up a person with the needed skills to respond, for 179 days, to a requirement elsewhere. We leave to the affected command the choice between continuing the reassigned individual's usual tasks or abandoning them altogether in his or her absence. There is rarely a deliberate policy established to make or codify these choices. In the face of a global war on terrorism, there has been very little discussion of whether there are peacetime objectives that are less important than meeting the emergent demands of terrorism.

Third, Asch and Hosek assert that the policies that govern promotion and tour length are the major bar to innovation and risk taking on the part of personnel. I have been quoted as having said some things that would comport with that assumption, and I probably did make such remarks. But on reflection, I believe that what the department needs is the ability to institutionalize successful innovation. We want to be able to institutionalize the results of prudent risk taking. We want our best and brightest to serve in assignments that allow them to lead us to capitalize on transformational opportunities.

A challenge for the Navy is being able to recognize that there are emergent requirements for knowledge, skills, and abilities that drive more than just a single assignment in a career field. Further, we are very slow in recognizing and adapting to new career paths or skill sets. The Navy tends to undervalue skills in information operations, for example, because those skills do not have a designator or subspecialty code. We have no way to communicate to selection boards that those skills are valuable. Officers, therefore, do not accept assignments that would allow the Navy, over time, to evolve an inventory of upwardly mobile people with new skills. Indeed, an officer has to perform well on individual assignments to receive a good evaluation. But this pressure to perform is not what keeps officers from being innovative or from taking risks on a scale that would lead to transformation. Rather it is the risk of taking an assignment that falls outside the normal pattern—outside the pattern expected by a promotion board—that keeps people from leading transformation.

Finally, the paper speaks to the features that are valued in the compensation system and argues that the level of attention they receive depends on how valuable they are perceived to be. But I believe a bigger concern is the need to examine some of the more basic assumptions of the current compensation system. Does it, indeed, matter to people that advancement occurs at the same rate in every skill set? Does it matter to people that advancement to the same highest pay grade is available in every skill set? Are the services recruiting and retaining a sophisticated enough force that they can accept that some skills are more germane to winning the fight than others? That there may be differences in how people enter the advancement window or in how high they can advance? We have not tested these assumptions, in my view. Instead, we have carried them with us as the volunteer military has matured from the draft-era force.

Earlier, I suggested that answering a different version of Asch and Hosek's title question would perhaps reveal more issues that would impel us to overcome the barriers to transformation. I would like to offer the logic behind that suggestion. The authors assert that today's manpower and personnel policies are inhibiting transformational opportunities. I am suggesting that the human capital strategy as a whole is in need of transformational thinking. The future vision for our force suggests a military that must be comprised, more uniformly, of highly capable people—capability that is not only a matter of entry-level test scores, but also a product of training, experience, attitude, and aptitude. To be affordable, such a force must be sized and shaped to enable a high degree of selectivity at recruitment and high per capita cost to retain under demanding conditions of service. The Asch and Hosek paper talks about decentralized action, agility, and innovation in the field as characteristics of the transformed force. I could not agree more. These characteristics are acquired through a combination of experience and knowledge that is typically

- a product of longevity in the job, but more importantly, in military service and in military activity

- a product of an ability to capture work force expertise, including being able, in the future, to bring people into the service with experience developed in the civilian work force, and to bring them in at a level that is appropriate given that experience

- a result of capitalizing on a richer education base as the department changes its paradigm about an enlisted member's education level upon joining the force

- a product of a reliable and robust capability to reach back on demand for support when an individual is in the field, under fire, and wants to be able to innovate or act in a decentralized fashion

These considerations imply to me that our department's entire system of manpower and personnel policies—from recruitment policies, to assignment policies, to the policies that govern how long we retain service members—deserves examination in order to meet the requirements for a transformed force. These requirements include those described below:

- An increased probability of hostile action—preemptive and preventative action, as well as defensive action, as described by Arthur Cebrowski (chapter 14, this volume)—requires a change in terms of service.

- A higher percentage of the force probably needs to be in combat support or combat service support specialties in order to sustain a higher level of real world activity.

- The active-reserve mix needs to change, as do the rules for active and reserve assignment and utilization.

- New policies are needed to manage operational tempo—policies that go beyond paying people to be gone from home longer than they would otherwise want to be, but that ensure that the troops can be regenerated, just as equipment has to be regenerated.

- We must better anticipate the market effects on recruiting and retention. The department is in a particularly golden period right now where it is able to be freer in managing the force without worrying about the impact on recruiting and retention. This period will not last forever, and when it turns, history suggests it will turn rapidly.

- Policy makers and force planners must recognize that military personnel are not a free good. Acquisition, force planning, doctrine, tactics, techniques, and procedures all need to be examined with an eye toward economy in the requirements for people.

- Training must be transformed so that it emphasizes experimentation and simulation, because these are the techniques that can help to substitute for longevity or field experience when they are lacking and create the confidence to innovate and take risks.

We experts in human resource management are the people who are creating the most important war-fighting asset: the war fighter. So that we may do this more effectively, manpower and personnel policies need to better accommodate the need for increased substitutability among skill sets. We need to work hard at defining the skill sets that actually match the transformed capabilities of the force, rather than holding onto legacy skill sets.

In closing, I come back to my initial premise that we who are responsible for the all-volunteer force need to be mindful of the three elements of the manpower and personnel policy equation. First are the compensation, promotion, and assignment policies and practices that encourage people to serve. These policies and practices need to be coupled with the right sets of decisions about how we equip and train people so that they can perform to the level of excellence that allows them to have pride in what they do—the second part of the equation. Finally, our service members have to know that what they do is valued. And even if the public ceases to value their work, military and civilian leaders need to remind them that they, and the work they do, are valued.

★ ★ ★ ★ ★

MICHAEL L. DOMINGUEZ

Our nation is now more than two years into the global war on terrorism. This war is unlike any other our nation has fought and, importantly, is unlike the conflicts for which our reserve component policies, authorities, and organizations were designed. The global war on terrorism will be a long conflict, possibly of the same duration as the cold war. This new war, however, has different characteristics that include the following:

- Sustained high operations tempo.

- Sustained high deployment tempo.

- Unanticipated spikes in operations and deployment tempos driven by opportunities to strike the enemy or by the need to parry one of the enemy's blows.

- Substantial uncertainty as to which capabilities or systems will be the weapons of choice in these offensive or defensive surges.

- Certainty that the sustained plateau in work load disproportionately burdens "support" forces and systems representing our "core capabilities." For example, in the Air Force, most of the fighters and bombers have returned home. At the same time, airlift, intelligence surveillance and reconnaissance, special operations, security, and expeditionary combat support (air base construction and operations) units—including reserve component units—remain heavily engaged.

The reserve components were conceived as a "force in reserve." Yet today's reserve components are essential contributors to the day-to-day work of the armed forces. The Air Force Reserve and Air National Guard, for example, provide from 10 to 25 percent of the capability embedded in the Aerospace Expeditionary Force—the new force presentation construct used by the Air Force. These are not "forces in reserve;" they are full-time forces manned by part-time people. Their skills are in constant demand, and their presence in the deployment rotation is essential.

Moreover, involuntary mobilization is the principal device through which the Department of Defense (DOD) accesses its reserve component capabilities, yet that policy tool was envisioned as a once-in-a-generation event. The word "mobilization" itself implies a vast marshalling of a nation's energies for a supreme sacrifice—a notion firmly grounded in the two world wars of the last century. Further, while DOD has made great strides in creating a "total force," this force is still composed of separate, distinct organizational components with policy and statutory barriers inhibiting cross-component movement of resources (money, people, and capital equipment).

Thus, the Department of Defense faces a 21st-century fight with policies, organizations, systems, practices, and biases firmly grounded in the last century's conflicts. The transformation challenge is to adapt to the demands of this conflict, and to do so quickly. Doing so requires that DOD make significant changes in its mix of active and reserve forces, and in how it allocates resources to and accesses its reserve components—a policy challenge of the first order.

The reserve components have been used heavily during the last two years. Many of these "part-time" warriors have served two full years on active duty; some have been called to active duty multiple times. This heavy use compels the department to reexamine the active-reserve mix for many types of units and capabilities. The past is, however, by itself an inadequate guide to the future. During the last two years, our homeland was attacked. The armed forces responded with an extraordinarily demanding defensive posture in the air above our nation, at our borders, in our airports, and at every one of our military installations. America went on the offensive, accomplishing two successful regime change operations (of immensely different scales). In both Afghanistan and Iraq, the American military is now engaged in creating the conditions for establishing stable, effective governments that will be able to prevent terrorist groups from using their territory and that will forge an enduring bond of legitimacy with their respective populations.

The questions before us are not what the department has done or what it is doing, but what it must be prepared to do next. Should the department size its force and evaluate its active and reserve mix to effect another regime change? Will future regime change operations be of the magnitude of that in Iraq or of that in Afghanistan? How often will they occur? The future undoubtedly demands construction and operation of military bases in austere locations. How many of these should the department expect to operate continuously? How far apart might they be, supporting how many troops? How will these functions affect the day-to-day and surge demands for airlift? While it is certain that we cannot know what the future will bring, it is critical to begin now to develop the planning assumptions that will guide the department's efforts to rebalance the mix of active and reserve forces.

Part of the "rebalancing" challenge is a rebalancing of resources. If the reserve components are now integral to accomplishing day-to-day missions and are rotating into the deployed "lineup," they will have to be trained and equipped for that role. If the future is characterized by the unanticipated parry or thrust—

depending on whether the nation sees and seizes an opportunity to strike the enemy, or it strikes us—the force in place at that moment must have the capabilities to do what is needed. At that place and time, it does not matter whether the forces engaged are from the active or reserve components; it only matters that the forces engaged can accomplish the mission. The "part-time" forces—or some significant segment of them—will have to be trained, equipped, and sustained at a readiness level indistinguishable from that of their "full-time" counterparts.

Arguably the most significant challenge facing the department is to transform the authorities, policies, and practices that are used to shape, control, and access the part-time forces. First and foremost, DOD has to recognize that it can no longer rely solely on mobilization as the policy device for bringing part-time forces into full-time engagement. Even in a volunteer force, mobilization is an exercise of the coercive power of the state. The reserve component volunteer has no choice but to comply at the time and for the duration dictated. Employers and families are put in the same position. Mobilization is disruptive, and its repeated use will undermine the web of support that is needed from the community to sustain the forces in a long conflict. Mobilization also takes time that might not be available or desirable in the quick-strike, rapid-parry engagements characteristic of this struggle with terrorist foes. Mobilization may have some utility in marshalling reserve component members for their unit's scheduled, anticipated turn in the deployment rotation. It will always be an essential tool for the most serious and severe national security challenges; but it is not the appropriate device for quick, effective access to needed skills and capabilities in the part-time force, exercised repeatedly over a long-term conflict.

Sustaining the commitment of the citizen-warrior, his or her family, and his or her employer over the duration of a long-term conflict requires creation of new access mechanisms characterized by voluntary agreements. The most immediate need, and the easiest policy remedies, involves removing barriers to volunteerism. The department has a complex web of policies that now govern a citizen-warrior's entry into full-time duty. For example, a reserve or guard member's service can be classified in a numbers of ways (such as inactive duty for training, active duty for training, or active duty for special work). Each of these duty statuses affects the work the citizen-warrior may do, the benefits to which he or she is entitled, and the duration he or she may remain on full-time duty. Furthermore, the methods for calculating pay entitlements are inconsistent and complex across the military services, and can discourage volunteers. Medical care, and in particular, the rules for determining when families are eligible and for what care they are eligible, are a perennial source of dissatisfaction for the citizen-warrior. This system is complex and frustrating, but effective in what it was designed to do—carefully regulate the full-time work performed by the part-time work force.

However, to achieve a real breakthrough in how it sustains reserve component participation in the global war on terrorism, the department needs to do more than merely redesign its policies to encourage rather than discourage volunteerism. It must also bring into the active-reserve contract a heretofore silent partner—the "other" employer. DOD has to recognize that the citizen-warrior is a shared resource, of extraordinary value to both the department and the civilian employer. Because of that value, it may make sense, for reserve and guard members with particular skills, to negotiate time-sharing agreements. (For example, DOD might agree to pick up employee medical costs in return for the right to use the employee on short notice for up to 120 days.)

Once DOD transforms its policies to encourage and facilitate voluntary contributions by its part-time force, trains and equips both full- and part-time members to the same standards, rotates forces in both components into the fight, and enables either component to provide immediate, decisive military capability when and where needed, it will have set the stage for the last transformation: elimination of the artificial distinctions among the components and the emergence of a true, seamless total force. This point was made clearly in the chapter by John Winkler (chapter 13, this volume). In a seamless total force, individuals could move easily from full-time to part-time status as their needs coincided with mission needs and resource availability. Civilian accomplishments in "cross-over" skills would be recognized in the part-time force and would be valued in promotion and assignment decisions. Blended units (composed of both full- and part-time forces) would be the norm, not the exception. And the need for separate congressional authorization and appropriation structures would evaporate.

Whether or not the department is ready to embrace this vision of a truly integrated total force, the demands of the global war on terrorism create an imperative to begin a journey to a new destination. The guard and reserve are and will continue to be essential participants in the fight. Voluntary associations will have to replace mobilization as the principal mechanisms for accessing reserve component warriors. In a long conflict, civilian employers, the department's silent partners, will have to be given a voice. When we in the DOD assign our part-time force full-time missions, we will have to match that tasking with the training and resources to do the job. The result will be a maturation of the total force, from its origins in the great global wars of the last century, to its fruition in the first global war of this one.

★ ★ ★ ★ ★

HEATHER WILSON

There are three endeavors to which I believe the Department of Defense (DOD) and the Congress need to make major commitments over the next year. These endeavors are to significantly increase military end strength; to reduce reliance on the National Guard and reserve; and to expand the special forces.

INCREASING END STRENGTH

I begin with the premise that the war on terrorism will define today's generation of service members, just as the cold war defined my generation. The war on terrorism is not a transient phenomenon. It is not a crisis for which the department can surge and then go back to business as usual. The nation needs to adjust to this new reality and to recruit, train, and support our military men and women in order to meet this threat.

In my view, there is no question that the Department of Defense needs to increase the size of the active duty military, particularly the Army. I believe somewhere between 90,000 and 150,000 additional personnel are needed on active duty. It is time to commit to that expansion. Guardsmen and reservists will be rotating back home over the next six months. Once the banners come down from the garage and the parades are over, these service members are going to be making decisions with their families about whether they stay in the guard or reserve. Guardsmen and reservists are not full-time soldiers. They have done a wonderful job, but the nation may be asking too much of them.

Since September 11, 2001, an average of 50,000 guardsmen and reservists have been called up per year, a much higher number than in years past. Eighteen percent of the U.S. soldiers serving in Iraq are members of the guard or reserve. And, perhaps most troubling, by March 2004, the Army expects that some reserve soldiers will be serving back-to-back year-long deployments in combat areas. At this pace, our military is going to start to burn out. Burnout will show up first as decreased retention rates for midcareer noncommissioned officers and junior officers—who make up the backbone of the American Army. These officers need to know that help is on the way. They cannot be expected to serve at this high tempo for an entire career. And the commitment to address operational tempo has to be made in Washington.

In 2003, at the request of the House Armed Services Committee, the military services conducted initial reviews of their manpower requirements to meet the demands of the war on terrorism. Every service judged that it required a significant increase in end strength. I think the Defense Department was right to review those requirements. It also needs to look at ways that current resources can be moved within today's force structure to meet growing demands.

Nevertheless, the reality is that the military will end fiscal year 2003 with 28,000 more people than authorized.[1] And even with its numbers thus augmented, the military's capacity to perform its missions is already nearing its limit. Congress and the Department of Defense must increase the active duty force's end strength or risk hollowing out the force.

REDUCING RELIANCE ON THE NATIONAL GUARD AND RESERVE

The second point I want to make is that the Department of Defense has to be able to tap a broader range of civilians to augment the military. I am married to a man who is in the National Guard. For the last 18 months, he has been receiving e-mails that say, "I have a three-hour window to come up with an O-5 to do 179 days of duty to an undisclosed location. Do you know anybody?" Are these messages locating people with skills appropriate for the jobs that need doing? What skills were the authors of these requests really seeking?

I saw in the newspaper recently an article about a 23-year-old staff sergeant in Iraq who was tasked with setting up a school board in the local community where she was assigned. She called back home to her father in Iowa, who happened to be the superintendent of schools in a little town. Now, this sergeant was probably successful. She was at least smart enough to get advice from somebody who knew something about the task. But there are over 20,000 towns with school boards in America, and in every one of those little towns, there is somebody who has spent an entire career working with the school board. Skills in the civilian community can be tapped to help the military accomplish its mission.

I represent a bilingual community. One third of my constituents speak Spanish at home. I was recently at Reginald Chavez Elementary School talking with the students. Sometimes when I attend town hall meetings or make formal presentations, where detailed issues are being discussed, I use a translator—someone trained and fluently bilingual who can make sure that the nuances are appropriately expressed. But if I am trying to sort things out on the playground at Reginald Chavez Elementary, I do not need a formally educated translator. I just put my hand on the shoulder of the nearest kid on the playground and say, help me out here. "¿Cómo se dice en español?" And the child can help me. One does not always require a Defense Language Institute–trained linguist wearing a battle dress uniform to provide the skills that are needed to get a job done.

I think the nation needs a civilian special skills corps made up of people who are not in the military, who do not drill once a month, and who may have minimal military training, but who have skills that are useful to the missions of the Department of Defense. Whether they are rural water engineers, retired utility company employees who can fix power lines, fluently bilingual bankers, or laypeople from a mosque, members of a civilian special skills corps would be called in for short assignments to assist the military in its work. If the department can embed journalists in a combat zone, it can similarly embed civilian specialists whose assistance will allow the military to do its combat-related job.

Developing mechanisms to access civilian specialists will be a challenge for the personnel system. If the department needs somebody who knows how to fix a 1962-vintage telephone system, the personnel system has to be robust enough to find the American civilian with that expertise who is willing to come and help. Personnel databases have to be better than they are now. The department needs to be able to anticipate the special skills that might be needed on short notice and then be able to reach out into communities to identify the right person when needed.

EXPANDING THE SPECIAL FORCES

Finally, I believe policy makers need to recognize that the war on terrorism is going to require some very specialized combat-related skills. Congress and the Department of Defense are going to have to continue to expand the special forces and the Special Operations Command. The authorized end strength for the special forces is currently 35,000; I think the authorized strength number should be increased to 50,000.

Because it is difficult to recruit individuals into the special forces and it takes time to develop their skills, the department needs to consider drawing from outside the military to fulfill some of its requirements for specialized skills. Some Americans possess skills that make them particularly good candidates for the special forces. For example, most police departments in the country now have special weapons and tactics (SWAT) teams; 20 years ago almost none of America's police departments had SWAT teams. This expertise could be useful in meeting DOD requirements.

I think it is possible to expand the department's special-purpose teams to be able to fight the war on terrorism effectively. Efforts to expand the membership of the special forces will have to be undertaken gradually so as not to compromise the standards that these special teams must have. But it is possible for the system to accommodate some growth, and it is necessary as well.

Congress and the Department of Defense must commit, now, to increasing the military's end strength, reducing its reliance on the reserve and National Guard, and augmenting the special forces. These actions are necessary if the military is to meet the increased demands placed upon it by the continuing war against terrorism.

NOTES

1. Authorized personnel levels (end strength) for the military services are set by Congress. The secretary of defense is permitted, under normal operating conditions, to allow actual levels of end strength to be up to 3 percent above authorized levels. In times of national emergency, such as was the case for the Army at the end of fiscal year 2003, title 10 waives the 3-percent limit, so that actual end strength can exceed authorized strength by a more significant amount.

★ ★ ★ ★ ★ ★ ★ ★ ★ ★ ★

PART V

THE NEXT DECADE

CHAPTER 15

OBSERVATIONS ON A REMARKABLE TRANSFORMATION

PAUL WOLFOWITZ

It is a privilege to celebrate the 30th anniversary of the all-volunteer force and to pay tribute to those who helped pioneer this tremendous transformation in American military history. Indeed, transformation has been the watchword in Washington and in the Pentagon for several years now. Many dramatic changes have been introduced since President Bush described a new strategic vision for our nation's military in a speech given at the Citadel during his campaign for the presidency.

Yet when one considers the transformation ongoing today and those that have occurred over the past half century, the move to a volunteer force is perhaps the most remarkable. One of the most notable aspects of this transformation is that it was not about technology — often perceived as the centerpiece of transformative events. Instead, the transition to the all-volunteer force was about people — about how the nation would man its armed forces.

As I travel around the world and observe our men and women in uniform responding to the difficult challenges they face in a dangerous and complex world, I am awestruck. Awestruck by their dedication and professionalism. Awestruck by their courage and patriotism. Awestruck by how they demonstrate the values that characterize this country, as well as ingenuity that is truly American. The members of our armed forces are brave when they fight, caring when they respond to humanitarian missions, and ingenious and imaginative when they deal with complex political and civil-military challenges. They are nothing short of incredible. And it is a tribute to our nation that we can attract such outstanding men and women to volunteer to serve their country.

Many examples of the exceptional performance of our armed forces come to mind; but I will share just a few from my recent travels in Iraq. When the horrible bombing took place in the Shia heartland of Iraq, in August 2003 in the city of Najaf, the U.S. Marines responded with extraordinary calm and maturity. As funeral processions traveled many miles through the streets, passing perhaps hundreds of thousands of people, not a single violent incident occurred. That stability can be largely attributed to our Marines and the remarkable success they have achieved in connecting with the Iraqi people. As they perform their duties, our Marines wave, they take off their sunglasses when they talk to people, they salute when funeral processions pass by, they bring cold water to the Iraqis. It is not uncommon to see young children holding the hands of the Marines as they patrol the streets. Their presence has been a tremendous influence.

Throughout Iraq, our soldiers and Marines have created functioning local governing councils—in Karbala, Najaf, and Kirkuk, for example—which in some areas are composed of a rich ethnic mix of Arabs, Kurds, Turks, and others. Council members in these cities have commended our troops for their efforts to provide security and services, to help solve problems, and to help establish stability in regions where violence and unrest were anticipated. These council members have expressed their gratitude to the coalition forces, and to our American soldiers, for liberating Iraq.

In Mosul, a young captain from the 101st Air Assault Division helped launch an association among the local butchers to resolve a problem with butchers who were slaughtering animals in the street and leaving garbage in front of their shops. In the old days, a few of the butchers would have been shot, to send a message to the rest. Instead, the association established a set of rules by which all agreed to abide. This young captain was not trained for this task at West Point; he relied instead on basic civics, imagination, and ingenuity—something our troops and coalition partners, including the Iraqis, are doing on a daily basis.

The all-volunteer force has been a key to America's success in Iraq. Recently, when I testified before the Senate with Army Vice Chief of Staff Jack Keane, he described what has been observed of our armed forces during this operation. He said of our service members, "[They] bring the values of the American people to this conflict. They understand firmness. They understand determination. But they also understand compassion. And those values are on display every day as they switch from dealing with an enemy . . . to taking care of a family" (U.S. Congress 2003, 64).

While the examples I have shared highlight some of the accomplishments of our armed forces in Iraq, our service members are accomplishing similar things in Afghanistan, in Kosovo, and in many other places around the globe. Their actions demonstrate why the all-volunteer force, including both the active and reserve components, constitutes the most effective fighting force in the world.

The all-volunteer force is effective because it is a high-quality force. We in the Department of Defense have set high standards for our volunteers. We are selective. Not everyone who volunteers gets to serve—only those who score well on the enlistment test and have a high school diploma. Sustaining these standards is critical, and we know it is critical because of past experience. In the draft era and even in the early years of the all-volunteer force, quality standards were not as high as they are today, and it was evident in the attitude and performance of the force. Empirical research has shown that high standards pay off — in higher performance and lower attrition. But they also come with a price.

Volunteers cost more than conscripts. As the department implemented the all-volunteer force, policy makers had to change their approach to recruiting and managing the force. No longer could manpower be viewed as cheap and abundant; rather it had to be treated as a scarce and expensive resource. It became essential to learn how to compete in the civilian labor market for recruits, to properly compensate the force, and to pay attention to and invest in quality-of-life matters. It costs money to maintain standards, but the cost is worth the resulting productivity of the force.

In fact, studies have shown that for a given level of force effectiveness, the all-volunteer force is less expensive than a conscripted one. This greater cost-effectiveness results from three principal factors. First, a conscripted force is associated with higher personnel turnover, shorter enlistment terms, and degradation in unit stability and performance. Higher turnover necessitates more recruits, and as a result more supervision and training. More training means more resources must be invested in basic and lower-level training rather than in core operational capabilities that enhance readiness. Second, because draftees are less likely to reenlist, a conscripted force has to be considerably larger than a volunteer force. It also tends to be younger and less experienced. Finally, as we are witnessing today, a volunteer force is more motivated. People perform better if they are doing what they choose to do.

Today more than 1.4 million men and women choose to serve on active duty in the armed forces, along with another 1.2 million who serve in the National Guard and reserves. It is a diverse force that reflects the rich culture, tradition, and values of America. Our all-volunteer force is high quality, well trained, and highly skilled. The men and women who serve in our armed forces are motivated, experienced, and compassionate. They are professionals in every sense of the word. They have defended America's interests and security for three decades and they are clearly prepared to meet the challenges of the war on terrorism.

America's all-volunteer force is held in high esteem, indeed in awe, both at home and around the world. It is recognized for what it does to advance democracy, peace, and freedom. I have no doubt that the all-volunteer force was the right choice for America 30 years ago and that it remains the right choice today. Indeed, its introduction in 1973 marked a return to the traditional practice of volunteerism that prevailed from the time of Lexington and Concord until the Civil War. It was the insatiable manpower needs of that tragic conflict that led to the use of the draft in both the North and the South. Now, 138 years after the Civil War that introduced the draft to America, we can confidently say that the United States has successfully and proudly returned to the great tradition of the all-volunteer force.

By any measure, the all-volunteer force has been an unqualified success. America owes an enormous debt to the visionaries who implemented this remarkable transformation 30 years ago. It is incumbent on all of us in the Department of Defense to protect and sustain this valuable resource long into the future.

REFERENCES

U.S. Congress. Senate. Committee on Foreign Relations. 2003. *Iraq: Status and prospects for reconstruction – resources.* 108th Cong., 1st sess. S. Hrg. 108–246.

CHAPTER 16

THIRTY YEARS OF AN ALL-VOLUNTEER FORCE: PERSONAL OBSERVATIONS

JOHN W. VESSEY JR.

Thirty years of the all-volunteer force! In light of the 43 years of American history that preceded those 30, it sounds like a great achievement. But as mentioned earlier in this volume, the soldiers at Concord and Bunker Hill, those who fought in the Army on the frontier both before and after the Civil War, the Philippine Insurrection soldiers, and those who fought in the Boxer Rebellion might ask what we are celebrating. They would surely say, "How about us? We were volunteers, too." Of course, many of them would probably tell us that they were not really volunteers but were "regulars," because "volunteer" was a term used to designate temporary formations for temporary operations.

This volume commemorates our nation's decision 30 years ago to return to a volunteer force. I would like to share some of my personal observations from the past three decades, as well as talk about a few challenges that I see for the future.

LOOKING BACK

In 1973, I had just returned from Laos and was assigned to be the director of operations on the Army staff. At that time, General Creighton Abrams, the Army chief of staff, and General George Brown, the Air Force chief of staff, were forming the new air-land battle team. It was an enormous effort. I believe it to have been one of the great transformations of the armed forces. I was one of the worker bees in that hive.

The all-volunteer force was a new ingredient—a new piece of untasted, untested meat—that was going into the stewpot. The Army had always had volunteers. As I recall, over half of those who entered the Army each year during the Vietnam War were volunteers, and certainly, in the rest of the services, almost everyone was a volunteer. In fact, the Selective Service System provided a great impetus for volunteers. It provided an opportunity for those people who did not want to serve in the Army to serve in the Air Force, the Navy, or the Marine Corps. It also provided some opportunity for those people who knew they had to serve in the Army to choose the type of service they might undertake.

The all-volunteer force changed the game for everyone. The Air Force and the Navy no longer had that large pool of smart kids who wanted to sleep in clean sheets, and poor old Mother Army had to find volunteers for every type of duty.

REBUILDING AFTER VIETNAM

By 1973, the Vietnam War had taken a tremendous toll on the Department of Defense. Not everything in the defense establishment was broken, but a lot of things were. Most of it needed major maintenance; a lot of it needed a complete overhaul or replacement. The war had delayed the modernization of the force, particularly the equipment modernization for that part of the force facing the nation's major enemy, the Soviet Union. For the Army particularly, the war had decimated the professional noncommissioned officer corps and that group of officers which provided the seasoned company commanders for the combat forces. Despite the need for rebuilding, the defense budget was declining. The size of the force was declining as well. The Army's end strength was falling to a level that history told us would support only 10 divisions. In general, things looked bleak. There was a lot of work to do.

Creighton Abrams, fortunately, was able to convince then Secretary of Defense James Schlesinger to allow the Army to keep 16 divisions if it could do so with the end strength that would ordinarily support a 10-division Army. Drastic changes were necessary if the Army was to be successful. We in the Army had to reduce overhead, reorganize headquarters, and get rid of unnecessary head-quarters and organizations. At the same time, we were changing the way we would train and fight. We had to find the money to both modernize equipment and support the new training concepts. As hard as many of these changes were, we generally knew how to accomplish them. But on top of all that, we were moving to an all-volunteer force. The all-volunteer force was a different business!

Yes, the Army had had volunteers before World War II. I was a volunteer. To me, 21 dollars a month, "three hots and a flop," and the opportunity to ride a motorcycle all looked pretty good during the Great Depression. But in 1973, the economy and society were very different than in the days of the Great Depression. The Army was also larger in size. Even at its reduced strength, the new all-volunteer Army would be four times the size of the pre–World War II volunteer Army.

As the Army began its transition to the all-volunteer force, I was involved in the structuring, equipping, and training aspects of the Army's rebuilding effort, not in the business of finding volunteers. Nevertheless, the whole Army staff was aware of the effort being placed on recruiting. At the time, many of the reports of the consultants being hired, task forces being formed, and ideas being generated sounded a little weird to me.

About a year and a half later, however, I was sent to Fort Carson to command the Fourth Mechanized Division, and then all of the ideas that other people had been working on involved me too. Many who were involved in the recruiting business at the time will remember putting curtains on the barracks windows to make them look like home and making sure that the food tasted like mother's. I always wondered whose mother we were trying to emulate. Being in Colorado, I was also getting regular suggestions from the staff of then Congresswoman Pat Schroeder about the need for rock concerts on the parade field on Saturday nights—suggestions aimed at the important task of attracting and retaining volunteers.

INTEGRATING WOMEN INTO THE FORCE

The volunteer aspect of the force was only one of many changes underway. Earlier in this volume, several authors wrote about the introduction of women into the force in much larger numbers. That change had an impact on those of us responsible for commanding the troops. I will share a story that illustrates what a significant impact that was.

General Bernie Rogers, one of the real giants of the all-volunteer force, had become the commander of the Army Forces Command. Bernie wanted to move quickly to integrate women into the units, and he wanted the women to live in the barracks of the units to which they were assigned. That change meant moving the women soldiers out of the Women's Army Corps (WAC) barracks and into the unit barracks.

In 1974, some new barracks were being built at Fort Carson, but most of the troops were living either in the old World War II wooden barracks or in barracks that were built in the 1950s according to the old squad-room concept. All of the barracks needed renovation except perhaps the WAC barracks, which were arguably the best soldier quarters on the post. I did not see a way to give women the privacy that I thought they needed in the unit barracks, and in particular a way to resolve the latrine problems. I told Bernie Rogers all of this at one of his commanders' meetings. Bernie told me very quickly that my ingenuity was not up to the standards of the Forces Command. He pointed out that General Bob Shoemaker, who then commanded the III Corps at Fort Hood, had solved these problems, and certainly I ought to be able to do so, too.

A few weeks later, the Fourth Division Cavalry Squadron was at Fort Hood in a training exercise, and I flew down to visit them. As Bob Shoemaker and I were flying around in a helicopter, I asked him about visiting one of the coed barracks. He agreed to the stop and added that the corps had only one coed barracks and it was the property of a division's support command.

A short time later, we landed close to the barracks and walked to it. The outside door was made of steel with a peephole in it, and there was a buzzer used to gain entrance. We buzzed the buzzer. After some rattling of chains and bars, the door was opened by a female staff sergeant or tech sergeant, who was about six feet tall. She had a Charge of Quarters armband and wore a web belt on which hung a pistol, a big ring of keys, and a hatchet. She guided us around the barracks and showed us how the latrines and showers had been allocated to men and women. I inquired about the hatchet. She said the doors between the men's and women's sides of the barracks had emergency fire locks on them, and they were secured on the women's side with heavy ropes. The hatchet was to enable her to chop through the ropes in case there was a fire and the doors had to be used. I inquired how the coed barracks idea was going generally, and she said she thought it was going okay. She said they had one problem. There was a little ledge that went around under the second-story windows, and soldiers were still getting back and forth on that ledge. She was sure that as soon as that ledge was barricaded, everything would be fine.

I decided I would have to accept General Rogers' criticism for lack of ingenuity until we at Fort Carson implemented a serious barracks renovation program.

FIGHTING THE NATION'S BATTLES

In the early days of the all-volunteer force, the services used a wide variety of recruiting inducements to encourage people to join the armed forces. Fighting the nation's battles was not necessarily one of them.

Early in my tour at Fort Carson, my new sergeant major and I visited one of the tank parks toward the end of a duty-day. A tank crew led by an inexperienced corporal was working on a tank that was not quite ready to go to battle. The crew had decided to quit for the day rather than fix a minor but nevertheless readiness-related problem in the tank. I gave the crew my "ready to fight" talk, stressing the importance of fixing the equipment and always being prepared to fight. One of the soldiers said, "Fight? I didn't join this Army to fight. I'm not fighting anybody." The sergeant major looked at me and I looked at him. We both sensed more agreement than disagreement with the nonfighter from the rest of the tank crew.

Sergeant Major Bill Tapp, a big, tough special forces soldier, looked at his new division commander and seemed to have question marks printed right on his eyeballs. I said, "Sergeant Major, take this soldier to his battalion commander. He should not be wearing a uniform or endangering this tank crew. He ought to be out of the Army by nightfall." The incident took place well before we in the Army had authority for quick administrative discharges, and I did not have any idea how I was going to make it work. The soldier was not gone by nightfall, but he left the Army the next day. It had a salutary effect. The word went through the division rather quickly.

As I mentioned earlier, lack of money was delaying barracks renovation by the normal contracting procedures, so we at Fort Carson did what the Army, the Navy, the Air Force, and the Marine Corps had done for years. We organized soldier teams to fix the plumbing and renovate the barracks. It was a lousy solution from the point of view of training soldiers or from the point of view of renovating barracks, but the job was not going to get done any other way.

About that time, a friend of mine told me about a new book that Robert M. Utley, the National Park Service historian, had written. The title was *Frontier Regulars*; the subject was the Army in the West after the Civil War. It was a follow-on to his earlier book, *Frontiersmen in Blue*, about the Army on the frontier before the Civil War. I had not read the first one, but I picked up the second one and read it, then promptly picked up the first one and read it as well. In both books, Utley pointed out that the frontier Army was severely constrained. Its units were usually understaffed. It had serious shortages of noncommissioned officers and junior officers, and the soldiers were detailed to all sorts of housekeeping tasks that had little to do with soldiering. At the same time, they were dealing with a very difficult and serious security matter for the nation. It seemed to me then that the post-Vietnam armed forces and the all-volunteer force in its early years mirrored the frontier Army in many ways.

It is important to recruit people for what we want them to be able to do. If the services are going to enlist people in a fighting force, then enlist them to fight.

ATTRACTING AND RETAINING GOOD SOLDIERS

Through the early years of the all-volunteer force, the nation was blessed with some giants in leadership positions, both civilian and military—people like George Brown, Chief of Staff of the Air Force; Lou Wilson, Commandant of the Marine Corps; and, in the Army, Abrams, Weyant, DePugh, Kerwin, and Rogers. To recall those people is to remember giants doing giants' work. The people working on today's transformation of the armed forces could learn valuable lessons from the transformation of the armed forces that took place at that time.

Recently I saw a wonderful greeting card sold by a Minnesota company called Artists to Watch. The card featured a wolf pack photo by Jim Brandenberg, a well-known Minnesota outdoors photographer who lives in the Boundary Waters area. The photo showed three very healthy-looking timber wolves in a snow-covered forest. Under the photo was a Rudyard Kipling quotation: "The strength of the wolf is in the pack, and the strength of the pack is in the wolf."

The giants of the early days knew what Kipling meant. Creighton Abrams probably understood the idea better than Kipling did when he wrote the words. Abrams knew that attracting and retaining good soldiers had very little to do with curtains on the windows or rock concerts on the parade field. It had a lot to do with having strong, capable, well-led, well-trained, well-equipped, mission-oriented military units. However, as Kipling noted, good wolf packs require good wolves. Unfortunately, in contrast to the wolf pack, the military services could not breed their own. They had to recruit them from the outside.

Many of the difficulties of the 1970s were recounted in part 1 of this volume. John White talked about the pay freeze and the mistake made in normalizing the entrance exams (chapter 4, this volume). Problems like those contributed to high attrition rates, high indiscipline rates, and poor readiness. Commanders struggled with the impact of these problems on the force. At the same time, the services attempted all sorts of gimmicks to attract and retain good servicemen and servicewomen.

One of these great ideas was to provide a desk, a chair, and a lamp for each soldier. I recall, after taking command in Korea in 1976, going into one of those 25-year-old Quonset huts with coal-fired space heaters housing Second Infantry Division soldiers along the demilitarized zone. There were the desk and the chair and the lamp. I saw that the lamp was not plugged in, so I said to the soldier, "Why isn't your lamp plugged in?" He said, "General, the only thing that comes out of that outlet is water, when it rains."

General Creighton Abrams died in 1974, but his legacy lived on. The people he had picked for leadership positions in the Army had the fever. Weyant, Kerwin, DePugh, Rogers, and those of us who followed them had all been infected with the virus. We were going to fix what was broken. We were going to make the armed forces—for us, the Army—better, and we were going to make it work despite the problems.

By the late 1970s, the pieces began to fall into place. The professional training that we had started for the noncommissioned officers began to pay off. The barracks' roofs no longer leaked. Some of the new equipment was coming into use, and a lot more of it was in sight. Then came the increase in the defense budget during the Reagan administration, and the problems that could be fixed with money began to fade. We were also beginning to learn a lot about recruiting.

We were beginning to realize that everything in the recruiting business was interrelated; it was difficult to separate cause and effect. For us in the Army, I think the real kick start came when General Shy Meyer and I decided to take the best major general we had on the staff, Max Thurman, and put him into recruiting. From then on, the goal was not to accept those who wanted to come into the Army but to go after the recruits we needed to make the Army effective. I hope that important lesson is never lost.

Max Thurman was in my office once a week with wall-to-wall spreadsheets that he called "horse blankets," analyzing every facet of the human-power acquisition business. One week, it was, "Do you have a minute to listen to this tape, see what you think about it." The tape was that wonderful "Be All You Can Be" recruiting song. Another time it was, "I've got a little video tape here, do you want to take an extra minute and look at this?" The video was that wonderful advertisement with the sergeant saying "We do more before 9:00 in the morning than most people do all day."

Thanks to these giants in the early years, we have marvelous armed forces today; but we also have new challenges. The question now is this: How will we meet those challenges?

CHALLENGES FOR THE FUTURE

Let me conclude with a few lessons and observations for the future, drawn from my view of the first 30 years of the all-volunteer force.

Number one: The armed forces have to be tied closely to the American people. It will not work any other way. The Defense Department can and should strive to equip its forces with the most advanced weapons. However, the greatest asset the nation can have for its defense is a society wherein the mothers and fathers, the school teachers and pastors, and the coaches and principals, say to young men and women from every rung of the social and economic ladders, "It would be a good thing for you to serve in the armed forces." That should be the number one goal.

Number two: The *people acquisition system* requires top-notch people. Those responsible for recruiting men and women into the armed forces have to be every bit as smart and as good and as innovative as the people buying weapons or looking for new technology and new fighting systems.

Number three: Recruit to fight. For the nation to sustain its fighting force, we must recruit people to fight. When every major television newscast shows reports that another soldier or Marine was killed in Iraq or Afghanistan, the services cannot try to hoodwink young people in America into thinking they are being recruited for something other than fighting, because fighting is what they are going to do.

We in the military services face a new world. There are no longer any low-tech soldiers, sailors, airmen, or Marines. It is a high-tech business, whatever task is being performed.

Several authors in this volume have referred to the Defense Science Board (DSB) report on human resources strategy (U. S. Department of Defense 2000). I served on that task force. I think many of the ideas in that report were understated, and they remain applicable to sustaining an all-volunteer force into the future. I highlight a number of them here.

One of the most important ideas was the recommendation to shape the force — to recruit, train, and reward — to do what it needs to do to defend the nation in the 21st century. In other words, recruit to fight.

I have heard some suggest that the service career should be longer and others suggest that it should be shorter. The fact of the matter is that the useful service time differs for different skills. For most Ranger infantrymen, the useful service time is about the same as that of an NFL lineman. Fighter pilots wear out after 10 or 12 years. The services should retain people for as long as they are needed in a particular job and at the same time work to keep them in the job that they are doing well. Why should a tank commander have to go into an administrative job to earn more pay when he has become a good tank commander? He should be rewarded for staying in the tank.

The DSB report also suggested moving toward early vesting of a 401K–style retirement benefit, readily transferable to the civilian economy. Such a system could help keep people in the armed forces for the time they are needed, and then reward them for that service when they go on to other pursuits. Every industry in the country desperately needs the leadership, innovation, and ingenuity that our soldiers, sailors, airmen, and Marines have demonstrated in their recent experiences in Iraq and Afghanistan.

The pool of high school graduates who are qualified for service, but who are not going on to college immediately, gets smaller and smaller every year. Perhaps the services should look elsewhere for eligible recruits. There are people who have completed a year or two of college who need a little break; two or three years in the armed forces might provide that break. Rising tuition costs at universities may help spur recruiting in this market.

The pay system used by the military services is a leftover from World War II. Before World War II, a soldier could earn extra pay by being a better radio operator or by being a better marksman, but the system was complicated to administer. So it was understandably simplified for the World War II mobilization. With today's computing capability, however, the department no longer needs to limit itself to a simplified pay system. Instead, the services should be able to pay for performance in every career field.

Clearly, the Department of Defense needs a seamless force of guard, reserve, and active duty service members. At the same time, the services must recognize the obligation they owe to guardsmen and reservists who dedicate part of their time, usually their vacation from their civilian job, to the nation's defenses. Short of general mobilization, members of the reserves should not be expected to serve the same amount of time overseas that the regulars serve.

I have touched here on some of the key challenges facing the armed forces in the years ahead. I have probably provided more questions than answers. Certainly, I don't know the answers to all the questions. But those responsible for our men and women in uniform are smart people with the benefit of all the lessons of the first 30 years of the all-volunteer force. I urge them not to relearn those same lessons by making the same mistakes, and I offer this advice. Examine the innovative ideas that have been suggested in this volume and in other studies and reports. Consider their applicability to today's challenges and implement those that will help to ensure an effective volunteer force into the future. Yet, at the same time, remember that the armed forces always benefit from stability and steadiness.

REFERENCES

U.S. Department of Defense. 2000. *Report of the Defense Science Board Task Force on Human Resources Strategy.* Washington, D.C.: Office of the Under Secretary of Defense (Acquisition, Technology, and Logistics).

CHAPTER 17

A BIGGER FORCE
OR A SMALLER EMPIRE

Ed Dorn

The under secretary of defense for personnel and readiness has the responsibility for procuring and managing the department's most important resource, its people: 1.4 million men and women on active duty, more than 1 million National Guard and reserve members, and 700,000 civilians. The Under Secretary holds a diverse portfolio; it includes recruitment, pay, family support, health care, equal opportunity employment, dependent schools, and commissaries. One of the most rewarding parts of the job, in my view, is getting out in the field to meet and learn from the terrific young men and women who are serving their country around the globe.

I am delighted that some of my predecessors and successors in the position of under secretary of defense for personnel and readiness have contributed to this volume — including John White, Christopher Jehn, Rudy de Leon, and Bernard Rostker. Each of us confronted a different mix of challenges, and each of us handled them well. But the current Under Secretary, David S. C. Chu, is confronting some unusually tough problems. He deserves our gratitude and commendation for the good job he is doing.

This volume has been built around two themes. The first theme, the subject of part 1, is the celebration of 30 successful years of the all-volunteer force. The second, explored in parts 2 through 4, is the nature of the challenges that lie ahead as the Department of Defense works to sustain the volunteer military. I will address each in turn.

CELEBRATING SUCCESS

All of us who have served in the Department of Defense over the past 30 years can take a small amount of pride in the contributions we made to the success of the all-volunteer force. In chapter 2, Martin Anderson's description of those important meetings in New York in 1967, at which he and others discussed the possibility of ending conscription, makes me feel like a real newcomer. Nevertheless, I too take pride in having made a small contribution to the success of our volunteer military during a challenging period.

The challenge during the first term of the Clinton administration was to downsize the force significantly without degrading military readiness. The department succeeded. I remember talking with Colin Powell shortly after arriving at the Pentagon in the spring of 1993. He was serving his last six months as Chairman of the Joint Chiefs of Staff. I asked him for advice about how I should approach my job and he said, "Ed, you guys in the Clinton administration are inheriting the finest military force ever assembled. Your job is not to screw it up."

We heeded that admonition, and we did so under a framework I called the "personnel triad." We developed a slogan to remind ourselves of what we were about: "recruit 'em, train 'em, and treat 'em right." We were able to continue bringing in high-quality men and women even as we downsized the force. We maintained readiness and improved quality-of-life programs. Let me say a bit more about each component of the triad.

Recruit Them

The Department of Defense must continue to emphasize the recruitment of high-quality young men and women, recognizing the link between an individual's educational background and his or her performance in military jobs. Through the mid-1990s, we in the department were able to maintain the high quality of our force. Personnel accessions had leveled to about 200,000 individuals each year as force reductions came to a close. But it was evident that sustaining quality recruiting was going to be more challenging in the years ahead. The propensity of American youth to enlist in the armed forces continued to decline; recruiting resources were falling; and, partly because of the drawdown, there was a perception that military service was no longer a secure profession.

My last full year in the department, 1996, demonstrated the services' success in recruiting. In that year, 96 percent of new enlistees were high school diploma graduates and 69 percent scored in the upper half of the enlistment test—numbers well above the Defense Department's minimum standards (U.S. Department of Defense 1997, tables 2.6 and B-5). On the other hand, we were not able to foresee the tough recruiting market that the services would face later in the decade.

Train Them

Training is the second component of the triad and is critical to force readiness. Investments in training improve the skills of individual service members and enhance unit performance. The department would be wise to continue investing in training technologies—such as simulation, computer-based training, and distance learning. The department also needs to continue to increase the involvement of active duty forces in reserve component training, given the rise in the number and frequency of guard and reserve deployments and the trend toward greater integration between the active and reserve components. Finally, the department needs to continue to emphasize joint training among the services.

TREAT THEM FAIRLY

The Department of Defense must also treat its service members fairly — the third part of the triad — by ensuring that compensation packages are adequate to recruit and retain a quality force. The recent targeted pay increases, which were based on the findings of the Ninth Quadrennial Review of Military Compensation, are significant steps toward pay comparability with the civilian sector. As I mentioned earlier, the department faced a special challenge during the drawdown to make sure those members leaving the force were treated fairly. We used carefully conceived personnel and compensation policies with special emphasis on voluntary separation incentives — financial inducements for members to leave the force voluntarily. We instituted programs to assist service members in their transition from military to civilian careers. With voluntary separations and reduced accessions, we were able to keep promotion opportunities steady, which was important not only for the morale of the force, but also to maintaining the correct force profiles for each service by pay grade and years of service.

In the mid-1990s, the department also transformed military health care services with a new delivery strategy termed TRICARE, which was intended to produce a more efficient, regionally based managed-contract system. Looking back on that period, I have concluded that military health care was funded adequately at that time. However, I suspect that this is not the case today.

CHALLENGES THAT LIE AHEAD

The second theme of this volume offers less to cheer about but a lot to think about. Representative Heather Wilson, Vice Admiral Pat Tracey, and others have challenged the department to be more creative and not to rest on its laurels. Admiral Tracey wrote about a number of concepts for personnel management with much transformative potential.

I want to suggest some other reasons for concern about the current and future state of the force. Today, the department faces two serious challenges. One challenge is the high deployment tempo that is driven by the many military operations in which the United States has recently been engaged. The second challenge is the high reliance on guard and reserve forces.

These two challenges are especially troublesome because there is little evidence to suggest that the current levels of stress on the force will subside any time soon. The largest current military operation, that in Iraq, is proving to be more difficult than the political leadership anticipated. Thus far, that experience has shown how difficult it is to project the true cost of invading a country. The Bush administration was not able to predict that the operation in Iraq would absorb such a large proportion of our forces for as many months as it has, or that it would cost upwards of $100 billion during the first year. Defense policy makers have not been able to make reasonable projections about the point at which the department can begin to significantly reduce its troop commitment in Iraq, and so they cannot tell us when the stresses on the force will start to abate.

The department has experience with deployments of this kind—in Bosnia and Kosovo, for example—and this experience suggests that during the first stages of a deployment, reenlistment rates go up. During the second rotation, they tend to return to normal. But when soldiers are rotated a third time into a dangerous area, their reenlistment rates begin to fall. The military services are likely to have large numbers of soldiers in Iraq for the next two years, at least. During that period of time, troops could experience three or four rotations, which could cause significant problems with retention.

Further, we have not yet found weapons of mass destruction in Iraq. At the same time, the costs of the operation are escalating in both monetary and human terms. If these problems are not resolved or ameliorated, we may see a decline in popular interest in, and support for, this operation. Popular disaffection could lead to a decline in propensity to enlist and, in turn, to reduced accessions. The recent, highly publicized "stop-loss" orders have made recruiters' jobs much tougher.[1] Every recruiter is now being pressed to answer the question, "If I complete my commitment and want to get out, will they let me out?" Reduced accessions will compound the problem of declining reenlistments.

The total force concept was created in response to Vietnam, but Operations Desert Shield and Desert Storm were the first conflicts for which the department actually deployed large numbers of guard and reserve personnel into combat zones for extended periods. When I arrived at the Pentagon two years later, the department was still addressing some of the fallout from the heavy use of reservists. Many reservists claimed to have suffered economic losses. And reservists were heavily represented among those who complained of the symptoms that have been referred to as "Desert Storm Syndrome." Even as the department was trying to address those problems, however, the services were relying more and more heavily on the reserve components for contingency operations.

As I traveled during my tenure as under secretary, I began to learn more and more about the stresses we were placing on guardsmen and reservists. Reliance on the reserve components has continued to grow, with some units being sent to Iraq for year-long assignments. I will be surprised if reenlistments do not decline in the reserve components even before they decline in the active force.

THE BOTTOM LINE

Let me move to the bottom line, which is this: *the department needs either a bigger force or a smaller empire.* Representative Wilson offered a very high number by which to increase the force: 90,000 to 150,000 additional military personnel. Other experts offer smaller numbers: 20,000 to 50,000. But I have not heard anyone outside the administration argue that the nation can maintain its present commitments, over the long run, with current personnel levels. Even so, the critical issue is this: could the department recruit 20,000 to 50,000 additional personnel if authorized to do so? I am not confident that the current recruiting processes would yield those additional numbers, particularly if public support for the operation in Iraq erodes and the economy begins to generate more jobs.

What is the alternative? One is a smaller empire. By a smaller empire, I do not necessarily mean that the nation must abandon its essential commitments to mutual security or that it must retreat from the global war on terrorism. What I mean is that it needs to find new, and perhaps more humble, ways to engage the rest of the international community. One thing should be very clear: we should not expect other nations to bear the cost of decisions that the United States has made unilaterally.

Even as we celebrate the success of the all-volunteer force, we need to face the future with concern and renewed creativity. The global war on terrorism is a new and different environment than that of the cold war. We are confronting an adversary that is as elusive as it is evil. At the same time, we have placed our military forces under pressures that will be unsustainable in the long run. I believe we face a situation that requires a more significant transformation than simply "tweaking the dials."

NOTES

1. Stop-loss orders prohibit members from leaving the service at retirement or upon the expiration of their contracts during the period of time the order is in effect. Stop-loss can only be initiated after a declaration of war, during a national emergency, or when members of any reserve component are involuntarily called to active duty.

REFERENCES

U.S. Department of Defense. 1997. *Population representation in the military services: Fiscal year 1996.* Washington, D.C.: Office of the Assistant Secretary of Defense (Force Management Policy).

★ ★ ★ ★ ★ ★ ★ ★ ★ ★ ★

CHAPTER 18

THE ALL-VOLUNTEER FORCE: RESILIENT AND PERISHABLE

RUDY DE LEON

With Americans serving in faraway combat theaters, the professionalism, integrity, and service of the dedicated men and women in the U.S. armed forces are the best evidence of the success of the all-volunteer force. Those of us who have played a modest role—in our current and past careers—in supporting these men and women are honored to have contributed to their substantial effort.

In addition to the department's military professionals, I would like to acknowledge its career civilian professionals. Career civilians have been committed to supporting the men and women in uniform for the past three decades and have made very important contributions to the all-volunteer force. From my perspective, the most important of these contributions is continuity. The department's professional civilian career force serves as the link from one era to the next. Therefore, one of the nation's highest national security priorities should be to improve the ability of the Department of Defense to recruit the next generation of career civilian professionals. The clock is ticking. The nation is headed toward a crisis unless it attracts the next generation of civilians. I want to acknowledge the effort and leadership exhibited by Secretary of Defense Donald Rumsfeld and Under Secretary of Defense David Chu in putting forth their current initiative on civilian personnel. It is an initiative I support.

I also want to recognize the leadership of Vice Admiral Patricia Tracey, former deputy assistant secretary for military personnel policy, and the work of her staff on the 1999 legislation to improve military pay and provide for military retirement equity. To Admiral Tracey, I say thank you for your critical work on behalf of military men and women.

At this 30-year milestone, the all-volunteer force has demonstrated that the concept of a volunteer military can work. The AVF has showed itself to be both resilient and perishable. It is resilient in the sense that it can work under a vari-

★

ety of challenging circumstances—a strong economy or a changing demographic base, for example. The AVF has endured despite debates within society about the value of military service. But the AVF is also perishable in the sense that America must always take care of the men and women who serve. Military pay, medical benefits, housing, and schools for dependents are important. But so, too, are capable leaders, training opportunities, and quality of life.

The success of the department's effort cannot be measured simply by the percentage of the budget that is invested in these areas. While proper funding is a first step, the true measure of this effort is an environment where military men and women can always answer the question, "Does the job I'm doing matter?" with a resounding "yes."

Much of this book discusses the tools necessary to keep the all-volunteer force resilient for the next 30 years. Several chapters discuss the need for change in various laws, regulations, and military personnel practices that are currently on the books. Other issues addressed include compensation; career management since the Goldwater-Nichols Act; and force structure, size, and composition.

Yet, for all the discussion of change—both at the margins and in the form of fundamental restructuring—I would remind everyone concerned with the future of the all-volunteer force that that force as it exists today is the product of two very bold presidential decisions. The first was the 1948 decision by President Harry Truman to racially integrate the armed forces of the United States. This decision was highly controversial in its time. Yet it changed not only the American military, but America as well. The second was President Nixon's decision, in 1973, to move from a draft to an all-volunteer force. These two decisions were initiated by leaders who, after some reflection, decided to change direction in a very bold way.

That brings us to today's policy makers and the decisions they face for the future. As noted, the all-volunteer force is perishable. To develop policies that ensure the future of the all-volunteer force and give honor to the men and women who serve their country is the challenge that those who are responsible for the all-volunteer force face today. Meeting this challenge is going to require a lot of work. And their success will be only as good as the effort and attention they invest.

★ ★ ★ ★ ★ ★ ★ ★ ★ ★ ★

CHAPTER 19

LOOKING AHEAD:
THE 40ᵀᴴ ANNIVERSARY

DAVID S. C. CHU

As we look back on the 30-year history of the all-volunteer force (AVF), the success of this enterprise is remarkable. There is now little argument about the wisdom of those who championed the volunteer concept in the early years. A common thread throughout this volume is the many accomplishments of the men and women who comprise the all-volunteer force. It is appropriate that we applaud their service. In this final chapter, I would like to raise four issues that must concern the department in the decade to come.

First, the success of the all-volunteer force was neither immediate nor guaranteed, so its success today should not be taken for granted. Indeed, the first decade of the all-volunteer force was very rough going. The possibility for failure, at times, loomed large. Even Richard Nixon appeared to lose hope, when he spoke about returning to the draft several years after leaving the Oval Office. But the AVF did not fail. Not only has it been successful over the past 20 years, its success has raised the bar on the standards and expectations against which the force is now measured. I can recall when Congress enacted legislation, in the 1970s, mandating that two-thirds of the male, non-prior service enlistees have high school diplomas. Today, such enlistment standards would be viewed as far too low.

While today's standards may be high in terms of both education and aptitude, they are the standards the department wants. The payoff for these standards is not only documented in studies, it is seen in the performance of the force. But high quality cannot be sustained without effort. The tendencies for cyclical swings that have characterized the department's personnel budgets — and have often occurred after periods of recruiting success — must be avoided. To ensure continued success, the department needs to maintain an appropriate compensation package, health care package, and family support package — an entire "incentive package" — that is consistent with aiming for a high-quality force. We have not yet

★ ——

made all the changes in manpower and personnel policies that are necessary to sustain a force of volunteers—and to elicit from them their best performance.

Second, I believe at this moment in history that we have taken the all-volunteer force concept beyond what the Gates Commission imagined in its report. In my judgment, the commission report did not adequately address the question of what happens when the department must go to war or conduct significant sustained operations—much like what the nation is now experiencing in the global war on terrorism. The solution offered by the Gates Commission was to call up the reserves, which the department is doing. But the report does not address what to do after that.

The department is currently asking a great deal from both its active and reserve forces. Since September 11, 2001, the average tour for a reservist has been over 300 days—twice the average tour length that reservists served during the first Persian Gulf War. And although we have not called up the entire reserve force, these long deployments reflect a substantially greater effort than we have asked of our reservists in the past. Despite this fact, our active and reserve personnel have realized an extraordinary level of achievement, even as they have endured significant personal hardship. It is truly remarkable that they have accepted this challenge with few complaints. As the department continues to prosecute this global war on terrorism, we will have to manage the force to ensure the burden on our troops is one they can reasonably bear over a prolonged period of time. As a start, the department can work to make the timing of deployments more predictable for reservists and provide more advance notice to help members, families, and employers prepare.

My third point is more of a reminder: the reserves are volunteers too. They have volunteered for service, even though it is under somewhat different conditions and expectations of service than the active duty force. Despite the high operational tempo, our reserve personnel have a positive outlook. In May 2003, the department conducted its second web-based poll, which reported that the retention intentions of the reserve force—which reflected a large number of reservists who had been mobilized—were actually somewhat better than in our last poll in 1999. Stories about reservists who intend to leave military service are normal, because even in peacetime 20–25 percent of reservists leave every year.

It is a great tribute to the manpower managers in the department that, over the last 10–15 years, they have built a remarkable reserve component. The reserves are no longer simply an insurance policy that sits on the shelf. They are a part of the total force; these volunteers will be used and they understand that fact. How often they will be used, and under what conditions, is a proper matter for debate, now and in the months and years ahead.

The department has shown that it can be successful in recruiting and retaining high-quality volunteers in the numbers needed to sustain the all-volunteer force. Indeed, one of the central issues in moving from conscription to a volunteer force was whether the department could, in fact, mobilize a sufficient *supply* of volunteers at a price and under conditions the nation was willing to bear. Today's all-volunteer force affirms that we know how to answer the supply question.

What about *demand*? How do we in the department best *use* our volunteers? That is the fourth issue on which the department must focus in the future. How do we manage the demands on our volunteer force; how do we manage the requirements, or to use another word, the trade-offs? What are alternative ways of doing business? What different options are available? Could civilian volunteers play a larger role, for example? How do we best motivate a force of volunteers to undertake the hardest tasks? Do the military services simply issue orders, as they would for a conscript force, or is there a better way?

The four challenges that I have identified here loom large among those the department must address in the next decade. If we can pronounce the volunteer force, on its 40th anniversary, as successful as it is on its 30th, then we will have met these challenges successfully.

★ ★ ★ ★ ★ ★ ★ ★ ★ ★ ★

EDITORS AND CONTRIBUTORS

EDITORS

Barbara A. Bicksler has been a senior policy analyst with Strategic Analysis, Inc. since 1996. While at Strategic Analysis, Ms. Bicksler has contributed to a variety of studies with the Defense Science Board, including the Defense Science Board Task Force on Human Resources Strategy (2000); served as lead writer on the staff of the Commission to Assess United States National Security Space Management and Organization, chaired by Donald Rumsfeld (2000–2001); participated in the Secretary of Defense Review of Military Morale and Quality of Life (2001); served as analyst and writer for the Ninth Quadrennial Review of Military Compensation (2002); and participated in a variety of studies for the Office of the Assistant Secretary of Defense for Reserve Affairs. From 1986 to 1995, Ms. Bicksler was a research staff member at the Institute for Defense Analyses. In 1985, she served as a program analyst on the Defense Guidance Staff in the Office of the Under Secretary of Defense for Policy; and from 1981 to 1984 was a consultant to the Office of the Assistant Secretary of Defense for Program Analysis and Evaluation. Ms. Bicksler holds a Bachelor of Science in Economics from James Madison University (1981) and a Master in Public Policy from the John F. Kennedy School of Government at Harvard University (1986).

Curtis L. Gilroy is the director of accession policy in the Office of the Under Secretary of Defense for Personnel and Readiness. Before this appointment he served as director of the Ninth Quadrennial Review of Military Compensation and was director of special projects and research within the Office of the Secretary of Defense. Dr. Gilroy has over 20 years of experience applying economic analysis and policy research to military manpower and force management issues and an additional 10 years of experience in studies of the civilian labor market. Prior to joining the Office of the Secretary of Defense, Dr. Gilroy was chief of the Manpower and Personnel Policy Research Office at the

Army Research Institute in support of the Deputy Chief of Staff for Personnel, U.S. Army. He has also served as a staff economist on several congressional and presidential commissions as well as with the Department of Labor, and has taught economics at the college level. Dr. Gilroy received his PhD in Economics from the State University of New York, his MBA from McMaster University, and his MA from the University of Toronto. He has published extensively on military manpower issues and is a referee for several professional journals. Dr. Gilroy has received the U.S. Army Recruiting Command Meritorious Service Award and the U.S. Army Superior Civilian Service Medal.

John T. Warner is professor of economics at Clemson University, where he has been a faculty member since 1980. Prior to joining the faculty of Clemson University in 1980, he was a visiting lecturer at the University of North Carolina at Chapel Hill from 1973 to 1974. From 1975 to 1980 he served as a member of the professional staff of the Center for Naval Analyses. Professor Warner was also a visiting professor at the U.S. Naval Academy from 1986 to 1987 and served as a visiting scholar in the Office of the Assistant Secretary of Defense for Personnel and Readiness from 1991 to 1992. Professor Warner has conducted and published numerous studies on military enlistment, retention, and compensation policy for the Department of Defense. He participated in the Third, Fifth, and Ninth Quadrennial Review of Military Compensation and most recently served on two DOD panels that reviewed human resource management and personnel policy in the department. Professor Warner received a BA degree from Wake Forest University in 1969 and a PhD degree from North Carolina State University in 1976. He is the coeditor of *Defense and Peace Economics*.

CONTRIBUTORS

Martin Anderson has been the Keith and Jan Hurlbut senior fellow at the Hoover Institution, Stanford University, since 1998. He has a BA, summa cum laude, from Dartmouth College (1957); an MS in Engineering and Business Administration from the Thayer School and Tuck School (1958); and a PhD in Industrial Management from Massachusetts Institute of Technology (MIT, 1962). Dr. Anderson held academic positions at the Thayer School, the Joint Center for Urban Studies at MIT and Harvard, and Columbia's Graduate School of Business. His executive branch posts include special assistant to the President (1969–70); special consultant to the President for systems analysis (1970–1971); and assistant to the President for policy development (1981–1982). He was also an advisor to several presidential candidates, including Nixon (1968), Reagan (1976 and 1980), Wilson (1995), Dole (1996), and Bush (2000); and was a delegate to three Republican Conventions. He was a second lieutenant in the Army Security Agency (1958–1959), a columnist for Scripps Howard News Service (1993–1994), and member of the President's Foreign Intelligence Advisory Board (1982–1985). Dr. Anderson has served on several boards and commissions, including the Defense Manpower Commission, the President's Economic Policy Advisory Board, the Ronald Reagan Presidential Foundation (trustee), the Congressional Policy Advisory Board (chair), and the Defense Policy Board. He is the author or editor of several books on Ronald Reagan, the draft, and other policy issues. His most recent book is *Reagan: A Life in Letters* (coauthor, 2003).

David J. Armor is a professor in the School of Public Policy at George Mason University, Fairfax, Virginia, where he is also director of the PhD program in public policy. He teaches graduate courses in statistics, culture and policy, and social theory and policy. He received a BA in Mathematics and Sociology from the University of California, Berkeley, and his PhD in Sociology from Harvard University, where he also taught as assistant and associate professor. From 1975 to 1982, Dr. Armor was a senior social scientist at RAND, and from 1986 to 1989 he was principal deputy assistant secretary and acting assistant secretary of defense for force management and personnel. He has conducted research and written widely in the fields of education and military manpower, and in 1999 he was appointed to the National Academy of Science Committee on the Youth Population and Military Recruiting. Recent publications include "Why is Black Achievement Rising" (*Public Interest*, 1992); "Maximizing Intelligence" (*Transaction*, 2003); "Race and Gender in the U.S. Military" (*Armed Forces and Society*, 1996); and *Attitudes, Aspirations, and Aptitudes of American Youth* (contributor, National Academies Press, 2002).

Beth J. Asch is a senior economist at RAND. Her research analyzes compensation, recruiting, retention, retirement, and performance incentive issues in the U.S. military and federal civil service. Her current research projects include retirement system alternatives for the reserve components, enhancements to the military compensation system to improve personnel management flexibility and support transformation of the armed forces, the recruitment of Hispanics in the military, analysis of retirement behavior of federal civil service employees and their response to buyouts and early retirement offers, and pay-for-performance incentives in the civil service. Past research includes studies of military recruitment of college-bound youth, analyses of enlisted supply, and assessments of how the level and structure of military compensation affects military personnel retention, retirement, and performance. Her work also includes several coauthored papers on the relative efficiency of military conscription versus a volunteer force. She has taught undergraduate labor economics courses at UCLA, and is currently a faculty member at the Pardee RAND Graduate School, teaching a course on economic incentives and organizations. She received her PhD in Economics in 1984 and her master's degree in economics in 1981, both from the University of Chicago. She received her bachelor's degree from UCLA in 1979.

Reginald J. Brown was nominated by President Bush to be the assistant secretary of the Army for manpower and reserve affairs on June 12, 2001, and was confirmed by the United States Senate on July 12, 2001. Mr. Brown previously served as assistant administrator Near East, U.S. Agency for International Development; a senior fellow at the Center for Strategic and International Studies; executive director of the President's Commission on Military Compensation; principal analyst at the Congressional Budget Office; and staff to the Cost of Living Council. Mr. Brown is a graduate of West Point and the John F. Kennedy School of Government at Harvard University. He served in the U.S.

Army with the Military Assistance Command (Vietnam), the Third Brigade, 82nd Airborne Division in Vietnam, the Fourth Infantry Division at Fort Lewis, Washington, and with the First Cavalry Division in Korea. As a member of the faculty at West Point, Mr. Brown taught economics and government. Mr. Brown's decorations include the Bronze Star, the Meritorious Service Medal, and the Army Commendation Medal.

Thomas L. Bush entered federal civil service in June 1998. He currently serves as the director for program integration and intergovernmental affairs for the Deputy Assistant Secretary of Defense for Manpower and Personnel in the Office of the Assistant Secretary of Defense for Reserve Affairs. He is responsible for developing legislative and policy initiatives affecting reserve component personnel and manpower programs. Prior to entering federal civil service, Mr. Bush was a career officer in the United States Navy. During his 28-year military career, Mr. Bush was assigned to increasingly demanding staff, operational, and command positions. As a naval flight officer, Mr. Bush accrued over 3,000 flight hours in a variety of tactical aircraft. He is a veteran of the Vietnam War, during which he flew over 150 combat missions. He retired at the rank of captain in May 1998.

Lieutenant General Dennis D. Cavin retired from the Army in May 2004 as the commanding general of the U.S. Army Accessions Command (USAAC). The USAAC is a major subordinate command of the U.S. Army Training and Doctrine Command and provides command, control, and coordination for Army recruiting and initial military training for all officers, warrant officers, and enlisted soldiers. General Cavin is a 1970 graduate of the University of Tennessee at Martin, where he received a bachelor's degree in agriculture. He also holds a Master of Arts in Management from Webster University, and is a graduate of the Army Command and General Staff College and the Department of Defense's senior executive level educational program, the Industrial College of the Armed Forces. General Cavin's other assignments include: commanding general, U.S. Army Recruiting Command; commanding general, U.S. Army Air Defense Artillery Center at Fort Bliss, Texas; director, Management Directorate for the Office of the Chief of Staff, U.S. Army, Washington, D.C.; and chief, Air Defense Division, Force Development Branch, Office of the Deputy Chief of Staff for Operations and Plans, U.S. Army, Washington, D.C. During his career, General Cavin received a myriad of decorations and awards including the Distinguished Service Medal, the Defense Superior Service Medal, and numerous Legion of Merit awards.

Arthur K. Cebrowski was appointed by the Secretary of Defense as director, force transformation in October 2001, and reports directly to the Secretary and Deputy Secretary of Defense. A retired vice admiral, Mr. Cebrowski served as president of the Naval War College in his final Navy assignment. As the force transformation director, Mr. Cebrowski serves as an advocate, focal point, and catalyst for transformation. He links transformation to strategic functions, evaluates transformation efforts of the military services, and promotes synergy by recommending steps to integrate ongoing transformation activities. Mr. Cebrowski monitors service and joint experimentation programs and makes policy recommendations to the Secretary and Deputy Secretary of Defense. Mr. Cebrowski entered the Navy through the Reserve Officers Training Corps in 1964. He is a naval aviator and commanded Fighter Squadron 41 and Carrier Air Wing EIGHT. He commanded the assault ship USS *GUAM*, the aircraft carrier USS *MIDWAY*, and the USS *AMERICA* battle group. He has combat experience in Vietnam and Desert Storm. Mr. Cebrowski retired from the Navy in October 2001, with over 37 years of military service. He is a 1964 graduate of Villanova University, holds a master's degree in computer systems management from the Naval Postgraduate School, and attended the Naval War College.

David S. C. Chu, Under Secretary of Defense for Personnel and Readiness, is the Secretary's senior policy advisor on recruitment, career development, pay, and benefits for 1.5 million active duty military personnel, 1.2 million guard and reserve personnel, and 680,000 civilians. He is also responsible for overseeing the state of military readiness. Dr. Chu oversees the $15 billion Defense Health Program; Defense Commissaries and Exchanges with $14 billion in sales; the Defense Education Activity supporting over 100,000 students; and the Defense Equal Opportunity Management Institute, the nation's largest equal opportunity training program. Prior to this appointment, Dr. Chu served in several senior executive positions with RAND, including director of the Arroyo Center and director of RAND's Washington D.C. office. Dr. Chu earlier served in government as the director and then assistant secretary of defense for program analysis and evaluation (1981–1993) and as the assistant director for national security and international affairs at the Congressional Budget Office (1978–1981). He was commissioned in the Army in 1968, serving a tour of duty in Vietnam. Dr. Chu received his undergraduate degree, magna cum laude, in economics and mathematics from Yale University in 1964 and his PhD in Economics from Yale in 1972. He holds the Department of Defense Medal for Distinguished Public Service with Silver Palm.

Colonel Gary L. Crone, U.S. Air Force is a special advisor to the Deputy Assistant Secretary of Defense for Reserve Affairs, Manpower and Personnel. Prior to this assignment, he completed the National Security Fellows Program at the John F. Kennedy School of Government at Harvard University. Colonel Crone has logged over 1,200 flying hours as a raven on the RC-135 Rivet Joint aircraft; served as a reserve air attaché in Muscat, Oman during Operation Desert Storm; was the deputy/acting chief of air operations for the U.N. Mission in the Western Sahara; served as the intelligence advisor to the general counsel's office at the Drug Enforcement Administration; completed a tour as the senior total force integration adviser to the Director of Air Force Intelligence, Surveillance, and Reconnaissance and Information Operations; and, in 1995, was an at-large delegate to the United Nations' first Congress on International Law and Peacekeeping. In 2000, the Air Intelligence Agency awarded Colonel Crone the Dr. James P. Gilligan Award for distinguished support to reserve intelligence forces. His highest military decorations to date include five Air Medals and the Defense and Air Force Meritorious Service Medals. Prior to returning to active duty full time, Colonel Crone served over seven years as a felony deputy prosecuting attorney in his home town of South Bend, Indiana.

Rudy de Leon is senior vice president of Washington, D.C. operations for the Boeing Company. He joined Boeing in July 2001 after more than 25 years of senior leadership experience in the executive and legislative branches of the U.S. federal government. In August 1997, de Leon was named under secretary of defense for personnel and readiness. During his three-year tenure, he was the principal architect of, advisor on, and spokesman for the 1999 compensation reform package, which at $42 billion was the largest pay increase for military members in a generation and restored retirement equity for military personnel. He was recognized by the National League of POW-MIA Families in 1999 and by the National Military Families Association in 2000.

Frederick B. Dent served as chairman of Mayfair Mills in South Carolina prior to retiring in 2001. His government service included active duty in the U.S. Navy in the Pacific theater (1943–1946); secretary of commerce for Presidents Nixon and Ford (1973–1975); and President Ford's special representative for trade negotiations (1975–1977). He also served on President Nixon's Commission on an All-Volunteer Armed Force (the Gates Commission), and on President Reagan's Commission of Industrial Competitiveness. Mr. Dent served on several boards of directors, including Armco Inc., General Electric Co., International Paper Co., MONY, Scott Paper Co., Comsat Corporation, and S.C. Johnson. He has been active in numerous civic groups and has served as a trustee for many organizations. Mr. Dent is a graduate of Yale University and has been awarded several honorary degrees. He was married to the late Mildred Harrison. They have five children. He lives in Spartanburg, South Carolina.

Michael L. Dominguez is assistant secretary of the Air Force for manpower and reserve affairs, Washington, D.C. A political appointee confirmed by the Senate, Mr. Dominguez oversees Air Force manpower and reserve affairs policies, practices, and operations. Mr. Dominguez entered the Senior Executive Service in 1991, serving as the director for planning and analytical support within the Office of the Assistant Secretary of Defense for Program Analysis and Evaluation. In this position he oversaw production of DOD's long-range planning forecast and its $12 billion in annual information technology investments. He also directed the modernization of computing, communications, and modeling infrastructure. He joined the Chief of Naval Operations staff in 1994 and assisted in the Navy's development of multi-year programs and annual budgets. Mr. Dominguez left the federal government in 1997 to join a technology service organization. In 1999 he began work at the Center for Naval Analyses, where he organized and directed studies of complex public policy and program issues. In 2001 he rejoined the staff of the Chief of Naval Operations where he worked until his current appointment.

Ed Dorn has been dean of the LBJ School of Public Affairs at the University of Texas at Austin since 1997. He previously served for four years as under secretary of defense for personnel and readiness. Prior to his presidential appointment in the Department of Defense, Mr. Dorn was a senior staff member at the Brookings Institution in Washington, D.C., where he developed executive education programs for government and private sector managers. From 1981 to 1990, he served as deputy director for research at the Joint Center for Political and Economic Studies. He has also been director of executive operations for the U.S. Department of Education; executive assistant in the U.S. Department of Health, Education, and Welfare; and deputy director of evaluation for the Model Cities Program of Houston. A native of Houston, Mr. Dorn graduated Phi Beta Kappa from the University of Texas at Austin and completed his PhD in Political Science at Yale. He was selected a Distinguished Alumnus of the University of Texas in 1998. His publications include *Rules and Racial Equality* (Yale University Press, 1979); *Who Defends America?* (editor, Joint Center Press, 1989); and several dozen articles, reports, and op-ed pieces. In addition to his duties as dean, Mr. Dorn is the University's faculty representative to the Big 12 and the NCAA. He also is a board member or advisor to several nonprofit organizations, including the Institute for Defense Analyses, the Kettering Foundation, the Children's Defense Fund, and the Capital Area United Way.

Peter D. Feaver (PhD, Harvard, 1990) is the Alexander F. Hehmeyer professor of political science at Duke University and director of the Triangle Institute for Security Studies. Professor Feaver is the author of *Armed Servants: Agency, Oversight, and Civil-Military Relations* (Harvard Press, 2003), and coauthor, with Christopher Gelpi, of *Choosing Your Battles: American Civil-Military Relations and the Use of Force* (Princeton University Press, forthcoming). He is coeditor, with Richard H. Kohn, of *Soldiers and Civilians: The Civil-Military Gap and American National Security* (MIT Press, 2001). From 1993 to 1994, Professor Feaver served as director for defense policy and arms control on the National Security Council at the White House, where his responsibilities included counter proliferation policy, regional nuclear arms control, the national security strategy review, and other defense policy issues. He is a lieutenant commander in the U.S. Naval Reserve (individual ready reserve).

Major Dave (David P.) Filer is an active duty Army officer who recently held positions at the United States Military Academy as assistant professor and course director for Introduction to American Politics, the core political science course required of all sophomores at West Point. He also served as the American Politics Program executive officer in the Department of Social Sciences there. A 1991 graduate of the United States Military Academy, Major Filer holds a Bachelor of Science in Economics, and a master's degree in political science from Duke University, where he focused his studies on American civil-military relations. Major Filer's research interests include the United States civil-military relationship and the military and homeland security; specifically, possible roles for the National Guard and reserves. Major Filer is an infantry officer with 14 years of active duty service. He has served with both the 24th Infantry Division at Fort Stewart, Georgia and the 82nd Airborne Division at Fort Bragg, North Carolina. He is currently serving as an Army strategist with United States Forces Korea in Seoul, Korea.

Milton Friedman, recipient of the 1976 Nobel Memorial Prize for economic science, has been a senior research fellow at the Hoover Institution since 1977. He is also the Paul Snowden Russell distinguished service professor emeritus of economics at the University of Chicago, where he taught from 1946 to 1976, and was a member of the research staff of the National Bureau of Economic Research from 1937 to 1981. Dr. Friedman was awarded the Presidential Medal of Freedom in 1988 and received the National Medal of Science that same year. He was a member of the President's Commission on an All-Volunteer Armed Force (the Gates Commission) and the President's Commission on White House Fellows. He served as economic advisor to President Richard Nixon and President Ronald Reagan. Dr. Friedman is past president of the American Economics Association and is a member of the American Philosophical Society and the National Academy of Sciences. His many books and articles appear in the scientific, public policy, and popular literature. He has been awarded many honorary degrees in the United States and abroad. Dr. Friedman received a BA in 1932 from Rutgers University, an MA from the University of Chicago, and a PhD from Columbia University.

Paul Gronke is chair of the Department of Political Science at Reed College. He received his BA from the University of Chicago and his PhD from the University of Michigan, and previously taught at Duke University. Professor Gronke's academic interests include public trust in institutions, social science methodology, U.S. Congress and congressional elections, and public opinion. He has published a book, *The Electorate, the Campaign, and the Vote* (Michigan 2000), and more than a dozen articles. Professor Gronke's current research focuses on the meaning of "trust" in abstract institutions such as the government, the media, and the military. He has written opinion pieces for a variety of newspapers, has served as a radio and television commentator, and manages a weekly e-mail list for students of American politics for W. W. Norton.

Thomas F. Hall was sworn in as the fourth assistant secretary of defense for reserve affairs on October 9, 2002. A Presidential appointee confirmed by the Senate, Secretary Hall is a retired two-star rear admiral, having served almost 34 years of continuous active duty in the United States Navy. He is a distinguished and decorated naval aviator who served a combat tour in Vietnam. His final military assignment was as the commander/director/chief of the Naval Reserve. His military awards include the Distinguished Service Medal, Defense Superior Service Medal, Legion of Merit, and Air Medal. He has been inducted into the Oklahoma Military Hall of Fame. Secretary Hall graduated from the United States Naval Academy in 1963 with a bachelor's degree in engineering. In 1971, he received a master's degree in public personnel management from The George Washington University. He is a graduate of the Naval War College, the National War College, and Harvard University's National Security Course. Secretary Hall served as the executive director of the Naval Reserve Association for six years.

Lieutenant General James R. Helmly took command of the U.S. Army Reserve Command, headquartered at Fort McPherson, Georgia on May 3, 2002, and became the chief, Army Reserve on May 25, 2002. Lieutenant General Helmly enlisted in the Army in 1966 and earned his commission through Officer Candidate School in 1967. He served on active duty until 1973 in a variety of assignments that included two tours in Vietnam, one with the 101st Airborne Division, the second as a district senior advisor. He also commanded an infantry company in Panama. As an Army Reserve soldier, Lieutenant General Helmly commanded at the division, area support group, and battalion level. He served in numerous staff officer positions, culminating with his assignment as military assistant, manpower and reserve affairs (individual mobilization augmentee), Office of the Assistant Secretary of the Army, Washington, D.C. His military education includes the Armed Forces Staff College and the Army War College. He has a bachelor's degree from the State University of New York at Albany. Among his awards and decorations are the Distinguished Service Medal, the Legion of Merit with two Oak Leaf Clusters, the Bronze Star with Valor Device and three Oak Leaf Clusters, the Combat Infantryman Badge, the Parachutist Badge, the Army Staff Identification Badge, and the Ranger Tab. He was inducted into the Infantry Officer Candidate School Hall of Fame in 1996.

Stephen E. Herbits served as a member of the President's Commission on an All-Volunteer Armed Force (the Gates Commission) from 1969 to 1970. Before that time, he provided research and editorial assistance for the book *How to End the Draft: The Case for an All-Volunteer Army* (National Press, Inc., 1967), authored by five members of Congress. Mr. Herbits also served as staff in both the House and Senate, focusing on the policy and subsequent implementation of the end of the draft. From May 1973 until March 1974, Mr. Herbits was the first special assistant to the Assistant Secretary of Defense (Manpower and Reserve Affairs) for All Volunteer Force Matters. From 1974 to 1975 Mr. Herbits was special assistant to the director of the Presidential Personnel Office under President Ford, and from 1976 to 1977, he served as the special assistant to Secretary of Defense Donald Rumsfeld. While an officer of the Seagram Company, Ltd., Mr. Herbits advised the defense transitions of Secretaries Weinberger and Cheney, and after retirement in 1997, the second Rumseld term. Since September 11, 2001, he has returned to the Department of Defense as a consultant.

Reverend Theodore M. Hesburgh is president emeritus of the University of Notre Dame. Father Hesburgh served as president of the University from 1952 to 1987, ending the longest tenure at that time among presidents of American colleges. He currently chairs the advisory committee of the Kroc Institute for International Peace Studies and is chair emeritus of the Kellogg Institute for International Studies, both housed at the Hesburgh Center for International Studies at Notre Dame. In 2000, he was awarded the Congressional Medal of Honor and in 1964 received the Medal of Freedom from President Lyndon Johnson. Father Hesburgh has been appointed to many important boards and commissions, including the President's Commission on an All-Volunteer Armed Force (the Gates Commission). His stature as an elder statesman in American higher education is reflected in his having received more than 150 honorary degrees—the most ever awarded to a single individual. Father Hesburgh was educated at Notre Dame and the Gregorian University in Rome where he received a Bachelor of Philosophy degree in 1939. He was ordained a priest in 1943 and was awarded his Doctor of Theology from the Catholic University of America in 1944.

Vice Admiral Gerry Hoewing, U.S. Navy, is the 53rd chief of naval personnel. A graduate of Iowa State University, he received his commission in May 1971 through the Navy's ROTC Scholarship Program and was designated a naval aviator in August 1972. Commands at sea include Strike Fighter Squadron EIGHTY-ONE; the fast combat logistics support ship USS Seattle (AOE 3); the aircraft carrier USS *John F. Kennedy* (CV 67); and Carrier Group SEVEN embarked in USS *John C. Stennis* (CVN 74). Vice Admiral Hoewing has served extensively in manpower and personnel-related capacities, including duty with the Bureau of Naval Personnel as head of the Aviation LCDR/Junior Officer Assignment Branch; senior military assistant to the Under Secretary of Defense for Personnel and Readiness; and assistant commander for distribution, Navy Personnel Command. He also served as commander, Navy Personnel Command. As chief of naval personnel he is responsible for planning and programming manpower and personnel resources, budgeting for Navy personnel, managing total force manpower and personnel resources, and assignment of Navy personnel.

Paul F. Hogan is senior economist and vice president at The Lewin Group. Mr. Hogan has conducted extensive research on the economics of the all-volunteer force and on military compensation. His most recent research interests include voluntary assignment systems for military personnel and financial incentives for performance in the military compensation system. Mr. Hogan was the chief analyst for President Reagan's Military Manpower Task Force and has served on the Transportation Research Council Committee on Staffing Standards for FAA Air Traffic Controllers, and on the National Research Council's Committee on Youth Population and Military Service. Mr. Hogan received his undergraduate degree in economics from the University of Virginia, and did his graduate work in applied economics and finance at the W. E. Simon School of Management of the University of Rochester. He is the author of papers appearing in journals such as the *Southern Economic Journal, Health Affairs, Diabetes Care, Compensation and Benefits,* and *Defense Management Journal*, and in National Research Council special reports. He has lectured at Johns Hopkins University, George Mason University, the Naval Postgraduate School, Gettysburg College, and the University of Rochester.

James R. Hosek's current research involves the effect of deployment on retention, the implication of defense transformation for personnel and compensation policy, the dynamic management of military personnel, and the reform of the reserve retirement benefit system. His past work has focused on a range of defense manpower subjects including enlistment, retention, supply of information technology personnel, military/civilian pay comparability, employment and earnings of military wives, military retirement benefit funding, and pay and management reform in the defense civilian work force. His research has been presented to many policy and professional audiences, and he was on the working group of the recent Ninth Quadrennial Review of Military Compensation. At RAND, Mr. Hosek has directed the Defense Manpower Research Center, headed the Economic and Statistics Department, served as a corporate research manager, is a member of the Board of Editors of the RAND Review, and is professor of economics at the Pardee RAND Graduate School. Since 1989 he has been editor-in-chief of the RAND Journal of Economics, which focuses on industrial organization, contracts, and regulation. Mr. Hosek chaired the Economic Advisory Council of the California Institute and was a founding member of the advanced transportation industry consortium. He received a doctorate in economics from the University of Chicago.

Christopher Jehn is vice president, government programs, of Cray Inc. He is an economist, educated at Beloit College and the University of Chicago. After several years on college faculties, Mr. Jehn began his career in military manpower as an analyst at the Center for Naval Analyses, directing studies of Navy recruiting and retention policies. The study and management of military manpower and personnel policy have been a key part of his professional career since then. In 1989 he was vice president and director of the Marine Corps Operations Analysis Group at CNA when the Senate confirmed him as the assistant secretary of defense for force management and personnel. He has also held executive positions at the Institute for Defense Analyses, ICF Kaiser International, Inc., and the Congressional Budget Office. He was the executive director of the National Defense Panel in 1997 and a member of the Commission on Servicemembers and Veterans Transition Assistance (1997–1998).

Ken Krieg serves as director of program analysis and evaluation and leads an organization that provides independent advice to the Secretary of Defense in a range of areas, as well as providing analytic support to planning and resource allocation. He joined the Department of Defense in July 2001 to serve and continues as the executive secretary of the Senior Executive Council, which is comprised of the secretary, deputy secretary, service secretaries, and under secretary of defense for acquisition, technology, and logistics. Prior to joining the Department of Defense, Mr. Krieg was the vice president and general manager of the Office and Consumer Papers Division, International Paper Company. Before joining International Paper, Mr. Krieg worked in a number of defense and foreign policy assignments in Washington, D.C., including positions at the White House, on the National Security Council staff and in the Office of the Secretary of Defense. Mr. Krieg received his BA in History from Davidson College and his Master in Public Policy from the John F. Kennedy School of Government at Harvard University.

Melvin R. Laird is senior counselor for national and international affairs for the Reader's Digest Association, Inc. He was secretary of defense from 1968 to 1973; counselor to the president for domestic affairs from 1973 to 1974; and, for nine terms, was a member of the U.S. House of Representatives, where he was chairman of the Republican House Minority, and served on the Appropriations Committee and the Republican Coordinating Council. Prior to his election to Congress, he served in the Wisconsin Senate and the U.S. Navy in the Pacific Fleet. Mr. Laird has served on numerous boards, including Martin Marietta, Metropolitan Life Insurance Co., and the Public Oversight Board of the American Institute of Certified Public Accountants. He also has been active in many nonprofit organizations, including the American Academy of Diplomacy, the Boys and Girls Clubs of America, the Laird Youth Leadership Foundation, the Laird Foundation for Historic Preservation, and the National Election Commission (chairman). Mr. Laird is a member of Disabled American Veterans and the Order of the Purple Heart. He has a BA from Carleton College, and has received over 300 awards and honorary degrees, including the Presidential

Medal of Freedom in 1974. Mr. Laird is the author of *A House Divided: America's Strategy Gap* (1962). He edited *The Conservative Papers* (1964) and *Republican Papers* (1968).

William A. Navas Jr. has served as the assistant secretary of the Navy for manpower and reserve affairs since July 17, 2001. In this capacity, he acts on matters pertaining to manpower and personnel policy within the Department of the Navy affecting active duty and reserve sailors, Marines, and Department of the Navy civilians. He retired as a major general and his last active duty assignment was as the director, Army National Guard. His prior assignments include service as vice chief of the National Guard Bureau, military executive of the Reserve Forces Policy Board, and deputy assistant secretary of defense/chief of staff for reserve affairs. Commissioned as a regular Army officer in 1965, he served both in Germany and Vietnam. After leaving active duty in 1970, he joined the Puerto Rico Army National Guard where he commanded military police and infantry battalions and a combat engineer company. His military decorations include the Defense Distinguished Service Medal, Army Distinguished Service Medal, Defense Superior Service Medal, Legion of Merit (two awards), Bronze Star Medal, Defense Meritorious Service Medal, Meritorious Service Medal (two awards), Air Medal, Army Commendation Medal (three awards), and numerous state awards.

Walter Y. Oi is an economist at the University of Rochester. He received his PhD from the University of Chicago in 1961 and has been teaching for over 40 years, mostly at the University of Rochester. His principal fields are labor economics and industrial organization. Professor Oi's publications include *Labor as a Quasi-Fixed Factor; A Disneyland Dilemma, Two-Part Tariffs for a Mickey Mouse Monopoly; Costs and Implications of an All-Volunteer Force; Work for Americans with Disabilities; Productivity in the Distributive Trades; Welfare Implications of Invention; and Firm Size and Wages.* He was the director of the economic analysis section of the Military Manpower Policy Study organized by William Gorham (Department of Defense, 1964–1965), and a senior staff economist for the President's Commission on an All-Volunteer Armed Force (the Gates Commission, 1969–1970). He was president of the Western Economics Association International (1992). He is a fellow of the Econometrics Society (1976), fellow of the American Academy of Arts and Sciences (1993), distinguished fellow of the American Economics Association (1995), and recipient of the Secretary of Defense Medal for Outstanding Public Service (1999).

Lieutenant General Garry L. Parks, Deputy Commandant for Manpower and Reserve Affairs, graduated from The Citadel in 1969. After attending The Basic School, he was assigned to the First Marine Division, Republic of Vietnam, where he served as a platoon commander, First Reconnaissance Battalion. General Parks' command tours also include company commander, Marine Corps Recruit Depot (Parris Island, South Carolina); company commander, Second Battalion, Ninth Marines; commanding officer, Recruiting Station (Raleigh, North Carolina); commanding officer, Second Battalion, Fifth Marines; and commanding officer, Ninth Marines. General Parks also served as commanding general, Marine Corps Recruit Depot (San Diego); and commanding general, Marine Corps Recruiting Command. General Parks' staff tours include joint program and budget coordination officer, OIC, III MEF Special Operations Training Group; director, Marine Corps Presentation Team; and chief of staff, Marine Forces Pacific. General Parks attended the Infantry Officers Advanced Course (commandant's list); Marine Corps Command and Staff College (honor graduate); and the Naval War College. He has a Master of Arts degree from Pepperdine University and the Naval War College. General Parks' decorations include the Defense Superior Service Medal, Legion of Merit, Bronze Star Medal with Combat "V," Meritorious Service Medal, Navy and Marine Corps Commendation Award, Navy Achievement Medal, and Combat Action Ribbon.

Aline Quester has worked on military manpower and personnel issues at the Center for Naval Analyses for the past two decades. While most of her work has been for the Marine Corps and the Navy, she has also undertaken studies for the Department of Defense and the National Science Foundation. Trained as an economist, her degrees are from Wellesley College and Tufts University. Her other experience includes work as a senior staff economist for the Council of Economic Advisors under President Reagan and teaching positions at Boston University, Cornell University, and the State University of New York College at Cortland. Dr. Quester is the author of many articles and papers in professional journals.

Martha Farnsworth Riche was confirmed by the U.S. Senate on October 6, 1994, as director of the U.S. Bureau of the Census, and served until January 1998. Through Farnsworth Riche Associates, Dr. Riche lectures, writes, and consults on demographic changes and their effects on policies, programs, and products. Dr. Riche began her career as an economist with the U.S. Bureau of Labor Statistics. In 1978, she became a founding editor of *American Demographics*, the nation's first magazine devoted to interpreting demographic and economic data for corporate and public executives. In 1991, she became director of policy studies for the Population Reference Bureau, a nonprofit organization devoted to educating the public about the demographic component of policy issues. A fellow of the American Statistical Association, she is the author of more than 200 articles, papers, and publications in academic and business journals.

Bernard D. Rostker rejoined RAND as a senior fellow in January 2001, after serving in the Department of Defense as the under secretary of defense for personnel and readiness (2000–2001) and the 25th under secretary of the army (1998–2000). Prior to those appointments, Dr. Rostker served as assistant secretary of the navy for manpower and reserve affairs (1994–1998). In 1996 he was also named special assistant to the Deputy Secretary of Defense for Gulf War illnesses—an assignment he continued until leaving government service in 2001. Since returning to RAND for the third time in 2001, Dr. Rostker has divided his time between leading a number of RAND projects and writing a comprehensive history of the all-volunteer force that begins with the early transition period and continues to the present. While in government service, Dr. Rostker received a number of awards including the Distinguished Service Medal from four agencies. He is also a fellow of the National Academy of Public Administration. Dr. Rostker received a Bachelor of Science from New York University in 1964 where he was a distinguished military graduate of the ROTC program and commissioned as a second lieutenant in the Army Reserve. He also holds master's and doctorate degrees in economics from Syracuse University.

Donald H. Rumsfeld serves as the U.S. secretary of defense. Secretary Rumsfeld was born in Chicago, Illinois. He attended Princeton University on scholarship and was captain of the varsity wrestling team. From 1954 to 1957, Secretary Rumsfeld served in the U.S. Navy as a naval aviator. In 1962, at the age of 30, he was elected to the U.S. House of Representatives from Illinois. He was reelected to Congress three times. In 1969, Secretary Rumsfeld resigned from Congress to serve as director of the Office of Economic Opportunity, assistant to the President, and a member of the President's cabinet. Later, he served as director of the Economic Stabilization Program, and then as U.S. ambassador to the North Atlantic Treaty Organization in Brussels, Belgium. In 1974, President Ford appointed Mr. Rumsfeld as the White House chief of staff. From 1975 to 1977, he served as the 13th U.S. secretary of defense, the youngest in the country's history. Secretary Rumsfeld was awarded the nation's highest civilian award, the Presidential Medal of Freedom, in 1977. Following his first tenure at the Defense Department, Mr. Rumsfeld had a successful career as a business executive and continued public service in a variety of posts. In 2001, Mr. Rumsfeld was asked by President Bush to return to government service, as the 21st secretary of defense.

Paul R. Sackett is a professor of psychology at the University of Minnesota. He received his PhD in Industrial and Organizational Psychology at Ohio State University in 1979. Professor Sackett served as the editor of *Personnel Psychology* from 1984 to 1990, as president of the Society for Industrial and Organizational Psychology, as co-chair of the Joint Committee on the Standards for Educational and Psychological Testing, as a member of the National Research Council's Board on Testing and Assessment, as chair of the American Psychological Association's Committee on Psychological Tests and Assessments, and as chair of the Association's Board of Scientific Affairs. His research interests revolve around various aspects of psychological testing and assessment in workplace settings. He chaired the National Research Council's Committee on the Youth Population and Military Recruitment from 1999 to 2003.

Congressman Edward L. Schrock represents Virginia's second district in the United States Congress. The second district includes the Virginia Beach area and large parts of Hampton Roads. Congressman Schrock serves on the House Armed Services, Budget, Small Business, and Government Reform Committees. He was commissioned as an ensign in the United States Navy in 1964. While in the Navy, he served two tours in Vietnam. Congressman Schrock retired from the Navy in 1988 with the rank of captain. He served as a member of the Virginia State Senate until his election to the 107th Congress in 2000. Among the primary reasons he sought a seat in Congress was to ensure that the United States military remained the finest in the world and to preserve and improve the quality of life for men and women serving in uniform and for their families. Congressman Schrock earned his undergraduate degree from Alderson-Broaddus College in 1964 and earned his master's degree in public relations from American University in 1975.

Curtis J. Simon received his BA in Anthropology from the College of William and Mary in 1981 and his PhD in Economics from the State University of New York at Binghamton in 1985. His initial work examined the relationship between unemployment and industrial diversity, extending this to include the role of wages in both the long run (with Charles Diamond) and short run (with Clark Nardinelli). He has also studied the role of internal labor markets (with John Warner), the interaction between human capital accumulation and college admissions standards (with Cheonsik Woo), customer racial discrimination (with Clark Nardinelli), and the interaction between city growth and human capital (with Clark Nardinelli). As part of a research team assembled by John Warner, he contributed to a Defense Department report, *Enlistment Supply in the 1990s: A Study of the Navy College Fund and Other Enlistment Incentive Programs*, and an article entitled "The Military Recruiting Productivity Slowdown: Resources, Opportunity Costs, and the Tastes of Youth," published in *Defense and Peace Economics*.

R. Wayne Spruell serves as the principal director to the Deputy Assistant Secretary of Defense for Reserve Affairs, Manpower and Personnel. In addition to principal director, he served as director for manpower requirements and programs and as program analyst in the Office of the Assistant Secretary of Defense for Reserve Affairs since 1985. Mr. Spruell received a BA in History from the Virginia Military Institute in 1968 and an MA in History from Georgetown University in 1981. In 1990 he attended the executive leadership course at the Federal Executive Institute. He served on active duty with the U.S. Marine Corps from 1968 to 1971, including service in the Republic of Vietnam, and completed 20 years in the Marine Corps Reserve, retiring in 1992 at the grade of lieutenant colonel after 23 years of service. Mr. Spruell's civilian career as a federal government employee includes service as an operations officer and intelligence analyst with the Central Intelligence Agency from 1972 until 1981. From 1981 to 1985, he was a training programs specialist with the Department of the Army, prior to assuming a position in the Office of the Assistant Secretary of Defense for Reserve Affairs. He was selected as a member of the Senior Executive Service in 1999.

Robert K. Steel is a vice chairman of The Goldman Sachs Group, Inc. He joined the firm in 1976 and served in the Equities Division of Goldman Sachs in Chicago until his relocation to London in 1986 to work in Equity Capital Markets. Mr. Steel became a partner in 1988 and shortly thereafter assumed the position of head of the Equities Division in Europe. In 1994, he relocated to New York and served as cohead of the Equities Division from 1998 to 2001, then as sole head until his appointment as a vice chairman of the firm in 2002. Mr. Steel is also a member of the New York Stock Exchange where he has served on various committees, and is a member of the Board of Directors of the Securities Industry Association. He is the vice chairman of the Board of Trustees of Duke University and is the chairman of the Duke University Management Company, the organization responsible for managing the University's endowment and other investment assets. He is a trustee of the Windward School and a director of The After-School Corporation. He received his undergraduate degree from Duke University and his MBA from the University of Chicago.

Vice Admiral Patricia A. Tracey is director, Navy staff. She serves the Chief and Vice Chief of Naval Operations and directs the Navy headquarters support functions for 1,200 personnel. Prior to this assignment, from 1999 to mid-2001, Admiral Tracey was the deputy assistant secretary of defense for military personnel policy, Washington, D.C. She has served in numerous manpower and training positions including chief of naval education and training and director of naval training for the Chief of Naval Operations (1996–1998); commander, Naval Training Center, Great Lakes (1995–1996); director for manpower and personnel, J-1, on the Joint Staff (1993–1995); head of the Enlisted Plans and Community Branch on the Chief of Naval Personnel's staff (1989–1990); and commander of the Naval Training Center at Treasure Island (1986–1998). Admiral Tracey assumed command of the Naval Station Long Beach, California, in 1990; following her command tour she reported as a fellow to the Chief of Naval Operations' Strategic Studies Group at the Naval War College. The Admiral's personal decorations include two Defense Distinguished Service Medals, the Distinguished Service Medal, three Legion of Merit Medals, three Meritorious Service Medals, and the French Legion d'Honneur. Admiral Tracey holds a Bachelor of Arts degree in Mathematics from the College of New Rochelle and a master's degree, with distinction, in operations research from the Naval Postgraduate School.

Rear Admiral Kenneth T. Venuto is the assistant commandant for human resources, United States Coast Guard. In this capacity, he is responsible for the leadership and management oversight of all aspects of the human resource systems and infrastructure supporting Coast Guard active duty, reserve, civilian, retired, and auxiliary personnel. As a flag officer, he was previously assigned as director of operations policy. Rear Admiral Venuto has served on board seven different cutters including command of three. His significant staff assignments include executive assistant to the Commandant, executive assistant to the Assistant Commandant for Human Resources, and training officer at Training Center Yorktown, Virginia. Rear Admiral Venuto graduated with high honors from the United States Coast Guard Academy in 1973. He earned a Master in Business Administration from the University of Massachusetts in 1978 and was a distinguished graduate of the National War College in 1994. He also completed a U.S. and Russian military executive development program at the John F. Kennedy School of Government at Harvard University. His awards include three Legions of Merit, three Meritorious Service Medals, four Commendation Medals, and an Achievement Medal.

General John W. Vessey Jr., U.S. Army (Retired) began his military career in 1939 as a private in the Minnesota National Guard; he ended it in 1985 in his second term as chairman of the Joint Chiefs of Staff. Following combat service in World War II, General Vessey had a long association with North Atlantic Treaty Forces. He also had extensive service in East Asia with combat tours in Vietnam and Laos, and additional service in Korea, Thailand, and the Philippines. His senior assignments included service as the Army's deputy chief of staff for operations and plans, commander United Nations Command and U.S. Forces Korea, and vice chief of staff of the Army. General Vessey continued to serve the nation after retirement. He was presidential emissary to Hanoi (1987–1993) and had long service on the Defense Science Board and Defense Policy Board. His numerous military decorations include the Distinguished Service Cross; the Army, Navy, Air Force, and Defense Distinguished Service Medals; and the Purple Heart. In 1992, President Bush awarded him the nation's highest civilian award, the Presidential Medal of Freedom. His civilian education earned him degrees from the University of Maryland and The George Washington University.

John P. White is presently on the faculty of the John F. Kennedy School of Government at Harvard University and is the managing partner of Global Technology Partners, LLC. He served as U.S. deputy secretary of defense from 1995 to 1997; deputy director of the Office of Management and Budget from 1978 to 1981; assistant secretary of defense for manpower, reserve affairs, and logistics from 1977 to 1978; and as a lieutenant in the United States Marine Corps from 1959 to 1961. His extensive private sector experience includes service as chairman and CEO of Interactive Systems Corporation from 1981 to 1988 and, following its sale to the Eastman Kodak Company in 1988, as a vice president of Kodak until 1992. In nine years with the RAND Corporation, he was the senior vice president for national security research programs and a member of the Board of Trustees. He serves as a director of IRG International, Inc., the Institute for Defense Analyses, the Concord Coalition, and the Center for Excellence in Government. He is a member of the Director of Central Intelligence's National Security Advisory Panel and the Council on Foreign Relations. Dr. White holds a Bachelor of Science degree from Cornell University and an MA and PhD in Economics from the Maxwell Graduate School, Syracuse University.

Congresswoman Heather Wilson is the first woman veteran in American history to serve in Congress. She was first elected in a special election in 1998. Her district is centered in Albuquerque and she serves on both the Energy and Commerce Committee and the Armed Services Committee. A distinguished graduate of the U.S. Air Force Academy in 1982, Congresswoman Wilson was a Rhodes scholar and earned her master's degree (1984) and doctorate (1985) in international relations from Oxford University in England. As an Air Force officer she worked with our NATO allies and in the United Kingdom. After leaving the Air Force in 1989, she became director for European defense policy and arms control on the National Security Council staff at the White House. In 1991, Congresswoman Wilson founded Keystone International Inc. in Albuquerque to work with senior executives in large American defense and scientific corporations with business development and program planning work in the United States and Russia. She was a cabinet secretary of the New Mexico Children, Youth, and Families Department from 1995 to 1998.

John D. Winkler was appointed deputy assistant secretary of defense for reserve affairs, manpower and personnel on August 6, 2001. He serves as the principal staff assistant and advisor to the Assistant Secretary of Defense for Reserve Affairs for all National Guard and reserve manpower, personnel, and compensation policies. He led the department's comprehensive *Review of Reserve Component Contributions to National Defense*, which proposed new ideas for building and rebalancing force capabilities and for creating flexibility in management that can assist the department in meeting it transformation goals,

★369

EDITORS AND CONTRIBUTORS

including establishment of a "continuum of service." Dr. Winkler was previously a senior behavioral scientist at RAND and associate director of the manpower and training program at the RAND Arroyo Center, a federally funded research and development center for the U.S. Army. He received his undergraduate degree from the University of Pennsylvania in 1975 and a PhD in Social Psychology from Harvard University in 1980.

Paul Wolfowitz is the 28th deputy secretary of defense. Prior to this appointment, he served as dean and professor of international relations at the Paul H. Nitze School of Advanced International Studies of the Johns Hopkins University. From 1989 to 1993, Dr. Wolfowitz served as under secretary of defense for policy. During the Reagan administration, Dr. Wolfowitz served for three years as U.S. ambassador to Indonesia. Prior to that posting, he served as assistant secretary of state for East Asian and Pacific affairs. He has held other senior positions at the Departments of State and Defense. Among his many awards for public service, he has received the Presidential Citizen's Medal, the Department of Defense's Distinguished Public Service Medal and Distinguished Civilian Service Medal, the Department of State's Distinguished Honor Award, and the Arms Control and Disarmament Agency's Distinguished Honor Award. Dr. Wolfowitz has taught at Yale University, the Johns Hopkins University, and the National War College. He has written widely on national strategy and foreign policy issues. He received a bachelor's degree from Cornell University in mathematics in 1965, and a doctorate in political science from the University of Chicago in 1972.

★ ★ ★ ★ ★ ★ ★ ★ ★ ★ ★

GLOSSARY

AFQT	Armed Forces Qualification Test. A composite of four subtests from the Armed Services Vocational Aptitude Battery that measures math and verbal skills (aptitude) and is used to determine enlistment eligibility. Scores on the composite are expressed in the following aptitude categories (percentiles): I (93–99), II (65–92), IIIA (50–64), IIIB (31–49), IV (10–30), and V (below 10). AFQT categories I–IIIA represent those potential recruits who score above average (50th percentile) on the AFQT and are often referred to as "high quality." The services accept no category V individuals by law and very few category IV individuals.
ASVAB	Armed Services Vocational Aptitude Battery. A standardized battery of math, verbal, science, and technical tests (a total of eight subtests) that are combined in various ways to form composites. These composites are used by all the military services to determine enlistment eligibility (AFQT) and job placement.
AVF	All-Volunteer Force
BAH	Basic Allowance for Housing
BAS	Basic Allowance for Subsistence
COLA	Cost-of-Living Allowance
Combat Arms	Units and soldiers directly involved in the conduct of actual war fighting such as air defense artillery, armor/cavalry, aviation, infantry, special forces, and the corps of engineers.
Combat Service Support	Units and soldiers that perform personnel, administrative, and logistics support in areas such as finance, medical, ordnance, and transportation.
Combat Support	Units and soldiers that provide critical operational assistance to combat arms such as the chemical corps, civil affairs, psychological operations, military intelligence, the military police corps, and the signal corps.
DMDC	Defense Manpower Data Center

★

DOD	Department of Defense
DOPMA	Defense Officer Personnel Management Act
DSB	Defense Science Board
ESGR	Employer Support of the Guard and Reserve
FY	Fiscal Year
GATB	General Aptitude Test Battery
GED	General Educational Development
Goldwater-Nichols Department of Defense Reorganization Act of 1986	The Goldwater-Nichols Act, sponsored by Senator Barry Goldwater and Representative Bill Nichols, resulted in the most significant reorganization of DOD since the of National Security Act of 1947. Operational authority was centralized through the chairman of the Joint Chiefs and the chairman was designated as the principal military advisor to the president, National Security Council, and secretary of defense. The act established the position of vice-chairman of the Joint Chiefs and streamlined the operational chain of command from the president to the secretary of defense to the unified commanders.
HOPT	Hands-On Performance Testing
IMT	Initial Military Training
I/O Model	Institution/Occupation Model
IRR	Individual Ready Reserve. A manpower pool consisting of individuals who have had some training, have previously served in the active component or in the selected reserve, and have some period of their military service obligation or other contractual obligation remaining. Members may voluntarily participate in training for retirement points and promotion with or without pay.
JPM	Job Performance Measurement
JROTC	Junior Reserve Officer Training Corps
Misnorming (of the ASVAB)	During the 1976 to 1980 period, the ASVAB was incorrectly calibrated to previous versions of the test. As a result, test scores were inflated and more than 250,000 low-aptitude personnel, who normally would not have been eligible for entrance into the armed forces, were erroneously enlisted.
NAEP	National Assessment of Educational Progress
NCESGR	National Committee for Employer Support of the Guard and Reserve
NCO	Noncommissioned Officer
NRC	National Research Council
NSC	National Security Council
OEF	Operation Enduring Freedom
OIF	Operation Iraqi Freedom
OMB	Office of Management and Budget
ONE	Operation Noble Eagle
PAYS	Partnership for Youth Success
PCMC	President's Commission on Military Compensation (also referred to as the Zwick Commission)
PCS	Permanent Change of Station

PRC	Presidential Reserve Call-Up. This authority is a provision of public law (U.S. Code, title 10, section 2304) that provides the president a means to activate, without a declaration of national emergency, not more than 200,000 members of the selected reserve and the individual ready reserve (of whom not more than 30,000 may be members of the individual ready reserve) for not more than 270 days to meet the support requirements of any operational mission.
QDR	Quadrennial Defense Review. Required by legislation, every four years the secretary of defense must conduct a comprehensive review of the national defense strategy, force structure, force modernization plans, infrastructure, budget plans, and other elements of the defense program and policies. The purpose of the review is to determine and express the defense strategy of the United States and establish a defense program for the next 20 years. Each review is to be conducted in consultation with the chairman of the Joint Chiefs of Staff.
QoL	Quality of Life
QRMC	Quadrennial Review of Military Compensation
REDUX	Military Retirement Reform Act of 1986
Renorming (of the ASVAB)	Because test scores by themselves have little meaning, norms allow of the ASVAB interpretation of an individual's score by comparing it to the scores of others in a reference population. Because the ASVAB was last normalized to the 1980 18 to 23-year-old civilian population, it did not truly reflect the cognitive ability of current military applicants and recruits compared to today's population because of increases in national achievement test scores, growth in high school and college attendance rates, and shifts in youth demographics. New norms to the ASVAB based on the 1997 youth population were introduced on July 1, 2004.
Reserve component	The reserve components of the U.S. Armed Forces are: the Army National Guard of the United States, the U.S. Army Reserve, the U.S. Naval Reserve, the U.S. Marine Corps Reserve, the Air National Guard of the United States, the U.S. Air Force Reserve, and the U.S. Coast Guard Reserve (part of the Department of Homeland Security). The Army and Air National guards are unique in that they have both a federal and state mission; the comprise the organized militias and can be used to enforce state laws. Most individuals in the reserve components are members of either the selected reserve or the individual ready reserve.
RMC	Regular Military Compensation
ROTC	Reserve Officer Training Corps
S&I	Special and Incentive
SD	Standard Deviation
Selected reserve	Those units and individuals within the ready reserve designated by their respective services and approved by the Joint Chiefs of Staff as essential to contingency or wartime missions. All selected reservists are in an active status. They are paid reservists, train a minimum of 38 days per year, and can be called for use by the president. The selected reserve also includes persons performing initial active duty for training.
SWAT	Special Weapons and Tactics

TDA	Table of Distribution and Allowances
Thrift Savings Plan	A federal-government-sponsored retirement savings and investment plan for civilians who are employed by the United States Government and for members of the uniformed services.
Tiers 1, 2, and 3	A description of an education credential applied to applicants for military service. Research shows that education credential is the best predictor of first-term attrition (separation before completion of the first term of enlistment). Based on predicted attrition, DOD places a credential in one of three groups or tiers. Tier 1 is given the highest enlistment priority and is for high school diploma graduates. Tier 2 includes alternate secondary school credentials, such as the General Educational Development certificate. Tier 3 is "no credential" or high school dropouts.
TIG	Time in Grade
TIS	Time in Service
TISS	Triangle Institute for Security Studies
Title 5	United States Code, Government Organizations and Employees, contains the laws relating to the organization of the government of the United States and to its civilian officers and employees. Title 5 was enacted by Public Law 89-554 on September 6, 1966.
Title 10	United States Code, Armed Forces, contains the law governing the armed forces of the United States and provides for the organization of the Department of Defense, including the military departments and the reserve components. The law relating to the administration of the National Guard is contained in title 32, United States Code. Titles 10 and 32 were enacted into law on August 10, 1956.
TRADOC	U.S. Army Training and Doctrine Command
TRIAD	A three-prong increase to military compensation, in the FY 2000 National Defense Authorization Act, which included (1) across-the-board pay increases, (2) pay raises targeted to particular pay grades and years-of-service cells in the military pay table, and (3) repeal of the Military Retirement Reform Act of 1986, restoring (increasing) military retirement benefits to amounts designated by the formula used prior to 1986.
TRICARE	A DOD regional managed health care program for members of the uniformed services, their families, retirees, and other eligible beneficiaries.
UIMS	USERRA Information Management System
Up or out	This military promotion policy requires an individual to be promoted to the next highest grade within a specified period of time in order to remain in the active duty military service.
USAAC	U.S. Army Accessions Command
USERRA	Uniformed Services Employment and Reemployment Rights Act
USJFCOM	U.S. Joint Forces Command
WAC	Women's Army Corps
YATS	Youth Attitude Tracking Study
YOS	Year of Service

INDEX

Abrams, Creighton, 335–36, 339–40
accession requirements, 58
access to battle space, concerns with, 311–12
activation, preparation of, time taken off work
    for, 184, 185f
active duty force
    age distribution of, 131, 131f
    attitudes of, 216–26
    disparities with reserve, efforts to correct,
        192–94
    diversity in, 131–32, 132f–133f
    integration with reserve force, 194–98
    sizing, 80–82
adaptability, transformation and, 318
adult roles, delay of, 126–28
advertising, 145–46, 158
    budgets for, 66–67
    DSB on, 67–68
    to older targets, 139n21
affiliation programs, 301–3
Afghanistan War, 21
African Americans
    in active duty force versus civilian work
        force, 131–32, 132f–133f
    and higher education, 125
    high school graduation rates of, 101f
    share of U.S. population, 118, 118f
Air Force
    and conscription, 35
    educational requirements in, 123
    mobilization of reserves in, 196
    pay variation in, 269, 270t
    promotion structure in, 86n21
    subculture of, 265
    in war on terrorism, 322
airline industry, and reserve force, 187

allies, and force size requirements, 59
all-volunteer force (AVF), xi–xii
    commentary on, 45–51
    debate on, 4–5, 16–21
    De Leon on, 348–49
    Dorn on, 343–45
    early troubles of, 12–13, 35, 48, 57
    establishment of, 6, 15–21
    functional and social imperatives of,
        reservist attitudes on, 221–24, 223t
    future of, 255–96; Chu on, 350–52;
        commentary on, 317–28; Dorn on,
        345–46; Vessey on, 340–42;White on, 43
    Keane on, 12
    Laird on, 3–7
    reputation and effectiveness of, 20, 155, 210;
        and recruitment, 67; reservist attitudes
        on, 216–18, 217f, 221, 221f–222f; Rostker
        on, 24; Wolfowitz on, 333
    Rumsfeld on, vii–ix
    success of, causes of, 24–25
    Vessey on, 335–42
    White on, 33–44
Anderegg, George, 16
Anderson, Martin, 15–21, 46
Arab-American Linguist Program, 303
Arends, Les, 6
Armed Forces Qualification Test (AFQT), 48, 124
    definition of, 371
    and force size, 59
    and job performance, 93–95, 95f, 149–50
    and recruit quality, 90–91, 91t
    renorming, 105–6, 105t
    and training performance, 92–93, 92f, 148–49
Armed Services Vocational Aptitude Battery
    (ASVAB), 149

definition of, 371
and hands-on performance, 94–95, 94*f*
misnorming episode, 22, 35, 48, 61, 98;
  definition of, 372
renorming, 152–53; definition of, 373
Armor, David J., 90–108
Army
  and establishment of AVF, 13
  subculture of, 265
Army Accessions Command, 146
Army Reserve
  history of, 200–201
  structure of, 202
Asch, Beth J., 257–96
assignment lengths, transformation and, 262
assignment system
  current, advantages of, 275–76
  incentive program for, 283–84
  pay differentials and, 75
attrition
  Army, 146
  high school completion and, 96–97, 97*t*
  Oi on, 48–49
  in reserve force, 246*f*
  White on, 42
auction, in assignment incentive program, 75,
  283–84
auxiliaries, volunteer, expansion of, 303
awards, 282–83

balance, in compensation structure, 39
base closings, and quality of life, 65–66–70
Basic Allowance for Housing (BAH), 79
basic pay, 71–75
Bayh, Evan, 81
Binkin, Marty, 26
Blackstone, William, 212
blended units, 298, 314–15
body-bag syndrome, 211
bonuses. *See* special and incentive pays
Brandenberg, Jim, 339
bridging role, of reservists, 207–8, 213–14
Brown, Charles, 28
Brown, George, 335, 339
Brown, Reginald J., 237–41
Buchanan, Pat, 16–17
Burk, James, 28
burnout, 326
Burns, Arthur, 46
Bush, George H. W., 21, 208
Bush, George W., 242
Bush, Thomas L., 297–306

call-ups, of reserve components
  by career field, 248*f*
  duration of, 247–49, 248*t*
  multiple, 247*f*
capabilities-based planning, 260–61, 292, 312–13,
  320
careerists, definition of, 59
career lengths

Oi on, 49
  transformation and, 262
  Vessey on, 341
career tracks, multiple, transformation and, 263
Carter, James E., 35–36
Cavin, Dennis D., 142–47
Cebrowski, Arthur K., 308–16
charter schools, 104
children
  of military personnel, 134–36
  See also dependents
Chu, David S. C., 343, 350–52
  on advertising, 68
  on civilianization, 82
  on continuum of service, 80
  on status of AVF, 36–37
  on veterans in population, 126
citizenship programs, 68
citizen-soldier image, 212, 309
Civil Air Patrol, 303
civilian-acquired skills, 325, 327
  in continuum of service, 302
  reservists and, 203
civilianization, 82–83
civilian market
  Cavin on, 144–45
  competing with, 82–83
  monitoring, 63–64
civilian participation programs, 301–3, 326–27
civilian professionals, career, 348
civil-military gap, 206–36, 308
  debate on, 208–11
  TISS survey on, 216–26
  Vessey on, 340–41
Clements, William, 13
cliff vesting, 77
Clinton, William J., 208
Coast Guard, 159–63
  functions of, 160
Coast Guard Auxiliary, 303
cognitive skills, of recruitment cohort, 103, 106
Cohen, William, 67
cohesion, in military culture, 265
Cold War era
  force planning in, 310–12
  See also post-Cold War world
college enrollments, 121
  and recruitment, 64
  trends in, 102–3, 125
College First program, 128
college students, in reserve programs, 81–82
combat arms, definition of, 371
combat service support, definition of, 371
combat support, definition of, 371
command climate, and recruitment/retention, 69
commissaries, access to, for reservists and
  families, 194
community partnerships, 303
compensation, 70–71, 71*t*, 263–76, 267*t*
  Carter and, 35–36
  Chu on, 350–51

current system: advantages of, 274–76;
    assumptions of, 320
  Dent on, 9
  Dorn on, 345
  increases in, 74–75
  Moskos on, 28–29
  new force-planning paradigm and, 315
  Oi on, 49
  and recruitment, 63–64, 63f
  for reservists, 80–81, 193–94, 203–4, 240
  by service and year of service, 268f
  structure: flexibility of, 266–71; and
    performance, 75–77
  traditional structure of, 39–41
  transformation of, 276–86; goals of, 287;
    obstacles to, 277–79
  variation in, 269, 270t
  Vessey on, 342
  White on, 35–36
  years-of-service distribution, by occupational
    code, 272t–273t
conscription
  alternative views of, 23–24, 34–35
  Laird on, 6
  and reserve force, 170–73
  See also draft
conscription tax, 22, 46–47
Constitution, and civil-military gap, 206
continuum of service, 80, 297–306
  advantages of, 307
  definition of, 298
  flexibility in, 304–6
contracting. See outsourcing
controlled-grade accounting, 304
cost-of-living allowances (COLAs), 266–67
costs
  of advertising, 66–67
  of assignment incentive program, 284
  of draft, 22, 46–47
  of establishment of AVF, 9–10
  personnel, insensitivity to, 41–43
  of recruiting, 59–60, 146
  of transformation, 321
  Wolfowitz on, 333
Crone, Gary L., 297–306
culture
  of Army, 200
  change in, definition of, 259
  and civil-military gap, 209–10
  definition of, 263
  joint, need for, 264–65
  military, 214; elements of, 265;
    transformation and, 263, 309–10
  and rebalancing, 308–9
  reservist attitudes on, 224–25, 225f
  transformation of, 204–5
Curtis, Tom, 46

databases, recommended
  of civilian-acquired skills, 302, 327
  of reservist employers, 188

decentralization, 320
Defense Integrated Military Human Resource
    System, 302
Defense Manpower Data Center (DMDC),
    recommendations for, 288
Defense Officer Personnel Management Act
    (DOPMA), 76
Defense Planning Guidance report /, 106
Defense Science Board, Task Force on Human
    Resources Strategy report, 39, 43, 67–68,
    277, 341
Defense Transformation for the 21st Century
    Act, 80
Defense Wireless Service Initiative, 303 degree
    ratio, 123
De Leon, Rudy, 348–49
demographic trends, 99–100, 102–4, 109–41
  commentary on, 154–59
  generational changes, 126–28
  global, 113–17
Dent, Frederick B., 8–11
Department of Defense (DOD)
  dependent schools, access to, for reservists
    and families, 194
  and establishment of AVF, 5
  White on, 39
dependents
  DOD schools for, access for reservists, 194
  military definition of, 134
deployment tempo, in war on terrorism, 322
developed nations, population trends in,
    115–16, 116f–117f
discipline, in military culture, 265
diversity
  active duty force versus civilian work force,
    131–32, 132f–133f
  and advertising, 146
  Navy and, 150
  of youth population, 120–21
Dominguez, Michael L., 322–25
Dorn, Ed, 343–47
draft
  Anderson on, 15
  costs of, 22, 46–47
  Dent on, 9
  Friedman on, 11
  Oi on, 46
  reinstitution of, 13–14
  and reserve force, 201–2
  standby, 10
  University of Chicago on, 23
  See also conscription
Duncan, Stephen M., 211–12, 214
duty-days, definition of, 171

economic issues, reservist attitudes on, 218–19,
    219f
education attainment
  and attrition, 96–97, 97t
  of recruits, 61–62

trends in, 100–102, 101*f*, 102, 121–25, 123*f*, 157–58
education programs, 68
Eisenhower, Dwight D., 16, 21
employers of reservists, 81, 169–90, 204, 240
   advance notice given to, 184, 184*f*
   benefits provided by, 177*f*
   definition of, 173–74
   economic impact on, 184–87
   firm size, 173, 174*f*
   with large complements of reservists, 187
   legal responsibilities of, 178–79
   motivation of, 176–84
   problems with, 179–84; expectations versus reality of, 179–81, 180*f*; types of, 181–83, 182*f*
   recommendations for, 188–89, 251
   research directions for, 187–89
   responses of, 174–76
   support by, 228; levels of, 175–76, 176*f*, 182*f*, 183; for time to prepare for activation, 184, 185*f*
   transformation and, 324–25
end strength
   after Vietnam War, 336
   recommendations for, 194, 325–26
   in reserve components, 246*f*
   White on, 33
enlisted
   education trends among, 121–24
   pay, 267*t*, 268*f*; variation in, 269, 270*t*; years-of-service distribution, by occupational code, 272*t*
   ratio to officers, 60
   retention rates, 73–74, 74*f*
equipment, for reserve force, 192–94, 196
escalator principle, 178
esprit de corps
   in military culture, 265
   and recruitment/retention, 68
ethnicity, trends in, 118–21
exit exams, 102, 104, 124, 152
expectations, 158–59
   for reserve force, 199–200
experience
   versus aptitude, 95, 95*f*
   distribution of, 59–60, 60*t*
   gap in, 210–11
extended service, opportunities for, 300–301
Exter, Thomas G., 136

family support, 204
   need for, 134–36
   recommendations for, 251
Feaver, Peter D., 206–36
fighting, Vessey on, 338–39, 341
Filer, David P., 206–36
flexibility
   characteristics of, 318–19
   in compensation structure, 39, 72–73
   in continuum of service, 304–6

in manpower management, need for, 279–81
   and reserve force, 251
   system-wide, need for, 319
force planning
   in Cold War era, 310–12
   new paradigms in, 312–15
   shift in, 260–61, 292, 312–13
force size requirements, 58–62
   Dorn on, 343–47
force structure, rebalancing, 308–16
Ford, Gerald, 3
Foster, John, 67
France
   population of, 115*t*
   population trends in, 116, 117*f*
Franklin, Benjamin, 23
free riding, 283
frequency of use
   definition of, 245
   of reserve force, 245, 247*t*
Friedman, Milton, 8, 11, 46
   Anderson on, 16
   and Gates Commission, 9, 19
   Herbits on, 13
   Rostker on, 23, 26
   Rumsfeld and, vii

Galbraith, John Kenneth, 16
Garment, Leonard, 16
Gates, Thomas S., 5, 9–10, 19, 46
Gates Commission, 8–14
   Laird on, 4–5
   makeup of, 9, 19
   Rostker on, 22–32
   social welfare argument of, 22–23
   staff of, 9
gender tracking, 134
General Aptitude Test Battery (GATB), and civilian training performance, 92–93, 93*f*
General Educational Development (GED) certificate, 61–62
   and attrition, 96–97, 97*t*
   trends in, 123–24
generational changes, 126–28
Germany, youth population in, 113–14, 114*f*
GI Bill program, 128, 309
global demographic trends, 113–17
G-7 nations, 137n2
   population distribution in, 113, 113*f*
Goldman Sachs, 175
Goldwater, Barry, 16
Goldwater-Nichols Department of Defense Reorganization Act, 261, 264
   definition of, 372
Gotz, Glenn, 188–89
Greenspan, Alan, 9, 16, 19
Gronke, Paul, 206–36
group-level awards, problems with, 283
Gruenther, Alfred, 9, 19

Haig, Alexander, 5

Hall, Thomas F., 241–52
Hamiton, Alexander, 24
hands-on performance testing (HOPT), 93–95, 94f, 149
Hansen, Ronald, 47
health care coverage
    assistance with, 186
    employer provision of, 176, 177f
    USERRA on, 178
Hebert, Eddie, 6
Helmly, James R., 199–205
Herbits, Stephen E., 9, 11–14
Herman Group, 150
Hesburgh, Theodore M., 8, 14
high-quality recruit, definition of, 91
high school completion
    alternative credentials for, 97, 104–5, 124
    and attrition, 96–97, 97t
    trends in, 100–102, 101f, 121–24
high school diploma, 61–62
    and recruit quality, 90–91
Hispanic population
    in active duty force versus civilian work force, 131–32, 132f–133f
    definition of, 119, 138n9
    demographic trends among, 119, 119t
    education trends among, 121–22
    and higher education, 125
    high school graduation rates of, 101f, 102
    and recruitment, 65
    recruitment among, 155
    share of U.S. population, 118, 118f
    underrepresentation in military, 132
Ho, Ming, 145
Hoewing, Gerry, 148–53
Hogan, Paul F., 57–89
Hollings, Fritz, 15
home schooling, 104, 124, 157–58
homosexuals in military, 209
    reservist attitudes on, 225–26
Hook Commission, 274
Hosek, James R., 57, 257–96
House Armed Services Committee, 6
housing allowance, 79
Humphrey, Hubert, 18
Huntington, Samuel, 5, 214
hybrid units, 298, 314–15

immigration. See migration
incentives
    Gates Commission on, 10
    at organizational versus individual levels, 288
    See also special and incentive pays
individual ready reserve (IRR), 302–3
    definition of, 372
influence behavior, 282
information-age force
    Navas on, 167
    as voluntary, 201–2

in-grade progress, variation in, transformation and, 262
in-kind benefits, 78–80
innovation
    in manpower management, 280–81
    obstacles to, 319–20
    in recruitment, 147
institution-occupation (I/O) model, 27, 162
intellectual change, definition of, 258
Internet, and recruitment, 147
interoperability, transformation and, 319
inventory used, percentage of, 245–47
Iraq War, 331–32, 345
    Anderson on, 21
    Keane on, 11–12
    reserve force in, 191, 194–95

Janowitz, Morris, 27–28
Jehn, Christopher, 55–56, 154
Jeremiah, David, 67
job performance, AFQT and, 93–95, 95f, 149–50
Johnson, Lyndon B., 4, 46
jointness, 259, 290
    and recruitment, Parks on, 157
    and training, 259
    transformation and, 319
Joint Services Job Performance Measurement (JPM) Project, 93, 149
JROTC Career Academy, 68
Junior Reserve Officer Training Corps (JROTC), 68

Kastenmeier, Robert, 46
Keane, Jack, 11–12, 332
Kelley, Roger, 3, 6, 12
Kennedy, Edward, 46
Kipling, Rudyard, 339
Kissinger, Henry, 5

labor force
    demographic trends and, 112
    reservists in, 172f
    shortages in, projected, 150
labor market, continuum of service and, 299–300
Laird, Melvin R., vii, 3–8, 11–12, 45, 49
lateral entry, 82, 138n10
    continuum of service and, 302
leadership
    and clarity of mission, 67
    in Coast Guard, 161–62
    Herbits on, 12
    Navy and, 152
    and recruitment/retention, 68–69
leavening
    definition of, 213, 232n7
    function of, 215
less-developed nations, population trends in, 115–16, 116f–117f
linguists, 303, 327

longevity
  and retirement trends, 129
  and United States population, 110–12, 111*f*
lottery system, 6, 7n1, 50

manpower, military, 255–96
  commentary on, 317–28
  system, Herbits on, 12, 201, 205
  transformation and, 259–64
manpower management
  and continuum of service, 304–6
  current system, advantages of, 274–76
  elements of, 318
  flexibility in, need for, 279–81
  future of, White on, 43
  Herbits on, 12
  Navy and, 150–52
  policy, versus personnel policy, 293n2
  special pays and bonuses for, 271
  transformation and, 262–76
  transformation of, goals of, 287
  White on, 33–44
manpower quality. *See* quality
Marine Corps, 332
  educational requirements in, 123
  subculture of, 265
marital status, by age and sex, military versus
      civilian, 134, 135*t*
marketplace philosophy, Moskos on, 27–28
married personnel, 134, 135*t*
  treatment of, 78–80
Marshall, Burke, 46
Marshall Commission, 50
maximal performance, 91
  HOPT and, 94
McCaffrey, Barry, 209
McCain, John, 81
McCarthy, James P., 259
McNamara, Robert, 46
Meckling, William H., 9, 26, 46, 50
median age, U.S., 118–19, 119*t*
medical personnel
  armed forces university for, 6
  Gates Commission on, 10
  recruitment/retention and, 203
Meyer, Shy, 340
migration
  assmptions on, 136, 137*f*
  and education trends, 122
  and global population trends, 115, 116*f*
  trends in, 130
  and United States population, 110
military culture, 214
  elements of, 265
  transformation and, 263, 309–10
Military Morale and Quality of Life (QoL)
      panel, 67
military service paradigms
  new, 298–99
  old, 297–98
military specialist, soldier as, 48–49

military work force, sizing, 82–83
militia, in Revolutionary War, 237–38
minorities
  education trends among, 121–22
  and higher education, 125
  share of U.S. population, 118, 118f
  See also representativeness
misnorming of ASVAB, 22, 35, 48, 61, 98
  definition of, 372
mission accomplishment, quality and, 162–63
mission clarity
  leadership and, 67
  and recruitment, 65
mobilization, 195–96
  disadvantages of, 324
  involuntary, 323
  of reserve, history of, 170–73, 171*f*
monopsony problem, 70
morale
  employer problems with, 186
  and recruitment/retention, 68
moral issues, reservist attitudes on, 220, 220*f*
Moskos, Charles, 27–29
Myers, Richard, 258, 290

National Assessment of Educational Progress
      (NAEP), 103, 103*f*
National Call to Service program, 81–82
National Committee for Employer Support of
      the Guard and Reserve (NCESGR), 175, 190n3
National Defense Act, 215, 238n8
National Defense Authorization act, 193–94
National Defense Panel, 291
National Guard, 200
  ChalleNGe program, 68
  role of, 191–92, 238; new, 313–15
  Wilson on, 326–27
  See also reserve force
National Military Strategy, 238
National Research Council (NRC), 92
National Security Council (NSC), and
      establishment of AVF, 5
National Security Personnel System,
      proposed, 83
national service proposal, 10
Navas, William A., Jr., 167–68
Navy
  assignment incentive pay in, 75, 283–84
  promotion structure in, 86n21
  recruitment/retention in, 25, 148–53
  subculture of, 265
  transformation in, 319–20
Neiburg, Michael, 214
networking. *See* leavening
Neuberger, Maureen, 46
Nineties
  challenges in, 257
  civil-military gap debate in, 208–11
  recruitment in, 57–58, 64
Nixon, Richard
  Anderson and, 16–20

De Leon on, 349
Dent on, 8, 10–11
Hesburgh and, 14
Laird and, 3–5
Rumsfeld and, vii
White on, 35
nonmilitary work force, sizing, 82–83
Norstad, Lauris, 9, 19
Nunn, Sam, 23–24, 34–35, 47

occupation
compensation by, 272t–273t
pay tables by, 73
occupationalism, 215
officers
education trends among, 125
pay, 267t, 268f; variation in, 269, 270t; years-
of-service distribution, by occupational
code, 273t
pay raises for, 74–75
ratio to enlisted, 60
Oi, Walter Y., 25, 45–51, 84n5
180-day rule, 305
operational tempo
new management policies for, 321
and reserve forces, 243–45
uncertainties regarding, 81
in war on terrorism, 322
"other race" category, 120, 120t
outsourcing, 249–50
for housing, 79
transformation and, 262

Packard, David, 3
Pakistan, population trends in, 116, 117f
paradigms, new
in force planning, 312–15
in military service, 298–99
parents, and recruitment, 68, 126, 139n21, 221,
222f, 340–41
Parks, Garry L., 154–59
participation
options for, 299–300
programs for, 301–3
Partnership for Youth Success (PaYS),
145, 240
pay-for-performance, 284–86
Peake, James B., 203
performance
compensation structure and, 75–77
Navy and, 150–51
pay for, 284–86
typical versus maximal, 91
performance appraisal, 281–82
Persian Gulf War, 26
Anderson on, 20
and reserve force, 171
reserve force in, 195, 200
personnel change of station (PCS), 65
personnel costs, insensitivity to, 41–43
personnel demand, 58–62

personnel policy, 255–96
commentary on, 317–28
elements of, 318
versus manpower policy, 293n2
and recruitment/retention, 70–80
personnel supply, 62–67
trends in, 109–17
personnel system
flexibility of, 266–71
tasks of, 76
personnel tempo, Rumsfeld on, viii
pillar distribution, 111–12, 111f
Posse Comitatus Act, 227, 238n15
post-Cold War world
Navas on, 167
recruitment in, 65
and reserve force, 171
Powell, Colin, 344
preconditioning, recommendations for, 144
Preisdent's Commission on an All-Volunteer
Armed Force. See Gates Commission
Preisdent's Commission on Military
Compensation (PCMC), 40
prescreening, recommendations for, 143
Presidential Reserve Call-Up, definition of, 373
Price, Raymond, 16, 18
privatization. See outsourcing
professionalism, 312
AVF and, 29
and civil-military gap, 206–7
in military culture, 265
promotion
criteria for, 58
current system, advantages of, 275
Oi on, 49
pay increase without, 284–86
and performance, 76
reform in, 281–82
pyramid distribution, 111–12, 111f

Quadrennial Defense Review, definition of, 373
Quadrennial Review of Military Compensation
(QRMC), Ninth, 39–40, 74
on education trends, 124
on planning, 260
on transformation, 258, 292
quality, 90–108, 148
Cavin on, 143–44
Chu on, 350–51
in Coast Guard, 160–63
indicators of, changing, 104–6
manpower, 90–108; trends in, 97–104, 99f
rank and, 62
of recruits, 60–62, 61t
of total force, 60–62
trends in, 97–104, 99f, 150
Wolfowitz on, 332–33
quality of life
expectations on, 158–59
and recruitment/retention, 65–66, 69
White on, 42–43

Quality of Life (QoL) panel, 67
Quester, Aline, 109–41

race
  issue of, 27
  trends in, 118–21
  See also demographic trends;
    representativeness
Rangel, Charles, 15
rank
  distribution of, 59–60, 60*t*
  and personnel quality, 62
rapid responsiveness, transformation and, 319
readiness
  in Coast Guard, 161
  recruitment and, 149–50
  reserve force and, 193, 196
Reagan, Ronald, 21
rebalancing, 249–50, 308–16, 316*f*
  commentary on, 323–24
  definition of, 249
  options for, 249–50
recruitment
  in Coast Guard, 160–61
  commentary on, 142–63
  costs of, 59–60
  demographic trends and, 109–41
  Dorn on, 344
  Jehn on, 55–56
  in Nineties, 57–58, 64
  for reserve forces, 199–205, 239–40, 244–45
  resources for: Parks on, 156–57; and
    personnel supply, 66–67;
    recommendations for, 146–47
  September 11, 2001 and, 228
  Vessey on, 339–42
  White on, 36–39
  without walls, 147
recruits
  characteristics of, 145
  quality of, 60–62, 61*t*; definition of, 90–91
  supply of, 62–67
REDUX, 278
regular military compensation (RMC), 70–71,
    71*t*, 266
renorming of ASVAB, 152–53
  definition of, 373
representativeness, 81
  definition of, 29
  issues in, 130–36
  Parks on, 155–56
  Rostker on, 29–30
reserve component, definition of, 373
reserve force, 167–68, 191–98
  Chu on, 351–52
  and civil-military gap, 206–36
  commentary on, 237–52
  continuum of service and, 304–6
  contribution to total force missions, 172*f*,
    191–92, 243–44, 243*f*, 244*t*

disparities with active force, efforts to
    correct, 192–94
  employers and, 169–90; research directions
    for, 187–89
  frequency of use of, 245, 247*t*
  funding for, 243*f*
  history of, 200–201
  importance of, 242–43
  integration with total force, 194–98
  in labor force, 172*f*
  mobilization of, history of, 170–73, 171*f*
  rebalancing and, 308
  recruiting for, 199–205
  role of, 169, 191–92, 211–12, 238, 297–98; new,
    170–73, 171*f*, 313–15
  sizing, 80–82
  transformation and, 322–23
  variable pool of, 300–301
  in war on terrorism, 322
  Wilson on, 326–27
Reserve Officer Training Corps (ROTC), 214
reservists
  attitudes of, 213–14, 216–26, 227*t*
  employment, by sector, 173, 174*f*
  problems with employers, 179–84;
    expectations versus reality of, 179–81,
    180*f*; types of, 181–83, 182*f*
  reasons for not volunteering for additional
    duty, 183, 183*f*
  responsibilities to employer, 179
Resor, Stanley, 57
retention
  in Coast Guard, 160–61
  commentary on, 142–63
  factors affecting, 39, 65–66
  Jehn on, 55–56
  rates: AVF and, 29; enlisted, 73–74, 74*f*
  in reserve forces, 199–205, 239–40, 244–45
  Vessey on, 339–40
  White on, 37–39
retirees, participation programs for, 301–2
retirement, trends in, 128–30
retirement benefits, 71
  assistance with, 186
  current system, advantages of, 275
  USERRA on, 178
  Vessey on, 341
retirement reform, 40–41
  obstacles in, 277–79
retirement system, 77–78
  purposes of, 78
Riche, Martha Farnsworth, 109–41
Ricks, Thomas, 209
risk taking
  characteristics of, 318–19
  encouragement of, 265–66
  obstacles to, 319–20
ritualization, in military culture, 265
Rivers, Mendel, 6
Rogers, Bernie, 337, 339
Rostker, Bernard D., 22–32

Rumsfeld, Donald H., vii–ix, 3, 46
  and combat capability, 34
  and Military Morale and Quality of Life
    panel, 67
  and reserves, 242
  on transformation, 249–50, 258, 290

Sackett, Paul R., 90–108
Schlesinger, James, 336
Schrock, Edward L., 191–98
seamless integration, of force components,
    194–98, 325, 342
Sears, John, 16
Sea Warrior program, 151–52, 151f
selected reserve, definition of, 373
self-employed reservists, 176
Semple, Robert, 17
separation pay, 279
September 11, 2001
  and airline industry, 187
  and civil-military gap, 226–28
  and employers, 174–75
  and reserve force, 169, 171, 197, 244
sergeants, on recruit quality, 35, 38
Shakespeare, William, 168
Shoemaker, Bob, 337
Simon, Curtis J., 57–89
single personnel, 134, 135t
  treatment of, 78–80
Sjaasted, Lawrence, 47
skilled occupational specialties, 239
  recruitment and, 202–3
small businesses, and reserve force, 176, 186–87
Smith, Gorman, 49
Smith Richardson Foundation, 210
social issues, reservist attitudes on, 218–19, 219f
social traditionalism, reservist attitudes on,
    220, 220f
soldiers, as military specialist, 48–49
special and incentive (S&I) pays, 71, 71t, 266,
    271, 274–75
  Oi on, 49
  reform in, 73
special forces, expansion of, 327–28
Spruell, R. Wayne, 297–306
Steel, Robert K., 169–90
Steiger, William, 3
Stevenson, Adlai, 16
Stone, Gregory L., 191
stop-loss orders, 346, 347n1
strength accounting, continuum of service and,
    304–6
Suddarth, Steve, 291
supervisors, support for reservists, 182f, 183
supply-side bias, White on, 37–39

table of distribution and allowances (TDA), 279
Tapp, Bill, 338
targeted pays, 71–75
tax, conscription, 22, 46–47
Tax, Sol, 46

technology
  and force size requirements, 60, 84n6
  Herbits on, 12
  keep-out, 313
  Oi on, 48
  and transformation, 259, 291
terrorism, war on, 200, 325–26
  characteristics of, 322
threat-based planning, 260–61, 292, 310–12
thrift savings plan, definition of, 374
Thurman, Maxwell, 36, 48, 142, 340
tiers 1/2/3, 100, 123–24
  definition of, 107n2, 374
time-in-grade (TIG) increases, 77
time-in-service (TIS) increases, 77
Title 5, definition of, 374
Title 10, definition of, 374
total-force concept
  and civil-military gap, 207
  Dorn on, 346
  Laird on, 4
  reevaluation of, 167
  seamless integration and, 194–98, 325, 342
Tracey, Patricia A., 317–22, 348
training
  Dorn on, 344–45
  for reserve force, 193, 196, 204, 251
  and transformation, 321
  Vessey on, 340
Training and Doctrine Command (TRADOC),
    279–80
training performance, AFQT and, 92–93, 92f,
    148–49
transformation, 255–96
  commentary on, 317–28
  of compensation, 276–86
  definition of, 258, 289–90
  duration of, 292
  goals of, 258, 289–90
  Hall on, 241
  and military manpower, 259–64
  obstacles to, 265–66, 277–79; overcoming, 320
  and rebalancing, 308–16, 316f
  and recruitment/retention, 57–89, 202–5
  requirements for, 321
  reservist attitudes on, 216–18, 218f
  system-wide, need for, 319
  Wolfowitz on, 291–92, 331–34
TRIAD, 38, 44n1
  definition of, 374
Triangle Institute for Security Studies (TISS)
    survey, 208, 210, 216–26
  data for, 230–31
  methodology of, 231–32
TRICARE coverage, 345
  definition of, 374
  for reservists and families, 194
Truman, Harry S, 349
tuition assistance, 128
typical performance, 91

unemployment, and recruitment, 63–64, 63*f*
Uniformed Services Employment and
      Reemployment Rights Act (USERRA),
      178–79 cases under, 181, 181*f*
United Kingdom, population change in, 115,
    115*t*
United States
    educational attainment in, 122, 123*f*
    population: change in, 110, 111*f*; distribution
        of, 111–12, 111*f*; minority share of, 118,
        118*f*; by race and Hispanic origin, 120,
        120*t*
    projected population, 115*t*; by age, 112*f*; by
        age-group and sex, 114*f*
    youth population in, 109–12, 110*f*
United States Joint Forces Command
    (USJFCOM), on transformation, 289
units, new types of, 261
University of Chicago Conference on the Draft,
    23
Up-Armored High Mobility Multipurpose
    Wheeled Vehicles, 194
up-or-out system
    alternatives to, 76
    definition of, 374
    transformation and, 263
Utley, Robert M., 338–39

value, feelings of, 318
    and recruitment/retention, 68
values
    and civil-military gap, 206–8
    of reservists, 213–14
    TISS survey on, 216–26
Venuto, Kenneth T., 159–63
Vessey, John W., Jr., 158, 335–42
veterans, in population, 126, 210–11, 229
    and recruitment, 64–65, 147, 158
Veterans Reemployment Rights, 179
Vietnam War
    and AVF, 4, 16, 23–24
    rebuilding after, 336–37
Volcker Commission, 83
volunteer auxiliaries, expansion of, 303
volunteerism
    enhanced, 81–82, 299–300, 324
    individual ready reserve and, 303
    before World War II, 336

Wallis, W. Allen, 46
Warner, John T., 57–89
warrior image, 309–10
Washington, George, 24
Weinberger, Casper, 26
Welch, Larry, 67
White, John P., 33–44
Wilson, Heather, 325–28
Wilson, Lou, 339
Winkler, John D., 297–306
Wolfowitz, Paul, 81, 291–92, 331–34
women

and higher education, 125
    in military: enlisted, 132–34, 133*f*; and force
        size requirements, 62; Meckling on, 26;
        Parks on, 155; reservist attitudes on,
        225–26; Vessey on, 337–38
Wool, Harold, 48
working conditions, and recruitment/retention,
    65–66, 69
youth aptitudes, trends in, 103, 103*f*
youth attitudes
    and recruitment, 65
    research on, 126–27
Youth Attitude Tracking Study (YATS), 100
youth population
    characteristics of, trends in, 102–4
    diversity of, 120–21
    global, 113–17
    large, nations with, 116, 117*t*
    trends in, 99–100
    in United States, 109–12, 110*f*

Zurcher, Louis, 213
Zwick Commission, 40